AMERICAN CINEMA/AMERICAN CULTURE

Second Edition

John Belton

Rutgers University

Boston   Burr Ridge, IL   Dubuque, IA   Madison, WI   New York
San Francisco   St. Louis   Bangkok   Bogotá   Caracas   Kuala Lumpur
Lisbon   London   Madrid   Mexico City   Milan   Montreal   New Delhi
Santiago   Seoul   Singapore   Sydney   Taipei   Toronto

Higher Education

AMERICAN CINEMA/AMERICAN CULTURE Second Edition
Published by McGraw-Hill, a business unit of The McGraw-Hill Companies, Inc., 1221 Avenue of the Americas,
New York, NY, 10020. Copyright © 2005, 2002, 1999, 1996, 1993, 1990 by The McGraw-Hill Companies, Inc. All
rights reserved. No part of this publication may be reproduced or distributed in any form or by any means, or
stored in a database or retrieval system, without the prior written consent of The McGraw-Hill Companies, Inc.,
including, but not limited to, in any network or other electronic storage or transmission, or broadcast for distance learning.

Some ancillaries, including electronic and print components, may not be available to customers outside the
United States.

This book is printed on acid-free paper.

2 3 4 5 6 7 8 9 0 DOC/DOC 0 9 8 7 6 5 4

ISBN 0-07-288627-7

Publisher: *Chris Freitag*
Sponsoring Editor: *Melody Marcus*
Development Editor: *Chris Narozny*
Marketing Manager: *Lisa Berry*
Media Producer: *Shannon Gattens*
Project Manager: *Roger Geissler*
Interior Designer: *Linda Robertson*
Cover Designer: *Cassandra Chu*
Art Editor: *Emma Ghiselli*
Photo Research Coordinator: *Natalia Pescheira*
Production Supervisor: *Rich DeVitto*
Compositor: *Thompson Type*
Cover Image: *Courtesy of Photofest*
Printer: *RR Donnelley*

Library of Congress Cataloging-in-Publication Data

Belton, John.
   American Cinema/American Culture/John Belton.—2nd ed.
      p. cm.
   Includes bibliographical references and index.
   ISBN 0-07-288627-7
   1. Motion pictures—United States—History.   2. Motion picture industry—United States—History.
3. Motion pictures—Social Aspects—United States.   4. United States—Popular culture—History—
20th century
PN1993.5.U6 B65   2005
R91.43—dc20   200425846

www.mhhe.com

ABOUT THE **AUTHOR**

John Belton teaches film at Rutgers University. He is the author of *Widescreen Cinema* (1992), winner of the Kraszna-Krausz Award for Books on the Moving Image (1994), and several other books on film.

To Mike Moore, a teacher of teachers

CONTENTS

PART II   GENRE AND THE GENRE SYSTEM

CHAPTER 6   SILENT FILM MELODRAMA   131

CHAPTER 7   THE MUSICAL   150

PREFACE

This book introduces the reader to basic issues related to the phenomenon of American cinema. It looks at American film history from the 1890s through the summer of 2003, but it does not always explore this history in a purely chronological way. In fact, it is not (strickly speaking) a history. Rather, it is a *cultural* history, which focuses more on topics and issues than on what happened when.

It begins with a profile of classical Hollywood cinema as a unique economic, industrial, aesthetic, and cultural institution. It considers the experience of moviegoing; the nature of Hollywood story-telling; and the roles played by the studio system, the star system, and film genres in the creation of a body of work that functions not only as entertainment but as a portrait of the relationship between an American national identity and an industrialized mass culture that has slowly evolved over the past century.

This book assumes that the reader has little or no formal training in film history, theory, or aesthetics. It presents fairly basic concepts in such a way as to encourage discussion, not so much of individual films, but of films in general. For this reason, the book concentrates on large groupings of films—on genres, topics, and periods of film history.

This textbook differs from the more traditional histories of the cinema for certain specific and important reasons. Over the past 30 years, the field of film study has undergone a tremendous transformation. This change has been spearheaded by the work of a new generation of scholars who challenge the traditional way in which film history has been written and taught. Introduction to Film courses that, 30 years ago, taught film as art, drew heavily upon the approaches of New Criticism. Contemporary film courses now teach film not only as art but also as film, and they attempt to situate film as an art form within a larger industrial, economic, social, and cultural context. They rely heavily on cultural studies, new historicism, psychoanalysis, and other contemporary critical disciplines.

Film history texts have changed over the years as well. In the past, histories consisted of simple, chronological accounts of who-did-what and what-happened-when, and of the stories of great men (sic) and their achievements, and of straightforward accounts of the influence of technology and economics on the course of a history that unfolds in a linear fashion up to the present. More recently, film scholars have begun to rewrite these traditional histories, creating what Thomas Elsaesser refers to as "The New Film History." At its best, this history is driven by a sophisticated, theoretically informed revisionism. It simply refuses to accept the easy answers to basic historical questions which had been offered up by past historians. "The New Film History" can best be seen in the work of David Bordwell, Janet Staiger, and Kristin Thompson (*Classical Hollywood Cinema: Film Style and Mode of Production to 1960*) and of Robert Allen and Douglas Gomery (*Film History: Theory and Practice*), though it can be found in a number of other scholarly efforts as well.

With the initial publication of *American Cinema/American Culture* in 1994, the methods and discoveries of "The New Film History," were applied to an introductory level text surveying the history of the American cinema. That book was an attempt to put the principles of "The New Film History" into action—to present and to make accessible the findings of contemporary film studies to college students taking introductory level courses in film, American Studies, or Cultural Studies. In other words, it sought to provide an updated map of the terrain of American cinema.

Traditional histories of the cinema rely upon certain unquestioned assumptions which underlie the way they are written and read. They assume, for example, that the meaning of history is best represented through the time-worn format of the chronological narrative of events. They suggest that the fact that one event takes place after another somehow automatically "explains" that event. In this view, each event derives from a prior event; it comes from a cause-and-effect chain that runs smoothly and linearly from some origin in the past to the present.

This book understands that history does not only consist of "one damned thing after another," but of ideas, problems, and issues. For that reason, the text gives a certain priority in its organization to thematic over chronological concerns. This textbook is designed not as a blow-by-blow account of who did what and when, but as an historically informed *portrait* of American cinema, provided through a clear and concise description of its most salient features.

Nonetheless, a sense of history strongly pervades the book, guiding the structure of specific chapters and of the book as a whole and providing a survey of the American cinema's major character traits as they take shape over the decades. Seen from the perspective of a cultural phenomenon, American cinema emerges as a stylistically unified body of work (as discussed in the chapters on classical Hollywood cinema), generated within a certain mode of production (see the chapters on the Studio System and the Star System) that is uniquely dependent upon modern technologies developed for the recording of images and sounds. These general characteristics of American cinema underlie the nature of the particular products which that cinema produces—the various genres of films discussed within the text, ranging from comedies and Westerns to war films and melodramas.

Traditional film histories tend to be unsuitable for introductory film courses in that they frequently omit any discussion of aesthetics, presuming that basic matters of film form have been dealt with in a prior course. This text, however, doubles as both a cultural history and an introduction to aesthetics and film form, introducing and explaining basic vocabulary in the chapters that discuss the narrative and stylistic practices of classical Hollywood cinema. Subsequent chapters refer back to these basic ingredients of narrative and stylistic form. Here, the function of mise-en-scene (lighting, set and costume design, camera angle and movement, etc.) and editing (eye-line matching, shot/reverse-shot editing, the 180-degree rule, parallel editing, etc.) is explored in terms of their relation to the overall system of classical Hollywood style.

Traditional film histories present themselves as purely objective accounts of "what happened in the past." They disguise their own position in relation to that past. This text, however, in addition to providing factual information and surveying what contemporary scholarship has revealed to us about the subject, develops a clearly delineated thesis and encourages instructors, students, and general readers to question and test that thesis by holding it up to close scrutiny. The core of that thesis rests on an assumption that American cinema reveals, both directly and indirectly, something about American experience, identity, and culture.

The relationship among American cinema and American identity, as mediated through American culture, is extremely complex. Each shapes and is shaped by the other in a constant process of mutual determination.

American cinema plays a crucial role in the process of identity-formation. Films not only serve as texts which document who we think we are or were, but they also reflect changes in our self-image, tracing the transformation from one kind of America to another. More importantly, the American cinema plays a crucial role in assisting audiences in negotiating major changes in identity; it carries them across difficult periods of cultural transition in such a way that a more or less coherent national identity remains in place, spanning the gaps and fissures that threaten to disrupt its movement and to expose its essential disjointedness.

The first major cultural crisis that American cinema addressed was the trauma in national identity brought about by the transition from an agricultural to an industrial nation, which took place in the United States after the Civil War. The period from roughly 1865 to the beginning of World War I (1916) witnessed a cataclysmic transformation of America from a largely rural to a predominantly urban culture, from an agrarian to an industrial economy, from a nation of producers (farmers, small businessmen, and shopkeepers) to one of consumers, and from a community of individuals to a mass society. Popular response to this rapid urbanization and industrialization combined an enthusiasm for technological progress and economic growth with an anxiety about the threats these changes posed to preindustrial American values. At the same time, urbanization, industrialization, and mass culture brought with them social and economic problems that justified those anxieties. On the one hand, preindustrial notions of individuality and personal agency (i.e., the ability of individuals to accomplish things on their own) were compromised by the social subject's new, disempowered status of anonymity within the mass. Victorian

America believed that the individual would be properly compensated for his/her integrity, energy, and hard work. But industrial trusts and monopolies had rigged the system in their favor, preventing the individual entrepreneur from securing an appropriate reward for his or her efforts.

At the same time, modern mass culture, according to Ann Douglas and others, was believed to have "feminized" traditional American virtues. In response to the "crisis of masculinity," leaders such as Theodore Roosevelt praised "the strenuous life," advocating a return to a more rugged way of life in the wilderness in an attempt "to reinvigorate American society." Roosevelt complained that the youth of America were brought up in a "slothful ease . . . that was creating a generation dominated by the over-civilized man, who has lost the great fighting, masterful virtues" and insisted that the country must struggle "to stave off effeminacy that is one of the dangers of nations that grow old and soft and unwilling to endure hardships."

Roosevelt sought to correct these problems. To protect the individual, he sought legislation to bust the trusts. In an attempt to preserve the manly virtues that made this country great, he created five national parks and 51 wildlife refuges where American boys and men could pursue the strenuous life. He also led by example, hunting bears in Yellowstone, leading safaris in Africa and expeditions up the Amazon. He also founded the Rough Riders, a crack company of soldiers he commanded in the Spanish-American War.

Two major reform movements—populism and progressivism—arose in an attempt to address the excesses brought about by industrialization, urbanization, and the rise of mass culture. The *politics* of populism and progressivism were short-lived, roughly spanning the period between the presidential campaigns of populist William Jennings Bryan (1896) and of two progressives, Theodore Roosevelt (1904/1912) and Woodrow Wilson (1912/1916). But as systems of belief, the *ideologies* of populism and progressivism outlived the rise and fall of the Populist and Progressive political parties.

Populist ideology was rooted in the ideals of the Jeffersonian democratic tradition. Thomas Jefferson envisioned America as "a republic of yeoman farmers, each man working his own land, free to develop in his own way." For Jefferson, the moral virtue of the American citizenry depended upon its association with the land. According to Jefferson, the American character was rescued from the corruption and decadence of the Old World through regenerative contact with Nature. But, more importantly, the land became, for him, the basis on which American democracy was to be built. The availability of free land in the West guaranteed each American an opportunity to own land, and, thereby, to have an equal stake in the affairs of the nation. The universal ownership of property would not only empower Americans but ensure their self-sufficiency and independence.

Populist ideology looked back with nostalgia to the "lost Eden" of preindustrial, agrarian America, to the nation of shopkeepers, artisans, farmers, and small towns that, as historian Richard Hofstadter wrote, existed "before the development of industrialism and the commercialization of agriculture." In returning to the original values and beliefs of Revolutionary-era America, populism advocated "democracy, honest and unobtrusive central government, leadership by decent men, equality of opportunity, [and] self-help." Responding to the post-industrial present, populism, as Jeffrey Richards noted, "opposed big business, the political machine and intellectualism as the things most likely to hamper the individual's pursuit of happiness."

Much of American cinema can be mapped in terms of its relation to notions of political, social, cultural, and economic reform articulated by populist and progressive ideologies. On the silver screen, American masculinity survived the onslaught of modernity in the form of countless male stars from Douglas Fairbanks and Clark Gable to Sylvester Stallone and Harrison Ford. In *Jaws* (1975), Chief Brody (Roy Schieder) opposes civic corruption *and* battles a great white shark, proving that in modern America one man [sic] could still make a difference. As for the "lost Eden" of small-town America, it can be found in the Bedford Falls of Frank Capra's *It's a Wonderful Life* (1946); its nightmarish alter-ego, Pottersville, turns out to be a bad dream, prevented from becoming a reality by the heroic efforts of populist reformers such as George Bailey (James Stewart). Even films that portray a world dominated by urban alienation, drugs, despair, crime, and corruption, such as *Taxi Driver* (1976) look back to populist and progressive mythology. They depict the consequences of an industrialization and urbanization that was not held in check. They turn populist and progressive ideology inside out, providing a portrait of their worst nightmares. The boundaries of the American cinema are defined by these two diametrically opposed visions—the utopian vision found in Capra, Spielberg and others and the dystopian vision found in film noir, Scorsese, Lynch, and others. These two visions constitute a single, larger, more complex vision that represents the deeper contradictions within the American psyche.

This book has been written in conjunction with the television course and series *American Cinema*, produced by the New York Center for Visual History as part of the Annenberg/CPB project collection. It also corresponds with a student study guide, written by Ed Sikov, which has been carefully designed to function equally well independently of these supplementary materials.

This book could not have been written without the help of a number of other film scholars. In particular, I would like to thank William Costanzo, Thomas Cripps, Douglas Gomery, William Paul, Ed Sikov, and Elisabeth Weis of the curriculum committee for the *American Cinema* television course project for the New York Center for Visual History, who read the bulk of this book in manuscript form and provided invaluable suggestions for improving it. Special thanks go to Angela Aleiss, Elizabeth Belton, Ellen Belton, Thomas Doherty, Howard Karren, Robert Lang, Charles Maland, Dara Meyers-Kingsley, and Alan Williams who read and commented on specific chapters. I am indebted to Jane Belton, David Bordwell, Aaron Braun, Fred Camper, Linda McCarthy, Al Nigrin, Jessica Rosner, Phil Shane, and Kristin Thompson for their advice, research help, and/or assistance in providing illustrative material for the book.

Also, I would like to thank the following for their careful reviews of the manuscript: Chuck Berg, University of Kansas; Jay Coughtry, University of Nevada, Las Vegas; Leger Grindon, Middleburg College; Douglas Gomery, University of Maryland; Eugene Huddleston, Michigan State University; Annette Insdorf, Columbia University; Kathryn Lasky, University of Southern Maine; Charles Maland, University of Tennesseee; Karen Mann, Western Illinois University; David Nasaw, College of State Island; Jere Real, Lynchburg College; Margaret Schrage, SUNY College at Old Westbury; Susan Scrivner, Bemidji State University; Steven Shields, University of Wisconsin, Whitewater; Kristin Thompson, University of Wisconsin, Madison; and Albert Wendland, Seton Hill College.

Molly Ornati and Lawrence Pitkethly of the New York Center for Visual History and Lin Foa of the Annenberg/CPB project proved instrumental in bringing this book about, along with my editors at McGraw-Hill, Alison Husting, Peter Labella, and Curt Berkowitz. A special thanks to Jeanine Basinger, Senior Academic Advisor for the *American Cinema* television course, who served as a catalyst for the development of this project.

John Belton

PREFACE TO THE SECOND EDITION

Changes to this Edition

- Full chapter on the Musical, spanning its history in film and cultural significance
- Analysis of David Lynch's *Mulholland Dr.* in Chapter 2, replacing that of *Goodfellas*
- Expanded coverage of "The Studio System" in Chapter 4 and of "The Star System" in Chapter 5, including a new case study of Tom Hanks' career
- Expanded coverage of the contemporary war film, including Gulf War films and an extensive comparison of *Saving Private Ryan* and *The Thin Red Line*
- More extensive discussion of *Unforgiven*, including a comparison to Jim Jarmusch's *Dead Man*
- Extensive updating in the final chapter to reflect the changes in the film industry
- Updated coverage of Film School Generation work such as that of Martin Scorsese and Spike Lee

Ancillary Support

A text-specific, Online Learning Center at **www.mhhe.com/cinema2** is available for student and instructor use. This website offers several tools to reinforce text content as well as various resources for extending knowledge of the material. Features include multiple-choice chapter quizzes, a glossary of key terms, links to related websites, and more.

Also available with the second edition is a student Study Guide (ISBN: 0-07-310287-3), written by Ed Sikov. This guide integrates the American Cinema instructional video series, produced by Annenberg/CPB, with the textbook. For more information on the Annenberg telecourse, please visit www. learner.org or call 1-800-LEARNER (1-800-532-7637).

Acknowledgments

The new chapter on the musical benefited from the careful reading given to it by Jerome Delamater who provided dozens of extremely helpful comments. The new edition is also indebted to the collective efforts of the highly professional staff at McGraw-Hill, including Cassandra Chu, Beth Ebenstein, Roger Geissler, Melody Marcus, Chris Narozny, and Natalia Pescheira. Scholars who reviewed the first edition and made useful recommendations for revisions were John Chapin, Pennsylvania State University; Renny Christopher, California State University, Channel Islands; Eugene J. Crook, Florida State University; Daniel Dootson, Edmonds Community College; Sam B. Girgus, Vanderbilt University; Bruce Haulman, Green River Community College; Jeanne Lynn Hall, Pennsylvania State University; Chris Jordan, Pennsylvania State University; Elinor Lerner, Richard Stockton College; Richard Sugg, Florida International University.

INTRODUCTION

During M-G-M's heyday as a studio, the end title of every M-G-M film read "Made in Hollywood, U.S.A." Though not every American film is or was made in Hollywood, the bulk of American cinema is the product of a specific mode of production which was perfected in Hollywood and which consists of a unique combination of various ingredients.

"Hollywood" is not only a place in California where movies are made. It does not only consist of studios, labs, and other buildings; nor of producers, stars, directors, screenwriters, and the other personnel who are actually involved in the making of movies. "Hollywood" is also a consistent and coherent set of aesthetic and stylistic conventions that audiences readily understand. Beneath these conventions lies an industrial infrastructure that works to maintain and support them. This industrial base includes the studio system and the star system, as well as the movie culture that grew up around these institutions.

Movie culture ranges in its scope from the discourses (or ways of representing things) of advertising, publicity, and fan magazines to the experience of moviegoing, which changes from decade to decade. The experience of watching a one-reel short film in a nickelodeon in 1908 differs dramatically from that of watching a silent feature film in a movie palace in the 1920s. These experiences, in turn, remain worlds apart from going to drive-ins in the 1950s, small-screen multiplexes in the 1960s and 1970s, and mall cinemas multiplexes (8 to 15 screens) and megaplexes (16 or more screens) in the present.

This book explores the *phenomenon* of American cinema. It investigates what it is and how it works. In order to understand what American cinema is and how it works, it is necessary to look at it as a mode of production. Hollywood has its own way of doing things. Over the years it has developed a unique system of studios, stars, distribution, exhibition, advertising, and marketing that enables it to make a profit. This mode of production not only forms the nature of Hollywood as an industry, but it also determines the kinds of films that get made, the way those films look, and the way those films tell stories.

The first section of this text (Chapters 1–5) concentrates on the notion of "Hollywood" as a unique system designed for the efficient production of a rather unusual product—motion pictures. An initial chapter on "The Emergence of the Cinema as an Institution" traces the evolution of American filmmaking from a toy, novelty item and fairground attraction to a carefully tailored mode of production which is designed to produce seamless narratives capable of entertaining a mass audience. Subsequent chapters on "Classical Hollywood Cinema" ("Narration" in Chapter 2; "Style" in Chapter 3), "The Studio System," and "The Star System" explore the nature of this institution, providing a descriptive account of the basic elements that constitute Hollywood as a distinct mode of production.

Much as Hollywood turns the craft of film production, distribution, and exhibiton into an efficient system, so it also systematizes its product. It makes and markets films according to yet another system—that of genres. The second section of the text (Chapters 6–11) looks at the way movies work by exploring the relation of major film genres to the specific industrial and cultural machinery that produced them—that is, to the institution of Hollywood and to the institution of American mass culture.

The system of genres duplicates, in the area of film product, the organizational strategies that underlie the film industry's institutional base. This system establishes broad categories of film types that have proven their economic viability over the years and that, as a result, work to stabilize the production process by reducing financial risk. Audiences go to movies that resemble films which they have seen before. That is, audiences go to comedies, melodramas, war films, Westerns, and other broad categories of film types.

This section will also relate these films to the more general cultural concerns which inform them and to which they, in turn, give form. The arrangement of these chapters follows a quasi-chronological line, corresponding roughly to the decades in which the individual genres are best represented by the production output of the studios.

Though the chapter on film comedy discusses the genre from the 1910s to the 1990s, it concentrates on the comedies of Frank Capra, Howard Hawks, and other directors of the 1930s. The chapter on the war film, though it includes discussion of Vietnam War films, devotes the bulk of its attention to the 1940s. And so on and so forth with the other genres.

In other words, each genre chapter focuses on a particular decade but also traces the history of that genre beyond that particular decade. At the same time, it attempts to link shifts within that genre's evolution to changes that occur within the larger profile of American cultural history.

Not all genres are covered here. There is no chapter on the gangster film, the horror film, the science-fiction film, or other major genres. Such coverage, though it might make the book more complete, would significantly change its focus and balance. Genres are a crucial part of the phenomenon of American cinema, but they need to be seen within the larger context of the institutional structure of the industry that produces them. And, as the chapters in the last section of the text suggest, individual genre films need to be seen within their larger cultural context—that is, within the history of culture.

Finally, the book concludes with a review of the history of recent American cinema. It provides an analysis of the postwar assaults on Hollywood by the anti-Communist witch-hunts of the late-1940s and 1950s, by the advent of television, by the social and political upheavals of the 1960s, and by the rise of new generations of filmmakers in the 1970s, 1980s, and 1990s. These filmmakers (and their audiences) grew up during the cold war, watched television as kids, and were shaped, in one way or another, by the counterculture of the 1960s, Vietnam and Watergate in the 1970s, and Reaganite America in the 1980s.

This history of Hollywood in the postwar years describes the dismantling of the old Hollywood as a unique system of production, distribution, and exhibition and the attempts to construct a new Hollywood out of whatever pieces of the old that could be salvaged and adapted to the needs of a changing marketplace. This section looks back to both the first part of the book, which describes the classical mode of production that is transformed in the postwar years, and the second part, which outlines the histories of various genres, which are themselves altered by this new mode of production. Indeed, the discussion of genres, which notes their postwar transformation, anticipates the final section. This segment of the book also traces the contemporary cinema's attempts to recover its initial integrity as a system through its interest in certain filmmaking practices, which are discussed in "The 1960s: The Counterculture Strikes Back," "The Film School Generation," and "Into the Twenty-First Century." This final chapter juxtaposes mainstream Hollywood cinema of the 1980s, 1990s, and early 2000s with a variety of countercurrent cinemas, ranging from films made at the fringe of the mainstream by directors such as Martin Scorsese, David Lynch, and others to films produced by independent and minority filmmakers such as Spike Lee, Jim Jarmusch, Todd Haynes, and Julie Dash.

Each chapter concludes with a chronological filmography of relevant motion pictures that the reader might wish to look at in order to explore a bit further the ideas and issues dealt with in the text. Each chapter also provides a select bibliography of books and articles that can be consulted for additional information about the subject. A glossary of technical and other terms is at the end of the text to assist the reader in defining crucial nomenclature and terminology.

The movies play a crucial role in our lives. They entertain us, but they also educate us. The education which they provide lies not so much in what they show—in what stories or situations we see on the screen. Rather it consists of the attitudes that the movies take to the underlying concerns with which our culture seems continuously preoccupied. The chief concern which this book examines is that of twentieth-century America as well—the traumatic shift in identity that takes place as the country evolves from a nineteenth-century, rural, agrarian-based, social, cultural, and economic community into a modern, urban, industrialized mass society. The movies, which were born in the midst of this crisis in American identity, emerge as a crucial factor in its resolution. They serve, in part, to help us to negotiate this transition. This book looks at how they do that.

PART ONE

The Mode of Production

Motion pictures are made in a variety of ways. Some films, such as home movies, are inexpensively produced by individuals who own or rent amateur filmmaking equipment. They use 16mm, super 8, 8mm, video, or digital video equipment to film everyday, non-fictional occurrences, such as birthday parties, weddings, holiday celebrations, vacations, and other family-related events. They do not bother to record sound or edit their footage; they show what they film as it was filmed. And they exhibit their films in the privacy of their own homes to audiences that consist of family members, relatives, and friends.

At the other end of the spectrum stand expensively produced, feature-length Hollywood productions. These works boast casts of thousands, high-priced stars, lavish costumes and sets, intricate narratives, complicated special effects, dangerous stunts, meticulous sound recording, and elaborate sound design. For their successful completion they require the facilities of a major studio or an independently assembled crew of several hundred technicians and craftspersons. These films take several months to a year to produce. They require painstaking preparation in the stage of preproduction, during which scripts are written, parts are cast, and budgets are planned. They demand the expertise of skilled professionals during the production process, when the efforts of the producer, director, screenwriter, cameraperson, actors, costume and set designers, sound recordists, and others are carefully coordinated to transfer the script to film. And they call upon the extensive skill and training of sound mixers, editors, and others personnel during postproduction to produce a high-class product that can then be sold to the general public. The distribution, advertising, marketing, and exhibition of the finished product enlist the aid of another team of experts, who design publicity campaigns and prepare marketing materials (such as posters, trailers, and television ads).

Between these two extremes are a variety of filmmaking practices. They include avant-garde films, which are made by individuals using amateur equipment and techniques but are designed for public exhibition. At the same time, industrial films are produced using professional equipment and staff. But, unlike experimental works, these films are intended to provide information about the business products and services that fund them. Another mode of production involves the making of documentaries, which rely upon similar kinds of equipment and personnel but are financed by public funds or grants and tend to explore topical or controversial public issues.

Although the largest body of motion picture production (in terms of sheer footage) undoubtedly consists of home movies, the mode of production with which the majority of Americans are most familiar is probably that of the Hollywood feature film. The chapters that follow examine the basic features of this mode of production, not experimental or avant-garde films, documentaries or industrials, or home movies. Individual chapters look at the emergence of narrative cinema as a medium and the growth of a movie culture that includes the creation of an industry to make films, an audience to support them, and movie theaters in which they can be shown. Other chapters also explore the basic narrative and stylistic features of the films that dominate this industry. And still other chapters examine the industrial systems—the studio and star systems—that evolve to ensure that motion pictures generate a profit for those who make them.

This section of the book argues that Hollywood's mode of production plays a central role in determining the basic features of American cinema and that these features reflect, in part, the nature of the system that produced them.

CHAPTER **1**

The Emergence of the Cinema as an Institution

"THE CATHEDRAL OF THE MOTION PICTURE"

For the better part of the last century, the movies enjoyed a unique status as the premiere entertainment activity for the majority of Americans. The movies, like baseball, became something of a national pastime. Americans not only supported their motion pictures but loved them as well. Going to the movies, though perhaps not a religious experience for most, was certainly an ecstatic experience for many. Ecstasy came not only from the movies themselves but also from the surroundings in which they were presented.

Movie palaces built in the 1910s, 1920s, and 1930s resemble gigantic cathedrals. Indeed, the 6200-seat Roxy, the world's largest theater, was described in advertisements as "the cathedral of the motion picture." Spectacular theaters like the Roxy inspired awe, and this awe inspired, in turn, cartoons like that in the *New Yorker* in which a little girl, staring in amazement at the interior of a theater lobby, asked, "Mama—does God live here?"

The cult status of movies extended to those who appeared in them. Movie fans helped to transform charismatic screen actors and actresses into movie stars, making them the objects of intense popular fascination and even idolization. Although mass-produced, movies have recovered a certain sense of aura or at least a unique sense of novelty and excitement for consumers of mass culture. Unlike preindustrial forms of entertainment such as the theater, the things represented (the characters, the story) were not really there before the audience. Instead, they were only there indirectly; they were present in the form of images on the screen. Although they were mechanically reproduced, they nonetheless continued to create an impression of immediacy and presence. At any rate, audiences regarded them as special. They waited for hours in lines several blocks long to see new films that had been highly publicized or critically acclaimed, were controversial—or that merely featured their favorite stars.

For 20 years, from the coming of sound in 1929 to the postwar period (1949), roughly 80 to 90 million Americans went to the movies *every week.* In other words, virtually every American between the ages of 6 and 60 went to the movies at least once a week. Although certain films, like *Gone with the Wind* (1939), drew more viewers than others, moviegoing had become a habit and increasing numbers of spectators religiously went to see whatever was playing at their neighborhood theaters. Though the movies may have resembled a religious institution, they were always primarily a social institution—going to the movies became a way in which people passed their leisure time. However, in even the most common sense of the term, by the 1920s the cinema had definitely become an institution—an integral feature of the experience of being an American in the twentieth century. Going to the movies became as commonplace as going to school, to work, or to church. For earlier generations, it was as familiar an activity as watching television has become today.

DEVELOPING SYSTEMS: SOCIETY AND TECHNOLOGY

The cinema is an institution in a number of senses of the term. It is an economic institution, designed to make money. In order to do this, it established itself as an industry. It is a complex organization of producers, distributors, and exhibitors whose job it is to make and market motion pictures. To accomplish its goals, the industry developed a basic technology that facilitates the production and exhibition of movies. It also established various systems—such as the star system (see Chapter 5) and the genre system—which are designed to ensure that individual films return a profit to the industry that produces, distributes, and exhibits them. Stars and genres serve as known commodities that guarantee, up front, a certain minimal amount of pleasure that can be expected by viewers. Thus, in addition to the basic technological machinery required for

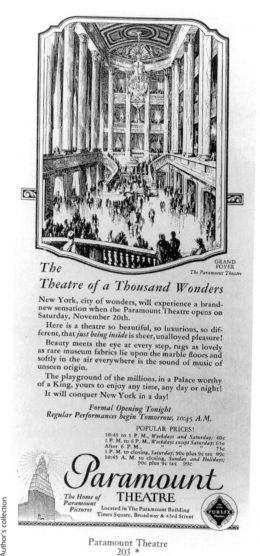

The
Theatre of a Thousand Wonders

GRAND FOYER
The Paramount Theatre

New York, city of wonders, will experience a brand-new sensation when the Paramount Theatre opens on Saturday, November 20th.

Here is a theatre so beautiful, so luxurious, so different, that *just being inside* is sheer, unalloyed pleasure!

Beauty meets the eye at every step, rugs as lovely as rare museum fabrics lie upon the marble floors and softly in the air everywhere is the sound of music of unseen origin.

The playground of the millions, in a Palace worthy of a King, yours to enjoy any time, any day or night!

It will conquer New York in a day!

Formal Opening Tonight
Regular Performances begin Tomorrow, 10:45 A.M.

POPULAR PRICES!
10:45 to 1 P. M., *Weekdays and Saturday;* 40c
1 P. M. to 6 P. M., *Weekdays except Saturday;* 65c
After 6 P. M. " " " 75c
1 P. M. to closing, *Saturday,* 90c plus 9c tax 99c
10:45 A. M. to closing, *Sunday and Holidays;*
90c plus 9c tax 99c

Paramount THEATRE

The Home of Paramount Pictures   Located in The Paramount Building
Times Square, Broadway & 43rd Street

PUBLIX Theatres

Paramount Theatre
203 *

Author's collection

An advertisement for a new movie palace, the Paramount Theatre, described it as "the playground of the millions, in a Palace worthy of a King."

making and showing films, the industry developed a secondary, "mental" machinery that makes audiences want to go to the movies.

In other words, the cinema, as an institution, developed on a variety of different levels at the same time. It functions as a social institution. That is, it is a means of providing an appropriate form of social contact for members of an emerging American populace born and bred in the world of mass culture. Indeed, it became an even more appropriate and more modern forum for leisure-time communal activity, for example, than were previous working-class social institutions such as churches, dance halls, social clubs, and saloons, which belong more properly to an earlier, preindustrial culture. At the same time, the cinema evolved as a technological institution that became dependent for its success on products of the Industrial Revolution—cameras, celluloid, microphones, amplifiers, magnetic recording tape, film laboratories, electricity, projectors, speakers, and screens. And it serves as a psychological institution whose purpose is to encourage the moviegoing habit by providing the kind of entertainment that working-class and middle-class Americans want.

The cinematic institution has changed from period to period, responding, in part, to technological changes, to the changing demands and leisure-time activities of audiences, and to social and economic changes that take place in American culture as a whole. But these changes have taken place within a more or less fixed notion of the cinema's identity as a medium. For roughly 100 years, no matter how often the face of the cinema has changed, the underlying structure of the cinematic experience has remained more or less the same. Going to the cinema has consisted of watching life-size images projected on a screen.

Yet even this fundamental feature of the cinema's identity was not always there. To understand what the cinema is and how it works, it is important to look at how it took shape. The identity of the cinema as an institution remains bound up with the sociocultural conditions in which it was conceived and developed by the growing film industry and in which it was experienced and consumed by an emerging society of habitual moviegoers.

EDISON AND THE KINETOSCOPE

Capturing Time

The origins of the cinema lie in the development of mass communication technology. The cinema serves as the culmination of an age that saw the invention of the telegraph (1837), photography (1826–1839), the typewriter (1873), the telephone (1876), the phonograph (1878), roll film (1880), the Kodak camera (1888), George Eastman's motion picture film (1889), Thomas Edison's motion picture camera (1891–1893), Marconi's wireless telegraph (1895), and the motion picture projector (1895–1896).

Edison, who had played a role in the development of the telegraph, the phonograph, and electricity, used the phonograph as a model for his "invention" of the motion picture. Actually, Edison did not so much invent as produce the first motion picture camera, the Kinetoscope. The actual execution of Edison's goal of creating an "instrument which [did] for the eye what the phonograph [did] for the ear" was accomplished through the effort of Edison's assistant, W. K. L. Dickson, which was itself based on earlier work by Étienne-Jules Marey.

The Kinetoscope, along with the telegraph, photography, the telephone, the phonograph, and the wireless telegraph, transformed the face of late nineteenth-century culture. Traditional notions of space and distance, which were based in part on how long it took to get from one place to another, were redefined by the virtually instantaneous transmission of information from one geographical location to another. Traditional notions of time underwent revision as still photographs captured moments of the present in ways that had eluded more primitive forms of representation. Photographs, unlike sketches, paintings, and sculptures, record events instantaneously before they vanish into memory. Thus the present and the past are rescued from the passage of time, lifted out of its continuous ongoing process, and frozen for all to see. Motion pictures record and reproduce the flow of time in a way that previously was impossible, even in photography.

Photography and the motion picture introduced—and *institutionalized*—a new, modern conception of time. Time could not only be caught but also replayed. It became, in a sense, a commodity. In the past, time was "spent" and then the experience of that time disappeared. But with still photography, the phonograph, and the motion picture, time was objectified. It could be marketed, in the form of photos, records, or movies, and it could be infinitely re-experienced. In short, the new communication technologies that arose at the end of the nineteenth century helped give birth to mass culture and the era of mass consumption, in part, by transforming time into a product that could be reproduced and sold. The cinema's ability to objectify and commodify time became crucial to its success.

As a medium, the cinema realized the goals of a twentieth-century consumer society whose desires were shaped by the Industrial Revolution. This society was encouraged by advertising and other forms of mass persuasion to consume what machines produced. These mass-produced products ranged from material goods such as cosmetics, clothes, household furnishings, and foodstuffs to less tangible items such as motion pictures. The cinema emerged as the perfect consumer product in that it not only gave audiences an experience to consume but also functioned as a display window for other mass-produced goods. As Charles Eckert argues, the movies serve as a showcase for consumer goods, including sewing machines, typewriters, telephones, automobiles, furniture, and fashions, which audiences then seek to obtain for themselves.

Peepshows versus Projectors

The cinema did not emerge as a form of mass consumption, however, until its technology evolved from its initial format of peepshow into its final form as images projected on a screen in a darkened theater. Edison's Kinetoscope was designed for use in Kinetoscope parlors, which contained only a few individual machines and permitted only one customer to view a short, 50-foot film at any one time. The first Kinetoscope parlors contained five machines. For the price of 25 cents (or 5 cents per machine), customers moved from machine to machine

Edison's peepshow Kinetoscope, featuring ear tubes for sound, entertained one customer at a time.

Courtesy of the Edison National Historic Site

to watch five different films (or, in the case of famous prizefights, successive rounds of a single fight).

These Kinetoscope arcades were modeled on phonograph parlors that had proved successful for Edison several years earlier. In the phonograph parlors, customers listened to recordings through individual ear tubes, moving from one machine to the next to hear different recorded speeches or pieces of music. The Kinetoscope parlors functioned in a similar way. More interested in the sale of Kinetoscopes (for roughly $250 apiece) to these parlors than in the films (which cost approximately $10 to $15 each) that would be run in them, Edison refused to develop projection technology, reasoning (quite correctly) that if he made and sold projectors, then exhibitors would purchase only one machine—a projector—from him instead of several.

Exhibitors, however, wanted to maximize *their* profits, which they could do more readily by projecting a handful of films to hundreds of customers at a time (rather than to one at a time) and by charging 25 to 50 cents for admission. About a year after the opening of the first Kinetoscope parlor in 1894, showmen such as Louis and Auguste Lumiere, Thomas Armat and Francis Jenkins, and Orville and Woodville Latham (with the assistance of Edison's former assistant, Dickson) perfected projection devices that were used in vaudeville houses, legitimate theaters, local town halls, makeshift storefront theaters, fairgrounds, and amusement parks to show films to mass audiences.

MASS PRODUCTION, MASS CONSUMPTION

A Public Spectacle

With the advent of projection (1895–1896), the motion pictures became the ultimate form of mass consumption. Previous audiences, of course, had viewed spectacles en masse at the theater, where vaudeville, popular dramas, musical and minstrel shows, classical plays, lectures, and slide and lantern shows had been presented to several hundred spectators at a time. But the movies differed significantly from these other forms of entertainment that depended on either live performance or (in the case of slide and lantern shows) the active involvement of a master of ceremonies who assembled the final program.

Although exhibitors regularly accompanied movies with live acts, the substance of the movies themselves was mass-produced, prerecorded material that could easily be reproduced for audiences by theaters, with little or no active participation on the audience members' part. Even though early exhibitors shaped their film programs by editing them together in whichever ways they thought would be most attractive to audiences or by accompanying them with lectures, their creative control remained limited. What audiences came to see was the technological marvel of the movies: the lifelike reproduction of the commonplace motion of trains, waves striking the shore, and people walking in the street, and the magic made possible by trick photography and the manipulation of the camera.

With the advent of projection, the viewer's relationship with the image was no longer private, as it had been with peepshow devices such as the Kinetoscope and the Mutoscope, which was a similar machine that reproduced motion by means of successive images on individual photographic cards instead of images on strips of celluloid. It suddenly became public—an experience that the viewer shared with dozens, scores, and even hundreds of others. At the same time, the image that the spectator viewed expanded from the minuscule peepshow dimensions of 1 or 2 inches (in height) to the life-size proportions of 6 or 9 feet. The spectator was no longer a Peeping Tom looking guiltily through a keyhole but a voyeur whose activity was shared (and thus semiauthorized) by a larger public.

Middle-Class Amusements

From 1896 to roughly 1905, when the nickelodeon era began, the audience that went to the movies (in the United States, at least) was the same more or less middle-class audience that had previously gone to vaudeville shows, variety theaters, and amusement parks. Indeed, the movies became variety acts of a sort, which played alongside live acts in places that provided a broad spectrum of different kinds of popular entertainment. Although the audiences consisted of all socioeconomic classes, the cost of admission tended to exclude the lower classes, as did the length of the program, which in vaudeville theaters was 2 hours or more. As a result, working-class laborers, who worked (ca. 1900) 60 hours a week or more and earned less than $4 a week, could only afford to attend on occasion.

The films mirrored the variety of contexts in which they were presented. Shown primarily in vaudeville houses until 1905, motion pictures appealed to audiences as attractions, a series of acts within the larger act of motion pictures, which was itself often only one of eight other variety acts. The kinds of films shown were actualities (documentaries, views of famous or distant places), recorded vaudeville acts, excerpts from popular plays, phantom rides (films shot from the front of moving vehicles), and trick films, which used the techniques of slow motion, reverse motion, substitution, and multiple exposure to perform tricks or acts of "magic."

Scholars of early cinema such as Tom Gunning (1990) describe this cinema of attractions as essentially an exhibitionist cinema. As attractions, films with self-descriptive titles like *The Execution of Mary Queen of Scots* (1895) or *Electrocuting an Elephant* (1903), presented or exhibited spectacles for viewers to admire. Strongmen such as Eugene Sandow flexed their muscles for the camera, and exotic dancers such as Fatima performed for the camera. Certain erotic films, such as *From Showgirl to Burlesque Queen* (1903), relied on a more traditional form of exhibitionism, as women undressed before and looked flirtatiously at the camera.

Early, pre-1906 cinema stressed showing rather than telling. Most films made in this period were actualities, which outnumbered fiction films until roughly 1906, when the percentage of story films began to increase dramatically and actualities became less and less popular. The shift from one kind of cinema to the other took place rapidly. By 1908, 96 percent of all American films told stories. The institutionalization of narrative as the primary category of American motion picture production marked the beginning of another stage in the development of the cinema as an institution. It was accompanied by a significant change in film exhibition.

The Nickelodeon: A Collective Experience

Starting in 1905, theaters devoted exclusively to the showing of motion picture films began to spring up in virtually every city in the country. Referred to as "nickelodeons" because the price of admission was initially only a nickel (this figure subsequently rose to 10 cents), these small, 200-seat theaters were quickly installed in or near shopping or entertainment districts in former stores that were converted, often in an extremely makeshift way, to movie theaters. The low cost of admission and the abbreviated length of the programs attracted a

Author's collection

The exterior of a typical nickelodeon, the Cascade Theatre in New Castle, Pennsylvania (ca. 1903).

new class of patrons, whom previous (and more expensive) forms of popular entertainment had ignored—the working classes.

Previously, working-class amusements had been confined to the home, the church, the saloon, or the social club. Nickelodeons drew the poorer elements of society, including recent immigrants, out of the ethnic social life associated with their local neighborhoods into a more diversified public space, where members of different classes and religions were transformed into a community of moviegoers. At the same time, these theaters continued to attract members of the middle-class audience that had earlier seen movies in vaudeville theaters.

Although the nickelodeons were never the melting pot of American democracy that certain historians have claimed, by 1910 they did provide the 26 million Americans who attended over 10,000 nickelodeons each week a common entertainment program. For the first time, millions of Americans from different backgrounds watched the same films and thus shared a collective experience as an invisible community. As the popularity of the nickelodeons increased and the moviegoing audience expanded, these theaters began to serve as the site for the creation of a homogeneous, middle-class American culture.

As a writer for *Harper's* magazine noted on visiting a nickelodeon in 1913, once the various members of the ethnically, socially, and economically diverse audience had taken their seats, they became part of a single crowd, caught up in the dreamlike images on the screen. This utopian ideal of a classless (or

Author's collection

Moviegoing as a social institution: The opening night audience at the (segregated) Rex Theater in Hannibal, Missouri, on April 4, 1912. Whites sat in the orchestra while blacks were seated in the balcony.

universally middle-class) community of spectators may never have been realized, but its potential was certainly there in the form of an institution of mass production and mass exhibition that was itself national in scope.

Cleaning Up: The Benefits of Respectability

The film industry was becoming more and more stabilized. In 1908, the major film producers banded together to form the Motion Picture Patents Company (MPPC), which sought to control all aspects of motion picture production, distribution, and exhibition (see Chapter 4, "The Studio System"). Shortly after the formation of the MPPC, exhibitors and film producers sought to expand the market of habitual moviegoers to include greater and greater numbers of those who had previously attended only "high-class" amusements, such as the theater and vaudeville.

However, in December 1908, the mayor of New York City ordered that all nickel theaters be closed, arguing that they posed a "threat to the city's physical and moral well-being." Exhibitors and members of the MPPC responded almost immediately with a campaign to improve the content of motion pictures and the conditions of theaters. At the same time, exhibitors consciously began to court middle-class customers by becoming more "respectable." They provided half-price matinees for women and children, they upgraded the quality of the physical structure of the theaters, they eliminated lower-class elements such as ethnic films and foreign-language sing-alongs, and they raised prices.

Producers joined the program to uplift the movies by making films that appealed to a higher class of clientele. They engaged in self-censorship to control any content of motion pictures that might prove offensive to middle-class tastes. And they voluntarily submitted their films to the national Board of Censorship (an independent body of censors) for review. In an attempt to appeal to middle-class sensibilities, they drew more and more on the classics. Prior to 1908, the source material for movies had come from newspaper headlines, vaudeville and burlesque routines, political cartoons, fairy tales, and popular songs. Between 1907 and 1911, however, Vitagraph released more than 50 films that were based on literary, historical, or biblical sources. Filmmakers began to adapt the works of Edgar Allan Poe, Charles Dickens, Emile Zola, Leo Tolstoy, Victor Hugo, and William Shakespeare.

SPECTACLE AND STORYTELLING: FROM PORTER TO GRIFFITH

The Camera as Recorder

The bourgeoisification of the movies involved considerably more than merely upgrading motion picture content from strongmen flexing their muscles to Shakespeare. In adapting more complex story material to the screen, filmmakers were forced to upgrade their own abilities as storytellers. While early American cinema had been exhibitionist in nature, content with showing attractions, subsequent (post-1908) American cinema became more and more intent on the perfection of narrative skills. Mere theatrical display proved less and less capable of conveying complex character psychology or intricate narrative complications. Middle-class audiences who had grown up with the highly involved plots and fascinating characters of authors such as Dickens began to demand more sophisticated film narratives than had their predecessors. Film directors like D. W. Griffith, who carefully crafted narrative personae for themselves, provided these new audiences with the kinds of narratives with which they were familiar in the theater or in literature.

Edwin S. Porter, the major filmmaker associated with early American cinema, epitomized the presentational style of pre-Griffith cinema. Intent on a theatrical style of spectacle, Porter composed his narratives out of a succession of separate attractions. In one of his most famous films, *The Life of an American Fireman* (1903), Porter showed the fireman's dramatic rescue of a mother and her baby from the second story of a burning building. In the final version of the film, Porter presented the action of the rescue as he had originally filmed it—in two successive shots. Filmed at two separate times as two separate spectacles staged in two separate spaces, the event remained that way for the audiences who saw it in 1903.

In the first shot, audiences saw the interior of a smoke-filled room: the fireman enters, rescues the woman, and returns a few moments later to rescue the infant. In the next shot, audiences saw the exterior of the building: the fireman enters, rescues the woman by carrying her down a ladder, and then, informed that her child is still in the room, returns to rescue the baby. In other words, Porter showed the same action from two different perspectives successively rather than cutting back and forth from the interior to the exterior of the building to follow the unfolding of the drama as it might have been told by a storyteller more intent on suspense and the act of narration itself. (In fact, the latter version of the film, assembled by subsequent distributors of the film, did circulate in the film library of the Museum of Modern Art for 30 or more years until the original version was discovered in the mid-1970s.)

The Camera as Narrator

Primitive cinema presented events but provided little or no reading of them. Events spoke for themselves without the intervention of a narrator or narrating presence that attempted to read or interpret them for the audience. Stories were told, but they were told directly; the camera did not read events but merely recorded them instead. The cinema of Griffith (and later) actively narrated events, shaping the audience's perception of them. This was accomplished in a variety of ways, but chief among them, for Griffith at least, was the device of parallel editing, which involves cutting back and forth from two (or more) simultaneous events taking place in separate spaces.

Gunning described the parallel editing in Griffith's *The Drive for Life* (1909), which cuts back and forth between a man who discovers that the woman he has jilted has sent a box of poisoned chocolates to his fiancée, and his fiancée, who is about to eat one of the pieces of candy. As the fiancée picks up a piece of chocolate and is about to eat it, Griffith cuts away, in midgesture, to her lover, speeding to her in his car to warn her of her danger. The suspense editing repeatedly interrupts her action, returning to show her being distracted by her sister, dropping the candy, or kissing it. Each time the film cuts away from her as she is about to eat the poisoned candy, the presence of Griffith as a narrator can be dramatically felt. The drama was clearly being constructed for the audience by these intrusions, as it was through similar editing patterns in *The Lonely Villa* (1909), *The Lonedale Operator* (1911), and other last-minute, race-to-the-rescue films directed by Griffith.

At the same time, Griffith used editing to contribute to the psychological development of his characters, giving the audience a sense of what they are thinking. Thus, in *After Many Years* (1908) he cut from a wife to the object of her thoughts—her shipwrecked husband. Other edits were used to explain the motivation or the behavior of his characters. Thus, in *Salvation Army Lass*

(1908), Griffith cut away from a burglar on his way to commit a crime to a shot of his girlfriend, still lying on the ground where he had left her after rejecting her pleas that he not go on the job. When Griffith cut back to the burglar, who then changes his mind about going ahead with the crime, he deftly conveyed to the audience the reasons for the burglar's change of heart. Similar cutaways served to explain character behavior in Griffith's historical epic, *The Birth of a Nation* (1915).

The "Feature" Film

With the emergence of a cinema of narration, which replaced that of monstration or showing, classical Hollywood cinema took one step further toward the institutionalization of the cinema as an American pastime. As narratives became more complex, the 1000-foot, one-reel (10-to-15-minute) format of the motion picture, which had only recently become an industrywide standard in 1908, became more and more restrictive. Critics in the trade magazine *Moving Picture World* observed that "the filming of some great opera or a popular literary or dramatic or historical subject requires more than a reel" and suggested that the longer the pictures, the more exhibitors could charge audiences to see them.

Multiple-reel "feature" films from abroad, such as *Dante's Inferno* (five reels, Italy, 1911), *Queen Elizabeth* (four reels, France, 1912), *Quo Vadis* (eight reels, Italy, 1913) and *Cabiria* (ten reels, Italy, 1914) were showcased in large, first-class legitimate theaters, which charged from 25 cents to a dollar for tickets. The financial success of these multiple-reel European films prompted American producers to release longer and longer films, including Griffith's biblical spectacle, *Judith of Bethulia* (four reels, 1914), his adaptation of Poe's "The Telltale Heart" and "Annabel Lee," *The Avenging Conscience* (six reels, 1914), and his historical epic, *The Birth of a Nation* (twelve reels, 1915).

The Birth, which sustains an intricate narrative for three hours of screen time, held audiences spellbound. One of Griffith's assistants, Karl Brown, reported his reactions to seeing the fully assembled film for the first time on opening night. "What unfolded on that screen was magic itself. I knew there were cuts from this and to that, but try as I would, I could not *see* them. . . . All I knew was that between the ebb and flow of a broad canvas of a great battle, now far and now near, and the roaring of that gorgeous orchestra banging and blaring battle songs to stir the coldest blood, I was hot and cold and feeling waves of tingling electric shocks racing all over me."

The Birth ran for 44 consecutive weeks at the Liberty Theater in New York City, where reserved-seat tickets were sold at the unprecedented price of $2. Its success transformed the nature of American film production and exhibition. It marked the end of "the lowly nickelodeon storefront theater, with its tinny honky-tonk piano and its windowless, foul-air smelliness" and introduced "the grandeur of a great auditorium with a great orchestra and a great picture that ran for three hours and filled an entire evening with thrills and excitement in a setting of opulent luxury such as the great masses of working people had never dreamed possible for them."

The Birth was notorious for other reasons as well, chief among them its racist agenda. *The Birth* illustrated the enormous power of the motion picture medium to communicate ideological arguments. Griffith's melodramatic retelling of the story of the Civil War and Reconstruction posited a villain. That villain was the African American (and the white politicians in the North who were determined to "overthrow civilization in the South" and to "put the white South under the heel of the black South"). For Griffith, the birth of the nation depended on the subjugation of the African American and the restoration of white privilege. If *The Birth of a Nation* marked the birth of classical Hollywood cinema, then that birth was grounded in white racism.

PRESENTING . . . THE MOVIE PALACE

"Gardens of Dreams"

The advent of multiple-reel, feature-length films was accompanied by a dramatic change in motion picture presentation as the uncomfortable, small, makeshift nickelodeons gave way to luxurious movie palaces and other large theaters especially built for the showing of motion pictures. Though the majority of movie theaters built in the 1910s and 1920s tended to be modest in size, seating from 500 to 800 spectators, more and more large movie palaces, seating from 1500 to over 6000 spectators, were built in urban areas. In contrast to the congestion and oppressive sense of city life experienced by urban residents outside the theater, inside the typical movie palace customers enjoyed the luxury of spacious, stately surroundings and a staff of obliging theater attendants who sought to answer their every need.

Movie palaces, boasting a palatial décor that ranged from the classical to the exotic, provided "an acre of seats in a garden of dreams." Contemporary interior decorator Harold Rambusch declared, in 1929, that "in our big modern movie palaces are collected the most gorgeous rugs, furniture and fixtures that money can produce. No kings or emperors have wandered through more luxurious surroundings. In a sense, these theatres are social safety valves in that the public can partake of the same luxuries as the rich."

The Great Showmen

The era of the movie palace began in 1913 with the opening of the 2460-seat Regent, "the first de luxe theatre built expressly for showing movies in New York." Shortly after the Regent opened, showman S. L. Rothapfel was hired to manage it. He made it the premier motion picture theater in the world. Like the movie palaces that followed it, the Regent featured an organ, an orchestra, a

Author's collection

The interior of a typical movie palace, the Brooklyn Paramount.

chorus and/or opera singers, ushers to show patrons to their seats, and a lavish atmospheric interior adorned with gilt.

Rothapfel, or "Roxy" as he was called by his associates, was subsequently lured away from the Regent, which was located uptown at 116th Street and Seventh Avenue, to operate the 3500-seat Strand (1914), which was downtown at Broadway and 47th Street. The *New York Times* reviewed opening night, was impressed by the neo-Corinthian decor and the plush seats, and compared the experience to "going to a Presidential reception." Roxy later lent his flair for extravagant motion picture presentation to the 1900-seat Rialto when it opened on Times Square in 1916.

By this time, the entertainment program of the movie palace had expanded to include (in addition to the theater orchestra's overture and musical accompaniment of the silent feature) dancers, opera singers, and other performers in live skits. The film program had also evolved to consist of not only the feature film but a newsreel and a comedy short as well. In fact, the feature presentation tended to occupy only about 68 percent of the entire program.

Roxy continued to provide bigger and better shows in a series of other New York theaters. He took over the management of the 2100-seat Rivoli (built in 1917) and of the 5300-seat Capitol (built in 1919, managed by Roxy in 1920), and

Author's collection

Grauman's Chinese Theater in the late 1920s.

then of his own 6200-seat Roxy theatre (1927). By the time he built the Roxy, the art of exhibition had developed into a science. Not only were uniformed ushers and other theater personnel drilled in their duties like military cadets, but spectators became part of this streamlined system of efficiency as well. As Richard Koszarski (1990) points out, "Each seat in the Roxy was wired to a central console so the house staff could immediately direct patrons to new vacancies."

In Los Angeles, impresario Sid Grauman followed Roxy's example, launching a series of movie palaces that were each more lavish than the other. While Roxy gave his audiences an entertainment program consisting of a variety of different live acts to accompany the film, Grauman provided a "Prologue," a show thematically related to the motion picture. His theater empire began with the Million Dollar Theatre (2100 seats) in 1917, then the Egyptian (1900 seats) in 1922, the Metropolitan (3485 seats) in 1923, and the Chinese (2500 seats) in 1927. As the names "Egyptian" and "Chinese" suggest, a number of movie palaces of the 1920s adopted exotic architectural styles, employing Oriental, Hindu, Italian, Persian, Moorish, or Spanish décor to create a romantic atmosphere in which audiences could consume onscreen fantasies.

Other major cities, such as Chicago, built movie palaces of their own. Theater magnates A. J. Balaban and Sam Katz, following the major routes of urban mass-transit lines, put their theaters within reach of a growing urban middle class, building the 2400-seat Central Park Theatre in 1917, both the 4700-seat Tivoli Theatre and the 3900-seat Chicago Theatre in 1921, and the 4000-seat Uptown Theatre in the mid-1920s. In addition to mighty Wurlitzer organs, full orchestras, and live stage shows, Balabar & Katz theaters provided patrons with "free child care, attendant smoking rooms, foyers and lobbies lined with paintings and sculpture, and organ music for those waiting in line." A staff of nurses and mother's helpers took care of the young children of patrons in the theater basement, which was equipped like a neighborhood playground with slides and sandboxes. At the same time, starting in 1921, Balaban & Katz theaters also had air conditioning, which gave them a crucial advantage over their competition throughout the summer months.

Noting the success of the Balaban & Katz theaters in Chicago, Paramount joined forces with that organization and put Sam Katz in charge of all Paramount theaters. As a result, the model for movie palaces developed by Balaban & Katz found widespread adoption in the Paramount theater circuit. It quickly spread to the circuits of other major studios as well, becoming the standard used by the film industry as a whole.

With the construction of theaters especially designed for the exhibition of motion pictures, the shift from one-reel films to the new phenomenon of the feature-length film that presented narratives and characters as sophisticated as those found in other typically middle-class forms of representation, and the development of a habitual, movie-going audience composed of a broad spectrum of the general public, the basic elements of the cinematic institution fell into place.

AN EVOLVING INSTITUTION

The cinema began as a technological marvel, as the latest invention from Thomas Edison, the "wizard of Menlo Park." The early cinema of the pre-nickelodeon days evolved from a primitive cinema of attractions into a modern cinema of compelling characters, engrossing stories, and hypnotic illusionism. Throughout the 1920s, the presentation of motion pictures retained its origin in the world of amusement parks, vaudeville, and burlesque. The movie palaces are themselves spectacles that frequently overwhelm the films shown in them. House orchestras and stage shows also foster an air of variety, as does the presence of newsreels, comedy shorts, and other filmed material that rounds out the program. Yet the feature film holds its own among these other attractions. Its ability to give expression to its characters' emotions, to explore their psyches, to trace their pursuit of their goals—in short, to tell their stories—has evolved to a point of near perfection. The coming of sound, color, widescreen, and stereo sound would add somewhat to the feature film's expressive capabilities but would not profoundly alter classical Hollywood cinema's ability to function as an efficient system of storytelling. Today's filmmakers draw on essentially the same set of stylistic practices and narrative techniques as those forged by Griffith and others during the period in which the fundamental elements of the feature film were established.

Other features of the cinematic institution, however, have been dismantled. The 1920s witnessed the creation of a general moviegoing public that habitually patronized the nation's cinemas. For over 20 years, from 1929 to 1949, an average of 83 million Americans went to the movies every week. In 2002, the average weekly attendance was only 31.5 million. The age of the nickelodeon gave way to that of the movie palace in the 1910s and 1920s. In the 1960s, the gigantic movie palaces of the past gave way to the new nickelodeons of the present—to small, minimally decorated multiplexes and mall cinemas. The Roxy was torn down in 1961. Radio City Music Hall, though still standing, ceased showing motion pictures on a regular basis in 1978. The cinematic institution of Hollywood past has disappeared. It slowly transformed itself, from the 1950s to the present, into a new institution designed to serve the different needs of contemporary audiences and an ever-changing, modern motion picture marketplace.

The chapters that follow are designed to provide an in-depth portrait of the cinematic institution in its heyday. They look at its stylistic foundations in classical Hollywood's stylistic and narrative practices, at its industrial roots in the studio system, and at its basic economic underpinnings in the star and genre systems. The goal is not only to draw a map of the terrain of the institution of American cinema, but also to recover for today's generation of moviegoers some sense of the *experience* that previous generations had when they went to the movies.

■ ■ ■ **SELECT FILMOGRAPHY**

*The Life of an American
   Fireman* (1903)
After Many Years (1908)
Salvation Army Lass (1908)

The Drive for Life (1909)
The Lonely Villa (1909)
The Lonedale Operator (1911)
The Birth of a Nation (1915)

■ ■ ■ **SELECT BIBLIOGRAPHY**

BORDWELL, DAVID, JANET STAIGER, AND KRISTIN THOMPSON. *The Classical Hollywood Cinema: Film Style and Mode of Production to 1960.* New York: Columbia University Press, 1985.
BOWSER, EILEEN. *The Transformation of Cinema: 1907–1915.* New York: Scribner, 1990.

BROWN, KARL. *Adventures with D. W. Griffith.* New York: Farrar, Straus & Giroux, 1973.

ECKERT, CHARLES. "The Carole Lombard in Macy's Window," *Quarterly Review of Film Studies* **3** (Winter 1978), 1–21.

ELSAESSER, THOMAS, ed. *Early Cinema: Space, Frame, Narrative.* London: BFI Publishing, 1990.

GOMERY, DOUGLAS. *Movie History: A Survey.* Belmont, CA: Wadsworth, 1991.

———. *Shared Pleasures: A History of Movie Presentation in the United States.* Madison: University of Wisconsin Press, 1992.

GUNNING, TOM. "The Cinema of Attractions: Early Film, the Spectator and the Avant-Garde" and "Weaving a Narrative: Style and Economic Background in Griffith's Biograph Films," in Thomas Elsaesser, ed., *Early Cinema: Space, Frame, Narrative.* London: BFI Publishing, 1990.

HALL, BEN M. *The Best Remaining Seats: The Story of the Golden Age of the Movie Palace.* New York: Bramhall House, 1961.

HANSEN, MIRIAM. *Babel & Babylon: Spectatorship in American Silent Film.* Cambridge: Harvard University Press, 1991.

KERN, STEPHEN. *The Culture of Time and Space, 1880–1918.* Cambridge: Harvard University Press, 1983.

KOSZARSKI, RICHARD. *An Evening's Entertainment: The Age of the Silent Feature Picture, 1915–1928.* New York: Scribner, 1990.

MAY, LARY. *Screening Out the Past: The Birth of Mass Culture and the Motion Picture Industry.* Chicago: University of Chicago Press, 1980.

MAYNE, JUDITH. "Immigrants and Spectators," *Wide Angle* 5, 2 (1982).

MUSSER, CHARLES. *The Emergence of Cinema: The American Screen to 1907.* New York: Scribner, 1990.

CHAPTER **2**

Classical Hollywood Cinema: Narration

A NATIONAL STYLE

"The Temper of an Age . . ."

A work of art is customarily associated with the name of the artist, and the history of an art form is traditionally written in terms of those names. Such a history assumes that individual artists either live and work in a social vacuum or so transcend the constraints of time and place that their work stands outside of social history. But if the individual artist transcends society, we should remember that society is also and above all *within* that artist and that every work bears at least two signatures—that of the artist and that of the world in which the work was created.

In the field of art history, Heinrich Wolfflin introduced the concept of "a history of art without names." Wolfflin wrote that history in terms of a typology of artistic styles or schools rather than in terms of isolated, individual works. By subsuming the individual styles of the Great Masters within the larger styles of the school or country at that particular moment in history in which they work, he drew attention to the multifaceted nature of style, which became for him an "expression of the temper of an age and a nation as well as an expression of the individual temperament."

The history of the cinema that is offered to students in introductory film courses has traditionally been written as a history of names: a history of actors, directors, producers, and writers whose works transcend the times and places in which they were produced. But in the American cinema, individual artistic styles exist in the context of a larger, national style. It was against the background of this general style, which has come to be known as classical Hollywood style, that the distinct individual styles of directors such as John Ford, Alfred Hitchcock, Howard Hawks, Josef von Sternberg, Orson Welles, Martin Scorsese, David Lynch and others took shape.

Every American film—from recognized masterpieces such as *Citizen Kane* (1941), which transcends stylistic convention, to run-of-the-mill program pictures such as *Andy Hardy Gets Spring Fever* (1939), which merely observes convention—draws on the fundamental stylistic principles of classical Hollywood cinema for its means of expression and, in doing so, conveys "the temper of an age and a nation" as well as that of the artists who produce it. Yet every film also articulates this style in a different way, inflecting the larger, national style with the individual accent(s) of particular studios, producers, directors, writers, stars, camerapersons, and other craftspeople who make films.

A Narrative Machine

Unlike the periods of art history, such as the Gothic, Renaissance, or Baroque, in which the overall stylistic features of each period are quite apparent even to the untrained eye, classical Hollywood cinema possesses a style that is largely invisible and difficult for the average spectator to see. Its invisibility is, in large part, the product of American cinema's proficiency as a narrative machine. Like the industry-based, assembly-line process innovated by Henry Ford and his peers in the business world to make the production of automobiles and other consumer goods as streamlined and economical as possible, American movies rapidly evolved during the 1910s and 1920s into a highly efficient mode of telling stories. Every aspect of the production operation was geared up to facilitate the smoothest possible flow of the narrative process.

As a result, the narrative is delivered so effortlessly and efficiently to the audience that it appears to have no source. It comes magically off the screen as if spontaneously creating itself in the presence of the spectators in the movie theater for their immediate consumption and pleasure. But, in fact, it is created; it is made according to classical principles of clarity, simplicity, elegance, order, economy, and symmetry. Classical works thus traditionally avoid excess, subjectivity, and undue emotionalism, striving for the Greek ideal of *meden agan,* or "nothing in excess."

EQUILIBRIUM AND DISRUPTION

Narrative process follows an orderly pattern in which an initial state of affairs is introduced, after which something occurs to disturb this equilibrium. Subsequent events attempt to restore the original status quo, but this is repeatedly frustrated, and order is recovered only at the end of the film.

For instance, Alfred Hitchcock's *Rear Window* (1954) begins with a statement of the narrative status quo, presenting a survey of the courtyard in which the action of the film will be set. The next few minutes of the film introduce the minor characters who live in the courtyard, as well as the film's major character, the news magazine photographer L. B. Jeffries (James Stewart), whose point of view provides us with a perspective on the action that will follow.

Once the world of the film is described, its equilibrium is suddenly disrupted with the introduction of a lovers' quarrel between Jeffries and his girlfriend, Lisa (Grace Kelly), and with a scream from a woman across the way, whom Jeffries subsequently suspects was murdered by her husband. The action that follows moves toward a resolution of the conflict between Jeffries and his girlfriend, toward the proof that a murder has taken place, and toward a solution of that crime. With the completion of these actions, order is restored

Courtesy of Paramount

The narrative status quo—the courtyard in which the action of *Rear Window* is set.

and the film concludes with another survey of the courtyard, revealing the new status quo.

Classical narratives routinely begin with an act that disturbs the original state of things and is answered, by the film's end, with another act that reestablishes a new order or balance. Thus a murder mystery, whether a private-eye film of the 1940s (*The Maltese Falcon*, 1941) or a police picture of the 1990s (*Se7en*, 1995), will begin with the discovery of a dead body and end with the solution of the crime.

An adventure story or quest (*Raiders of the Lost Ark*, 1981) is launched with the loss, absence, or lack of a desired object and concludes with its attainment (or at least discovery). A love story (*Pretty Woman*, 1990) starts with a chance encounter and culminates with a proposal of marriage. A monster (*Jaws*, 1975) or horror (*Halloween*, 1978) film begins with the death of an innocent victim and ends with the actual or symbolic death of the thing, which is routinely reincarnated for the sequel(s).

In between the beginning and the end of the film's overall narrative action, a series of additional, smaller disturbances take place, followed by tentative restorations of order, with each scene or sequence recapitulating the larger process of balance, disruption, and rebalancing of the film as a whole. In this way, the narrative moves ceaselessly toward closure, completion, conclusion.

CHARACTERS AND GOALS

Problem Solving

As David Bordwell explains, classical Hollywood cinema is primarily a character-centered cinema. Its characters are more or less stable, knowable, and psychologically coherent individuals who possess clearly defined, specific goals. Although this cinema is also a plot-driven or action cinema, characters stand at the center of the action and interact with events. Filmmakers use these interactions in accordance with the classical principles of narrative economy and efficiency to further the exposition of their characters. Plot expectations are set by the specific goals that individual characters possess or by the problems they are asked to solve.

Over the course of the narrative, characters struggle to achieve their goals or solve their problems. They overcome those who stand in their way (such as the villains), triumph over adverse circumstances (such as physical disability, nature, or some other force), and/or transcend their own limitations (such as individual fears or weaknesses). The narrative ends with the character's triumph or failure, with the resolution (or conclusive nonresolution) of the problem, and with the attainment (or clear-cut nonattainment) of the goal.

In *Vertigo* (1958), former detective Scottie Ferguson (James Stewart), who suddenly discovers that he suffers from acrophobia, becomes the unwitting victim of an elaborate murder scheme that takes advantage of his fear of heights in order to effect a perfect crime. Though Scottie's larger goals in the narrative remain obscure, by the end of the film, his more immediate goals have been satisfied. He reestablishes the balance or equilibrium with which the film begins: he not only discovers the deception and solves the mystery, but also cures his vertigo (although he loses the great love of his life in the process).

Much as classical mystery narratives such as *Vertigo* enlist audiences in the process of problem solving, classical suspense narratives regularly take shape around the forward movement of characters' attempts to attain goals and around the backward or sideways movements of the delays they experience in trying to overcome the various obstacles that stand (or are placed) between them and their goals. For example, the action in *The Terminator* (1984) is constructed around the efforts of a cyborg (Arnold Schwarzenegger) who was sent back in time by a totalitarian regime in the future (ca. 2029). He has been programmed to kill a woman, Sarah Connor (Linda Hamilton), to prevent her from bearing a child who is destined to lead a rebellion against that dictatorship.

At the same time, Kyle Reese (Michael Biehn), a (human) rebel freedom fighter, is also sent back in time to prevent the cyborg, or Terminator, from accomplishing his task. The dramatic structure of the film consists of alternating sequences in which each of these major characters sets about attempting to solve problems and to reach goals only to discover that his or her attempts have been frustrated by the countereffort of the other. Both Reese and the Terminator pursue their goals relentlessly—to their own self-destruction. At this point, the film concludes (with Reese dead but victorious)—only to find its narrative resolution reopened seven years later in *Terminator 2: Judgment Day* (1991).

Through Time and Space

Often the goals that organize a classical Hollywood narrative are given a precise temporal dimension—a specific deadline has to be met or a certain task has to be completed by a definite time. Near the start of *Brewster's Millions* (1985), the sixth remake of a popular plot idea that first reached the screen in 1914, Brewster (Richard Pryor) is told by a somewhat sadistic philanthropist that he will be given $300 million, provided that he can spend $1 million a day for 30 days without acquiring any tangible property or assets. The remainder of the film documents his efforts to meet this deadline.

Buster Keaton also milks the inheritance idea for suspense comedy in *Seven Chances* (1925), in which his character discovers that he will inherit $7 million if he can get married by 7:00 P.M. on his 27th birthday, which happens to be that very day. After getting a quick brush-off from his first seven choices for possible brides, Keaton literally runs through the rest of the movie looking for someone to marry, racing against the clock to meet the 7:00 deadline. In *48 Hours* (1982), the deadline gimmick plays a central role in a plot in which a detective (Nick Nolte) gives a convict (Eddie Murphy) 48 hours to help him catch a couple of cop killers, promising to reward the latter with a parole if they succeed.

Courtesy Universal Pictures

Fred Haise (Bill Paxton, left), Jack Swigert (Kevin Bacon, center), and Jim Lovell (Tom Hanks) journey to the moon in *Apollo 13.*

In a similar way, stories are routinely designed along spatial lines, with their characters moving toward precise destinations or geographical goals. Journeys and cross-country treks have served as the fundamental organizing principle for narratives since Homer's *Odyssey.* The journey provides the basic structure for a number of extremely popular motion pictures, ranging from *The Wizard of Oz* (1939), *Around the World in 80 Days* (1956), and *North by Northwest* (1959), to *2001: A Space Odyssey* (1968), *Close Encounters of the Third Kind* (1977), *Apocalypse Now* (1979), and *Apollo 13* (1995). Even in those instances in which the final destination is never announced, made clear, or reached, the voyage becomes sufficient in itself to hold the narrative on course, giving it an all-important sense of forward movement.

By the ends of these journeys, the characters not only move from point A to point Z, but they realize other nonspatial goals as well, making deadlines, solving mysteries, falling in love, discovering new worlds, and coming to terms with themselves and their fellow travelers. The purely physical movement of the characters through space provides a sense of narrative development that is immediately coherent, no matter how obscure or incoherent the logic of the dramatic action actually is (as in *2001*). The journey film always looks forward to getting there; as a result, the spectator always arrives, even when the characters do not and even when "there" is only a hastily tacked-on title that reads "The End."

The Audience's Journey

In the broadest possible sense, then, every film is a journey that begins with the distributor's logo and the credits and ends with an end title; every spectator is a traveler whose trip to the theater and whose short sojourn there takes him or her on a narrative journey that only ends when the lights come up. The popularity of goal-centered, deadline-driven, and journey narratives undoubtedly owes something to the ways in which these particular narrative forms rework the all-too-familiar movie-going experience in the most exciting and pleasurable ways imaginable. The invisibility of the narrative patterns of classical Hollywood cinema remains indebted, in part, to such "cloaking devices."

Going to the movies becomes "going to the movies." What we see on the screen is what we are doing at that very moment; that is, looking for goals, participating in deadlines, and undertaking journeys. The invisibility of classical Hollywood cinema is an integral product of its transparency—in both senses of the word. By concealing all signs of their artifice and constructedness, the movies encourage us to see through them, and what we see is what they are. They are us going to the movies; we identify with onscreen characters who do what we do—who look for clues and solve problems; who look forward to, yet also dread, the deadline that marks the end of the film; and who reach our destination at the same time that they reach theirs.

HIGH ARTIFICE, INVISIBLE ART

Denial and Recognition

Ironically, the invisibility of classical Hollywood cinema is the result of great artifice. Its transparency is only an illusion. Beneath the apparent artlessness of the surface lies a solid foundation of highly crafted narrative techniques that all share the same common goal and participate in the same dual mission. They function to deliver the story as powerfully as possible without interrupting its flow with intrusive marks or signs that might betray the fact that the story is itself a product of careful construction.

Most spectators are aware, either consciously or unconsciously, that films are not real—that is, that the blood they see in the shower sequence of *Psycho* (1960) is really chocolate sauce; that the dangerous stunt sequences in the Indiana Jones films are made using doubles; that the attack on the Death Star in *Star Wars* (1977) is shot using models and miniatures at George Lucas's special-effects house, Industrial Light & Magic; and that no one really dies during the making of either of the Terminator films. At the same time, most spectators also deny—out of necessity—their awareness of this artifice, or the fiction of the reality, in order to participate in the reality of these fictions.

Moviegoing engages audiences in what is known as a willing suspension of disbelief; and audiences are all the more willing to be thus engaged because the pleasures provided by doing so prove to be both rewarding and significant. Although a certain amount of denial works wonders in enabling audiences to enter into the onscreen fiction, considerable pleasure also derives from the recognition of the artifice. Audiences appreciate what they refer to as "particularly good films," that is, technically well-crafted films or stories that are told in an especially exciting manner; and they distinguish these works from what they consider to be average films.

The pleasures of watching a Hitchcock film, for example, come as much from the audience's complicity with the storytelling interventions of the director, who repeatedly nudges his viewers to notice this or that important detail or encourages them to react in this or that specific way, as it does from their absorption into the fictional world of the narrative. Hitchcock described his films as "slices of cake" rather than slices of life. By this, he meant that his films are not merely transparent records of reality.

Defining drama as "life with the dull bits cut out," Hitchcock cut those dull bits out with a razor-sharp narrative sensibility and rearranged the exciting bits that were left over into breathtaking suspense thrillers. Yet unlike other, more self-effacing directors, Hitchcock left his mark on the finished film, and his imprint became an integral element of the film's appeal, openly acknowledging its status as a concoction, that is, as a slice of cake. As a result, Hitchcock enjoyed a special relationship with his audiences, who both lose themselves in the story being told and simultaneously derive pleasure from a recognition of how it is being told.

Underlying Patterns

The narrative patterns of mainstream Hollywood cinema are less clearly visible than the storytelling presence that can be found in every Hitchcock film; but, even so, they function to provide audiences with pleasure. But while the structure of a Hitchcock narrative lies more or less on or near the surface of the film, the structure in the typical classical Hollywood film is buried much deeper; it shapes audiences' responses on a less visible level.

Audiences unconsciously sense the classic principles of economy, regularity, symmetry, and order that inform the most compelling narratives to emerge from this system of storytelling, and they derive pleasure from the order that these elements impose on the entertainment experience. Any attempt to come to grips with the phenomenon of classical Hollywood cinema must therefore acknowledge the importance of these basic narrative patterns and examine the role they play in the overall effectiveness of classical Hollywood cinema as a system.

Average spectators are fully aware that the films they watch are constructed out of bits and pieces of celluloid that have been shot at a variety of different times and in an assortment of different settings and that have been assembled to tell a specific story in a certain way. Every time they watch a film, they are necessarily reminded of its artifice by a number of factors—not the least of which is the opening or closing credit sequence full of the names of those who worked on the film. However, spectators rarely *experience* films in this way.

ANALYZING FILM NARRATIVES: SEGMENTATION

Though 90- to 120-minute films consist, on the average, of 600 to 800 individual shots and 5 to 40 separate sequences, audiences generally experience films as continuous instead of fragmented, as seamless wholes rather than as a string of discrete episodes. As we shall see in the next chapter, this illusion of continuity is the product of a body of stylistic practices that are specifically designed to conceal the essential discontinuity of the filmmaking process. In order to understand how narratives work, film studies has developed an analytical technique designed to expose this underlying discontinuity. It breaks the film down into its basic narrative units. This process of structural analysis is known as *segmentation*, which is a term that has been used in literary studies to describe the process of dividing works into their constituent parts to study them in greater detail.

Segmentation can be used in the analysis of single scenes, parts of scenes, or entire films. Various criteria can also be used to organize the segmentation, based on their appropriateness to the narrative structures of individual films. In general, the strategy involved in the segmentation of entire films is to break the films down into their largest units, which can then be subdivided into increasingly smaller units. These larger units tend to be based on the traditional *dramatic unities* (as they are defined by Aristotle and others); that is, the unities of action, time, and/or space.

For example, Sophocles' *Oedipus the King* possesses all three unities: it consists of a single action—Oedipus's investigation into the causes of the plague that besets Thebes; it takes place more or less continuously during the course of a single day; and it plays itself out in a single setting in front of the king's palace at Thebes. Analyzed using these three traditional criteria, *Oedipus* would thus break down into only one segment.

Only a handful of motion pictures observe all three unities as thoroughly as does Sophocles in *Oedipus*. Hitchcock's *Rope* (1948) is one of them. *Rope* is an adaptation of a play set in the living room of the central characters' apartment (unity of space). It takes place in real time; that is, without any abridgment or expansion of the time of the action (unity of time). And it traces the beginning, middle, and end of a single action—a murder—that is committed, then concealed, and finally discovered (unity of action). *Rope*, like *Oedipus*, can possibly be segmented according to the arrivals and departures of various characters, but, in terms of its action, time, and space, it is not segmentable.

The Hitchcock films *Lifeboat* (1944) and *Rear Window* (1954) observe the unities of action, dealing with the survivors of a shipwreck and a murder mystery, respectively, and unities of space—they are set in a lifeboat and a Greenwich Village courtyard. But they do this without strict observance of the unity of time: *Lifeboat*'s action occupies roughly a week, and *Rear Window*'s approximately four days.

Most films, however, violate the traditional unities. They lend themselves quite readily to segmentation, and the process of breaking them down into large units quite often reveals crucial elements of their dramatic structure. This structure, in turn, can be read in terms of the role it plays in shaping the film's thematic concerns. In other words, segmentation serves as a potentially productive first step in the larger process of film analysis.

A CIRCULAR PATTERN: CHAPLIN'S *THE GOLD RUSH*

Charles Chaplin's *The Gold Rush* (1925), if broken down into spatial units, proves to be a paradigm of classical narrative construction. A segmentation of the film into large units, organized around its various locations and settings, discloses the following seven-part, circular pattern:

I. Prologue (journey to the Alaskan gold fields by Charlie, the lone prospector)

II. The cabin (Charlie and Big Jim take refuge in the outlaw Black Larsen's cabin during a snow storm; Larsen leaves to get help; Charlie and Big Jim enjoy a Thanksgiving feast of boiled boot; the storm subsides and they set off on their separate ways)

III. The dance hall (in town, Charlie discovers Georgia and falls in love with her at first sight, though she ignores him)

IV. The cabin in town (on New Year's Eve, Charlie prepares dinner for Georgia and her girlfriends, falls asleep when she stands him up, dreams that she is there, and performs the dance of the rolls to entertain her).

V. The dance hall (Georgia apologizes to Charlie; Big Jim rediscovers Charlie and falls in love with [pursues] him, much as Charlie pursued Georgia earlier)

VI. The cabin (Charlie and Big Jim return to the cabin—this time with plenty of food—in search of Big Jim's claim; another snowstorm; the storm returns Big Jim to the exact spot where he was at the start of segment II)

VII. Epilogue (Charlie and Big Jim, having struck it rich, return by boat to the States; Charlie is reunited with Georgia who mistakes him for the lone prospector whom she met in segment III)

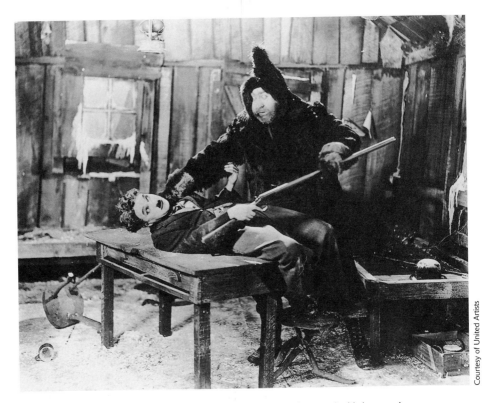

Courtesy of United Artists

The Cabin—Charlie tries to protect himself from Big Jim, who is crazed with hunger in *The Gold Rush.*

Symmetry

Chaplin's narrative observes a strict classical symmetry. The prologue (I), in which Charlie travels to Alaska, is answered by an epilogue (VII), in which he returns to the States, casting the narrative in the form of a journey. An initial cabin sequence (II) introduces the characters of Big Jim and Black Larsen; Big Jim reappears in the final cabin sequence (VI). The first cabin sequence also introduces the characters' fixation on material or physical needs (the desire for gold, then for food), which is answered in the final cabin sequence when physical survival once again becomes paramount as the cabin is blown about in a blizzard and finally settles on the edge of a cliff where it teeters precariously.

By an uncanny coincidence, the wandering cabin ends up at the exact spot where Big Jim is introduced discovering gold. Thus the pursuit of wealth, which motivates Charlie's journey to the gold fields in the prologue and which is echoed and doubled in the figures of Big Jim and Black Larsen whom he meets in the cabin (II), finds resolution in segment VI in which all these elements reappear.

If the search for gold structures the overall narrative, other goals emerge to give shape to the central section of the film, which is set in the town rather than in the wilderness. These three segments introduce another set of characters and a second body of thematic concerns. This time, Charlie interacts not with men but with women (Georgia and her friends), and his chief desire is not for gold or for physical survival but for more abstract needs—he longs for Georgia's love. In this central narrative section, two public scenes in the dance hall (III, V) frame a more private sequence (IV) in the cabin which Charlie is taking care of for a friend.

The film's two fantasy or dream sequences, which provide one of the film's many parallel or paired scenes, underscore this thematic turnabout. During Thanksgiving at the wilderness cabin, Big Jim fantasizes that Charlie is a chicken, turning him into food. On New Year's Eve at the cabin in the settlement, Charlie transforms food into a phantasmical person, combining his own head with dinner rolls on the ends of forks to produce the dance of the rolls. In the former sequence, physical appetite produces the fantasy; in the latter, romantic desire feeds Charlie's imagination. The contrast between the two holidays and the two settings is further driven home by another variation on the film's central theme. In one scene, Charlie turns a boot into a meal; in the other, he turns food into feet, transcending the purely physical world of blizzards, hunger, and greed for gold with an escapist fantasy that celebrates imagination, creativity, and romance.

At the Center: Imagination

The film reveals itself to be a perfect example of the interdependency of form and function in classical Hollywood cinema. The narrative organization of *Gold Rush* is designed around the central character, Charlie, whose goals the plot explores and whose personality serves as a barometer that governs the audience's perception of and reaction to the events which take place. Charlie's desire, feelings, and imagination stand at the literal center of the film—segment IV—in which he realizes his romantic desires through a fantasy sequence. This central sequence looks back to the physical hardship that precedes it in the prologue and in the wilderness cabin sequence, and it looks forward to the epilogue, in which this fantasy is made real. Charlie, now a millionaire but dressed once again in his tramp's outfit for news photographers, is reunited with Georgia, who, unaware of his wealth, befriends him, much as he befriends her in his New Year's Eve dream sequence.

JOURNEY TO A NEW PLACE: *SOME LIKE IT HOT*

Flight and Pursuit

The orderly narrative patterns of classical Hollywood cinema are not always circular. The journey format often takes characters into new, unexplored terrains. That is, it takes them to a destination other than where it begins, as is the case in *Some Like It Hot* (1959). The action of the film begins in Prohibition-era

Chicago and follows its central characters, a saxophone player named Joe (Tony Curtis) and a bass player named Jerry (Jack Lemmon), on their journey to Florida in flight from gangsters who want to kill them because they are the sole surviving witnesses to the St. Valentine's Day Massacre.

The narrative pattern of the film is simple, with the action falling under three basic spatial groupings that range from Chicago to the train and finally to Florida. The goals that drive the narrative are similarly simple, even though their comic realization seems a bit improbable. Joe and Jerry need jobs and to get out of Chicago if they are to escape "Spats" Columbo (George Raft) and his mob. Having no money, they are forced to take jobs impersonating women musicians in an all-female jazz band on its way to Miami.

On the train to Miami, they meet Sugar Kane (Marilyn Monroe), the band's lead singer, who is, like them, also in flight. However, the men she flees are not gangsters but rather saxophonists, with whom she always falls in love but who always abandon her, leaving her holding what she describes as "the fuzzy end of the lollipop."

In Florida, the characters' initial goals are modified; instead of focusing on flight, they shift their attention to pursuit. Sugar hopes to change her luck and find a millionaire to marry. Joe, who has fallen in love with Sugar, concocts a plan that would permit him to become her millionaire. To do this, however, he is forced into yet another impersonation—he plays the role of "Shell Oil, Jr.," the sexually impotent, millionaire yachtsman who seeks Sugar's help in restoring his interest in women. Meanwhile, Jerry, masquerading as Daphne, enjoys unprecedented success as a woman. S/he is romanced by a genuine millionaire, Osgood, who showers her/him with expensive gifts and even proposes marriage.

Just as the characters are about to realize their romantic goals (even Jerry/Daphne looks forward to marrying Osgood and then divorcing him for a nice alimony settlement), the gangsters reappear, having come to Miami from Chicago for a convention of The Friends of Italian Opera. Pursued by Spats and his men, Joe and Jerry take refuge under a banquet table, where they once again witness a mob bloodbath. Spats is rubbed out in retribution for his murder of Toothpick Charlie and others at the St. Valentine's Day Massacre. Although Spats has been eliminated as a threat, Joe and Jerry suddenly find themselves pursued by a new mob for observing his murder.

As Josephine and Daphne, they "elope" with Sugar and Osgood, fleeing to the supposed safety of the latter's yacht. For this escape, however, Joe and Jerry remove rather than put on their disguises; Joe confesses to Sugar that he is not only Josephine, but Shell Oil, Jr., as well; and Jerry informs Osgood that he cannot marry him because he is a man. The film ends with Osgood's reply: "Nobody's perfect."

Narrative Structure and Sexuality

Some Like It Hot uses the journey format to provide a background for its central characters' sexual odyssey, which takes them from a comic-book world of

Courtesy of United Artists

In *Some Like It Hot,* Joe/Josephine (Tony Curtis) and Jerry/Daphne (Jack Lemmon) flee the male world of Chicago gangsters for the female world of Sugar (Marilyn Monroe) and Sweet Sue and Her Society Syncopaters.

sexual stereotypes (Chicago), through a duplicitous, unstable world of disguise and sexual role-playing (the train, Florida), to an uncharted world where sexual differences no longer determine social structure (the boat trip in the last scene). In Osgood's world, nobody is perfect; that is, no one's sexuality is perfect and traditional notions of sexual difference no longer have any significance. As in Shakespeare's *The Tempest,* the film's characters survive a harrowing experience and enter a brave new world, having "suffer[ed] a sea-change into something rich and strange." At any rate, they are not in Chicago anymore.

Chicago emerges as the city of gangsters. It is dominated by male violence. Spats and his henchmen, ironically referred to as "all Harvard men," are caricatures of masculinity. They are two-dimensional tough guys with too many muscles and too few brains. In Chicago, Joe embodies male insensitivity, repeatedly taking advantage of women. He borrows money from the girls in the chorus without intending to pay it back and sweet-talks Nellie, an agent's receptionist, into lending him her car.

When Joe and Jerry are forced to become Josephine and Daphne, they are plunged into the all-female world of Sweet Sue and Her Society Syncopaters, where they find themselves on the other end of male insensitivity and sexism. This world is dominated by the "masculine" presence of Sue, the leader of the band, and by the effeminate presence of Mr. Bienstalk, the band's manager. In Florida, the reversal of sexual roles continues. Gold diggers in the band, such as Sugar, aggressively pursue local millionaires who, like Shell Oil, Jr., are inadequate as men; and millionaires, like Osgood, whose sexuality is similarly "abnormal," fall in love with men in drag, such as Daphne. Joe's creation of Shell Oil, Jr., serves as an unconscious expression of his own sense of male inadequacy and as an indirect critique of the hypermasculinity that characterizes his own earlier attitudes toward women as the womanizer, Joe.

Resolution/Irresolution

The sexual confusion of the central section of the film is resolved by the reinstitution of clear-cut sexual differences, in the form of the excessively masculine gangsters, who, unlike Osgood, see through Joe's and Jerry's masquerades. Through their threatening presence, they force the reinstitution of a simplistic sexual duality, whereby men are men and women are women.

Yet the film suggests that their stereotypical male sexuality is inadequate, much as is that of Sugar's ideal man, whom she envisions as "gentle, sweet, and helpless." Sugar's ideal proves to be pure fantasy, and she is ultimately forced to recognize and give in to her irrational desire for tenor saxophone players (Joe). On the other hand, if Daphne is Osgood's ideal, then Jerry emerges as the next best thing, as an imperfect Daphne. *Some Like It Hot* illustrates how the impossible perfection imagined in the romantic dreams and sexual fantasies of the central characters gives way to the more immediate, concrete realities of their sexual desires. In other words, all of them, even Osgood, discover that nobody is perfect.

NARRATIVE INCOHERENCE: *MULHOLLAND DR.*

There is perhaps no more extreme instance of this testing of the limits than David Lynch's *Mulholland Dr.* (2001), a film that has repeatedly baffled those who have attempted to decipher its meaning, not to mention recounting its basic plot. Even though it remains difficult to explain exactly what happens in the film, segmenting it is not all that difficult. Because the film observes certain classical patterns of displacement, condensation, alternation, symmetry, repetition, variation, and resolution, it is possible to analyze its formal structure and to discuss the meaning of that structure. In this way, the film opens itself to productive readings of its themes. A segmentation of the film's narrative action would look something like the plot segmentation in the following section.

PLOT SEGMENTATION OF MULHOLLAND DRIVE

Precredit sequence; jitterbug contest; Diane's apartment: heavy breathing off-screen. FADE OUT.

  I. Betty and "Rita." Desire in pursuit of its object.

    A. The couple.

      1. Rita; hit men; car crash; flight to Aunt Ruth's; Rita falls asleep; Dan at Winkie's; Rita continues to sleep; mobsters' phone montage.

      2. Betty; LAX; Aunt Ruth's apartment; discovers Rita, who then falls asleep.

    B. The third element: Kesher and his film.

      1. Adam Kesher and Castigliani brothers discuss casting at Ryan Entertainment.

      2. Betty and Rita (still sleeping) at Aunt Ruth's.

      3. Mr. Roque orders film shut down. FADE OUT.

    C. Partial resolution of two narratives: Betty meets Adam.

      1. Searches for solutions: hit man continues his search, Betty and Rita try to solve a mystery, and Adam gets his film back.

        a. Alternation between hit man and Betty and Rita (hit man kills three; Betty discovers Aunt Ruth does not know Rita; hit man looks for brunette; Betty and Rita discover money and key in Rita's purse).

        b. Alternation between Betty and Rita and Adam. (Betty and Rita discuss money and key; Adam learns his film has been shut down; Betty and Rita make plans to call police; Adam discovers his wife in bed with the pool man; Betty and Rita hide the money; call cops outside Winkie's; inside Winkie's, Rita remembers "Diane Selwyn"; mobster at Adam's house; Adam at Park Hotel; Betty and Rita get Diane's address; Adam goes to meet the cowboy). FADE OUT. Betty rehearses her scene, then auditions; Betty exchanges glances with Adam at studio.

      2. Temporary solutions that solve nothing: Diane appears; Betty and Rita disappear.

        a. Diane's: Betty and Rita discover dead body.

        b. Aunt Ruth's: Rita goes blonde; Betty and Rita make love; Rita murmurs in her sleep, "Silencio . . . There is no band."

        c. Club Silencio: "It's all recorded . . . it's all a tape . . . There is no band." Betty and Rita hear Rebekah Del Rio sing Roy Orbison's "Crying" in Spanish. Blue box found in Betty's purse.

        d. Aunt Ruth's: hatbox, key, box; Betty disappears; Rita opens box and disappears; Aunt Ruth returns to find the apartment empty.

Betty (Naomi Watts, left) helps "Rita" (Elena Harring) try to regain her memory in *Mulholland Drive.*

II. Diane Selwyn and Camilla Rhodes: the death of desire/the desire for death.
  A. The couple: Camilla as Diane's fantasy.
    1. Diane's apartment; body on bed; the cowboy: "Hey, pretty girl. Time to wake up." FADE OUT.
    2. Diane's apartment; neighbor retrieves her things; Diane sees Camilla (fantasy); Diane, in bathrobe, makes coffee alone; Diane, now topless, puts glass of whiskey down; tries to engage a topless Camilla in sex; Camilla resists.
  B. The third term: Adam, Camilla, and Diane's reality. Studio: Rehearsal. Adam shows actor how to kiss Camilla as Diane watches (triangle completed; see I C1 *b*). FADE OUT.
  C. The couple: Diane's fantasy. Diane's apartment; Camilla begs to be let in; Diane refuses, masturbates; Camilla invites Diane to a party on Mulholland Drive. FADE OUT.
  D. The third term: Adam, Camilla, and Diane's reality.
    1. Mulholland Drive/Adam's house. Diane's backstory. Reprise of Coco, the original Camilla, the cowboy, Vincenzo Castigliani.
    2. Winkie's: Diane puts out a contract on Camilla with hit man; waitress's name tag says "Betty"; Dan stands near register; dumpster person puts the blue box into a paper bag; old couple (in miniature) escape from the bag on their way to

3. Diane's apartment; blue key (hit man has killed Camilla). Diane in same robe and with same coffee cup as in II *A* 2. Old couple (in miniature) crawl under door and, now full-size, attack Diane, who runs to bedroom, gets gun, and shoots herself. Smoke fills the room.

Final montage: face of dumpster person; faces of smiling Betty, and Betty and Rita, and Rita in her blonde wig, and Betty at LAX; and the woman in the blue wig at the Club Silencio: "Silencio." FADE OUT.

Hollywood: Love and Ambition

The film was dedicated to Jennifer Syme, an actress who played a minor role in Lynch's *Lost Highway* (1997) and subsequently died in an automobile accident. The film is about aspiring actresses, Los Angeles as a city of dreams, Hollywood as a criminal conspiracy (the Mafia types, the hit man), memory (and its opposite—amnesia), love, jealousy, and revenge. The film falls into two large segments—the story of Betty and "Rita" and that of Diane Selwyn and Camilla Rhodes. In the film's two parts, the same actress, Naomi Watts, first plays Betty and then Diane, while Laura Elena Harring is first "Rita," then Camilla.

The focus of one of the film's chief narrative threads is Betty/Diane's desire to make it as an actress in Los Angeles. Narrative movement here is optimistic and looks forward to the achievement of certain goals (making it as an actress, solving the mystery of Rita, finding true love with Rita). The first half traces Betty's professional trajectory as an actress from her winning of a jitterbug contest in Deep River, Ontario, and her arrival in Los Angeles to her brilliant audition for *The Sylvia North Story* at Paramount. (The director for whom she auditions is Bob Brooker; we later learn that he directed *The Sylvia North Story*.) But Betty abruptly walks out on a chance to meet a famous director (Adam Kesher) who might help her career, to keep an appointment with Rita. The remaining action in this part of the film finds Betty playing detective ("just like in the movies") in an attempt to help Rita discover who she is.

Hollywood: Jealousy and Failure

Narrative movement in the second half is pessimistic and looks backward towards Betty/Diane's failure to achieve certain goals (to become a star, to win Camilla's love). If, for Betty, Hollywood was a bit like Heaven, here, for Diane, it is a kind of Hell. This part begins with a Diane who has lost everything. She failed to get the coveted part in *The Sylvia North Story*, losing it to Camilla. Even worse, Camilla has thrown her over for Adam Kesher. Instead of trying to help Rita/Camilla, Diane pays a hit man to kill her. This downward spiral ends with Diane's suicide.

In part one, the theme of identity takes the form of a double movement looking both forward and backward. There is Betty's pursuit of her own future as an actress and her attempt to discover Rita's past identity. In part two, it is

Camilla who has a future as an actress and attempts to forget Diane (a possible connection with her amnesia in part one). It is Diane who is mired in the past, unable to move forward. She has no future, only memories. Instead of actively pursuing her goals, Diane can only recall her failure as an actress and fantasize that Camilla is still in love with her.

Desire

Desire necessarily exists in relation to some object, to that which is desired. When that which is desired is obtained, desire disappears. In other words, desire always demands the absence of its object. *Mulholland Dr.* explores desire in precisely this sense. The first half of the film lays out various desires (to become an actress, to direct a film, to recover one's memory). The pursuit of these concrete goals, however, turns out to be illusory. When the characters arrive at what they've been searching for, it has no substance. It's all an illusion. At Club Silencio, what we see and hear is not real: the musician does not really play the trumpet, and Rebekah Del Rio does not really sing "Crying" in Spanish: "It's all recorded." After finding the blue box, Betty and Rita disappear. Even they prove to be without substance.

The second half of the film explores the death of desire (and the desire for death, which is the negation of all desire). Here, the objects of desire are not absent, but have already been attained. Camilla does not have amnesia: she knows who she is. She has become the famous actress that Betty wanted to be. Camilla has Adam Kesher and no longer wants Diane. Adam has his film back and has Camilla as well. Diane, who as Betty almost never slept, is repeatedly seen asleep in bed in part two. Her costuming and makeup suggest that she has given up all ambition and repudiated all desire. But this is not quite the case. In two fantasy scenes that are clearly detached from the abysmal reality in which she finds herself, Diane first acts out her desire for Camilla, only to be rejected, and then rejects Camilla in turn, refusing to let her in the door. Forced to witness the reality of romantic moments between Adam and Camilla, Diane's desire self-destructs, leaving her only with the desire for Camilla's death and her own.

Fantasy and Reality

"It's just like in the movies," says Betty. "We'll pretend to be somebody else." Popular readings of the film understand part one as Diane's fantasy or dream at the moment of her death, a fantasy that rewrites the reality of part two. In this fantasy, Diane, as Betty, is a success at the audition and wins the love of Rita/Camilla, who miraculously escapes the hit men Diane had hired to kill her. The second part of the film presents Diane's reality—her failure to realize her dreams of becoming a great actress, her loss of Camilla, and her own suicide. These attempts to figure out the plot of the film not only fail to account for central elements of it (the blue box and key, the money, the bum behind the dumpster) but also mistakenly approach the film as if its meaning—its se-crets—existed on the level of its plot. The assumption is that by figuring out what happened one could then discover what it was about.

Spectatorship

On one level, Lynch's narrative is crystal clear. It is about spectatorship. It en-gages us, as spectators, in assembling the various threads of narrative infor-mation into a master narrative. More accurately, it engages us in a *process* of narrative construction that resists closure, that refuses to provide us with a coherent master narrative. Unlike classical Hollywood cinema that relentlessly attempts to read the narrative for us, Lynch's film does not. Like the *Twin Peaks* television series (1990), *Mulholland Dr.* engages its spectators in a seemingly endless process of sense-making, and it is this process that provides the bulk of the viewer's pleasure.

MODERNIST NARRATION: *CITIZEN KANE*

Unresolved Questions

Mulholland Dr. might be described as a modernist film. Modernist works tend to reject the illusionistic transparency of classical realist texts and to bring to the foreground the process of the text's construction, laying bare its parts, or to expose the process by which its meaning is constructed, or both. Modernist texts convey the spirit of crisis that characterizes the modern (post–Industrial Revolution, twentieth-century) age. They do this, in part, by rejecting the prin-ciples of order, regularity, and invisibility that dominate representation in its classical, romantic, and realist forms. The particular form that modernism takes depends on the particular tradition that it rebels against; in American narrative filmmaking, modernism is best exemplified by *Citizen Kane* (1941), a film that breaks the rules of classical narration in several ways.

Kane belongs to several film genres. On one level, it is a newspaper film; on another, a mystery; on yet another, it is a fictional biography (or biopic). If it is difficult to classify *Kane* in terms of its exact narrative type, it is also hard to identify its central character. Is it Charles Foster Kane, who dies in its opening minutes? Or is it Thompson, the investigative reporter who is assigned to solve the mystery of Kane's last word—"rosebud"?

What are the goals of these characters? If what both Kane and Thompson want is "rosebud," then neither succeeds in getting it. "Rosebud" remains, as far as Kane is concerned, a lost object that he both possesses and can never find; it lies concealed in the vast storehouse of Kane's possessions. For Thompson, "rosebud" remains a mystery that he never solves. In other words, the goal that structures the narrative is never reached by its central characters (though the audience does penetrate at least one layer of the mystery of "rosebud" in discovering the object to which the word refers).

Artifice Exposed

Though the narration of *Citizen Kane* is extremely fragmented and complex, it can be broken down into three segments. The first segment consists of Kane's death at Xanadu and public reactions to it, seen in the *News on the March* newsreel. It concludes with the reporter Thompson's assignment to discover the meaning of Kane's last words, "rosebud." The second segment documents Thompson's search. It is structured around a series of five flashbacks presented through Thatcher's papers and interviews with Mr. Bernstein, Jed Leland, Susan Alexander Kane, and the butler, Raymond. It concludes with Thompson's admission of failure in finding out what "rosebud" meant. The final segment is extremely brief—only five or six shots. It surveys Kane's possessions, reveals the identity of "rosebud," and returns us to the images of Xanadu and the "No Trespassing" sign that began the film.

The narrative structure of *Kane* also plays havoc with the norm; it is built around a complex series of overlapping flashbacks in which five different characters present their perceptions of Kane. Though Thompson serves as the audience's guide through the maze of information presented about Kane, he never processes that information for us. In fact, he refuses, declaring that he "doesn't think any word [could] explain a man's life" and that "rosebud" is "just a piece in a jigsaw puzzle—a missing piece."

Thus, the audience is left with the difficult task of assembling these separate portraits of Kane into a coherent figure. The persistent refusal of the film to give the audience access to its central character serves as the chief mark of its modernism. A "No Trespassing" sign greets us at the beginning of the film; doors are repeatedly closed in our faces; and, once we finally get to see "rosebud" at the end, it goes up in smoke just as we begin to grasp its possible meanings.

Kane stands at the very fringe of classical Hollywood cinema and draws much of its power from its violation of the codes and conventions that audiences take for granted when they go to the movies. *Kane* makes visible much of that which the machinery of Hollywood cinema seeks to keep invisible. But even this visibility provides pleasure for audiences, engaging them on a heightened level of narrative awareness that plays a crucial role in their understanding of the narrative.

Several more recent films engage in a similar kind of modernist play with classical narrative conventions, including films such as *Pulp Fiction* (1994), *Memento* (2001), and *Mulholland Dr.* (2001). In each of these films, traditional narrative linearity gives way to a confusing rearrangement of the temporal relationship between scenes that demands an active and alert spectator who can figure that relationship out and construct a coherent story from the films' fragmented scenarios. In *Pulp Fiction,* the spectator needs to puzzle through a

Courtesy of RKO

Citizen Kane paints a modernist portrait of its central character, played by Orson Welles, as the sum total of various reflections.

convoluted series of events to reconstruct their logical order so that the killing of Vincent Vega (John Travolta) by Butch (Bruce Willis) occurs *after* all the other narrative action we see in the film. *Memento* presents a narrative that runs, more or less, backwards from the final action in which Leonard (Guy Pearce) kills Teddy (Joe Pantoliano) to the event that initially prompted this action—the murder of Leonard's wife. Presented in a succession of 10-minute scenes that lead up to and briefly overlap with each previous scene, the film ironically calls on the short- and long-term memories of its spectators to make sense of the narrative that explores the hero's short-term-memory loss. *Mulholland Dr.,* as discussed earlier, enlists the spectator in a process of reading that becomes an end in itself and never produces a coherent master narrative.

These narratives not only echo the modern condition in their formal rebelliousness but *become about it,* representing a contemporary sense of frustration, lack of closure, and dissolution. In other words, they serve, much as does the seamless classical Hollywood cinema of the past, as an "expression of the temper of an age and a nation as well as an expression of the individual temperament" of the artists who make them.

■ ■ ■ SELECT FILMOGRAPHY

The Gold Rush (1925)　　　*The Terminator* (1984)
Citizen Kane (1941)　　　　*Pulp Fiction* (1994)
Rear Window (1954)　　　*Memento* (2001)
Vertigo (1958)　　　　　　*Mulholland Drive* (2001)
Some Like It Hot (1959)

■ ■ ■ SELECT BIBLIOGRAPHY

BORDWELL, DAVID. "Classical Hollywood Cinema: Narration Principles and Procedures," In Philip Rosen, ed., *Narrative, Apparatus, Ideology*. New York: Columbia University Press, 1986.

BORDWELL, DAVID. *Narration in the Fiction Film*. Madison: University of Wisconsin Press, 1985.

BORDWELL, DAVID, JANET STAIGER, AND KRISTIN THOMPSON. *The Classical Hollywood Cinema: Film Style and Mode of Production to 1960*. New York: Columbia University Press, 1985.

BORDWELL, DAVID, AND KRISTIN THOMPSON. *Film Art: An Introduction*, 7th ed. New York: McGraw-Hill, 2003.

BRANIGAN, EDWARD. *Narrative Comprehension and Film*. New York: Routledge, 1992.

GAINES, JANE, ed. *Classical Hollywood Narrative: The Paradigm Wars*. Durham, NC: Duke University Press, 1992.

WOLFFLIN, HEINRICH. *Principles of Art History*. Translated by M. D. Hottinger. New York: Dover Publications, 1932.

CHAPTER 3

Classical Hollywood Cinema: Style

FILM FORM AND CHARACTER DEVELOPMENT

Classical Hollywood cinema is a character-centered cinema. Not only are narratives structured around the goals of individual characters, but basic elements of film style are also put at the service of character exposition and dramatic development. Even at the level of setting, the narrative machinery seeks to maximize its use of the medium—to use it to describe character psychology, to visualize the goals and desires of characters, and to convey their development as characters through the action that follows.

Classical Economy:
The Opening Sequence of *Shadow of a Doubt*

The introductory sequence of Alfred Hitchcock's *Shadow of a Doubt* (1943) provides a perfect example of classical economy and efficiency in character delineation. A series of establishing shots connected by dissolves identifies the

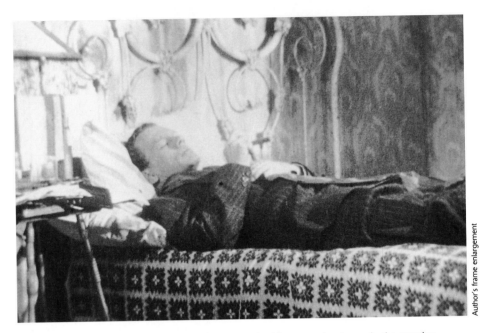

Author's frame enlargement

Uncle Charlie (Joseph Cotten) lies stretched out on a bed in a rooming house in the opening sequence of *Shadow of a Doubt.*

setting of the action as a lower-class neighborhood in Philadelphia. Establishing shots function to present the spatial parameters within which the subsequent action of a scene takes place. Here, long shots of the city, with derelicts, trash, and abandoned cars in the foreground, establish an aura of decadence and decay that dominate our perception of the world into which the dissolves bring us, and of the character who occupies the center of that world. Dissolves (a fluid form of shot transition which involves fading out on one shot while fading in on another) gradually narrow the spectator's field of view from the entire city to a specific block, kids playing stickball in the street, a rooming house on that block, and finally a specific window in that rooming house.

In a low-angle shot, the camera looks up from below at the second-story window of the rooming house. Then there is a dissolve to the second-floor interior. The camera tracks (that is, moves bodily) across a room to reveal Uncle Charlie (Joseph Cotten) lying fully dressed in a business suit on a bed in midday and smoking a cigar. On the nightstand next to him lies a wad of high-denomination currency; some of the bills have fallen to the floor. There is also a half-empty whiskey glass.

The landlady enters through the door, pulls down the blinds of the window, and announces that two men have called, looking for him. The lowering of the blinds casts shadows on Charlie's face. Once she has left, Uncle Charlie rises, drinks the whiskey, and angrily throws the empty glass into the basin in the adjoining bathroom, smashing it. Then he walks to the window, raises the blinds, and looks out onto the street where the two men stand. In an internal monologue in which we hear his thoughts, Charlie challenges the men to prove that he has done anything wrong, declaring that they have nothing on him. Finally, Charlie leaves the room, defiantly walks by the men, and subsequently eludes them in a chase through the surrounding tenements.

The Art of Details

This introductory scene establishes Uncle Charlie as an enigmatic figure. His clothing and bearing suggest that he is clearly out of place in this lower-class setting. Yet the money, the whiskey, and his violent reaction to the news that he is being followed suggest that he belongs in a criminal milieu. The mise-en-scène (that is, the staging of the sequence) presents Charlie as a man who is at the end of his rope. His posture is that of a dead man, a fully dressed corpse stretched out on a bier in the funeral parlor. The crumpled bills on the floor convey his disregard for money. His depressed state is clearly less a result of material wants than of unstated spiritual needs.

Yet there is also something monstrous about him. Charlie rises, like Dracula from his coffin, when the room is made dark by the landlady's lowering of the blinds. His subsequent behavior expresses his potential for violence: when he gets up, one of the first things he does is to smash his glass by throwing it across the room into the bathroom sink. At the same time, his actions express tremendous hubris: his internal monologue voices defiance toward his pursuers. At the end of the scene, he goes out to confront them, behaving like a character in a Dostoevsky novel who is driven by a desire for such challenges.

At the same time, the sequence epitomizes the narrative economy and efficiency of classical Hollywood cinema. Every detail in the scene serves a purpose, advances the narrative, and gets used up by the conclusion of the scene. The window is there for the camera to enter at the beginning of the scene, for the landlady to pull the blinds down on, and for Charlie to raise the blinds on and look through to see the men outside. The bed is there for Charlie to lie on and get up from; the nightstand is there to provide a surface on which the money and the whiskey can be placed. The whiskey glass is there for Charlie to drink out of, and the bathroom sink is there for him to use to smash the whiskey glass. The door is there for the landlady to enter and for Charlie to use when exiting. By the time Uncle Charlie leaves, every prop and every feature of the room have been used to advance the narrative; the room has been narratively exhausted, so to speak, and it is time to move on to the next space.

MISE-EN-SCÈNE

Not every Hollywood film is so meticulous in its use of décor and mise-en-scène; *Citizen Kane,* for example, overwhelms the spectator with detail, much of which never finds its way into the narrative except as atmosphere. But films like *Shadow of a Doubt* reflect the general principles of narrative economy that informs the majority of Hollywood films and sets a standard for efficiency that a surprising number of narratives meet. Elements of film style are not merely ornamental. They are not the superficial coating of a story that could be told in a thousand different ways. Classical Hollywood style becomes *the means by which* narratives are realized; it provides the formal system that enables them to be told. Elements of style serve to shape the narrative. They function to read it for the audiences. They draw attention to, underline, and point out what it is that the audience needs to see or hear in order to read or understand the scene.

In presenting stories on the screen, the cinema relies on actors and actresses to stage events, much as they are staged in the theater. The term "mise-en-scène" describes this activity. Mise-en-scène encompasses a variety of theatrical categories related to the staging of action. These range from purely theatrical areas of expression such as set design, costume design, the blocking of actors, performance, and lighting to purely filmic techniques such as camera movement, camera angle, camera distance, and composition. Strictly speaking, mise-en-scène (or "putting on the stage") includes the relation of everything in the shot to everything else in the shot—of actors to the décor; of décor and actors to the lighting; of actors, décor, and lighting to the camera position; and so forth.

In the theater, mise-en-scène serves as a reading of the action. Set design, costume, lighting, and the movement of actors are designed by the stage director (or producer) to present the ideas in the script to the audience in a more or less predigested way. That is, these elements of stagecraft, which are used to organize the drama, process the action for the audience. Mise-en-scène translates the contents of a scene into the language of the theater, producing a reading of the action that guides the audience's attention in specific ways.

THE CAMERA

In the cinema, theatrical mise-en-scène provides a primary interpretation of the drama. Costume and set design become a reflection of character, as we saw in the introduction of Uncle Charlie lying fully dressed on a bed at midday in *Shadow of a Doubt*. Lighting becomes an extension of the character's psychological makeup into the surrounding space. The shadow of the blind which falls over Charlie's face becomes the "shadow" of his doubt, conveying the concern that creeps over him about the two men waiting outside for him in the street. The mise-en-scène's theatrical reading of the action is driven home, in turn, by means of a variety of uniquely cinematic techniques such as camera position (which includes the camera's angle on and distance from the action) and camera movement (which includes pans, tracks, zooms, and combinations of all three).

Thus, the low-angle shot of Uncle Charlie from below as he looks out of the window, coupled with the high-angle shot from above of what he sees (the two men outside), communicates ideas. The shots function in terms of both their narrative context and their relation to one another in a system of other shots to convey a sense of conflict or opposition between his view and physical position in space and theirs. These two seemingly insignificant shots help to set up the tense confrontation that follows, when Charlie walks directly toward, then past, the two men.

Meaning through Context: Camera Angle and Distance

Camera angle and distance become expressive devices as a result of their participation in systems of difference. They possess no absolute meaning but derive their meaning through a relative process that depends on the specific dramatic context in which they are used and their relation to other possible angles and distances. Thus, a low-angle shot, in which the camera looks up at the action, might acquire meaning through a process of association, becoming identified with a specific character or situation that it is repeatedly used to film.

At the same time, the particular meaning of a low-angle shot derives not only from the content of the shot but also from the relation of that particular angle to the other angles used in the film, that is, from its place in a system of differences. Thus, a particular low-angle shot differs not only from other low-angle shots (which look up at different angles), but also from eye-level and high-angle shots, in which the camera looks at the action straight on or from above, respectively.

It is often tempting to view low- or high-angle shots in somewhat literal terms as descriptive of the relative power of a character; thus, when the camera looks up at a character, it (and we) occupy an inferior position in relation to that character. As a result, our impression of that character's power or stature is thereby magnified. Similarly, high-angle shots automatically position viewers above the action, giving them a quasi-omniscient, quasi-omnipotent, god's-eye view of the action, indicating the relative weakness or inferiority of any onscreen character. However, this literal interpretation of camera angle proves to be rather limited, especially when it ignores the context in which the shot occurs.

Thus the low-angle shot of Charles Foster Kane (Orson Welles) in *Citizen Kane* (1941) as he stands in his deserted campaign headquarters and talks to his friend Jed Leland (Joseph Cotten) after his defeat in the race for state governor conveys contradictory ideas. Kane's power and mystery are suggested in the camera angle—yet in losing the election he has just proven how vulnerable he is. The extremity of the low angle actually captures his powerful powerlessness, making it appear as if the character is about to topple over.

Something similar takes place at the end of *Ace in the Hole* (1951). The film's central character, a newspaper reporter named Chuck Tatum (Kirk Douglas), turns the simple rescue of a man trapped in a cave accident into a sensational

A low-angle shot of Kane (Orson Welles) and his friend Leland (Joseph Cotten) after Kane's defeat at the polls.

Frame enlargement by Kristin Thompson

front-page story, then delays the rescue process in order to further his own career as a journalist.

After the man dies, Tatum is fatally wounded by the man's wife. Back at his newspaper office, he renounces the fame he has won through his coverage of the story. As he does so, director Billy Wilder films him in an extreme low-angle shot. The exaggeration of the angle serves to caricature his excessive abuse of the power of the press and to look askance at his greed and self-interest; the shot concludes as Tatum drops dead on the floor, falling right into the camera. This particular low-angle shot can hardly be understood as a signifier of his power; rather, it dramatizes the terrible consequences of too much power.

Systematic Meaning: Some Definitions

At the same time, camera angle and distance determine meaning systematically. They participate in a system of differences that varies from film to film. Thus the extreme camera angles and distances employed in a Welles film, such as *Citizen Kane,* differ significantly from the more moderate angles and distances found in a film directed by Howard Hawks, such as *Bringing Up Baby* (1938) or *His Girl Friday* (1940). In *Kane,* the extreme close-up of Welles's lips as he utters the word "rosebud" and then dies *underlines* the importance of that moment and that word in a way that would be unthinkable in a Hawks film. In other words, the Welles system depends on exaggeration for effect, while the Hawks system employs a more subtle variation from shot to shot to drive home the meaning of its scenes.

Although camera distance is clearly a relative phenomenon, the terms used to describe it are more or less fixed. The scale on which the terms rely is that of the human body (though the content of shots, of course, is not restricted to human or even animate forms). Thus an extreme close-up presents only a portion of the face—Kane's mouth in *Kane* or the gunfighters' eyes as they face off against one another in *Forty Guns* (1957). A close-up frames the entire head, hand, foot, or other object, such as the shot of the wad of money on the floor in *Shadow of a Doubt* or the close-up of Kane's hand as he drops the glass ball to the floor in his death scene in *Kane.*

Medium close-ups give a chest-up view of individuals, as seen in most sequences in which two characters converse with one another, while medium shots tend to show the body from the waist up. Shots of characters that frame them from the knees up are referred to as medium long shots, while long shots range from full-figure images of characters as well as a bit of the surrounding space immediately above and below them (such as the first image of Uncle Charlie lying on the bed), to shots in which the human figure is only a small part of the overall scene (as in the point-of-view shot in which the two men are seen waiting in the street below for Charlie). In extreme long shots, the human body is overwhelmed by the setting in which it is placed, as in countless Westerns in which distant figures are seen as specks in a larger landscape.

Camera Movement

Camera movement emerges as a powerful element of mise-en-scène that (in most classical Hollywood films) serves the interests of narrative exposition. The term "camera movement" encompasses a variety of different formal devices, including one—the zoom—in which the camera makes no movement whatsoever. A zoom involves the use of a special lens that possesses a variety of different focal lengths ranging from wide-angle to telephoto. Manipulation of the lens produces the impression of movement toward or away from objects by shifting from wide-angle to telephoto focal lengths or vice versa. These shifts simply enlarge or decrease the apparent size of the image.

Since the camera does not literally move during a zoom shot (unless it is combined with other camera movements), its sense of movement is illusory. The famous vertigo effect in *Vertigo,* when the acrophobic central character, Scottie, looks down from a height, is achieved by the combined effects of zooming in and tracking out. This makes the space appear to expand and to contract at the same time. Zooms, which are frequently used to designate a character's subjective point of view or reaction to something, function as a kind of consciousness that surveys, studies, or scrutinizes the drama unfolding before it.

Actual camera movements consist of pans, tracks, and dolly or crane shots. In a pan, the camera rotates horizontally and/or vertically on its axis. Typically, it presents a panoramic view of a space by rotating from right to left (or from left to right) a certain number of degrees to reveal what lies before the camera

The camera, mounted on a makeshift crane (center), descends to photograph the key in Ingrid Bergman's hand in *Notorious,* as director Alfred Hitchcock looks on.

on either side. At the start of the cattle drive in *Red River* (1948), the camera pans 180 degrees as the owner of the herd (John Wayne) surveys his cattle and the men (including his adopted son, Montgomery Clift) who will drive them to market. The pan not only conveys the enormous size of the herd, but also sets up the conflict between Wayne and Clift that will dominate the rest of the narrative.

In tracking shots, the camera moves bodily through space in any of a variety of directions parallel to the floor. To facilitate smooth movement, the camera is either mounted on tracks fixed to the ceiling (as in the long tracking shot of the man's rendezvous with the woman from the city in the swamp in *Sunrise,* 1927) or to the floor. In the majority of instances, however, it is affixed to a movable camera support, such as a dolly, as seen in the continuous camera movements in *Rope* (1948). If mounted on a dolly, the camera can track in a variety of different directions. It can move laterally, either to follow the movements of a character walking parallel to it or to explore space in one direction or the other. It can move circularly, tracking around a central subject or observing a scene that is taking place around it from the center of a circle. The camera is also capable of moving circuitously in, out, and around the scene.

Most typically, the camera tracks in or out on an axis, moving at an angle to or perpendicularly to the dramatic action. In a crane shot, the camera can not only move forward, backward, or circuitously on the ground, as in any dolly shot, but can also rise or descend. The party sequence in *Notorious* (1946) begins with a crane shot that descends from an overhead long shot of the ballroom floor and surrounding staircase to an extreme close-up of an important key clutched in the hand of the heroine (played by Ingrid Bergman). Like other camera movements, this crane shot reads the action for the spectator, singling out a crucial detail that might otherwise have gone unnoticed.

LIGHTING

Though set and costume design remain the most obvious and most forceful elements of expression among all the techniques of mise-en-scène, lighting has played an increasingly important role in the articulation of the meaning of a particular sequence. For the most part, lighting is a fundamental requirement. A certain minimal amount of lighting is necessary for the camera to photograph the contents of any scene. But there is more to lighting than ensuring proper exposure. Lighting has become a tool for reading the contents of a scene; and directors of photography carefully build their lighting setups to accomplish this goal.

Three-Point Lighting

In classical Hollywood cinema, the lighting setup begins with what is called general set lighting, which is designed not only to ensure proper exposure but also to establish overall lighting directionality. Natural or realistic lighting always establishes (or refers to) the source of the light. In exterior daytime sequences, light typically comes from above—from the sun. For many interior daytime or nighttime sequences, the same rule also applies because most interiors are lit from lighting fixtures located on the ceiling. In these instances, the key or dominant source light comes from above. In other instances, however, the major illumination for a scene comes from the front, the side, or the rear. Its source is a table or floor lamp, a fireplace, or a doorway or window through which exterior light comes. These lighting setups are realistically *motivated*; their source and direction are determined by the location or setting specified in the script.

The standard lighting setup employed in Hollywood films is called *three point lighting*. The three points to which the term refers are dominant sources of illumination. Most three-point lighting setups involve dozens of actual lights, not just three, but they are so arranged as to suggest three basic sources or lights. These lights are known as the *key light* (or chief directional light sources), the *fill light* (or weaker light sources that fill in the shadows cast by the key

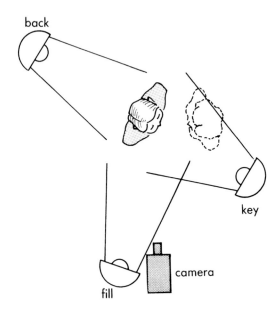

Artist's sketch of the three-point lighting system.

light), and the *back light,* the minor lights that are used to light the space between the back of the set and the characters to separate or distinguish them from the background. In certain situations, lights are also positioned to the sides or beneath characters to delineate important features. At the same time, a number of back lights are deployed to create the illusion of depth by lighting various levels of the set, curved surfaces of the set, or the shoulders of the characters; the latter are known as *clothes lights.*

High-Key/Low-Key Lighting

Three-point lighting can be manipulated to produce a variety of different lighting effects. However, most of these effects fall under two basic stylistic categories. These are either high-key or low-key lighting. The terms "high" and "low," unlike their use in connection with camera position, have nothing to do with the position of the lights. Rather, they describe the ratio of fill light to key light. In a high-key lighting system, this ratio is high; that is, there is a high amount of fill light, which washes out shadows cast by the key light. This produces a more or less brightly lit scene in which light is evenly distributed throughout the set. This style of lighting is associated with upbeat genres, such as comedies and musicals.

In a low-key lighting system, the ratio of fill to key light is low. Shadows cast by the key light are not fully filled in, producing a shadowy effect and an uneven distribution of light. This style of lighting is used in conjunction with

Courtesy of Warner Brothers

The dark side. Low-key lighting engulfs a cynical and embittered Rick (Humphrey Bogart) as he tries to drown his memories of Ilsa and Paris in *Casablanca.*

downbeat genres, such as mysteries, thrillers, and horror films, and with films noirs. These conventional associations of different lighting systems with different moods are occasionally violated. Billy Wilder, for example, used low-key lighting to film a number of comedies, including *Love in the Afternoon* (1957) and *The Apartment* (1960). Yet his appropriation of the low-key style is done deliberately to match the bittersweet moods that dominate these films' narrations. In other words, the low-key style retains its darker associations, even in a comedy.

The key light in a Western filmed outdoors in the daylight is normally the sun. Shadows cast by the sun on the faces of actors wearing cowboy hats are regularly filled in with light from reflectors or lamps positioned on or near ground level. This fill light violates the logic of nature; in daylit exteriors, light always comes from above and never from below. Yet it seems perfectly natural; it has established itself as a convention, which owes its existence to the necessity that faces be as legible or readable as possible. In fact, Westerns such as *Tom Horn* (1980), which do not always fill in the shadows under the brims of hats, appear unrealistic because they do not abide by this timeworn lighting convention.

Courtesy of Warner Brothers

The bright side. High-key lighting distributes the light evenly across the scene, filling in shadows, as Rick (Bogart) and Ilsa (Ingrid Bergman) plan their future together in *Casablanca.* They'll always have Paris.

Star Lighting

Readability plays a major role in the development of lighting styles and conventions, serving to justify their violation of the dictates of realism and directionality. The building of the lighting setup begins with a nonrealistic foundation—with general illumination that is merely there to secure proper exposure (that is, to achieve literal readability). Over this is laid directional lighting, which is realistically motivated. On top of this, in turn, is placed star lighting, which highlights (or conceals) certain features of the major performers and makes the expressions on their faces readable.

Star lighting singles out the chief figures in a scene by giving them their own special lighting system. Star lighting thus functions to guide the attention of the audience to the actors and actresses whose roles in the scenes are of primary importance and to relegate other figures to the literal or figurative background. At the same time, star lighting serves to heighten the charismatic presence of certain performers. Directional lighting casts shadows on the faces of the minor players, whose faces become mere surfaces that reflect light coming from elsewhere. Star lighting, on the other hand, works to transform the faces of the major performers into apparent sources of light. Since the light on their faces has no identifiable origin in the scene, it appears to come from within them—to radiate from them as if they were, indeed, astral bodies or stars. In other words, every scene in a Hollywood film combines realistic, directional, motivated lighting with unrealistic star lighting. And audiences never seem to be bothered by the apparent contradiction.

SOUND

Miking and Mixing

A blend of the realistic and the unrealistic, similar to star lighting, takes place in sound recording. Microphones are positioned to pick up sound effects and dialogue in a quasi-realistic way; the microphones duplicate, as it were, the general position of the camera, recording the sounds of what it sees. However, the intelligibility (or readability) of dialogue always takes precedence over that of other sounds in determining actual microphone positions. As a result, the overall realism and directionality of sound is combined with *star miking*. Specially placed microphones ensure that the words of major performers and crucial lines of dialogue will be heard, and sound-mixing practices lift them out of the general hubbub of sounds in the scene.

Sound mixing, which takes place on the set, in a recording studio, or in a sound-mixing facility, involves the combination of three different categories of film sound—dialogue, sound effects, and music. Sound mixers combine the various tracks in order to "hear" the scene for the audience. The hearing of a scene is the aural equivalent of the reading of the scene—that is, sound recordists and mixers provide an aural perception of the action. For example, the sound effects of the noise of an automobile engine might accompany the introduction of a scene in which two characters converse while riding in a car. But after establishing the aural atmosphere through the presence of engine noise, the sound mixer will normally lower these particular sound effects to make the dialogue more intelligible. The same sort of manipulation will take place with the music track during dialogue sequences.

The Musical Score

The musical score of a film, which is written by the film's composer, functions as a commentary on the action. Music serves to direct the audience's attention to specific characters or details, to provide information about the time or place of the action, or to establish mood. Thus characters are frequently associated with or identified by specific musical motifs. In Westerns, for example, Indians are routinely introduced with the familiar ¼ allegretto drumbeat that signifies

"Indian territory." Melodramatic moments are underlined with musical crescendos, and the season of the year is cued by appropriate traditional music, such as Christmas carols, "Auld Lang Syne" (for New Year's), and so forth.

Like camera angle, distance, and movement, the musical score comments on the action without the characters' knowledge. Much as the characters cannot (or pretend they cannot) see the camera, so they cannot hear the underscoring. However, they can obviously hear music that emanates from the space of the drama, such as that from radios, record players, and musical instruments played by characters within the fiction. The musical score provides yet another level of interpretation of the drama in addition to those already built into the mise-en-scène.

Sound and Continuity

Sound is a feature of both mise-en-scène and editing. Sounds occurring within the shot, whether dialogue, sound effects, or music, automatically interact with one another (as do the visual elements of mise-en-scène) to provide narrative information. In other words, sound is not only a part of mise-en-scène but also behaves and functions just as mise-en-scène does. But sound, both as a phenomenon and as an aesthetic category, cannot be as easily confined as is mise-en-scène to the borders of the frame or the limits of the shot. Offscreen sound penetrates the borders of the frame. We see characters react to unseen voices or noises that come from outside the frame. And sound continues over cuts. Dialogue, sound effects, and music extend from one shot to the next. Sound editing becomes an integral aspect of the film-editing process. Thus, much as film editors cut from shot to shot, they also cut from sound to sound; or they use sound to bridge shots and to make cuts between them less visible.

Musical scoring plays a major role in transporting spectators smoothly through highly edited sequences by giving them a melodic line that can carry them over disjunctive edits. In conversation sequences, the dialogue provides a stream of continuous aural information that helps to bridge the cuts from one speaker to another. Sound effects are orchestrated to accomplish a similar goal. In all of these instances, the flow of the sound serves to stabilize the audience, to hold them in place across the visual discontinuities that appear on the screen.

EDITING FROM SCENE TO SCENE

Classical continuity editing serves a purpose similar to that of sound editing. Often referred to as invisible editing, classical editing is designed to render more or less imperceptible the 600 to 800 separate shots that constitute the average feature-length film. The goal of this editing strategy is to disguise the transitions from shot to shot, making the film appear to be a seamless flow of images.

At the same time, invisible editing provides yet another level of interpretation of the onscreen action for audiences by singling out details or making connections from one shot to another. Thus a cut to a close-up proves to be an efficient and relatively unobstrusive way of conveying important plot- or character-related information.

Shortly after the title characters in *Strangers on a Train* (1951) accidentally meet on a train, the film cuts from a medium shot of one character, Bruno (Robert Walker), to a close-up of his lobster-patterned tie and his tie clasp. The unusual pattern of the tie and the tie clasp (which bears his name, Bruno) communicate vital aspects of Bruno's character (his eccentricity and his narcissism), as well as his name, to the audience. The physical juxtaposition of shots could be used to express ideas that cannot be conveyed through the more theatrical means of mise-en-scène. At the beginning of *Modern Times* (1936), for example, Chaplin cut from urban workers entering the subway to a herd of sheep. This simple shot transition establishes the film's dominant metaphor—that modern workers in industrialized society are like sheep.

Transitions

Editing serves as a primary means of organizing the film. On the most basic level of organization, shots are assembled to create a scene. A shot is an unbroken strip of film made by an uninterrupted running of the camera. A scene is the film's smallest dramatic unit; it consists of one or more shots that present an action that is spatially and temporally continuous; that is, an action taking place in a single space at a single time. Certain scenes consist of two or more actions set in two or more spaces and times that are intercut to form a single complex scene. At a larger level of organization, scenes or groups of scenes are assembled to create a sequence of scenes, a large segment, or an entire film. Thus the term "editing" encompasses two different forms of organization— editing within a scene and editing from scene to scene.

Editing from scene to scene provides the fundamental structure for the film as a whole. It employs five basic transitional devices—the cut, the fade, the dissolve, the iris, and the wipe. The cut is a simple break where two shots are joined together. The fade involves the gradual darkening of the image until it becomes black (the fade-out) or the gradual brightening of a darkened image until it becomes visible and achieves its proper brightness (the fade-in). The dissolve is achieved by simultaneously fading out on one shot while fading in on the next so that the first shot gradually disappears as the second gradually becomes visible; during the middle of the dissolve, the two shots will briefly be superimposed.

Though rare in contemporary cinema, the iris-in or iris-out serves as a major transition in the silent cinema; an adjustable diaphragm or iris in the camera or a movable mask placed over the camera lens will gradually open, in an iris-in, to reveal more and more image within an expanding, geometrically shaped frame. Or it will gradually close down, in an iris-out, to narrow the field of view, which is surrounded by more and more blackness. The wipe, which has also become something of a dated device, is a transition in which the second shot appears to wipe the first shot off the screen.

Cuts figure significantly in both editing from scene to scene and editing within scenes. The other transitions, however, are generally used to signify shifts from scene to scene. The fade, like the lowering or raising of the lights between scenes or acts in the theater, marks a change in time or place. The iris functions like the opening or closing of a theater curtain to designate major transitions. However, the dissolve and the wipe, which communicate similar information, provide a more fluid, less discrete marking of temporal or spatial change.

Editing and Narrative Structure

Editing from scene to scene provides structure for the narrative in a variety of ways. Scenes can be organized in a purely linear fashion, as seen in the journey structure of *Some Like It Hot* (1959) analyzed in the previous chapter. Or they can be narratively linear and structurally circular or symmetrical, as seen in the seven-part, A-B-C-D-C-B-A pattern found in *The Gold Rush* (1925). Or they can be organized into a flashback structure, as in *Citizen Kane* (1941), which commences with Kane's death at his mansion, Xanadu; reviews his life through five flashback interviews with his friends, associates, former wife, and butler; and concludes, roughly a week after the film began, with a return to Xanadu, where the mystery of "rosebud" is solved. Yet again, films can be organized around an alternating pattern that interweaves two or more story lines, as in D. W. Griffith's *Intolerance* (1916), which cuts back and forth from stories of social intolerance set in four different periods of history, or around the dovetailed pattern of successive stories, such as Jim Jarmusch's *Mystery Train* (1989), in which three separate plots unfold over the course of a single evening in a Memphis hotel.

Crosscutting or parallel editing provides the structural backbone of countless Hollywood narratives, from the silent cinema of Griffith to the sound films of Hitchcock and George Lucas. Crosscutting or parallel action involves shifting back and forth between two or more characters or stories, which are occurring in two or more separate spaces more or less simultaneously. (*Intolerance* is an exception to this rule in that its events, although thematically parallel, take place in different centuries.) Hitchcock's *Strangers on a Train* alternates between the exploits of a tennis star and a psychopathic killer, while his *Family Plot* (1976) juxtaposes the actions of two couples, a phony medium and her boyfriend, and a pair of kidnappers/jewel thieves, whose paths repeatedly intersect.

In *American Graffiti* (1973), Lucas's narrative shifts from character to character on a summer night in 1962. Robert Altman perfected this pattern of shifting from character to character in his multicharacter narratives, especially *Nashville* (1976), with its 24 characters; *The Player* (1992); *Short Cuts* (1993), with 22 "main" characters in 10 separate stories; and *Gosford Park* (2002). Steven Soderbergh's *Traffic* (2001) takes Altman's multicharacter storytelling pattern and spreads it out geographically; Altman's films tend to be set in a single location, but

Traffic's narrative moves from Mexico to San Diego to Washington, D.C., to Ohio, following the flow of the drug traffic. From Griffith to the present, cross-cutting builds toward a climax where the various narrative strands cross and where the dramatic tensions and conflicts they represent are finally resolved.

EDITING WITHIN SCENES

The transitions employed in editing from scene to scene are marked as such; that is, they are necessarily visible, functioning to convey dramatically significant shifts in time or place. Editing within scenes, on the other hand, pursues a strategy of self-effacement that disguises its operations and makes the scene appear to be more or less seamless. This is accomplished through a variety of matching techniques that make transitions from shot to shot smoother. These techniques involve the careful observance of narrative logic in the analytical dissection of dramatic action and the strict adherence to certain rules of thumb that ensure that the space in which the action takes place will be perceived by audiences as coherent and unified. Editing serves the narrative logic; it "reads" the drama in a purely logical and descriptive way. Thus a conversation sequence will cut back and forth from the person speaking to the reactions of those listening and then to the next speaker; the discovery of a safe that has just been robbed might be followed by a shot of the open window through which the burglar has escaped.

Scene dissection tends to follow an orderly pattern. It begins with an establishing or master shot, which is followed by a series of shots (scene dissection) that analyzes the dramatic contents of the space presented in the establishing shot, and it closes with a return to either the master shot or to some other shot marking the ending of the scene. The establishing or master shot, which is frequently a long shot, establishes the space in which the subsequent action will take place. It occasionally also indicates the time of day or year.

In *Shadow of a Doubt,* the shots of kids playing ball in the street and the crane shot up to Uncle Charlie's window serve as establishing shots, informing the viewer where and when the action is taking place. Charlie's conversation with his landlady and his subsequent behavior alone in his room constitute the body of the scene, which concludes with a medium long shot of his open door just after he has left his room to confront the men waiting outside. The interior shot of the door echoes the exterior establishing shot of the window and conveys to audiences that the scene is over.

In more recent years, a number or filmmakers have dispensed with traditional establishing shots, opting to begin scenes more abruptly in the middle of an action or with a close-up of a significant detail. In these instances, the space in which the action will occur is indicated in subsequent shots that are not reserved exclusively for establishing the location but are part of the scene dissection.

Matches

Scene dissection relies on a system of matches to provide continuity for the action. This system involves the matching of shots in such a way that potential discontinuities are cosmetically concealed. Matches include graphic matches, matches on action, and eyeline matches. In a graphic match, major features of the composition in one shot will be duplicated in the next shot, providing a graphic continuity that serves to bridge the edit. The editing of most conversation sequences employs rough graphic matches, in that characters retain their approximate positions in the frame from shot to shot. The introduction of Xanadu during the opening sequence of *Citizen Kane* involves an extremely subtle series of exact graphic matches. Successive shots of the mansion from different perspectives (with different objects in the foreground) are linked by dissolves. They are all united by a common feature—a single window with a light in it—that occupies the same place in each frame of each shot as the editing gradually brings the viewer close and closer to the window.

Matches on action use the carryover of physical movement from one shot to the next to conceal cuts. Thus, as a character begins to sit down in medium long shot, an editor often cuts to a closer shot as the action continues. Or as a character opens a door and begins to walk through it, there is often a cut to a different camera position on the other side of the door as the same character walks through the open door and closes it. Yet the cut and the change in camera position are more or less imperceptible, disguised by the continuity of the character's movement.

Eyeline matches and point-of-view editing play crucial roles in the continuity system, serving the interest of character exposition and character psychology. Eyeline matching involves two shots in which a character in the first shot looks offscreen at another character or object. The next shot shows what that character sees from a position that reflects, in its angle, the character's position and the direction in which he or she looks, but that remains more or less objective in nature. That is, it does not duplicate that character's actual perspective. In effect, the second shot obliquely answers the first, presenting the space to which the character's eyeline refers or looks from the neutral position of the camera.

Point-of-View Editing

Point-of-view editing is a subset of the eyeline match that involves a series of three separate shots—a shot of a character looking offscreen, a point-of-view shot of what the character sees, and a reaction shot of the character as he or she reacts to the thing seen. Thus in *Rear Window* (1954), Hitchcock cut from a shot of his hero (James Stewart) looking out his window at Miss Torso, one of his neighbors, to a point-of-view shot from his perspective of her dancing in a halter and shorts, and back to a reaction shot of Stewart as he smiles somewhat lecherously. Unlike the second shot in the standard eyeline match, the point-of-view shot duplicates what the character sees, representing his or her actual per-

Point-of-view editing in *Rear Window:* Jeff (James Stewart) looks, an insert shot of what he sees (Miss Torso), and a shot of Jeff's reaction.

spective. In other words, in point-of-view editing, the second shot is subjective rather than objective. Thus, while the eyeline match describes the character's interactions with others from the outside, point-of-view editing involves the audience in the mental processes of the character and gives them privileged access to character psychology.

The 180-Degree Rule

At the center of the continuity system stands its fundamental principle—the illusion of spatial reality. This illusion is created and maintained in the cinema through the observance of one simple law, which is known as the 180-degree rule. To guarantee matches in screen position and movement and to construct a realistic playing space for the characters, filmmakers film the action from one side of an imaginary line (the axis of action) that runs through the center of the scene's major action. By remaining on one side of this line, the camera ensures that screen direction remains constant. That is, if one character stands on the right of the frame and another on the left, those characters retain their relative screen positions from one shot to the next (unless, of course, they moved).

If, however, the camera crosses the axis of the action after one shot and films the next shot from the other side of the 180-degree line, the original screen position of the characters is reversed in this second shot, making them appear to switch positions as the film cuts from one shot to the next. If there is any onscreen movement from right to left (or vice versa) and the axis of action is crossed, that movement appears to change direction from shot to shot. Certain directors, such as John Ford, repeatedly violate the 180-degree rule; others, such as Howard Hawks, scrupulously obey it. Hawks's respect for and Ford's lack of respect for the rule reflect their different attitudes toward the representation of space, which Hawks conceives of quite physically and Ford quite abstractly.

In observing the 180-degree rule, filmmakers rely extensively on shot/reverse-shot editing. This editing pattern employs paired shots to cover conversations or other actions. The shots alternate back and forth between an angled shot from one end of the 180-degree line and another from the other end. The second shot views the action from the same angle as the first, though that angle is now reversed, that is, the shot is taken from the opposite direction.

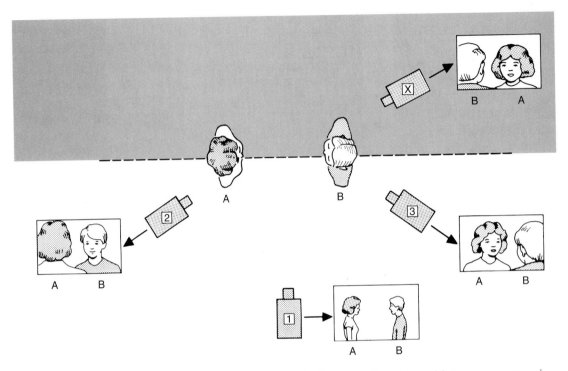

Artist's sketch illustrating the 180-degree rule. Camera positions 1, 2, and 3 preserve screen position; X reverses it.

Classical Hollywood style achieves semitransparency by putting itself at the service of film narrative. Elements of mise-en-scène and editing function to advance the narrative or to further character exposition. As a result, the narrative's visibility relegates technique to the status of a facilitating tool. Stylistic invisibility becomes a goal of the system, which its technicians and craftspersons seek to achieve on both a conscious and an unconscious level. Cinematographers, editors, and directors in Hollywood declare that if audiences notice their technique, it is no good, and they immediately set to work to hide it. Ironically, their art consists of its own self-effacement. Yet that art remains visible no matter what they do to hide it. It can be seen in its invisibility, for it is a style and system of conventions that *work* to convince audiences that no work is taking place. And that *work* can never quite disappear. For in making the film legible for audiences, classical Hollywood cinema leaves the marks of this legibility on the film itself. But these marks remain hard to see because classical Hollywood style is not superficially superimposed on the narrative. It cannot be seen as something that is separate from the narrative because it is the means by which that narrative is realized. In other words, it is invisible because it *is* the narrative.

■ ■ ■ SELECT FILMOGRAPHY

Intolerance (1916)
Bringing Up Baby (1938)
His Girl Friday (1940)
Citizen Kane (1941)
Shadow of a Doubt (1943)
Notorious (1946)

Red River (1948)
Strangers on a Train (1951)
Rear Window (1954)
American Graffiti (1973)
Traffic (2001)
Gosford Park (2002)

■ ■ ■ SELECT BIBLIOGRAPHY

ALTON, JOHN. *Painting with Light.* 1949. Reprint, Berkeley: University of California Press, 1995.

BORDWELL, DAVID, AND KRISTIN THOMPSON. *Film Art: An Introduction,* 7th ed. New York: McGraw-Hill, 2003.

GORBMAN, CLAUDIA. *Unheard Melodies: Narrative Film Music.* Bloomington: Indiana University Press, 1987.

REISZ, KAREL, AND GAVIN MILLAR. *The Technique of Film Editing.* New York: Hastings House, 1973.

CHAPTER **4**

The Studio System

MANUFACTURING DREAMS

Movies and Mass Production

When Hortense Powdermaker, in her 1950 anthropological study of the movie colony, described Hollywood as "a dream factory," she put into words the essential contradiction that lies at the heart of the American cinema: it is both an art and an industry. It manufactures images, sounds, characters, situations, and stories. Film is a product of the so-called second Industrial Revolution, the late nineteenth-century upheaval that took place in the scientific technologies of electricity, steel, chemistry, and communications. The cinema arose as a result of the scientific research and technological development of American industry—from Thomas Edison's machine shops that produced the motion picture camera; George Eastman's photographic works that innovated motion picture film; and the research labs of Bell Telephone, Western Electric, American Telephone & Telegraph, General Electric, and Westinghouse that pioneered the basic sound recording and transmission technologies, ranging from the telephone and tele-graph to the phonograph and radio, which provided the foundation for the si-lent motion picture's subsequent transition to sound.

At the same time, the motion picture industry is genuinely an industry in that it draws on the techniques of modern mass production—the centralization of production, the division of labor, the increasing specialization and profes-sionalization of the work force, and the assembly line. Even before the studio era, film companies such as Edison and American Mutoscope relied on cheap, sweatshop labor (consisting mostly of women) to operate film-drying drums, to retouch negatives, to handpaint (or tint and tone) sequences from films, and to assemble prints for distribution.

The development of the studio system in the 1910s and 1920s was based on industrial models developed by Henry Ford and others to streamline the pro-duction process. Although the motion picture does not pass from hand to hand on a continuously moving conveyor belt (like the machine parts in the comic assembly-line sequence of Charlie Chaplin's *Modern Times*, 1936), it nonetheless depends on the coordinated efforts of each member of the production team, including not only highly paid producers, directors, and stars but also other workers from the middle and lower end of the salary scale, such as screenwriters, art directors, costume designers, camerapeople, carpenters, and electricians.

Author's collection

The studio as a factory: An overview of the Warner Bros. Lot.

Like other machine-based industries, the motion picture industry relies on an elaborate, heavily capitalized system of production, employing precision, state-of-the-art machinery and hundreds, if not thousands, of skilled workers whose efforts are carefully coordinated by a centralized management. Its efficiency hinges on the ownership or control of raw materials (including not only mechanical equipment but also, in the unique case of motion pictures, talented artists), the standardization of the production operation, and the implementation of modern mass-distribution and marketing strategies that maximize the accessibility of the product for the consumer and minimize competition from others. It is no accident that the motion picture business is referred to as an industry and that motion picture studios are called, by Powdermaker and others, factories.

Intangible Goods

As Powdermaker's phrase "dream factory" suggests, the products of this system of mass production are unlike the typical products of American industry. It does not make cars, household appliances, toothpaste, or laundry detergent; it manufactures dreams. The consumers of motion pictures do not purchase a durable good, that is, a commodity designed to last for three or more years. Nor do they purchase a nondurable good, an item that is intended to be used up more quickly. Instead, they purchase an intangible good, an entertainment experience that lasts for a few brief hours and then vanishes into memory.

Other machine-based industries produce standardized merchandise. Each bar of Ivory soap, each box of Total cereal, each 2004 Ford Taurus is more or less identical to each other bar, box, or car bearing the same name. Such items can be distributed and sold as products to a public that knows, more or less, what it is getting. Once manufacturers have established the brand names of their wares, through advertising or other means, they can predict with reasonable certainty how their products will fare in the marketplace. In this way, they are able to avoid excessive underproduction or overproduction and thus stabilize their operations.

Motion pictures, however, are one-of-a-kind items. They are unique products, never before seen by an audience. Though films, in general, have enjoyed a relatively stable following (from the 1920s through the 1940s, at least), each individual film is an unproven commodity for which there is no built-in, guaranteed audience. As a result, producers take a gamble each time they make a film. The fact that a previous film has done well at the box office in no way ensures the success of the next film. The studio system evolved to reduce the risks inherent in the production of intangible goods such as motion pictures. Its business practices developed in the way that they did in order to stabilize an unstable business.

Hollywood generates its own form of brand names—the star system; the identifiable personalities of well-known producers, directors, and screenwriters whose names attract audiences; and the familiar visual iconography and story patterns of film genres. In this way, the studios attempt to provide audiences with a variety of fundamental known quantities that can serve as a basis for selling a larger, essentially unknown quantity. At the same time, producers engage in an assortment of monopolistic business practices, such as blind bidding; block booking; and runs, zones, and clearances, to ensure that whatever films they do make will provide them with a secure return on their investment.

THE MAJORS AND THE MINORS

In its heyday (1930s–1950s), the studio system was dominated by five major and three minor studios, most of whom continued to play a significant role in Hollywood long after the demise of the studio system. In fact, many of them still dominate the film industry today. The majors included Paramount, Loew's/ Metro-Goldwyn-Mayer (M-G-M), Fox/20th Century-Fox, Warner Bros., and Radio-Keith-Orpheum (RKO); the minors consisted of Universal, Columbia, and United Artists. These studios came into being over a relatively short, 16-year period stretching from 1912 (Universal) to 1928 (RKO). (Though 20th Century-Fox was not created until 1935, the Fox Film Corporation on which it is based was founded in 1915.) Paramount was founded in 1914, Columbia Pictures in 1922, Warner's in 1923 (though it came into existence as a distributor in 1917), and M-G-M (formerly Metro, 1919) in 1924.

Origins

The studio system took the place of an earlier organization, Thomas Edison's Motion Picture Patents Company (MPPC), a trust that, through its control of basic motion picture patents, governed production, distribution, and exhibition. The structure of this trust was oligopolistic; that is, it was controlled by a handful of companies, including Edison, Vitagraph, Pathé, Biograph, and others. The origins of the studio system can be traced to the attempts by independent exhibitors and distributors, such as William Fox and Carl Laemmle, to break up this trust. They finally succeeded in doing this in 1915, when U.S. courts declared the MPPC to be in violation of the Sherman Antitrust Act.

The trust had served to stabilize the industry during the nickelodeon era. Its overthrow led to the establishment of another stabilizing system, designed to suit the needs of an expanding film industry. The trust oversaw an industry in which short, one-reel films were sold, like sausages, by the foot. The dramatic content of the films played little or no part in their marketing strategy. Though the actors in trust pictures were occasionally identified in the trade press as early as 1909, the trust resisted the publicization of its stars in the popular press in a deliberate attempt to prevent the creation of a costly star system, similar to that which had developed in the legitimate theater.

Independents such as Fox and Laemmle fought the trust both in the courts and in the theaters, where they gave the public what it seemed to want—

feature-length films with sensational dramatic content and stars. In particular, the formation by Adolph Zukor in 1912 of the Famous Players Company, which boasted motion pictures with "famous players from famous plays," capitalized on these two selling points to differentiate its product from the trust's more anonymous and less distinguished fare. The studio system arose to maximize the exploitation of feature-length films and the star system, dramatic innovations in the nature of the wartime and postwar film industry that the trust had ignored. But the studio system's greatest strength, as an institution, lay in its development of a vertically integrated marketplace, which virtually ensured its economic future.

Vertical Integration

The term "vertical integration" refers to the structure of a marketplace that is integrated (rather than segregated) at a variety of crucial levels; in the case of the motion picture industry, the studio system established a market in which the studios are owners of their production facilities, distribution outlets, and theaters. In other words, the studios control every level of the marketplace from the top down, from production to exhibition.

Vertical integration began in the 1910s, when the trust denied motion pictures to independent exhibitors such as Fox, who refused to pay arbitrary weekly license fees to the trust to operate his theaters, and to independent distributors like Laemmle, who resented the trust's stranglehold on the supply of product, which his exchanges purchased and then rented to exhibitors. Their search for product to distribute and exhibit led them into production themselves. Vertical integration inspired the postwar consolidation of the studio system as national distribution companies, such as Paramount, merged with production companies, such as Famous Players and Lasky, and subsequently began to purchase theater chains; and as exhibitors such as First National added distribution and production to their overall operations.

The creation of M-G-M in the mid-1920s is an example of the vertical integration that was taking place during this period. In 1920, Marcus Loew, who owned an extensive chain of theaters, entered production and distribution by purchasing a small company called Metro Pictures. Early in 1924, Loew obtained another independent production company, Goldwyn Pictures, and, later that year, purchased the Louis B. Mayer Picture Corp., whose chief assets consisted of Mayer and his star producer, Irving Thalberg. The result of Loew's expansion was Metro-Goldwyn-Mayer, a fully integrated corporation that extended its control of motion picture product through the production, distribution, and exhibition stages.

All of the major studios owned theater chains; the minors—Universal, Columbia, and United Artists—did not. The minors distributed their pictures, by special arrangement, to theaters owned by the majors; and the majors regularly booked one another's films in their theaters. Vertical integration results in a fairly efficient economic system. The major studios produced from 40 to 60 pictures a year—enough films to supply their own and even other studios'

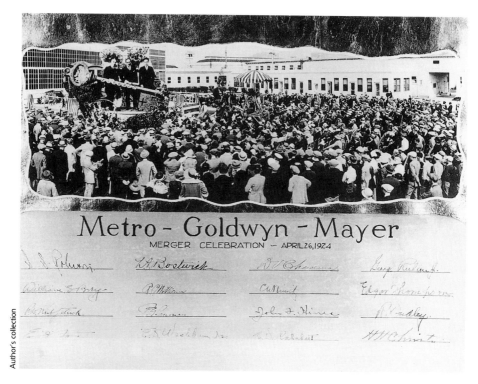

Author's collection

The formation of M-G-M via a merger of Metro Pictures, Goldwyn Pictures, and Louis B. Mayer Pictures in 1924.

theaters. The majors owned only a fraction of the nation's theaters—in 1945, for example, they owned 3,000 of the 18,000 theaters around the country. The remainder were owned and operated by theater chains or independents. But the theaters owned by the majors tended to be large, first-run houses, situated in the biggest cities. As a result, these theaters generated over 70 percent of all box-office receipts.

Block Booking, Blind Bidding, and Runs, Zones, and Clearances

The majors ensured the profitability of their own theaters and controlled the independents by instituting a series of special distribution practices known as block booking, blind bidding, and runs, zones, and clearances. Block booking refers to the rental of films in large quantity. If exhibitors wanted to rent films, they had to rent the studio's entire yearly output. And since they had contracted with distributors for films before the films were actually made, they were forced to bid for them without seeing them—a procedure called blind bidding.

These practices evolved out of the power of the star system. Paramount insisted that theater owners who wanted to book a popular Mary Pickford or

Douglas Fairbanks picture take other pictures as well, including cheaply made films that featured no stars. In this way, Paramount could sell the bad with the good, ensuring that even its worst films would find a market. The studios protected their own first-run theaters from the competition of independents and attempted to get the most rental income from first-run independent theaters by implementing a system of runs, zones, and clearances.

As a result of this system, a film that opened in the first-run movie palaces in early September would not get to play in the cheaper neighborhood theaters until late October or early November. New films would initially be rented only to first-run theaters—to large houses that generated the lion's share of box-office receipts. The majority of these tended to be owned by the studios. At the same time, distribution was guided by a system of zones; only one theater in any particular area was permitted to exhibit a new picture. This practice also tended to favor studio-owned theaters.

Finally, smaller second-run and sub-run theaters were forced to wait until a picture had completed its run in the larger houses before they could obtain it. As a film moved through successive runs, clearances of between 7 and 30 days were observed, during which time the film was unavailable. This practice reinforced the hierarchical structure of exhibition and protected each tier of theaters from competition with theaters farther down the scale that charged audiences less for tickets. Delays between runs were designed to renew demand for the picture.

These practices, which were subsequently outlawed by the courts, effectively prevented independent producers from entering the marketplace and competing with the eight major studios by arming the latter with contractual advantages that enabled them to control first-run exhibition. Without access to first-run exhibition, independent producers could not make a profit on their films. These procedures also served to squeeze the maximum rental income out of the marketplace. Independent producers of first-run films did not exist in Hollywood. David O. Selznick, Walt Disney, Samuel Goldwyn, Walter Wanger, Howard Hughes, Alexander Korda, and others worked effectively within the studio system, largely by distributing (and occasionally financing) their films through existing studios such as United Artists, which had been established in 1919 for just such a purpose.

STUDIO PRODUCTION: FROM STORY IDEA TO AD CAMPAIGN

Under Contract

The efficient organization of distribution and exhibition operations was matched by that of actual film production. The oligopolistic control by a small cartel of major studios extended to production personnel, who were contracted to various studios or producers and who existed as a pool of resources from which studios could draw at any time. Actors and actresses functioned as commodities, much as baseball players and the members of other professional athletic teams did. Unlike the stars of the silent era who secured short-term contracts for two or three pictures, studio stars worked under restrictive, long-term, seven-year contracts, which forbade their engaging in nonapproved acting activities (such as the theater, radio, and television) and regulated their personal behavior, demanded that they adhere to a morals clause, and even governed other features of their offscreen appearance, including their hair styles, choice of clothing, and weight.

The *1937 Academy Players Directory Bulletin* provides a photo gallery of that year's contracted and noncontracted players, listing them by category and including their studio affiliations. The categories for women range from "Ingenues" (Lucille Ball, RKO-Radio) and "Leading Women" (Marlene Dietrich, Paramount) to "Characters and Comediennes" (Gracie Allen—of George Burns and Gracie Allen fame, Paramount). Male categories range from "Younger Leading Men" (John Wayne, Universal) to "Leading Men" (Spencer Tracy, M-G-M) and "Characters and Comedians" (Edward Everett Horton, Universal). At the back of the book are "Children" (Judy Garland, M-G-M; Mickey Rooney, M-G-M), "Colored Artists" (Stepin Fetchit, 20th Century-Fox), and "Oriental Artists" (Keye Luke, 20th Century-Fox, who played Number One Son in the Charlie Chan films). The fact that minority performers occupy only five of the *Bulletin's* 245 pages indicates their marginality in the studio system.

Studio contracts required contract players to act in whatever films the studios cast them in (or undergo suspension without pay, which time was added to the seven years of their contract), attend studio publicity functions, publicize their own films, promote product tie-ins, and, occasionally, be loaned out to other studios to fulfill the same obligations there for one or two pictures. During the early 1930s, in particular, the actors' lives were no picnic. They worked six days a week—often for 14 hours a day. During his first year at M-G-M (1931), Clark Gable appeared in 14 pictures; during her first year at Warner's (1932), Bette Davis made 8 films. It was tough on directors as well. In the early 1930s, Michael Curtiz (who made *Casablanca* in 1942) directed, on the average, five films a year for Warner Bros.

A Self-Contained World

The studio kept everyone under contract, including producers, directors, screenwriters, cinematographers, art directors, costume designers, sound recordists, and other technical staff. With such a sizable pool of talent held in constant readiness for each new project, it was relatively easy to cast a picture and get it into production. The physical layout of the studio was similarly designed to facilitate production. In fact, the studio functioned as a self-sufficient world unto itself—with its own police force and fire, sanitation, water, and electrical departments, and with its own commissary or restaurant, gymnasium, and infirmary.

A story department housed readers, whose job it was to pore through recent books, magazines, and newspapers in search of story ideas. Nearby stood the offices of studio screenwriters, who prepared story synopses or treatments, wrote dialogue, and generated shooting scripts for stars under contract. These scripts were then analyzed by unit managers or production assistants and broken down scene by scene by assistant directors, who estimated overall budget and shooting time and organized a shooting schedule. This schedule was planned in such a way as to economize on costs.

Scenes from films were rarely shot in the order in which they appeared in the screenplay (in continuity), but rather they were shot out of order. Thus, all the scenes staged in one setting or location were shot back-to-back; scenes containing the same groups of actors or actors who were only available for a short time period were shot together; shots requiring the rental of expensive equipment not owned by the studio, such as special camera cranes, or the use of studio equipment in high demand by other studio production units were shot on a single day; and so forth. Shooting scripts were sent to the casting department, which suggested actors for those roles not already cast by the producer or director.

The scripts were also sent to the art department, which designed the sets and perhaps drew up a storyboard, or a sketch of what scenes would look like, for the use of the art director, costume designer, and cinematographer. Carpenters in the studio workshop built sets according to the instructions of the art director; scenic artists painted them; staff set decorators dressed the set with tables, chairs, and other furnishings provided by the prop department, which stored a supply of such items in the prop room. A wardrobe department was staffed with seamstresses to make alterations in existing costumes, which were stored on the lot (or rented from Western Costume), and to execute designs for new costumes.

The studio's camera and sound departments provided the necessary equipment for filming scenes and recording dialogue and sound effects (and repaired this equipment when necessary). Additional equipment for the filming of stunts or sequences involving special effects, such as explosions, bullet holes, or fires, were made in the studio's special-effects department. Electricians wired the set for both on-camera props (such as table lamps) and off-camera equipment (such as incandescent or arc lamps, cameras, sound-recording equipment, and other machinery to produce special effects such as wind, rain, snow, or fog).

The Chain of Command

The coordination of all of these individual efforts was the responsibility of the producer and/or director and their assistants, who relied on the screenplay to serve as a blueprint for production. During shooting, the division of labor was coordinated according to various areas of specialization. The director's crew, consisting of assistant directors, script girls, dialogue coaches, and second-unit directors, assisted the director. Actors were attended by makeup artists, hairdressers, lighting doubles, and stand-ins. The photography unit, consisting of camera operators, grips, and gaffers, assisted the cinematographer; and the

Author's collection

Harry Cohn (left), head of production at Columbia, and Frank Capra share an Academy Award for Best Picture for *You Can't Take It With You* (1938).

sound unit, including boom operators and technicians who laid cables and placed microphones, facilitated the job of the sound recordist.

After filming, editors prepared a rough cut of the film that was synched with dialogue and sound effects. To this was added a musical score written by a studio composer and recorded by the studio orchestra. The montage department assembled montage sequences, which condensed the passage of time or space (as seen in montages of newspaper headlines summarizing the course of events over time or in travel montages conveying the characters' European vacation through stock shots of the House of Parliament in London, the Eiffel Tower in Paris, and the Coliseum in Rome); the studio's own laboratory added optical effects, such as fades, dissolves, or wipes; and the titling department prepared the credit sequence and any intertitles to be inserted in the film.

At the top of the production process stood the studio's chief executive or head of production—Jack Warner at Warner Bros., Darryl Zanuck at 20th Century-Fox, Louis B. Mayer at M-G-M, or Harry Cohn at Columbia. Actual production was supervised by a team of unit producers such as Irving Thalberg, Harry Rapf, Eddie Mannix, Hunt Stromberg, and others at M-G-M during the early 1930s. These producers selected story properties and planned a program of films to be put into production for the year; the unit producer was responsible for selecting a director, helping in the casting of the film, and supervising the preproduction, production, and postproduction phases, including the final editing of the film.

Next in command was the director. Certain major directors worked with the producer and screenwriter in preproduction, consulting on the preparation of the script and the casting of actors. Other directors might have been assigned to the picture only a few days before actual shooting is to begin. In the former case, the director consulted with the art director and costume designer in working out the overall design of the film. In either instance, the director was responsible for rehearsing and directing the actors, staging the action, and giving instructions to the cinematographer on how each shot should look in terms of lighting, camera angle and distance, and camera movement. After shooting was completed, the director supervised postproduction, working with the editor, sound mixer, and composer on a version of the film that might be screened for audiences at a sneak preview. In general, the unit producer had final say on changes made to the film between the preview and its release to theaters.

During production and just prior to the film's release, the publicity department orchestrated promotion for the film in the media, designing posters and ad campaigns as well as supervising the production of publicity photographs and pressbooks to be sent to newspapers, magazines, and exhibitors, as well as trailers to be run in theaters.

STUDIO STYLE

The structure of the studio resulted not only in the streamlining of the production process but also in the creation of a studio style or look. The seven-year contract kept actors, producers, directors, art directors, cinematographers, and composers at individual studios for decades. Gable remained under contract at M-G-M from 1931 to 1954. Producers Henry Blanke and Bryan Foy worked for Warners from 1928 through the mid-1950s. Cecil B. De Mille directed films for Paramount for over 40 years, from 1914 *(The Squaw Man)* to 1956 *(The Ten Commandments)*—except for one brief 6-year stretch (1925–1931) when he worked first as an independent producer and then at M-G-M, where he made his first sound films. Michael Curtiz and Roy Del Ruth directed films for Warner's from 1926 to 1953–1954.

Cedric Gibbons supervised art direction at M-G-M for over 30 years, from 1924 to 1957; Anton Grot served as a production designer for Warner Bros. From 1929 to 1950; and Hans Drier worked more or less exclusively for Paramount from 1924 to 1951. Arthur Miller was a director of photography at Fox from 1932 through 1950; William Daniels, Greta Garbo's cinematographer of choice, was under contract to M-G-M from 1923 to 1946; and Charles B. Lang shot films at Paramount from 1926 to 1952. Alfred Newman scored films for 20th Century and 20th Century-Fox from 1934 to 1962; Max Steiner did the same for both Warner Bros. and RKO from 1929 to 1956.

The presence of these and other contract personnel contributed to the unique stylistic and thematic personality that each studio constructed for itself during different periods of the studio era. As a result, the studio system permitted each studio, by focusing on certain kinds of genre story types and establishing an individual style, to differentiate its product from that of the other studios. A

M-G-M's stable of stars in 1948–1949. Ricardo Montalban (row 4) represents the studio's postwar nod to diversity.

1st row (left to right for all rows): Lionel Barrymore, June Allyson, Leon Ames, Fred Astaire, Edward Arnold, Mary Astor, Ethel Barrymore, Spring Byington, James Craig, Arlene Dahl, Lassie

2nd row: Gloria De Haven, Tom Drake, Jimmy Durante, Vera-Ellen, Errol Flynn, Clark Gable, Ava Gardner, Judy Garland, Betty Garrett, Edmund Gwynn, Kathryn Grayson, Van Heflin

3rd row: Katharine Hepburn, John Hodiak, Claude Jarmon, Jr., Van Johnson, Jennifer Jones, Louis Jourdan, Howard Keel, Gene Kelly, Alf Kjellin, Angela Lansbury, Mario Lanza, Janet Leigh

4th row: Peter Lawford, Ann Miller, Ricardo Montalban, Jules Munchen, George Murphy, Reginald Owen, Walter Pidgeon, Jane Powell, Ginger Rogers, Frank Sinatra, Red Skelton

5th row: Alexis Smith, Ann Sothern, J. Carroll Naish, Dean Stockwell, Lewis Stone, Clinton Sundberg, Robert Taylor, Audrey Totter, Spencer Tracy, Ester Williams, Keenan Wynn

comparable system of product differentiation exists today on television. Cable channels provide viewers with markedly different programming; there are, for example, shopping, weather, news, sports, children's, classic-movie, and new-movie channels. The studios functioned in a somewhat similar way. Along with their movement toward the standardization of production, which was built into the structure of the studio system, there was a complementary drive for product differentiation.

M-G-M and Paramount

The most visible form of product differentiation was the star. M-G-M, which boasted "more stars than there are in heaven," developed a roster of glamorous

The famous Bronson Gate, as seen in Paramount's *Sunset Boulevard* (1950).

actresses who dominated the screen from the late 1920s to the 1940s. Greta Garbo, Joan Crawford, Norma Shearer, Louise Rainer, Myrna Loy, and Greer Garson brought sincerity, refinement, and sophistication to their screen roles. (There were, of course, exceptions to M-G-M's image of polish and gloss, for the studio was also home to the more earthy Marie Dressler and to Lassie; it was also the producer of Tod Browning's *Freaks*, 1932, which functioned as a kind of *Grand Hotel* for freakish circus attractions.) By contrast, Paramount's leading ladies, such as Clara Bow, Marlene Dietrich, Mae West, Claudette Colbert, and Carole Lombard, combined sexual savoir-faire with tongue-in-cheek wit.

The differences between the two studios can best be illustrated by contrasting the anarchic, pretension-deflating comedies made by the Marx Brothers for Paramount (such as *Animal Crackers*, 1930; *Monkey Business*, 1931; *Horse Feathers*, 1932; and *Duck Soup*, 1933) with the more sober, restrained, and calculated comedies they made a few years later for M-G-M (*A Night at the Opera*, 1935; *A Day at the Races*, 1937; and *Room Service*, 1938). Even Paramount's Jeannette MacDonald, who costarred with Maurice Chevalier in a series of Ruritanian musical romances, shed her self-irony and penchant for sexual innuendo when she moved to the more restrained operettas at M-G-M, where she teamed up with the decidedly less continental Nelson Eddy.

Paramount's deft European stylishness, epitomized in the subtle ironies of Ernst Lubitsch's comedies (such as *The Love Parade*, 1929; *Monte Carlo*, 1930;

Photofest

Studio logos: The Warner Bros. Shield.

Trouble in Paradise, 1932; and *Design for Living,* 1933) and in the exotic erotic fantasies concocted by Josef von Sternberg for Marlene Dietrich (such as *Morocco,* 1930; *Shanghai Express,* 1932; and *The Scarlet Empress,* 1934) had its counterparts in the earnest celebration of American middle-class family values in M-G-M's series of Andy Hardy comedies and teen musicals, starring Mickey Rooney or Judy Garland or both (*Babes in Arms,* 1939, and *Strike Up the Band,* 1940) and in the solid seriousness of prestige melodramas such as *The Good Earth,* 1937; *Boys Town,* 1938; *Mrs. Miniver* and *Random Harvest,* 1942; and *Madame Curie,* 1943.

Warner Bros.

In contrast to the middlebrow style and content of M-G-M, Warner Bros. earned its reputation as the working man's studio. Photographic style at M-G-M was carefully polished; that at Warner's looked hasty and rough and conveyed a gritty realism that suited the studio's narrative interests. Warner's specialized in gangster films, such as *Little Caesar* (1930), *The Public Enemy* (1931), *The Petrified Forest* (1936), and *The Roaring Twenties* (1939), starring tough-guy performers such as James Cagney, Edward G. Robinson, and Humphrey Bogart, whose proletarian acting styles matched the looks and sounds of the ethnic characters they were asked to play.

Even the swashbuckling action heroes played by Errol Flynn in Warner's costume dramas championed the downtrodden lower echelons of society—the unjustly imprisoned doctor-turned-pirate in *Captain Blood* (1935) and the title character in *The Adventures of Robin Hood* (1938). Exposés such as *I Was a Fugitive*

© Shooting Star

Studio logos: The Fox searchlight.

from the Chain Gang (1932), *Wild Boys of the Road* (1933), and *Confessions of a Nazi Spy* (1939) were ripped from the headlines of the tabloids and pitched, like these newspapers, at a lower- and lower-middle-class audience. Warner's actresses (such as Ruby Keeler, Joan Blondell, Bette Davis, Olivia de Havilland, Ida Lupino, Ann Sheridan, and Lauren Bacall) played girls-next-door, gold diggers, molls, and down-to-earth dames who could trade wisecracks with the guys without losing their femininity.

20th Century-Fox

Warner's pitched its product to an urban audience, tailoring its crime films, mysteries, films noirs, musicals, and even costume pictures to blue-collar workers and shop girls who appreciated hard-hitting films with a social conscience. 20th Century-Fox, jokingly referred to by rival studios as "16th Century-Fox" because of all the period and costume pictures it produced, targeted a rural rather than an urban audience. Major Fox stars of the 1930s, such as Will Rogers, Stepin Fetchit, Shirley Temple, and (in the late 1930s) Henry Fonda, spoke to an agrarian, preindustrial, populist concern for homespun, grassroots values. Even Fox stars of the 1940s, such as Tyrone Power, Betty Grable, and Don Ameche, were all-American types who bore no traces of the urban ethnicity found in Warner's stars such as Robinson, Cagney, and even Paul Muni.

Fox, which was run by an Irish Catholic former cop named Winfield Sheehan and then by a Methodist from Nebraska named Darryl Zanuck, was also known as "the goy studio" because, after the ouster of its founder William Fox in 1930, it was the only studio that was neither owned nor operated by Jews (though the Jewish Joe Schenck did serve as chairman of the board and executive producer during Zanuck's reign). This image only served to reinforce the

Photofest

Studio logos: The RKO radio tower.

studio's appeal to nonurban audiences in the Midwest and the South. Ironically, while Jewish executives at Paramount, M-G-M, Warner's, Columbia, Universal, and elsewhere rarely dealt with subject matter that might be considered Jewish or that openly condemned anti-Semitism at home or abroad, Zanuck, perhaps because of Fox's reputation as a Christian studio, was one of the first studio heads to sponsor an exposé of anti-Semitism in his production of *Gentleman's Agreement* (1947), starring Gregory Peck. Zanuck discovered that there was a market for films with a certain social consciousness and prided himself on his productions of John Steinbeck's *The Grapes of Wrath* (1940), which dealt with exploited migrant farm workers; Erskine Caldwell's *Tobacco Road* (1941), a drama about the plight of sharecroppers; *The Ox-Bow Incident* (1943), a Western in which vigilantes lynch the wrong man; *Boomerang* (1947), an exposé of legal corruption; *The Snake Pit* (1948), a story about mental illness that looks at the brutal conditions in American mental asylums; and *Pinky* (1949), a film about racial prejudice and a black woman passing for white.

RKO

RKO, famous for an unlikely combination of films that range from *King Kong* (1933) to Fred Astaire and Ginger Rogers musicals and *Citizen Kane* (1941), was governed by a succession of different heads of production during the 1930s and 1940s, including David Selznick (*What Price Hollywood?* and *Bill of Divorcement*, 1932); Merian C. Cooper (*The Lost Patrol*, 1934); George Schafer (*Abe Lincoln in Illinois*, 1940; *Citizen Kane*, 1941); Charles Koerner (Val Lewton's films, such as *The Cat People*, 1942, and *I Walked with a Zombie*, 1943; *The Spiral Staircase*, 1946);

Studio's logos: Columbia's lady
with a torch.

Dore Schary, who supervised a number of films noirs (*Crossfire, Out of the Past,* 1947; *They Live by Night,* 1948); and finally, Howard Hughes (*I Married a Communist,* 1950; *Vendetta,* 1946–1950; *Jet Pilot,* 1950–1957), whose mismanagement of the studio led to its sale and dismantlement in 1955. Though certain directors (John Ford, George Stevens, Robert Siodmak, Jacques Tourneur) and stars (Katharine Hepburn, Cary Grant, Robert Mitchum) worked for the studio at various times during his period, RKO lacked the thematic and stylistic consistency enjoyed by the other majors. United Artists, which merely distributed the work of independent producers such as Samuel Goldwyn, David Selznick, and Walter Wanger, shared a similar fate.

Columbia Pictures

Columbia earned a reputation for witty and urbane screenwriting and served as the home base for much of the screwball comedy talent in Hollywood. It was also the studio where Frank Capra directed populist melodramas (*American Madness,* 1932; *The Bitter Tea of General Yen* and *Lady for a Day,* 1933; *Lost Horizon,* 1937; *Mr. Smith Goes to Washington,* 1939) and comedies (*It Happened One Night,* 1934; *Mr. Deeds Goes to Town,* 1936; *You Can't Take It with You,* 1938) for over ten years (1928–1939). Capra's own *It Happened One Night* is generally acknowledged as the first screwball comedy, but Howard Hawks's contribution to Columbia comedies, *Twentieth Century* (1934), written by Ben Hecht and Charles MacArthur, runs a close second.

Photofest

Studio logos: Universal's globe.

Columbia scenarists such as Robert Riskin, Sidney Buchman, Jo Swerling, Vina Delmar, Donald Ogden Stewart, Hecht, and MacArthur lent their big-city cynicism to a string of screwball comedies at Columbia in the 1930s, including John Ford's *The Whole Town's Talking* and Gregory La Cava's *She Married Her Boss*, 1935; Richard Boleslawski's *Theodora Goes Wild*, 1936; Leo McCarey's *The Awful Truth*, 1937; George Cukor's *Holiday*, 1938; Hawks's *His Girl Friday*, 1940; Alexander Hall's *Here Comes Mr. Jordan*, 1941; and George Stevens's *The Talk of the Town*, 1942.

Forced to borrow stars such as Clark Gable, Gary Cooper, James Stewart, and Cary Grant from other studios for Columbia pictures in the 1930s, studio chief Harry Cohn decided to build his own stable of stars in the 1940s, including William Holden (*Golden Boy*, 1939; *Picnic*, 1955); Rita Hayworth (*Cover Girl*, 1944; *Gilda*, 1946; *The Lady from Shanghai*, 1948; *Salome* and *Miss Sadie Thompson*, 1953; *Fire Down Below*, 1957); Kim Novak (*Picnic*, 1955; *Bell, Book and Candle*, 1958); Judy Holliday (*Born Yesterday*, 1950; *The Marrying Kind*, 1952; *The Solid Gold Cadillac*, 1956); and Glenn Ford (*Gilda*, 1946; *Loves of Carmen*, 1948; *The Big Heat*, 1953; *Jubal*, 1956; *3:10 to Yuma*, 1957).

Universal Pictures

The golden age of Universal Pictures took place in the first half of the 1930s when the studio was under the guidance of Carl Laemmle, Jr., who supervised the production of two innovative sound films in 1930, the Academy Award–winning *All Quiet on the Western Front* and a Technicolor musical, *The King of Jazz*. He also launched a series of classic horror films, stretching from Bela Lugosi's *Dracula* (1931) and Boris Karloff's *Frankenstein* (1931) to *The Mummy* (1932), *The Invisible Man* (1933), *The Black Cat* (1934), and *The Bride of Franken- stein* (1935). At the same time, John Stahl directed a series of emotionally restrained melodramas—*Back Street* (1932), *Imitation of Life* (1934), and *Magnifi- cent Obsession* (1935)—bringing a sophistication and elegance to the studio that gave way, in the 1940s and early 1950s, to crude program pictures for Abbott and Costello, Ma and Pa Kettle, and Francis, the Talking Mule. Douglas Sirk remade a number of Stahl's melodramas in the mid-1950s, including *Magnificent Obsession* (1954) and *Imitation of Life* (1959), and brought both prestige and profits back to the studio.

Sirk helped to build Universal's latest leading man, Rock Hudson, into a star in *Has Anybody Seen My Gal?* 1952; *Magnificent Obsession* and *Taza, Son of Cochise*, 1954; *Captain Lightfoot* and *All That Heaven Allows*, 1955; *Written on the Wind*, 1956; *Battle Hymn*, 1957; and *Tarnished Angels*, 1958. The studio subsequently took over where Sirk left off, pairing Hudson and Doris Day in a series of financially successful sex comedies such as *Pillow Talk* (1959) and *Lover Come Back* (1961).

Poverty Row

These eight studios dominated a system that included a number of smaller studios, such as Republic and Monogram, that sprouted up in the early 1930s to make B pictures to accompany the major studios' more expensively produced A picture on the bottom half of a double bill. The demand for cheaply made B films gave rise to other poverty-row studios, such as Grand National, Producers Releasing Corporation (PRC), Eagle-Lion, and Allied Artists. The advent of broadcast television in the postwar era eliminated the demand for B pictures, although certain producers of teen-exploitation films, such as American International Pictures, survived into the 1970s.

COLLAPSE: THE END OF THE STUDIO ERA

Divestment, Independent Production, and a Changing Marketplace

The dismantling of the studio system began just before World War II when the U.S. Department of Justice's Antitrust Division filed suit against the eight major studios accusing them of monopolistic practices in their use of block booking, blind bidding, and runs, zones, and clearances. Hollywood avoided prosecution by agreeing to refrain from some of these practices, but in 1944 the government, after hearing complaints from independent exhibitors that the studios had persisted in antitrust activity, reopened the suit. The Paramount Case, as the suit was now called, was finally settled in May 1948 when the U.S. Supreme Court ruled against the studios. The majors were forced to divorce their operations from one another, separating production and distribution from exhibition. They were also forced to divest themselves of their theater chains, which were to be sold off or operated by a separate group of owners who had no involvement in production and distribution. United Artists, Columbia, and Universal, though named in the suit as coconspirators for collaborating with the Big Five

Photofest

Studio logos: United Artists.

studios in these practices, owned no theaters and thus were not subject to this ruling. The major studios delayed the process of divorcement and divestiture as long as possible, maintaining a certain degree of control over their theaters until the mid- to late 1950s. As a result, the initial mechanism or structure that gave rise to the studio system remained more or less in place until roughly 1960.

Other factors contributed to the demise of the studio system, including lengthy postwar strikes against the studios by labor unions, changing patterns in leisure-time entertainment that resulted in a sharp drop in attendance (see Chapter 13, "Hollywood in the Age of Television"), competition with television, and the rise of independent production. After the war, actors and directors went into business for themselves, forming their own production companies. Instead of weekly salaries, they negotiated for lump-sum payments to their privately owned corporations. Instead of being taxed as income, these payments were taxed at a much lower rate as corporate capital gains.

During the war, actor James Cagney had formed an independent production company with his brother William, financing and distributing films through United Artists. In 1946, directors Frank Capra, William Wyler, George Stevens, and producer Sam Briskin formed Liberty Films, which folded after the release of one production, *It's a Wonderful Life* (1946). Alfred Hitchcock and British theater owner Sidney Bernstein set up Transatlantic Pictures in 1948, releasing *Rope* (1948) and *Under Capricorn* (1949) under that logo. Humphrey Bogart's Santana Productions, named after his yacht, produced *Knock on Any Door* (1949), *In a Lonely Place* (1950), and several other pictures that were released through Columbia. In 1951, John Wayne set up Batjac, which produced *Blood Alley* (1955), *The Alamo* (1960), *The Green Berets* (1968), and many other pictures starring Wayne. In 1956, producer Harold Hecht, screenwriter-director James Hill, and actor Burt Lancaster created their own company, which produced *Sweet Smell of Success* (1957), *Run Silent, Run Deep* (1958), and three other films.

At the same time, fewer but more expensive films were being made to satisfy a changing market of fewer but more demanding spectators. The era of the

Studio logos: The Paramount mountain.

blockbuster had begun, and the studio system was not equipped to service that mode of production with any efficiency. As the studios lost their grip on major talent and fewer and fewer films were put into production, the studios deliberately let other contract personnel go, closed down their newsreel and animation departments, rented empty studio space to producers of television shows, and entered television production themselves.

The 1960s saw the ownership of the major and minor studios shift to the hands of conglomerate corporations, such as Gulf + Western, which acquired Paramount; Kinney National Services, which purchased Warner Bros.; and MCA (Music Corporation of America), which bought Universal. Conglomerates did not confine their business activities to manufacturing or distributing a single product but engaged in several unrelated economic ventures. Gulf + Western, for example, manufactured automobile bumpers and owned the Consolidated Cigar Corp., New Jersey Zinc Co., and the South Puerto Rico Sugar Co. It also owned Simon & Schuster (publishers), Sega Enterprises (video arcade games), and Madison Square Gardens Corp. (the New York Knicks and Rangers). In this new economic structure, the making of motion pictures became only one of many corporate activities. Studio assets, ranging from real estate to libraries of older films, were sold so the studios could show a profit and increase the value of the company's shares for stockholders.

Near the end of the 1960s, a number of studios, including Fox and M-G-M, began to sell off their back lots, which now had more value as real estate than as production space. M-G-M even auctioned off its collection of props and costumes, including Dorothy's ruby slippers from *The Wizard of Oz* (1939). Symbolically, the studio era was over.

Starting from Scratch: The New "Studios"

Today, many of the studios of the old studio era exist but do so primarily as the distributors of films produced by a growing number of independents. The cur-

Studio logos: The M-G-M lion.

rent studio system consists of six major media companies that are engaged in film production and distribution; broadcast, cable, and satellite television; publishing; the music industry; theme parks; and even motion picture exhibition (the studios can now own theaters as long as they do not conspire with one another to set prices or engage in other restrictive contract terms). Warner Bros. is now a subsidiary of Time Warner, which also owns Castle Rock, Morgan Creek, Village Roadshow, New Line, and Fine Line. Columbia Pictures belongs to a multinational, Japanese-owned conglomerate—the Sony Company, which also includes TriStar, Mandalay, Revolution, and Sony Pictures Classics. Paramount Pictures is part of the Viacom Corporation, while Universal is an entertainment arm of General Electric, which, through Universal NBC, also owns Working Title and Universal Focus. The hyphen in 20th Century-Fox has been dropped, and 20th Century Fox Film Corp. is now run by Rupert Murdoch's News Corp. Fox Searchlight is also part of this group. Disney, which includes Buena Vista, Walt Disney Pictures, Touchstone, Hollywood Pictures, Spyglass, and Miramax, has become one of the most powerful and successful new majors. In addition to these conglomerates, there are also a number of smaller producer-distributors, including Dreamworks, the old M-G-M/UA, Artisan, and Lions Gate.

The new conglomerates maximize their profits and minimize their risks through synergy, a process of cross-promotion. Time Warner, for example, owns most of the Harry Potter franchise. Though the Harry Potter books are published by a separate entity, Scholastic Books, the Harry Potter films are produced and distributed by Warner Bros., a Time Warner company. AOL, a part of the Time Warner family which has more than 30 million customers, provides Internet links to information about the film and to Harry Potter merchandise that the company sells. Moviefone, another Time Warner subsidiary, promotes the film and sells tickets for it. Time Warner magazines, ranging from *Time, People,* and *Fortune* to *Entertainment Weekly,* generate news and feature coverage of the films, while Time Warner cable outlets such as Turner Broadcasting saturate the airwaves with trailers and advertisements for the films. Meanwhile, the Warner Music Group markets the soundtracks to the films on CDs and tapes. In effect, the entire Time Warner company pools its efforts to sell Harry Potter.

Each time a new film is made today, a studio must be assembled from scratch to produce it. Screenwriters must be found to produce treatments and shooting scripts; producers, directors, stars, cinematographers, art directors, costume designers, and others must be assembled before production can go ahead; and, most crucial, financing must be secured from banks or other investors. Picture making today takes more time than it ever did; the six-week shooting schedules of the 1930s and 1940s have given way to three- to four-month shooting schedules. Films once made in two or three months now took a year or more to finish. As Billy Wilder once said, "In the old days we used to spend our time making pictures; these days we spend it making deals."

And since time is money, the cost of making motion pictures has skyrocketed as well; the average negative cost (the cost required to produce a finished negative, excluding print costs and advertising and distribution expenses) has grown from $200,000 to $400,000 in the 1930s ($1 million to $3 million in the 1950s and $27 million to $30 million in the early 1990s) to almost $59 million in 2002. With the collapse of the studio system, another system has taken its place. Since the courts have outlawed certain practices that formerly reduced the financial risks of film production, producers today face greater and greater uncertainty when they make a film. Because the system that guaranteed a profit has disappeared, these guarantees must be built into the films themselves in the form of bankable stars, sequelization, presales to cable television and various forms of corporate synergy and cross-promotion.

With the demise of the studios, the production of motion pictures has left the factory and returned to a kind of preindustrial workshop in which the final product is custom-made to express the unique interests of the transitory assortment of artists who come together for this particular project and then move on to new ventures. Though we still refer to motion pictures as an industry, the traditional industrial model based on principles of mass production no longer applies. Indeed, with the loss of a mass audience, mass production suddenly became inappropriate. Now Hollywood tailor-makes films for a diminishing film-going elite. The term "studio," which once served as a euphemism for "factory," finally means a studio in the truest sense of the word: an interrelated group of artisans whose unique talents contribute to the handcrafting of individual motion pictures.

■ ■ ■ SELECT STUDIO PRODUCTIONS   (From Four Sample Studios)

Columbia
It Happened One Night (1934)
Twentieth Century (1934)
Mr. Deeds Goes to Town (1936)
Lost Horizon (1937)
The Awful Truth (1937)
Holiday (1938)
Golden Boy (1939)
Mr. Smith Goes to Washington (1939)
His Girl Friday (1940)
Here Comes Mr. Jordan (1941)
Cover Girl (1944)
Gilda (1946)
The Jolson Story (1946)
The Lady from Shanghai (1948)
All the King's Men (1949)
Born Yesterday (1950)
The Big Heat (1953)
From Here to Eternity (1953)
On the Waterfront (1954)
Picnic (1955)
The Solid Gold Cadillac (1956)
Pal Joey (1957)

M-G-M
Greed (1924)
The Merry Widow (1925)
The Big Parade (1925)
Ben-Hur (1926)
Flesh and the Devil (1927)
Anna Christie (1930)
Grand Hotel (1932)
A Night at the Opera (1935)
Camille (1936)
The Good Earth (1937)
The Wizard of Oz (1939)
Goodbye, Mr. Chips (1939)
Mrs. Miniver (1942)
Meet Me in St. Louis (1944)
The Pirate (1948)

Singin' in the Rain (1952)
The Band Wagon (1953)
Ben-Hur (1959)
Home from the Hill (1960)

Paramount
Manslaughter (1922)
Manhandled (1924)
It (1927)
Wings (1927)
Morocco (1930)
Trouble in Paradise (1932)
Shanghai Express (1932)
Duck Soup (1933)
She Done Him Wrong (1933)
I'm No Angel (1933)
The Scarlet Empress (1934)
Cleopatra (1934)
Desire (1936)
Swing High, Swing Low (1937)
Midnight (1939)
The Lady Eve (1941)
Going My Way (1944)
The Lost Weekend (1945)
Sunset Boulevard (1950)
A Place in the Sun (1951)
Roman Holiday (1953)
The Ten Commandments (1956)
Vertigo (1958)

Universal
Blind Husbands (1919)
Foolish Wives (1922)
Phantom of the Opera (1925)
The Cat and the Canary (1927)
Lonesome (1928)
All Quiet on the Western Front (1930)
Dracula (1931)
Frankenstein (1931)
Back Street (1932)

The Mummy (1932)
The Invisible Man (1933)
Imitation of Life (1934)
Magnificent Obsession (1935)
Destry Rides Again (1939)
Cobra Woman (1944)
Phantom Lady (1944)
Scarlet Street (1945)
The Killers (1946)
Letter from an Unknown Woman
   (1948)

Winchester '73 (1950)
All I Desire (1953)
The Glenn Miller Story (1954)
The Far Country (1955)
All That Heaven Allows (1955)
Written on the Wind (1956)
The Incredible Shrinking Man
   (1957)
Touch of Evil (1958)
Imitation of Life (1959)
Pillow Talk (1959)

■ ■ ■ SELECT BIBLIOGRAPHY

BORDWELL, DAVID, JANET STAIGER, AND KRISTIN THOMPSON. *The Classical Hollywood Cinema: Film Style and Mode of Production to 1960.* New York: Columbia University Press, 1985.

FRENCH, PHILIP. *The Movie Moguls: An Informal History of the Hollywood Tycoons.* London: Weidenfeld and Nicolson, 1969.

GOMERY, DOUGLAS. *The Hollywood Studio System.* New York: St. Martin's Press, 1986.

GUSSOW, MEL. *Don't Say Yes Until I Finish Talking: A Biography of Darryl F. Zanuck.* New York: Doubleday, 1971.

LITMAN, BARRY R. *The Motion Picture Mega-Industry.* Boston: Allyn and Bacon, 1998.

PIRIE, DAIVD, ed. *Anatomy of the Movies.* New York: Macmillan, 1981.

SCHATZ, THOMAS. *The Genius of the System: Hollywood Filmmaking in the Studio Era.* New York: Pantheon, 1988.

WASKO, JANET. *Hollywood in the Information Age.* Austin, University of Texas, 1994.

CHAPTER **5**

The Star System

THE MECHANICS OF STARDOM

Making Stars

Exposed Artifice: Singin' in the Rain

In the late 1920s, it was estimated that over 32,250,000 fan letters were received each year by movie stars in Hollywood. From the mid-1930s through the early 1950s, over 500 journalists and newspaper correspondents gave Hollywood as their dateline, generating more than 100,000 words per day about the film industry and making Hollywood the third largest source of news information in the country, lagging behind only New York and Washington. Most of that news concerned the public and private activities of movie stars.

Though motion pictures may have been an industry, the general public has always tended to see Hollywood less as a factory town than as a place where royalty resides. Indeed, few eyebrows were raised when screen stars such as

Pola Negri, Gloria Swanson, and Grace Kelly married European counts, princes, and even kings. Stars inhabit a different world from the rest of us and live by different rules. To paraphrase Lina Lamont (Jean Hagen) in *Singin' in the Rain* (1952), stars are not people. They are celestial bodies.

Convinced by the media of her own stardom, Lina (quoting a newspaper puff piece) explains that she is a "shimmering, glowing star in the cinema firmament." But Lina, alas, is not a real star; she does not radiate her own light but merely reflects the light cast on her by others. Her image as a star has been carefully fabricated. It is partly the product of studio press releases, which are reprinted verbatim by the media and consumed without question, not only by the public but by Lina herself. And it is partly the product of film technology that functions to conceal her flaws. Though Lina may look like a star, she doesn't sound like a star—her shrill, lower-class voice lacks refinement and fails to match the glamour and sophistication of her appearance.

This imperfection, which the silent cinema easily ignored, threatens to betray her when she is forced to speak in the talkies. Her image, however, is preserved when another actress, Kathy Seldon (played by Debbie Reynolds), dubs her, substituting her own voice for Lina's in all of Lina's dialogue and song sequences. Lina's phoniness is ultimately unmasked, however, when the curtains are drawn back to disclose to the public part of the previously invisible machinery that has made Lina a star; we see Reynolds—now revealed as the real star—singing the film's title song in the background as Lina pathetically lip-syncs the lyrics in the foreground.

In the opening sequence of *Singin' in the Rain,* a radio columnist (Dora) interviews stars attending the preview of a new Lockwood and Lamont picture. Dora's presence indicates, in part, the role that the media play in Hollywood's construction of stardom. She becomes the willing vehicle for the transmission of Don Lockwood's exaggerated reconstruction of his past to the listening public. Yet again, the film exposes the artifice involved in the construction of stardom through a mismatch of voice and image.

Lockwood's duplicity differs from that of Lina's in one crucial way, however. Here, we *see* the truth—Lockwood's less than glamorous personal history—while we *hear* the official, sanitized studio biography, which paints a far more elegant portrait. With Lina, the audience has been tricked into forming a certain set of expectations (into assuming her perfection as a star)—expectations that are then revealed to be incorrect. With Lockwood (Gene Kelly), there is no deception because his verbal construction of his image is simultaneously undercut by what we see on the screen. Our knowledge of the truth turns us into his allies and makes us complicit in his playful manipulation of the press. At the same time, the images reveal Lockwood to be hardworking, forthright, and unpretentious—unlike Lina, who emerges as a self-centered prima donna.

Lockwood has concocted a charming tale, carefully tailored to project a dignified image that matches the elegance of his onscreen roles. The story he tells is designed for the consumption of not only the radio gossip columnist but also the public, whose fascination with stars drives the economy of two interrelated industries: it draws cash customers to the box office, and it supports the fan magazines (which can be seen in the hands of members of the crowd waiting for the arrival of stars outside the preview of the new Lockwood and Lamont film) and other popular publications that seek to satisfy the public's almost insatiable appetite for news about stars.

Stars, Fans, and Profits

Indeed, it was a film studio that gave birth to the first fan magazine. In 1911, Vitagraph's head of production, J. Stuart Blackton, launched the *Motion Picture Story Magazine,* the first film magazine designed for a general readership, which publicized Vitagraph's players and recent releases. Carl Laemmle at Universal followed suit in 1913 with *Moving Picture Stories.* The independently produced *Photoplay,* which was published once a month from 1911 to 1980 and enjoyed a circulation of more than 2 million in the 1920s, took up where the studios left off, providing photo-illustrations of the stories of films and feature articles on film stars. Major fan magazines of the sound era, such as *Modern Screen, Photoplay, Silver Screen,* and *Movie Stars,* enjoyed wide circulation (in 1950, *Photoplay* had 1.2 million readers) and furnished, through their probes into the offscreen lives of movie stars and their rehashes of studio press releases, free publicity for the studios, which, in turn, indirectly supported a number of these publications by advertising heavily in them.

Producer Samuel Goldwyn would have had us believe that "God makes the stars. It's up to the producers to find them." God, however, has little to do with it. The industry that makes motion pictures also manufactures movie stars, with the aid of the press and other media—movie stars who have played and continue to play a crucial economic role in the history of that industry. In a business in which each new picture is an unproven commodity, the presence of an established star guarantees a certain return on the high-venture capital invested in a film. Since a star's name on the marquee drew audiences, it was to the advantage of the studios to perpetuate the star system.

The star provides the studio with a tangible attraction, an image that can be advertised and marketed, offsetting the less tangible qualities of the story, direction, acting, art direction, costume design, and overall studio style. Though these latter elements can be marketed as well, they rarely achieve the identifiability of the star and cannot, in themselves, guarantee that a film will make a profit.

Mary Pickford's popularity (she was receiving 18,000 fan letters per month in 1919) not only ensured the profitability of her pictures but enabled her studio, Paramount, to sell its other, non-Pickford films as well, instituting a system of block booking and blind bidding that was forced on exhibitors who wanted to rent Pickford's films (see Chapter 4, "The Studio System"). Years later, Mae West, the buxom burlesque and vaudeville performer who gave new meaning to the art of sexual innuendo through her double entendres and her tongue-in-cheek delivery, was credited with saving Paramount when it went into receivership and was taken over by its creditors in 1933. M-G-M owed its survival during the Depression to its stable of stars, which included Greta Garbo, Joan Crawford, Clark Gable, Marie Dressler, Norma Shearer, Mickey Rooney, Judy Garland, and Spencer Tracy; while the youthful singing star Deanna Durbin is said to have rescued Universal in the recession of 1938.

Star Power

Stars can save studios because stars sell films. When the investment firm of Kuhn, Loeb and Company decided to bankroll Paramount in 1919, its decision was based, in large part, on the studio's stable of stars, which included Gloria Swanson, Douglas Fairbanks, William S. Hart, and Pauline Frederick. Stars were assets that the studios could take to the bank. Some major stars even took themselves to the bank, forming their own studio. In late 1919, Hollywood's premiere stars—Mary Pickford, Douglas Fairbanks, and Charles Chaplin (along with "star" director, D. W. Griffith)—formed their own company, United Artists, to distribute their films. But, for the most part, from the 1920s to the 1950s, the studios "owned" the stars, who were bound to them through multiyear contracts. As that system of contracts started to crumble in the 1950s and 1960s, the stars began to assume more and more power in the marketplace. In 1969, in a gesture that recalled the formation of United Artists, a handful of major stars (including Barbra Streisand, Sidney Poitier, and Paul Newman) created First Artists Production Company to finance the production of their films. These stars were soon joined by Steve McQueen and Dustin Hoffman, but the company was unable to generate enough income to finance subsequent films. It effectively went out of business in 1982 after releasing such films as *The Getaway* (McQueen, 1972), *The Life and Times of Judge Roy Bean* (Newman, 1972), *Uptown Saturday Night* (Poitier, 1974), and *A Star Is Born* (Streisand, 1976).

The power of the stars in contemporary Hollywood is reflected in the focus of entertainment journalism, ranging from daily, syndicated television shows such as *Access Hollywood* and *Entertainment Tonight* to weekly magazines such as *People* and *Entertainment Weekly*. News about stars is headlined on such TV shows, and photographs of stars dominate the covers of these magazines. Every year, *Premiere* magazine publishes a list of "the 100 most powerful people in movies." Though the top 10 tend to be the CEOs of production companies and star producer-directors (such as Steven Spielberg and George Lucas), more than a third of the exclusive 100 are stars, ranging in 2003 from Tom Hanks (no. 13) to Tom Cruise (no. 14), Mel Gibson (no. 15), Julia Roberts (no. 16), Jackie Chan (no. 94), Halle Berry (no. 96), Colin Farrell (no. 98), and Kate Hudson (no. 99). People on the power list can get pictures made; their pictures make money; and, because their pictures make money, top stars such as Hanks, Cruise, Gibson, and Roberts can command per-picture fees of $25 million as well as percentages of the box-office gross.

As Mike Sullivan in *Road to Perdition,* Tom Hanks goes against type to play a mob hit man.

Tom Hanks: A Case Study

Tom Hanks's films make money ($266 million in 2002; $2.8 billion in box-office grosses over the length of his career from 1981 to 2002). But Tom Hanks is also a star whose talent as an actor has repeatedly been recognized by various institutions in the film industry. Highly respected by his peers, Hanks won back-to-back Academy Awards for Best Actor for *Philadelphia* in 1993 and *Forrest Gump* in 1994. He's also won three Golden Globe Awards, as well as awards from the Los Angeles Film Critics Association and the Screen Actors Guild.

Like a number of other contemporary stars, Hanks got his start in film through his apprenticeship on a successful TV series. But unlike Halle Berry (*Knots Landing*), Jim Carrey and Jennifer Lopez (*In Living Color*), George Clooney (*ER*), Leonardo DiCaprio (*Growing Pains*), Eddie Murphy and Mike Myers (*Saturday Night Live*), Will Smith (*Fresh Prince of Bel Air*), John Travolta (*Welcome Back, Kotter*), and Bruce Willis (*Moonlighting*), Hanks's rise to stardom began by his dressing up as a woman on *Bosom Buddies*. Hanks's career can be charted in terms of a sexual trajectory from the amiable, soft, sensitive, quasi-feminized, curly-haired youth in his films of the 1980s to the older, harder, more masculine figures he played in the 1990s. The curly-headed youth surfaced in a string of 1980s comedies, from his first hits in *Splash* (1984), *Bachelor Party* (1984), *Volunteers* (1985), and *The Money Pit* (1986) to his first megahit, *Big* (1988). In *Big*, Hanks played a 13-year-old kid trapped in the body of a 35-year-old man, a role that captured the boyish innocence and essential sweetness of his roles in this period. To some extent, this Hanks recalls the all-American earnestness of Harold Lloyd (without the athleticism), though Hanks is clearly no clown. He is a straight actor who plays multidimensional characters who possess a certain comic aspect.

In *A League of Their Own* (1992), in the minor role of Jimmy Dugan, a former baseball great forced into retirement due to injuries who has hit the skids, taken to alcohol, and been reduced to coaching in a women's baseball league, Hanks refashioned his image from a kid with a future to a man with a past. His character's insistence that "there's no crying in baseball" echoes his gruff behavior but masks an inner, repressed sensitivity to his players' needs. Subsequent roles as veteran astronaut Jim Lovell in *Apollo 13* (1995), the battle-fatigued marine captain John Miller in *Saving Private Ryan* (1998), death-row prison guard Paul Edgecomb in *The Green Mile* (1999), and mob hit man Michael Sullivan in *Road to Perdition* (2002) present a world-weary figure who is no stranger to disappointment, failure, physical pain, and self-doubt. If, in *Big,* Hanks is a kid in the body of a man, in *The Green Mile,* he turns out (in the frame story) to be a 100-year-old man in the body of an 80-year-old. In both *League* and *Perdition,* Hanks plays against type; indeed, in *Perdition,* he plays a cold-blooded killer. But his character in *Perdition* nonetheless resembles that of earlier Hanks characters. Hanks has been described as an American everyman. That description fits him in the sense that his films are modern morality plays in which he emerges as the moral compass whose behavior exemplifies an internalized and intuitive adherence to an abstract, unwritten set of moral guidelines. Characters around him—for example, the members of his platoon in *Ryan*—do their duty inasmuch as they do what is necessary for the mission; they play by the book. Hanks's character seems to be guided by an inner sense of what he *must* do and he does it. When he breaks the rules (and the law) in *Green Mile* and takes death-row prisoner John Coffey (Michael Clarke Duncan) out of jail to the warden's house where Coffey cures the warden's wife of a brain tumor, we understand that Hanks is observing a higher law. Like the populist heroes in Frank Capra's American morality plays of an earlier era (such as *Mr. Smith Goes to Washington,* 1939, and *Meet John Doe,* 1941), Hanks knows in his heart what is right and does it. In avenging the murder of his wife and child in *Perdition,* Hanks never swerves from his mission, but he also makes every attempt to secure what he sees as a just resolution to his grievance. It is the mob that emerges as hypocritical in its behavior, not Hanks, who respects his enemies and understands their moral dilemmas, yet knows that the injustice done to him and his family gives him the right to do what he does to exact vengeance and to protect the life of his sole surviving son. And he knows that his chief enemy John Rooney (Paul Newman) and mob boss Al Capone (Anthony LaPaglia) understand this as well. Of his generation of actors, Hanks is the only one who brings a moral clarity to his roles. Certainly Tom Cruise does not, nor do Gibson, Clooney, DiCaprio, Brad Pitt, or others.

The roles that won Hanks his two Oscars—that of lawyer Andrew Beckett in *Philadelphia* and that of Gomerish Alabama simpleton *Forrest Gump*—exemplify this notion of Hanks as moral center. As Beckett, Hanks seeks not revenge but justice, bringing the idealism of Jimmy Stewart's Mr. Smith to his crusade against the impersonal forces of corporate America. Every problem has a solution, and his solution is Joe Miller (Denzel Washington), a lawyer who earns his living by representing the unrepresented. The alliance between Beckett, an AIDS victim, and Miller, an African American, underscores the moral nature of the film's project to challenge bigotry in all of its forms. Over the course of the film, the Hanks character undergoes a physical deterioration that is presented in the form of an ethical-moral passion in which he reaches a personal state of bliss like the passions of Christ or Joan of Arc.

As Forrest Gump, Hanks again undergoes a Christlike agony, playing an everyman character who suffers for the sins of others. Through the figure of Jenny (Robin Wright), the girl-woman with whom he falls in love, Forrest bears the burden of the major social problems of postwar America—child abuse, Vietnam and the antiwar movement, free sex, drugs, and, ultimately, AIDS. But he bears these sins without fully understanding them; thus he remains blissfully innocent of all the knowledge that oppresses others such as the bitter, disabled war veteran Lt. Dan (Gary Sinese). Therefore, Gump can serve as an agent that reconciles such others to their lot in life. Hanks's thick southern accent coupled with Forrest's childlike speech patterns threaten to expose the performance as allegorical commentary on the character, but Hanks's grounding of the performance in his body (his gestures, physical movement, eyes, and exchanges of looks with others) rescues him from self-parody. Only Tom Hanks could have pulled off this part and made Gump credible.

Persona

A Variety of Masks

Every star houses several different personalities, though they all tend to coexist graciously with one another rather than battle for control. At the base of the human pyramid known as the star lies an actual person, whose physical attributes and, in some instances, psychological makeup provide the foundation for the construction of the personality of the actor, or actress, who appears on screen.

The phenomenon of the star "Cary Grant" thus began with the biological birth of Archibald Leach, who would subsequently change his name to Cary Grant; that of "Judy Garland" can be traced back to Frances Gumm, the name with which she was born. Archie Leach and Frances Gumm, however, remained inaccessible to us for the most part, as do the real Harrison Ford, Denzel Washington, Michael Douglas, Glenn Close, and Meryl Streep. Even if we met them in the flesh, so to speak, our firsthand knowledge of them would be limited to the public persona, or game face, that they put on for personal appearances. Our knowledge of movie stars is necessarily secondhand; we can only experience screen personalities *as personalities*. We have contact with them only through the roles they play, and we come to know them as personae rather than as persons.

Literally, the term "persona" refers to the mask worn by a character on the ancient Greek stage. Actors develop a persona or portrait of themselves out of the personalities of the various characters they have played over the course of their careers and out of elements of their personal lives that have become public knowledge. Actors either use these traits in their performances or audiences impose them on the actors, reinvesting their performances with added significance, as was the case with James Dean, whose accidental death in a highway accident became part of his star legend.

John Wayne's persona, for example, included the inflexible, sometimes violent determination of the Western (*The Searchers,* 1956) and war (*Sands of Iwo Jima,* 1949) heroes he played as well as his public political stance as an anti-Communist (*Big Jim McLain,* 1952), a conservative Republican (*The Alamo,* 1960), and a supporter of the war in Vietnam (*The Green Berets,* 1968). Even his highly publicized personal bout with cancer (which prompted him to proclaim after one of his lungs was removed, "I licked the big C") provided crucial material for his last film, *The Shootist* (1976), in which he played an aging gunfighter dying of cancer. Wayne himself died of cancer three years after the film was made.

Stars essentially consist of three personalities—the star, the actor, and the actual person. Each of these personalities consumes the entity that lies immediately beneath it. With actors, the real person disappears in the creation of a fictional character. Indeed, some actors so transform their physical features, including their voice and bodily appearance, that they give the illusion not only of becoming the characters they play but of becoming different characters from film to film. They efface themselves not only as persons but also *as actors,* as in the case of chameleonlike performers such as Chris Cooper who, as Sam Deeds in *Lone Star* (1996), plays a romantic lead as the crusading sheriff, and then, as Col. Frank Fitts in *American Beauty* (1999), is a military martinet who tests his son for drugs. Years later, Cooper plays the toothless orchid thief John Laroche in Spike Jonze's *Adaptation* (2002), and then reincarnates himself virtually unrecognizably as the enigmatic horse trainer Tom Smith in *Seabiscuit* (2003).

Types and Typecasting

More commonly, actors become "typed," playing similar kinds of characters from film to film. Over the course of several films, these actors develop a distinct persona, or public image. In certain instances, an actor will become associated with a specific character, whose attributes become fused with his or her own. Thus, Charles Chaplin became identified with the Tramp, Sean Connery and Roger Moore with James Bond, William Shatner with Capt. James Kirk, and Sylvester Stallone with Rocky Balboa and John Rambo.

More frequently, an actor will consistently play a certain character type from film to film. Thus, Humphrey Bogart tended to play hard-boiled, anti-authoritarian, romantically vulnerable tough guys (*The Maltese Falcon,* 1941; *Casablanca,* 1942); Marilyn Monroe was regularly cast as a gold digger or dumb

Courtesy of Universal

Sean Connery, in a departure from his role as James Bond, played opposite 'Tippi' Hedren in Alfred Hitchcock's "sex mystery," *Marnie* (1964).

blonde (*Gentlemen Prefer Blondes* and *How to Marry a Millionaire*, 1953); and Woody Allen has played neurotic New York Jewish intellectuals who quote Kierkegaard, hate Los Angeles, and fantasize about love and death (*Annie Hall*, 1977; *Manhattan*, 1979).

Many actors resist typecasting and try to alter the kinds of characters they play on the screen from film to film. Dustin Hoffman, for example, went from a female impersonator–soap opera queen in *Tootsie* (1982) to Tom Cruise's autistic older brother in *Rain Man* (1988). Even those actors closely identified with specific roles will cast themselves against type in an attempt to broaden their range and thus rewrite their screen persona. Sean Connery resisted his James Bond image from the very start, taking parts as a Philadelphia publisher sexually intrigued by a neurotic kleptomaniac in Alfred Hitchcock's *Marnie* (1964) and a rebellious prisoner of war in Sidney Lumet's *The Hill* (1965). Later, Connery even took off his toupee to play older parts such as the seasoned soldier of fortune in John Huston's *The Man Who Would Be King* (1975) and the aging, incorruptible Irish cop in Brian DePalma's *The Untouchables* (1987).

Stardom and Mass Culture: From Persona to Star

The Role of the Media

Every actor and actress constructs a persona over the course of his or her career, but few become stars. A star is an actor whose persona transcends the sum total of his or her performances. The star's image may be rooted in specific roles, but it extends beyond them, establishing itself in subsidiary forms, in secondary representations of the actor's persona such as those found in fan magazines or supermarket tabloids. The star's persona recirculates in these other media, where it acquires new meanings more or less on its own, beyond the control of the individual actor or actress.

A star's persona thus differs from that of an actor. For an actor, the persona provides a primary mask that disguises the real person underneath. For a star, the persona includes the actor's persona as well as the star's persona. This secondary mask of stardom covers the earlier one, reproducing and reshaping the original persona and often transforming it in the process.

In other words, stardom is constructed not solely in films themselves but in the larger terrain of mass culture as well. As an image reflected back to the performer from the mirror of popular culture, stardom colors the actor's persona on which it is based, rewriting that personality in certain identifiable ways. Thus, Elizabeth Taylor's stardom includes not only her films but her representation in the media, which have tended to portray her as a troubled figure—a former alcoholic plagued by recurrent weight problems and a succession of tragic or unhappy marriages. In the 1980s and 1990s, Taylor successfully harnessed her stardom to fight AIDS, raising money for AIDS research and increasing public awareness about the disease. Though she has not acted regularly in films since 1989, she continues to "star" in supermarket tabloids, where articles about her appear on a routine basis.

The same might be said of Elvis Presley, whose stardom continues to thrive in the tabloids, even though he died in 1977. Reported sightings of Elvis in malls and shopping centers testify to the supernatural existence that certain stars enjoy when they transcend the media (records, films) in which they originally excelled and achieve a different order of celebrity, becoming (even after their own deaths) stars in another medium. In other words, stars become stars when they lose control of their images, which then take on a life of their own.

By the same token, Jeremy Irons and Anthony Hopkins, in spite of their Oscars for *Reversal of Fortune* (1990) and *The Silence of the Lambs* (1991), respectively, and their obvious talents as actors, have yet to become major stars, largely because (1) the different roles that they have played do not lend themselves to the construction of a coherent screen persona, (2) their images have not found widespread circulation in the media, and (3) their personal lives have remained private rather than public. As a result, the nature of their offscreen personalities is obscure and ill-defined for the majority of filmgoers.

Mickey Mouse: A Case Study

The transcendent nature of stardom is perhaps best illustrated not by Taylor or Presley, whose physical realities served as solid foundations for their appeal with the public, but by Mickey Mouse, whose star status rests on a purely imaginary form of existence. Alfred Hitchcock, who once described actors as cattle, declared Mickey Mouse to be the perfect actor because he didn't draw a salary, he did whatever you wanted him to do, he never asked what his motivation was for a scene, and he could be erased. Mickey was not only the perfect actor,

Courtesy of Buena Vista

Mickey Mouse skyrocketed to stardom in
Steamboat Willie (1928).

but he became a star as well, christened by no less a Hollywood luminary than Mary Pickford (who once proclaimed him to be her favorite star).

Mickey's stardom was phenomenal. Mickey Mouse Clubs, introduced by theater owners in 1929 shortly after Mickey's first talkie, *Steamboat Willie*, quickly spread throughout the country and, by 1931, boasted more than a million members. Merchandising tie-ins worth tens of millions of dollars soon followed. By the mid-1930s, there were Mickey Mouse dolls, watches, stationery, ice cream cones, lunch boxes, clothing, wallpaper, toys, and games.

Though he had no private life or tabloid existence, Mickey's image was widely circulated, not only through consumer products but through the media, including newspapers, fan magazines, and comic strips, making him one of the most recognizable figures in the world. Even today, Mickey's image is better known than that of any world leader, rock star, sports figure, or other national or international celebrity. If Mickey was the perfect actor, he was also the perfect star; he was a purely fictional construction whose image circulated independently of not only the control but also the physical existence of any real person.

Playing Themselves

It could be said of Mickey Mouse that he was a star without ever being an actor. In other words, Mickey always played himself (even when nominally playing the sorcerer's apprentice in *Fantasia*, (1940). The same is often said of star actors such as John Wayne, James Stewart, and countless others. It may even account for the fact that many great stars—including Charles Chaplin, Greta Garbo, Marlene Dietrich, Cary Grant, Fred Astaire, Barbara Stanwyck, Marilyn Monroe, and Judy Garland—never win an Academy Award for Best Actor or Actress (though Grant, Stanwyck, and Chaplin did win special, honorary, career-achievement Oscars). If stars are only playing themselves on the screen, then they are not really acting and are thus undeserving of an Oscar, or so most members of the Academy would have us believe.

Though ostensibly playing different characters, John Wayne (who finally won an Oscar in 1969 for his role as Rooster Cogburn in *True Grit*) employed the same speech and phrasing patterns, gestures, and physical movements (especially his famous walk) in roles as diverse as that of a tyrannical empire builder in *Red River* (1948), a memory-haunted ex-prizefighter who has retired to Ireland in *The Quiet Man* (1952), and a genial naval officer serving in the Pacific on the eve of World War II in *In Harm's Way* (1965). In each instance, Wayne played two characters—the character created in the script and John Wayne, a persona that it took the actor almost 10 years (1929–1939) and scores of B Westerns and serials to create. Though Wayne's persona overlapped and created a fit with the characters he portrayed, what audiences saw (and went to the movie theater to see) was not the fictional character he played but Wayne *as* the character. In Wayne's case, the reality of the star overpowered that of the character, preventing the full realization of the character as an autonomous being.

The nature of star acting helps to explain why stars have difficulty playing famous historical personages; the persona of the star refuses to fit that of the well-known character from history. Thus, Spencer Tracy was more Spencer Tracy than Thomas Edison in *Edison, the Man* (1940), and James Stewart was more James Stewart than Glenn Miller in *The Glenn Miller Story* (1954) or Charles Lindbergh in *The Spirit of St. Louis* (1957). It's unlikely that John Wayne could have played anyone other than John Wayne, though he did take a stab at William Tecumseh Sherman in *How the West Was Won* (1962).

For this reason, Hollywood tends to cast unknowns in the parts of familiar figures. Milos Forman chose Tom Hulce, whose chief previous credit had been a supporting role in *National Lampoon's Animal House* (1978), for the role of Mozart in *Amadeus* (1984); Gary Busey played Buddy Holly in *The Buddy Holly Story* (1978); Kurt Russell, relatively unknown at the time, starred in the TV movie *Elvis* (1979); and Ben Kingsley debuted on film as *Gandhi* (1982), winning an Oscar for his performance. *Gandhi*, however, did not turn Kingsley into a star. Nor did his Oscar translate itself into drawing power for Kingsley at the box office.

Stars, the System, and the Public

Marilyn Monroe: A Case Study

Perhaps Marilyn Monroe gave the best account of stardom when she declared that "only the public can make a star. . . . It's the studios who try to make a system out of it." In other words, stars are indeed made, but it is not necessarily the studios, producers, press agents, or even the stars themselves who make them. However, once a star has been made, the studios attempt to harness the power of the star and transform it into a system.

Monroe's swipe at the studios refers, in part, to the successful efforts of her own studio, 20th Century-Fox, to build her up as a star in the early 1950s and, in part, to its less successful attempts to manufacture stars to take her place if she should ever refuse a part, fail to report to the set, chronically arrive late on the set, or temperamentally walk off the set in midproduction (which she did repeatedly in the late 1950s and early 1960s).

At first, Fox groomed the platinum-blonde starlet Sheree North to take Monroe's place, giving her the same sort of publicity buildup given earlier to Monroe; but North failed to catch the attention of the public. Fox tried again in the mid-1950s, launching another shapely blonde, Jayne Mansfield, on a somewhat more successful career as a Monroe type in films that parody Monroe's (and Mansfield's) image as blonde bombshell, such as *The Girl Can't Help It* (1956) and *Will Success Spoil Rock Hunter?* (1957). Though Mansfield achieved some success, Mamie Van Doren, the next Fox entry in the field of Monroe substitutes, did not fare nearly as well, becoming a familiar fixture in teen-exploitation pictures such as *Running Wild* (1955) and *Untamed Youth* (1957) and ending her film career with *The Navy vs. the Night Monsters* (1966).

Stardom and Public Acceptance

The most famous attempts to manufacture stars are associated with the studio era (roughly from the mid-1920s through the late 1950s), when male producers revealed their obsessions with certain actresses by trying to make them stars. William Randolph Hearst established Cosmopolitan Pictures in the late 1920s to produce films for Marion Davies; Samuel Goldwyn imported Soviet actress Anna Sten in the mid-1930s, hoping to make her into another Garbo or Dietrich; Darryl Zanuck tried to turn Bella Darvi into a star in the 1950s. In the late 1970s and early 1980s independent producers, agents, and publicists tried to turn models or covergirls, or *Playboy* centerfolds into film stars and failed, as the disappointing careers of Christopher Atkins (*Blue Lagoon,* 1980), Bo Derek (*10,* 1979), Morgan Fairchild (*The Seduction,* 1982), and Pia Zadora (*Butterfly,* 1981) indicate.

If Monroe was right and it is the public that makes a star, then why does the public select certain performers for stardom and reject others? Although producers may view the public as capricious or whimsical in this regard, there is often a method to the public's madness or, to phrase this relationship more positively, a foundation for the fanaticism about certain stars.

The star answers a particular need that the public either consciously or unconsciously has at a particular time for a particular figure of identification. In other words, the star functions as a sociocultural barometer of sorts, giving expression to and providing symbolic solutions for specific fears, desires, anxieties, and/or dreams that haunt popular consciousness.

But before examining the intimate nature of the relationship between the public and its stars, it is important to recognize two significant features of this

Ingrid Bergman's highly publicized affair with director Roberto Rossellini clashed dramatically with her screen image as the title character in *Joan of Arc* (1948).

Courtesy of RKO

relationship. First, stars may be figures of fantasy, but their fans are not fools. Audiences are quite aware of the machinery that studios and others set in motion in their attempts to produce stars, and they knowingly participate in the manufacturing of stars. Indeed, much of their enjoyment of stars comes from this knowledge. Second, the public that makes stars can also break them, especially if the stars violate their public image, as the much-beloved silent comedian Fatty Arbuckle did when he was accused of raping a young actress at a wild party in 1921, or as Ingrid Bergman (briefly) did when, having just starred in *Joan of Arc* (1948), she deserted her husband and daughter to live with director Roberto Rossellini, with whom she then had a child out of wedlock.

STARS AND CULTURE: A HISTORICAL SURVEY

The Early Years

The First Stars

The star system, of course, preexisted the advent of motion pictures, thriving in the legitimate theater, vaudeville and the music hall, and the opera throughout the nineteenth century. Histories tend to cite Florence Lawrence, an actress who appeared in Biograph films in 1908–1909 and who was heavily publicized as a star by Carl Laemmle when she left Biograph in 1909 to join his IMP Company, as the first movie star. However, she was not the first star to appear on film.

In 1894, Edison's Kinetoscope Exhibition Co. signed the first movie star—the prizefighter Gentleman Jim Corbett. His exclusive contract forbade him to appear in anyone else's films. Edison brought before his cameras stars from a variety of fields, including Wild West performers Buffalo Bill and Annie Oakley, strongman Eugene Sandow, dancers Ruth St. Denis and Annabelle, and other attractions from the New York stage and the Barnum and Bailey Circus. One of the most sensational early films, *The May Irwin–John C. Rice Kiss* (1896), was an adaptation of a scene from a Broadway stage play, *The Widow Jones,* featuring theater stars May Irwin and John Rice.

However, Lawrence, who, unlike these earlier stars, enjoyed little prior celebrity on the stage or elsewhere, was one of the first stars to be created by the medium of film. These extracinematic stars of the cinema's first decade did not act; rather, they performed feats for which they were well-known—some of which, as in the case of Sarah Bernhardt, involved the staging of famous theatrical scenes for the camera to record. For the most part, their stardom was merely recorded; it was not created on the screen, as was Lawrence's. And Lawrence's stardom derived not from studio publicity (Biograph refused to publicize its performers) but from fans who were drawn to her without knowing her name, fascinated by her radiance, refinement, beauty, and dramatic range, which enabled her to play both comedy and tragedy. As one of a succession of director D. W. Griffith's heroines, including Blanche Sweet, Mary Pickford, Lillian and Dorothy Gish, and Mae Marsh, she served as an embodiment of American energy and Victorian virtue.

Late Victorianism

The stars of the 1910s represented transitional figures for audiences whose nineteenth-century Victorianism was slowly giving way to a more modern sensibility in which many of the more restrictive aspects of Victorianism were relaxed. American Victorianism consisted of somewhat more than the negative virtues of sexual repression and restraint. It involved a code of positive values that included hard work and an aversion to idleness; a sense of moral orderliness and self-control, discipline, self-confidence, and self-sufficiency. However, it did prize obedience and it also set forth fairly circumscribed roles for women to play within the family and the community, relegating their activities to the private sphere of the home and barring proper ladies (wives, mothers, and daughters) from taking part in the more public sphere of the workplace or politics. The nineteenth-century ideal of womanhood insisted, as one critic put it, on their "piety, purity, submissiveness, and domesticity."

In *Broken Blossoms* (1919), for example, the options for Griffith's lower-class heroine, played by the delicate, Victorian ideal of femininity, Lillian Gish, consisted of the virtuous drudgery of an oppressive marriage or the depraved misery of prostitution. There was no question (in Griffith's mind at least) of her getting a job, supporting herself, and living alone.

During the 1910s and 1920s, the status of women changed as the American economy shifted from a rural and agricultural to an urban and industrial base. More and more women entered the workplace, securing jobs in emerging corporations and businesses as "typewriters" (that is, office secretaries) and in the growing consumer industries such as department stores, where women found jobs as clerks and salesgirls. These economic changes produced profound social changes, resulting in—among other things—greater freedom for women. Certain stars functioned to bridge these transformations.

Pickford, Fairbanks, and Chaplin

Mary Pickford embodied the profound social changes taking place in that she retained her screen image as "Little Mary, the girl with the long, golden curls," "America's sweetheart," and the ideal embodiment of Victorian virtue, while a more modern, offscreen image of the actress as a working woman and as a businesswoman managing a successful career evolved alongside this earlier image. Though her screen roles, such as those in *Tess of the Storm Country* (1914) and *Rebecca of Sunnybrook Farm* (1917), continued to portray her as a doll-like child, her more modern image in the media made her a figure of identification for an emerging class of "new women," which included independent working women, suffragettes, and other nontraditional women who took their place alongside men in the post-Victorian world of modern America.

In similar fashion, Douglas Fairbanks constructed a double image: he often played a hard-working young businessman in an emerging corporate America; yet his occasional bouts of boredom registered his frustration as an individual in a stifling atmosphere dominated by the Protestant work ethic. But rather than give in to a decadent idleness, Fairbanks energetically threw himself into the guilt-free enjoyment of pleasure and relaxation through healthy leisure-time pursuits. He engaged in sports, athletic exercise, or other physical adventures.

Charles Chaplin combined, in the persona of the Tramp, the old-world, aristocratic values of Victorian society, and the new-world egalitarianism of the immigrant, whose hunger and homelessness made him the defiant opponent of all arbitrary authority—especially policemen. Thus, his costume of derby, dress coat, and cane looked back nostalgically to a former elegance. And his concern for proper behavior and social manners identified him with more traditional values.

The enormous popularity of Pickford, Fairbanks, and Chaplin during the 1910s testified to their ability to address the anxieties of audiences who were themselves confronting a modern, twentieth-century world with old-fashioned, nineteenth-century values and ideas. One measure of their popularity can be seen in the dramatic escalation of their salaries: in 1909, Pickford earned $10 a day at Biograph; by 1915, she was being paid $10,000 a week by Famous Players. Chaplin's earnings grew from $150 per week (Keystone, 1913) to $10,000 a week at Mutual in 1916; Fairbanks multiplied his weekly salary from $2,000 in 1915 to $10,000 in 1916.

By the end of the decade, all three achieved per-picture salaries in excess of $150,000, as well as percentages of the box-office returns on their films, making them the most highly paid and most powerful stars in the industry. When they became so expensive that their studios, in an attempt to limit their salaries, secretly agreed not to bid against one another for their services, the stars left and formed (along with Griffith) their own company, United Artists, which served as a distributor for their independently made films.

Exoticism, Eroticism, and Modern Morality: Stars of the 1920s

The Jazz Age

During the 1920s, more exotic and erotic stars such as Rudolph Valentino and Greta Garbo joined the ranks of Pickford, Fairbanks, and Chaplin. The American nature of the latter (in spite of Pickford's Canadian and Chaplin's English origins) was expressed in both their pragmatic ingenuity and their new-world innocence. Their sexuality was that of the child or the naive adolescent rather than that of the worldly adult. The appeal of Valentino and Garbo was that of sophisticated, sexually experienced Europeans. Their popularity with American audiences reflected the new atmosphere of sexual liberation that followed the war.

The woman's suffrage movement had secured women the vote in 1920, and the women's temperance movement had played a major role in the institution of Prohibition in 1919, demonstrating the power women could exert in the public sphere. But the involvement of women in political reform proved to be only the first stage of a larger social revolution in which a new generation of women began to usurp traditionally male roles. The male double standard slowly gave way to a new permissiveness for those women who dared to enjoy it. The daughters of the women's movement discovered that it was fun to dance, drink, smoke, and "pet." And although more conservative elements of society objected, unconventional sexually liberated young women of the Roaring Twenties (referred to as "flappers" and "jazz babies") defended their actions in terms of a modern morality.

The Victorian Puritanism of major filmmakers such as Griffith was replaced by a new explicitness in dealing with female desire and behavior by filmmakers such as Cecil B. De Mille. De Mille specialized in titillating topics (and film titles) such as adultery (*The Cheat*, 1915), promiscuity (*Manslaughter*, 1922), and "modern" marriages in which women and men engaged equally in infidelity (*Old Wives for New*, 1918; *Don't Change Your Husband*, 1919; *Why Change Your Wife?* 1920; *The Affairs of Anatol* and *Forbidden Fruit*, 1921). Yet, although De Mille's characters experimented with the new morality, their adventures taught them a lesson. More often than not, they returned, by film's end, to the same

Publicity material for Clara Bow in Elinor Glyn's *It* (1927).

Courtesy of Paramount

old-fashioned values they had initially rejected, often going back to their husbands and wives with a new appreciation of the more traditional virtues of sexual fidelity, marriage, and family.

Having "It": Clara Bow and Rudolph Valentino

The extent to which the new interest in sexuality now dominated the screen can be seen in the emergence of a novel criterion for stardom—the possession of "It." Elinor Glyn, English author and Hollywood tastemaker, wrote several popular novels and more than a dozen screenplays in the 1920s about the new, sexually aggressive and sexually provocative flappers. Her 1926 novel, called *It*, was adapted for the screen and starred the quintessential Hollywood flapper—the pretty, sexy, fun-loving, impudent, worldly-wise Clara Bow. Glyn, who defined "It" as "an inner magic, an animal magnetism," declared Bow to be the "It Girl." (Glyn also acknowledged that Valentino, John Gilbert, and Rex the horse had "It" as well; apparently "It" was a quality that not only crossed sexual boundaries but also those between different species.)

Although Bow's sexuality breathed rebellious life into models of female behavior in the 1920s, it remained, like that of De Mille's heroes and heroines, more or less within the moral confines of what F. Scott Fitzgerald and other spokespersons associated with the Jazz Age outline as typical of the wilder, more bohemian American youth of that era. Bow's characters, again like De Mille's, had fun and sowed their wild oats but ultimately married and settled down.

The sexuality of Valentino, Garbo, and other foreign-born screen idols of the 1920s differed in nature from the wildness of American youth epitomized by Bow. The screen behavior of the former was not part of a larger rite of passage through which they passed on their way to sexual maturity (as it was with Bow). The threat posed by Valentino, for instance, cannot be explained away as some youthful fad, though his role in *The Sheik* (1921) did produce a generation of American couples who referred to one another as "sheiks" and "shebas." As the sheik, Valentino wooed the heroine by abducting her, enslaving her, and holding her, not only against her will but under the constant threat of rape. Valentino's image as a menacing and brutal but romantic lover was extended in his roles as the passionate bullfighter in *Blood and Sand* (1922) and as the vengeful woman-hater in *The Son of the Sheik* (1926); but films such as *The Four Horsemen of the Apocalypse* (1921) and *A Sainted Devil* (1924) also promoted his image as a sultry Latin lover.

American men hated Valentino almost as passionately as American women loved him. Men regarded his skill as a dancer with suspicion, envied his good looks, resented his status as a great lover, considered him to be effeminate, and distrusted him as a foreigner. They preferred the more American onscreen lovemaking of male stars such as John Gilbert.

But when Valentino died suddenly in the summer of 1926, more than 100,000 fans, most of them women, mobbed the streets of New York outside the funeral home. The actress Pola Negri, with whom Valentino was reportedly having an affair, collapsed on the set of her latest film when she heard the news. When she recovered, she rushed to New York (along with a studio publicist) to be near him. And, for more than 65 years, on the anniversary of his death, a mysterious woman in black visited his tomb and brought a bouquet of roses to place upon it.

Greta Garbo: From Divinity to Humanity

The passionate Mediterranean sexuality introduced by Valentino ignited his female fans. The more distanced Nordic allure of Garbo smoldered on the screen, generating a more cerebral, less visceral response among her audiences. There was virtually no precedent among American actresses for Garbo's world-weary sexuality on the screen. Hollywood had created vamps before; Theda Bara enjoyed a brief career of luring men to their doom as a femme fatale in films such as *A Fool There Was* and *Carmen* (1915), *Cleopatra* (1917), and *Salome* (1918). Similar roles had subsequently been played by (and become exclusively reserved for) European actresses such as Alla Nazimova and Pola Negri, in the 1920s. But Garbo lacked the manipulative power that the vamp exerts over men and the destructiveness of the femme fetale. If Garbo was a femme fatale, then she was more "fatale" for herself than she was for the men who fell in love with her.

The passion of Garbo was not only romantic but religious as well. She was the Joan of Arc of screen vamps, femme fatales, and courtesans; she suffered and died for love. Garbo's most characteristic roles were as Leo Tolstoy's Anna

Courtesy of M-G-M

Greta Garbo and John Gilbert in *Flesh and the Devil* (1927).

Karenina in *Love* (1927) and in *Anna Karenina* (1935)—as the unhappily married woman who falls desperately in love with another man and who pays for her infidelity with death. This was a part she also played in *The Temptress* (1926), *Flesh and the Devil* (1927), *A Woman of Affairs* (1928), and a number of other films. In *Mata Hari* (1932) and *Camille* (1937), Garbo was the older, more experienced woman of the world who seduced and fell in love with younger men but died tragically, the victim of her own self-destructive nature and past behavior.

The stars of the late silent era achieved the status of screen idols whom fans worshiped from a distance. Garbo's reclusiveness, memorialized in the utterance for which she has become most famous—"I vant to be alone"—lasted even after her departure from Hollywood and her retreat to anonymity on New York City's East Side, where she continued to play the moody Swede. Though Garbo's onscreen and offscreen mystery might have exceeded that of other stars, it symbolized the quasi-religious divinity that stars possessed in the eyes of the movie-going public.

But, with the down-to-earth realism associated with the coming of sound, with the social upheavals introduced by the stock market crash and the Depression, and with the redefinition of American notions of individualism brought about by the New Deal, the aloof, aristocratic nature of silent screen stars came under increasing criticism and attack. Though American audiences remained fascinated by stars, they wanted their stars to be more human and more accessible. The transformation of Garbo's screen persona in the 1930s provided a perfect illustration of the way in which silent stars were forced to step down from their pedestals and come alive in order to prolong their careers.

The initial stage in the dedivinization of Garbo took place with her first sound film, *Anna Christie* (1930), which was sold to the public through an ad campaign that humanized her by simply declaring "GARBO TALKS!" Later in the decade, when top stars such as Katharine Hepburn and Fred Astaire were denounced by exhibitors as "box-office poison" because fans supposedly found them to be too sophisticated, highbrow, and elitist, Garbo briefly reclaimed her popularity by switching from tragic costume melodramas, such as *Camille* (1937), to appear in her first comedy, *Ninotchka* (1939). This film was not only done in modern dress but also featured Garbo as an avid consumer of contemporary female fashion (she fell in love with a hat). This time, M-G-M publicity struck another blow in its attempt to make Garbo more accessible, proclaiming "GARBO LAUGHS!"

Depression/Repression: The 1930s

New Realities, New Images

The transition to sound ushered in a new breed of movie star made up of actors and actresses from the theater (George Arliss, Ruth Chatterton, Fredric March), vaudeville (the Marx Brothers, Mae West), the recording industry (Al Jolson, Eddie Cantor), and radio (Bob Hope, Bing Crosby, Jack Benny). Distinct vocal styles provided the basis of stardom for many performers, ranging from the charming French and German accents of Maurice Chevalier and Marlene Dietrich, respectively; the cultivated English accents of Ronald Colman and Herbert Marshall; and the urban, lower-class voices of Wallace Beery, James Cagney, Edward G. Robinson, Mae West, and Barbara Stanwyck to the regional speech of Will Rogers and the racial dialect of Hollywood's first black star, Stepin Fetchit.

The major stars of the early 1930s (with one or two exceptions) did not belong to the sophisticated royalty of the silent era but to the working class. American audiences fell in love with burly, homely types such as Wallace Beery and Marie Dressler; with hard-working shopgirls such as Janet Gaynor and Joan Crawford; with proletarian tough guys such as Cagney and Robinson; with homespun humorists and broad slapstick comics such as Will Rogers and Joe E. Brown; and with an adorable little "orphan" whose only possessions were her dimples, her curls, and her boundless optimism for the future— Shirley Temple.

All-American Kids: Shirley Temple and Judy Garland

Between 1934 and 1938, Temple's films earned more money than those of any other star. By the mid-1930s, she was earning more than $300,000 a year and received more than 3,500 fan letters a week. Her endorsement of products,

Courtesy of 20th Century-Fox

Shirley Temple dances with Bill "Bojangles" Robinson in *The Littlest Rebel* (1935).

ranging from dresses to dolls, brought in another $300,000 a year. For Depression audiences, Temple provided sentimental solutions to national problems. In her films, Temple's character was often an orphan (*Captain January,* 1936) or motherless (*Little Miss Marker,* 1934) and came from working-class backgrounds (*Marker, Dimples,* 1936). The perfect democrat, she befriended both servants (*Curly Top,* 1935) and blacks (*The Littlest Rebel,* 1935).

More important, she became the focus for a new social order. Her unqualified love melted the hardened hearts of both rich and poor and prompted uncharacteristic generosity among her wealthy guardians and/or benefactors, who then vowed to take care of those less fortunate than themselves. Temple was America's answer to the Russian Revolution; she awakened the benign forces of paternalistic capitalism, which healed the nation's wounds and united formerly antagonistic factions of society. Rescued, adopted, and rewarded with untold wealth for her simple trust and love, the miraculous fortune of Temple's screen characters made her the embodiment of every spectator's desires.

Temple's popularity decreased as she approached puberty, but so did the dangers facing the typical American family as it weathered the economic turmoil of the 1930s. Other young stars, such as everybody's boy-next-door and girl-next-door couple Mickey Rooney and Judy Garland, took up where Temple left off and provided a similar optimism for audiences of the late 1930s. As Andy Hardy, Rooney applied energy and resourcefulness to the problems that beset bourgeois, middle-class America at the end of the decade. Given a meager allowance by his FDR-like father, the judge, Andy Hardy managed to buy a jalopy, take his girl to the drugstore for a soda, rent a tuxedo for the senior prom, and, working with the other kids in the neighborhood, assemble an amateur show or musical revue that would put Broadway to shame.

Garland, whether as Andy's sweetheart or Dorothy (of Kansas and Oz), paid similar tribute to the inventiveness and innate talent of the average American teenager. Garland infused everything she did, from singing to coping with the trials and tribulations of adolescence, with emotion. She suggested that the happiness that lay just over the rainbow could be obtained if only you could pursue it, as Judy did, through an intense, wholehearted commitment to pure feeling.

Clark Gable: Populist Hero

The most representative star of the 1930s was not an old man (Beery, Rogers), a child (Temple), or a teen (Rooney, Garland), but rather a rugged, all-American guy. In *Broadway Melody of 1938* (1937), Garland sang to his photograph. She declared, like other female fans who worshiped him, that he was "Not like a real actor. . . . But like a fellow you'd meet at a party." That fellow was named Clark Gable. The foundation of Gable's screen persona was laid by Frank Capra in *It Happened One Night* (1934), in which Gable, in an Oscar-winning performance, played a cynical, big-city newspaper reporter. His character advocated the lower-class, populist virtues of dunking donuts, eating raw carrots, hitchhiking, and giving piggyback rides just like the great Abe Lincoln used to do. Gable's regular guy educated runaway heiress Claudette Colbert in all of the above and taught her how to survive without money on the road in Depression America.

Whether an adventurer in *Red Dust* (1932) or *Call of the Wild* (1935), a gambler in *No Man of Her Own* (1932) or *Manhattan Melodrama* (1934), or a con man in *Hold Your Man* (1933), Gable projected a no-nonsense honesty and self-irony that made him an ideal antagonist for and complement to Vivien Leigh's incurably romantic and self-deluding dreamer, Scarlett O'Hara, in *Gone With the Wind* (1939).

Sex, Censorship, and Star Images

Sex continued to play a major role in the construction of stardom in the 1930s, but it did so largely through its overt repression. The comparatively unbridled sexuality of stars such as Bow or Valentino in the 1920s became the object of censorship in the 1930s when the Motion Picture Producers and Distributors of America reinstituted the Production Code in 1934 in response to protests by certain civic organizations and members of the clergy.

Directed against depictions of not only crime and violence but also sexual themes such as adultery; scenes of passion, seduction, or rape; sexual perversion, and miscegenation, the Code handcuffed the rampant sexuality of early 1930s stars such as the sexy platinum blonde Jean Harlow and the sexually suggestive Mae West. It turned the sex comedy into the screwball comedy; it made stars out of presexual child and teen performers (such as Temple, Rooney, Garland, and Deanna Durbin) and old men (such as Beery and Rogers). And it forced otherwise sexually healthy and attractive stars to find socially acceptable substitutes for sex, such as Joan Crawford's onscreen drive toward success in a career. In the 1920s, Rex (the horse) may have had "It," but in the 1930s, Gene Autry's horse, Champion, not only didn't but couldn't.

In *It Happened One Night* (1934), which was made just after the Code was put in force, Gable found himself in the unusual position of having to deny himself to Claudette Colbert until they could be properly married and the "walls of Jericho" (the makeshift curtain that Gable erected between their twin beds) could come tumbling down. Sexual self-censorship made actors such as Gable even more desirable for their female fans, but it also drove sex underground, where it built up steam during the war years and finally exploded in the resexualization of Hollywood that took place in the postwar years in film noir and in films with more sexually explicit themes and sexier stars.

World War II and Its Aftermath

A New Generation

After the Japanese attack on Pearl Harbor, a number of American actors (including Clark Gable, James Stewart, Tyrone Power, Henry Fonda, Robert Montgomery, and Mickey Rooney) enlisted in the military, creating a vacuum of sorts that a new generation of male stars struggled to fill. Established male stars such as Humphrey Bogart, James Cagney, Gary Cooper, Errol Flynn, Cary Grant, and Spencer Tracy were joined by relative newcomers such as Abbott and Costello, Don Ameche, Dana Andrews, Joseph Cotten, Bing Crosby, John Garfield, Bob Hope, Van Johnson, Ronald Reagan, John Wayne, and Orson Welles. Musical star Betty Grable became a favorite with the GIs in her incarnation as a pinup whose leggy picture adorned more than 2 million posters on the walls of U.S. military barracks around the world.

At the other end of the spectrum, a desexualized Greer Garson epitomized home-front sacrifice as *Mrs. Miniver* (1942). Ginger Rogers in *Tender Comrade* (1943) and Jennifer Jones in *Since You Went Away* (1944) represented the girls back home for whose safety the war was being fought, as did Judy Garland and child star Margaret O'Brien in the period musical *Meet Me in St. Louis* (1944). Finally, Ingrid Bergman emerged as the perfect combination of romance and patriotism as a member of the Resistance in both *Casablanca* (1942) and *For Whom the Bell Tolls* (1943).

Transformations

Stardom changed during and after the war as performers began to push the limits of classical social, sexual, and psychological behavior. Cary Grant, a handsome romantic lead in 1930s screwball comedies such as *The Awful Truth*

(1937), *Bringing Up Baby* and *Holiday* (1938) began to explore the darker side of his screen persona as a suspected murderer in *Suspicion* (1941), as a small-town radical in flight from the police in *Talk of the Town* (1942), and as a disreputable cockney tramp in *None but the Lonely Heart* (1944). Musical comedy song-and-dance man Dick Powell and easygoing Fred MacMurray underwent a similar image overhaul for their roles as Detective Philip Marlowe in *Murder, My Sweet* (1944) and as slick insurance salesman and husband-killer Walter Neff in *Double Indemnity* (1944).

Bogart's transformation from 1930s gangster (*The Petrified Forest*, 1936; *The Roaring Twenties*, 1939) to 1940s romantic lead (*The Maltese Falcon*, 1941; *Casablanca*, 1942) represented the flip side of these attempts by leading men to redefine their images: instead of tarnishing his persona, he polished it up; but in the process, Bogart brought something of the gangster to his roles as a good guy. In all of these instances, an amalgam of opposing traits led to the creation of the sort of antihero that would dominate film noir.

The postwar period also witnessed the reemergence of the femme fatale, but this time the femme fatales were homegrown, girl-next-door types rather than vamps from abroad. Stars such as Rita Hayworth (*Gilda*, 1946; *The Lady from Shanghai*, 1948), Lauren Bacall (*To Have and Have Not*, 1944; *The Big Sleep*, 1946), and Lana Turner (*The Postman Always Rings Twice*, 1946) brought an erotic sexuality to the screen that had formerly been reserved for European imports. (The exception that proved the rule was Theda Bara, who, though born as Theodosia Goodman in the United States, was given an Afro-European ancestry and an exotic name by studio publicists.)

American female sexuality that had previously been channeled into the positive enterprises of creating a family or a career suddenly rebelled, revealing its disastrous potential. And though this sexuality was ultimately contained (as in the case of Bacall, who was "tamed" by Bogart) or proved to be self-destructive (as in the case of Hayworth and Turner, whose greed, lust, and/or improper desire brought about their own deaths in *Shanghai* and *Postman*), that sexuality nevertheless emerged as revolutionary, empowering (albeit briefly) the women who possessed it.

The Darker Side: Psychology and "the Method"

If perfection characterized classical stardom, postwar stars exposed and took advantage of their flaws—all in the interest of a greater realism. The good looks of a Tyrone Power, Errol Flynn, or Robert Taylor gave way to the rough features of a Bogart or Robert Mitchum (who once described himself as looking "like a shark with a broken nose"). Actors began to explore the psychological dimensions of their screen personae, revealing the apparent transparency of their mental makeup to be clouded with psychological complexities. Bogart started talking to himself in *Treasure of the Sierra Madre* (1948) and developed psychotic tendencies in *In a Lonely Place* (1950). Edward G. Robinson heard voices in *Scarlet Street* (1945), and James Cagney became a psychopathic killer with an Oedipus complex in *White Heat* (1949).

James Stewart evolved from the naive, small-town, populist hero of Frank Capra's 1930s comedies (*You Can't Take It With You*, 1938; *Mr. Smith Goes to Washington*, 1939) to the bitter, anxiety-ridden, vengeance-obsessed cowboy in Anthony Mann's 1950s Westerns (*Naked Spur*, 1953; *Man from Laramie*, 1955) and the disturbed voyeur and sexual fetishist in Alfred Hitchcock's 1950s suspense thrillers (*Rear Window*, 1954; *Vertigo*, 1958). Even John Wayne developed neuroses as the iron-willed, dictatorial cattleman in *Red River* (1948) and the socially estranged, broodingly violent, racist Indian fighter (with a quasi-incestuous fixation on his brother's wife) in *The Searchers* (1956). But by the mid-1950s, Wayne, Stewart, and others were merely acting à la mode. Hollywood was now populated by a new generation of tormented, high-strung young actors such as Montgomery Clift, Marlon Brando, and James Dean, who embodied the alienation, anguish, and sensitivity of 1950s teenagers.

Clift, Brando, and Dean, along with Barbara Bel Geddes, Ben Gazzara, Julie Harris, Paul Newman, Jack Palance, Lee Remick, Rod Steiger, Eli Wallach, Shelley Winters, and Joanne Woodward, had studied acting in New York at the Actors Studio, where the dramatic theories of the Soviet theater director Constantin Stanislavski had been adopted and reworked by Lee Strasberg, Elia Kazan, and others. Stanislavski's techniques became the foundation for "the method," training exercises that require actors to use their own past experiences and emotional histories as a basis on which to build an inner identification with the characters they portray. The Actors Studio became so famous for its success in training actors in the 1950s that even established stars, such as Marilyn Monroe, began to take lessons there.

However, not all 1950s actors and actresses achieved stardom by means of the method, that is, by baring their psyches and their souls to the public. Bob Hope, Bing Crosby, Gary Cooper, Gregory Peck, Doris Day, Rock Hudson, Jane Wyman, William Holden, and Randolph Scott dominated the box office during the decade. But the general moviegoing audience of the prewar years had fragmented into a number of special-interest audiences in the 1950s, which ranged from rebellious teens (who idolized Dean, Brando, and later Elvis Presley), college-age men and women (who liked sexier, older stars such as Marilyn Monroe, Kim Novak, William Holden, and Gregory Peck), and housewives (who were fans of Rock Hudson, Jane Wyman, Ava Gardner, June Allyson, and Susan Hayward) to conservative older viewers and family audiences who patronized Dean Martin and Jerry Lewis comedies and Biblical epics starring Robert Taylor or Charlton Heston.

Stars and Anti-Stars

Many of the more stable stars of the 1950s continued to be top box-office attractions in the 1960s. Dean had died in a car crash in 1955, after completing *Giant*; Clift had been seriously injured in another car accident while making *Raintree County* in 1957 and never quite recovered his earlier form; and Brando floundered in a series of oddball items, including *Mutiny on the Bounty* (1962), *The*

Courtesy of Warner Bros.

Director Elia Kazan (left) and actors Marlon Brando, Julie Harris, and James Dean on the Warner Bros. Lot during the making of *East of Eden* (1955).

Ugly American (1963), *Bedtime Story* (1964), and *The Countess from Hong Kong* (1967), though his performances in *The Chase* (1966) and *Reflections in a Golden Eye* (1967) proved that he had not lost his ability to rivet audiences.

Doris Day and Rock Hudson emerged as the biggest box-office attractions from 1960 to 1964, costarring in a number of bedroom farces including *Pillow Talk* (1959), *Lover Come Back* (1961), and *Send Me No Flowers* (1964). Cary Grant and John Wayne continued to hold sway over American screen comedies and Westerns, respectively, but were challenged by a new international star, Sean Connery, whose characterization of Ian Fleming's British secret agent, James Bond, made him one of the most popular male actors between the years 1962 (*Dr. No*) and 1972 (*Diamonds Are Forever*).

Resisting Tradition: Nicholson, Eastwood, and Their Peers

A number of contemporary stars resisted the traditional star image. They played the role of the reluctant star or anti-star, refusing to give interviews to the press or do extensive publicity for their pictures. Apparent by-products of a 1960s counterculture, they not only refused to behave like stars, but also didn't even look like stars (with the notable exceptions of Warren Beatty, Paul Newman, and Robert Redford). Many of them didn't live in Hollywood (Woody Allen, Marlon Brando, Robert De Niro, Clint Eastwood, Paul Newman, Robert Redford, Bill Murray, George C. Scott, Shirley MacLaine, Meryl Streep, Sean Connery, Michael Caine, and Dustin Hoffman); some didn't bother to pick up their Academy Awards on Oscar night (Allen, Brando, and Scott). Other anti-stars included Warren Beatty, Jack Nicholson, and Barbra Streisand.

Uncomfortable with celebrity, these anti-stars not only refused typecasting, selecting parts that problematized their personae, but also preferred to play anti-heroes rather than heroes. Eastwood, for example, alternated his role as Sergio Leone's man-with-no-name in the Italian spaghetti Westerns and the tough supercop Dirty Harry Callahan with a series of parts that explored the hypermasculinity of his screen image, questioning its rigidity and exposing its flaws. Thus, he played a phony cowboy from New Jersey in *Bronco Billy* (1980) and a self-reflective cop sensitive to women's issues and critical of his own male chauvinism and excessive violence in *Tightrope* (1984).

Nicholson went from antiauthoritarian rebel (*One Flew Over the Cuckoo's Nest*, 1975) to Mafia hit man (*Prizzi's Honor*, 1985), though a certain demented subversiveness has given some consistency to his image from his rebellious youth as an actor (*Easy Rider*, 1969, and *Five Easy Pieces*, 1970) to his roles in the 1980s as the maniacal killer in *The Shining* (1980), the devil in *The Witches of East-wick* (1987), and the Joker in *Batman* (1989). By contrast, more conventional stars, such as Schwarzenegger and Stallone, have continued in stardom's classic mold, building consistent screen characters for themselves by playing a fairly narrow range of character types, such as Conan and the Terminator or Rocky and Rambo.

Television as Training Ground

Since the breakup of the studio system, contemporary stars have entered Hollywood from a variety of other media, developing a star status outside of motion pictures that they then translate into stardom in Hollywood. Television serves as the training ground for many actors, replacing the B pictures and low-budget motion picture mills that provided past performers with experience in front of a camera. Actors who have moved from television series to motion picture stardom range from Steve McQueen, Burt Reynolds, James Garner, and Clint Eastwood to John Travolta, Michael J. Fox, Sylvester Stallone, Robin Williams, and Bruce Willis. (Actresses seem to have been less successful.)

Saturday Night Live gave us John Belushi, Eddie Murphy, Steve Martin, Chevy Chase, Dan Ackroyd, Bill Murray, and Gilda Radner, as well as Michael Myers and Dana Carvey of "Wayne's World." A handful of television gag writers and nightclub comics, such as Woody Allen and Mel Brooks, have graduated to the motion pictures, where they perform their own material. Cher, Diana Ross, Kris Kristofferson, Dolly Parton, Liza Minnelli, and Barbra Streisand came to the cinema by way of the recording industry. Cover girls whose careers in modeling led them to the movies have included Brooke Shields, Farrah Fawcett, and Cybill Shepherd.

Stars' Children: Déjà Vu

A related phenomenon is the emergence of second-generation stardom—the children of stars whose features and mannerisms recall those of their parents, giving audiences an uncanny sense of déjà vu. Thus Jane and Peter Fonda (chil-

dren of Henry); Liza Minnelli (daughter of Judy Garlar
(son of Kirk); Jeff and Beau Bridges (sons of Lloyd); Emilio L.
Sheen (sons of Martin Sheen); Keith, David, and Robert Carl.
John); Isabella Rossellini (daughter of Ingrid Bergman); Melanie Griffit.
ter of 'Tippi' Hedren); Laura Dern (daughter of Dianne Ladd and Bruce L.
Carrie Fisher (daughter of Debbie Reynolds); Jamie Lee Curtis (daughter o.
Janet Leigh and Tony Curtis); Kiefer Sutherland (son of Donald); Timothy Hut-
ton (son of Jim); and Angelina Jolie (daughter of Jon Voight) bring to the screen
a kind of self-reflexivity that is quite consistent with contemporary Hollywood's obsession with its glorious past (see Chapter 15, "The Film School Generation"). In effect, contemporary stars enable us to see the ghost of Hollywood
past in the faces of Hollywood present.

Different Faces: The Rise of Black Stars

From Sidney Poitier to Blaxploitation

In the late 1960s, as the political and cultural climate polarized, a growing segment of the moviegoing public, comprised largely of younger spectators under
the age of 30, moved to the left, embracing certain aspects of the women's,
youth, and civil rights movements. In the right place at the right time, Sidney
Poitier enjoyed unprecedented success at the box office in this period, emerging
as the first black star who could draw a significant number of white spectators.
His *A Patch of Blue* landed among the top 10 moneymakers of 1965, earning
$6.3 million; *To Sir with Love* did the same in 1967, making more than $7.2 million. Then, in 1967, *Guess Who's Coming to Dinner* placed second only to *The
Graduate* in profits, returning an incredible $25.1 million to its distributor,
Columbia, while in 1968 another Poitier picture, *For the Love of Ivy,* pulled in
$5 million.

The blaxploitation movement of the early 1970s sought to build on Poitier's
pioneering efforts in creating a crossover audience of whites who went to black
films and to address the interests of an increasing number of black spectators,
who, industry analysts estimated, made up from 25 to 30 percent of the total
moviegoing audience. The phenomenal success of *Shaft* and *Sweet Sweetback's
Baadasssss Song* (1971), which grossed $7 and $11 million, respectively, proved
that black was beautiful at the box office. But unlike the Poitier vehicles, which
catered to a middle-class and lower-upper class audience, this cycle of black
films addressed lower-middle-class and lower-class concerns, dramatizing
crime in the streets and creating a black urban landscape peopled by private
eyes, drug dealers, numbers runners, petty criminals, pimps, and prostitutes.

Fame in Other Fields

The course of stardom for young black actors and actresses in this period followed a somewhat different line of development from that taken by white

Courtesy of Columbia

Sidney Poitier and Katharine Houghton in *Guess Who's Coming to Dinner* (1967).

performers, though black stars also came from other media. For the most part, blacks had to come from noncinematic backgrounds because Hollywood had never invested in the development of more than a handful of black stars. In the postwar era, only Poitier had evolved into a leading man, achieving celebrity in *The Defiant Ones* (1958), *Lilies of the Field* (1963), and *In the Heat of the Night* and *Guess Who's Coming to Dinner* (1967). One or two other black actors such as Brock Peters (*To Kill a Mockingbird*, 1962) and James Edwards (*The Manchurian Candidate*, 1962) put together careers as talented supporting performers but were unable to find vehicles that would secure for them the singular kind of success enjoyed by Poitier.

If television proved to be the station along the way to stardom for white actors in the 1960s and 1970s, this was not the case for black actors, who found it difficult to secure work on TV (though Bill Cosby achieved some recognition in the *I Spy* series in the late 1960s). It was not until the late 1970s that television provided roles for black actors in any significant numbers. As a result, the studios turned to black stars from other media. Hollywood had done this in the past with black performers whom it had recruited from the world of music and dance, such as Cab Calloway, Paul Robeson, Bill "Bojangles" Robinson, Pearl Bailey, Lena Horne, Dorothy Dandridge, Harry Belafonte, and Sammy Davis, Jr. More recently, women of color who topped *Billboard*'s pop music charts, such as

Whitney Houston (*The Bodyguard*, 1992) and Jennifer Lopez (*Out of Sight*, 1998; *Maid in Manhattan*, 2003), have also gained recognition as film stars.

During the 1960s and 1970s, Hollywood capitalized on the celebrity of African Americans, but it found them not so much in the traditional media of theater and television as in other fields in which nonacting skills are perfected. Black actors came from the world of fashion; white executives cast former models such as Richard Roundtree (*Shaft*, 1971) and Tamara Dobson (*Cleopatra Jones*, 1973) in films. New stars also came from the world of athletics: Hollywood turned to track and football stars such as Woody Strode (*Sergeant Rutledge*, 1960), Rafer Johnson (*Soul Soldier*, 1972), Jim Brown (*Slaughter* and *Black Gunn*, 1972), Fred Williamson (*Black Caesar*, 1973), O. J. Simpson (*The Towering Inferno*, 1974), Jim Kelly (*Enter the Dragon*, 1973), and "Rosey" Grier (*The Thing with Two Heads*, 1972).

The Eddie Murphy Generation

Unfortunately, Hollywood's interest in producing black films and developing black talent declined as the box-office revenues from blaxploitation films fell off during the mid-1970s—a turn symbolized by the failure of *The Wiz* (1978), which starred Diana Ross and Michael Jackson. Though mainstream black actors such as Poitier, Belafonte, Cosby, and Richard Pryor continued to attract large crossover audiences in films such as *Uptown Saturday Night* (1974), black actor-athletes failed to establish themselves as stars. Muscle and good looks only carried black stars so far; it was raunchy nightclub comedy, however, that led the way for the next wave of African American stars. The polite restraint of Cosby plays quite well on the living room TV (which proved to be the best setting for Cosby, who never enjoyed the same success in movies that he did on television). But the less conventional, raw humor of Pryor, who starred in a number of concert films as well as in the box-office smashes *Silver Streak* (1976) and *Stir Crazy* (1980), and of Eddie Murphy, who appeared in a string of commercial hits in the mid-1980s ranging from *48 Hours* (1982), *Trading Places* (1983), and *Beverly Hills Cop* (*I* in 1984 and *II* in 1987) to *Coming to America* (1988), made stars out of both Pryor and Murphy and provided a new format for the showcasing of other black performers such as Whoopi Goldberg, whose skills as a comic actress produced a popular nightclub act as well as hit films such as *Ghost* (1990) and *Sister Act* (1992), and Arsenio Hall, who parlayed his costarring role in *Coming to America* into a steady berth as a late-night talk show host.

During the 1980s, an increasing number of minority actors and actresses established careers for themselves on television and in the movies, including Emilio Estevez, Raul Julia, James Earl Jones, Rae Dawn Chong, Lou Diamond Phillips, Oprah Winfrey, James Smits, and Red Foxx. At the same time, black actors such as Lou Gossett, Jr. (*An Officer and a Gentleman*, 1982), Danny Glover (the *Lethal Weapon* films), Morgan Freeman (*Driving Miss Daisy* and *Glory*, 1989), and Denzel Washington (*Glory*, 1989; *The Pelican Brief*, 1993; *The Siege*, 1998), found more or less regular employment in a new Hollywood dominated by liberal white executives who grew up in the 1960s. These moguls seem to have inherited some of that decade's racial sensitivity. At the very least, they have seen a potential market growing out of the liberal counterculture, and have made films for the children of those (like themselves) who grew up in the 1960s.

Economics and Contemporary Stardom

The fact that Hollywood has opened its heavens for minority stars remains a significant step forward (especially for those stars of color who have made it), but this development has more to do with simple economics than it does with notions of fair play. Stars are and always have been commodities. Today's marketplace, though culturally more diverse, is nonetheless still a marketplace, where an increasing number of star images trade places with one another on the floor of the film industry's own form of stock exchange, in which images are worth money. It is from this perspective that the essential artifice of stardom emerges most clearly. Stars are not born but made; and they are made with a purpose—to sell films. Throughout the history of the theater, the movies, and television, stars have been rated in terms of their bankability, that is, their value at the box office. The star system took shape around the economic reality into which the unique attractiveness of each star was translated. In this way, the star system played a crucial role in the perpetuation of the studio system. After the demise of the studio system in the 1950s and 1960s, the star system became, along with the genre system (see the introduction to Part II), the most important stabilizing feature of the motion picture industry. Though the path to stardom in the contemporary film industry has become increasingly complex and the attainment of stardom increasingly haphazard, the phenomenon of stardom has remained essential to Hollywood because of its ability to lure spectators into the theater.

In the early 1980s, Robert Redford's presence in a film was considered to be worth $5 million at the box office; Clint Eastwood's was worth $4 million; and Robert De Niro's, $3 million. In 1991, *Premiere* published a list of stars whose appearance in a film "virtually guarantee[d] a foreign presale [i.e., the sale of the film to potential exhibitors overseas *prior* to its production], regardless of the script, director, or other stars brought to the package." The most bankable stars included (in order of their box-office appeal) Arnold Schwarzenegger, Mel Gibson, Tom Cruise, Sean Connery, Harrison Ford, Jack Nicholson, and Julia Roberts.

Today, that list of top stars (each earning about $20 million or more per picture) has a few new names: Tom Hanks, Julia Roberts, Denzel Washington, George Clooney, and Russell Crowe. And in the mix of contemporary box office attractions are more women and minority performers than ever before, including Nicole Kidman, Reese Witherspoon, Will Smith, Jennifer Lopez, Cameron Diaz, Drew Barrymore, Renée Zellweger, Sandra Bullock, Angelina Jolie, Jodie Foster, Eddie Murphy, Jackie Chan, and Halle Berry. A possible indication of changing times is the industry's recognition of black performers at the 2002 Academy Awards ceremony, at which Denzel Washington won the Best Actor

© AP/Wide World Photos

At the 2002 Academy Awards ceremony, Halle Berry won an Oscar for Best Actress and Denzel Washington for Best Actor.

award for *Training Day* (2001) and Halle Berry won a Best Actress award for her role in *Monster's Ball* (2001). Sidney Poitier (*Lilies of the Field*, 1963) had earlier won an Oscar for Best Actor, but Berry was the first African American woman to win for Best Actress.

A few veteran actors have remained top stars, such as Bruce Willis, Jack Nicholson, Mike Myers, Nicholas Cage, and Harrison Ford, but these have been joined by a new generation of acting talents, including Adam Sandler, Jim Carrey, Matt Damon, Ben Affleck, Leonardo DiCaprio, Brad Pitt, Vin Diesel, Keanu Reeves, Tobey Maguire, and Ben Stiller.

Stars continue to play a stabilizing role in the contemporary film industry, providing filmmakers with built-in audiences who regularly watch films in which their favorite actors and actresses appear. However, in recent years, a number of films that feature no major stars have performed exceedingly well at the box office, suggesting that those who are willing to take risks and gamble on the public's potential interest in particular projects can quite often reap even greater rewards than those who hedge their bets by hiring proven (and pricey) stars. *Variety's* list of the top-grossing films of all time includes *E.T.: The Extra-Terrestrial*, the *Star Wars* films, *Batman*, *Jurassic Park*, *The Lost World*, *Twister*, *Home Alone*, *Ghostbusters*, *Jaws*, and the *Indiana Jones* trilogy—films that feature no well-known stars (except for Harrison Ford, who was more or less unknown at the time of *Star Wars*, and Jack Nicholson, who played only a supporting role in *Batman*). In other words, stars are not indispensable. Yet Hollywood, the media, and motion picture audiences seem unable to do without them for any length of time.

For nearly 100 years, Hollywood's biggest attractions have been stars and stories. Audiences have come to see Gentleman Jim Corbett, Mary Pickford, Greta Garbo, Clark Gable, John Wayne, Robert Redford, Barbra Streisand, Eddie Murphy, Arnold Schwarzenegger, and others. To some extent, the stars make the stories, driving them forward with the force of their personalities. More often than not, the stars and the stories collaborate with one another: the stars build their screen personalities on the backs of the characters they play and on the story patterns that writers provide for them; and the fictional characters and stories come to life through/in the bodies of individual stars. Yet the pleasure that stars provide to audiences has remained unique, because it always depends on the audience's recognition of the differences between the star and the character which he or she plays. Unlike the novel, in which no such distinction exists—in which there is only character—the movies can never quite collapse a star into a mere character. Our delight in stars comes from an appreciation of them *as performers*—from the interplay between star and character. Ironically, in order to be caught up in and carried away by a star, we must be fully conscious of the essential artifice that underlies stardom.

■ ■ ■ SELECT FILMOGRAPHY

Tess of the Storm Country (1914)
The Cheat (1915)
Broken Blossoms (1919)
The Sheik (1921)
It (1927)
Steamboat Willie (1928)
It Happened One Night (1934)
The Littlest Rebel (1935)
Camille (1937)
Gone With the Wind (1939)
Ninotchka (1939)
The Maltese Falcon (1941)
Casablanca (1942)
Red River (1948)
Singin' in the Rain (1952)
Gentlemen Prefer Blondes (1953)
Giant (1956)
The Searchers (1956)
Will Success Spoil Rock Hunter? (1957)

Guess Who's Coming to Dinner (1967)
In the Heat of the Night (1967)
True Grit (1969)
One Flew Over the Cuckoo's Nest (1975)
The Shootist (1976)
Silver Streak (1976)
Annie Hall (1977)
Bronco Billy (1980)
The Shining (1980)
Stir Crazy (1980)
48 Hours (1982)
Trading Places (1983)
Beverly Hills Cop (1984)
Tightrope (1984)
Coming to America (1988)
Ghost (1990)
Pretty Woman (1990)
Philadelphia (1993)
Monster's Ball (2002)

■ ■ ■ SELECT BIBLIOGRAPHY

DYER, RICHARD. *Heavenly Bodies: Film Stars and Society.* New York: St. Martin's Press, 1986.

DYER, RICHARD. *Stars.* London: BFI, 1979.

GLEDHILL, CHRISTINE, ed. *Stardom: Industry of Desire.* New York: Routledge, 1991.

MORIN, EDGAR. *The Stars: An Account of the Star-System in Motion Pictures.* New York: Grove, 1960.

PIRIE, DAVID, ed. *Anatomy of the Movies.* New York: Macmillan, 1981.

STUDLAR, GAYLYN. *This Mad Masquerade: Stardom and Masculinity in the Jazz Age.* New York: Columbia University Press, 1996.

THOMPSON, DAVID. *The New Biographical Dictionary of Film.* New York: Knopf, 2002.

WALKER, ALEXANDER. *Stardom: The Hollywood Phenomenon.* New York: Stein and Day, 1970.

WEIS, ELIZABETH, ed. *The Movie Star Book.* New York: Penguin, 1981.

PART TWO

Genre and the Genre System

"Genre" is a French word that refers to a kind, type, or category of a particular phenomenon or thing. In the cinema, genre is a term that is used to designate various categories of motion picture production. Major movie genres include such broad types of films as musicals, comedies, action and adventure films, Westerns, crime and detective films, melodramas, science-fiction and horror films, gangster films, war films, suspense thrillers, epics, and disaster films.

These genres can frequently be broken down into subgenres, or subdivisions of the major genre. Thus, horror films can be subdivided into specific types such as vampire, mad doctor, demon-seed/evil-child, splatter, or slasher films. Comedies can be categorized as slapstick, romantic, screwball, and so on.

Genres serve to stabilize an otherwise unstable film industry. Motion picture production is extremely expensive. In 2002, for example, the average negative cost (i.e., the amount of money it cost to produce a finished negative of the film before prints were made or costly advertising and distribution expenses were incurred) was $58.8 million. (By comparison, in 1950, average negative costs were approximately $1.1 million which translates into $8.4 million in today's dollars.) Marketing, advertising, and print costs in 2002 averaged an additional $30.6 million. Industry analysts estimate that, for any film to break even (whether it was made in 1950 or 2002), it would have to earn roughly 2 to 2½ times its negative costs.

Given these costs, motion picture producers face tremendous risks each time they make a film. These risks are increased by the very nature of the motion picture product. Unlike other consumer products, such as cars, household appliances, and fashions, that rely on brand-name recognition for much of their market appeal, motion pictures are essentially one-of-a-kind products. Each film is necessarily different from every other film, featuring a story and a cast that are more or less unique. Each film is thus an unknown quantity; its producer has no assurance that it will make a profit at the box office because, unlike other consumer items, it has no brand name status in the marketplace. The star system and the genre system attempt to compensate for the dangers involved in this process. They serve to hedge producers' bets against the unknowns and variables that underlie the production of every film.

Unlike cars and other merchandise, movies are not durable goods. They have no physical existence; they are not objects that can be bought, taken home, and used. They are, of course, consumed, but the consumer has little or nothing to show for that consumption. Audiences take home no tangible product but only the memory of an entertainment experience. The genre system that structures the American film industry represents an attempt by the film industry to control the entertainment marketplace in a way that is similar to the control over the consumers of durable goods exerted by brand-name products.

Genres result from the proven success of one-of-a-kind films in the marketplace. The box-office fortune of one particular kind of film results in the production of another film that resembles it in terms of plot and character type. The film industry assumes that the audience that came to the earlier hit will return to see a film similar in nature to it. This can be seen most clearly in the proliferation of sequels (and prequels) that accompany so many box-office hits of the 1960s, 1970s, 1980s, and 1990s.

Thus, the exceptional profits of the first James Bond film, *Dr. No* (1962), led to a succession of others. This also explains the string of *Godfather, Jaws, Rocky, Star Wars, Superman, Star Trek, Indiana Jones,* and other films of the 1970s and 1980s. In terms of more traditional notions of genres (rather than the series or sequels mentioned above), the financial success of one disaster film, such as *Airport* (1970), leads directly to the production of others, such as *The Poseidon Adventure* (1972), *The Towering Inferno* (1974), and *Earthquake* (1974).

Films that belong to a specific genre draw from a more or less fixed body of character and story types, settings and situations, costumes and props, thematic concerns and visual iconography, and conventions that are shared by other films in that particular genre. Westerns, for example, regularly contain certain character types such as cowboys, town marshals, Indians, dance hall girls, schoolmarms, cavalry officers, saloon keepers, Indian agents, gamblers, and rustlers who are readily identifiable by the costumes they wear, the props they use, the things they do, and the situations in which they find themselves. The films are set in the West and feature certain kinds of landscapes or settings, ranging from the vast stretches of the Great Plains, Rocky Mountains, and barren deserts to cattle ranches, bunkhouses, and frontier towns.

Each new film in the genre banks on a number of familiar genre elements, motifs, and themes but combines them in a novel way. The audiences that go to genre films are lured to them by the promise of seeing a film that is similar in kind to films they have seen and enjoyed in the past. They are drawn to the genre much in the way they are drawn to a brand-name product. But they are also enticed by the prospect of seeing a film that *differs* in a number of respects from films they have seen before. In this way, the system of genres relies on a combination of the familiar and the unknown, conventionality and novelty, similarity and difference. It uses the basic ingredients of the genre to produce certain expectations in the audience, but it also adapts, modifies, or plays with those conventions in order to provide audiences with a unique entertainment experience.

Because of the economic role that genre plays in the American film industry and because the major genres not only contain a large number of films but also span several decades (or more) of film production, a study of genre and the genre system is crucial to any understanding of what classical Hollywood cinema is and how it works. Even more important, by looking at the large body of films in individual genres, we can see how those genres help to shape our understanding of American culture, character, and identity. In the following chapters, we explore the role that a handful of American genres play in expressing "the temper of an age and a nation" and conveying the unique nature of the American experience in the twentieth century.

CHAPTER 6

Silent Film Melodrama

THE ORIGINS OF MELODRAMA

"Melodrama" literally means "a drama accompanied by music." The term was coined by Jean-Jacques Rousseau in 1770 to describe a dramatic monologue that he had written, entitled *Pygmalion,* that alternated speech with passages of pantomime and music. The emergence of melodrama in France in the 1770s and 1780s can be traced to the royal monopoly, which was held by officially approved, classical repertory companies such as the Comédie Française and which granted them the exclusive rights to stage verbal dramas. Secondary theater groups were restricted to nonverbal dramatic forms such as juggling or acrobatic acts, ballets, puppet shows, and pantomimes. Marcel Carne's *Children of Paradise* (France, 1945) provides a vivid portrait of this popular tradition, which was built upon carnivalesque street theater and mime acts. After the French Revolution (1789), this "verbal monopoly" came to an end, and all theatrical groups were able to use words. But even though melodramas could now make full use of dialogue, they never lost their ability to communicate on a nonverbal level.

Theatrical melodrama, which began without a voice, perfected the craft of visual expression, translating thought and emotion into gesture, costume, decor, and other elements of mise-en-scène. It discovered how to say all without literally saying anything. Melodrama even developed its own sign language. Adapting acting techniques from classical theater, it produced a system of gestures and hand movements, which were subsequently recorded and catalogued by a French scholar, François Delsarte. At the same time, melodrama manipulated traditional mise-en-scène in an attempt to wring even greater expressiveness from it, freezing the action at particularly significant moments into a tableau. In tableaus, which frequently came at act endings, the actors assumed particularly revealing and characteristic positions and then held them for several moments in an attempt to underscore or crystallize events, feelings, or ideas for the audience.

Melodrama works on a purely emotional level, rooting its drama in a common base of feeling that crosses over all linguistic barriers. In the science-fiction tearjerker *E.T.: The Extra-Terrestrial* (1982), the heart of the film resides in E.T.'s large, expressive eyes and poignant facial movements rather than in anything anyone says. This is typical of contemporary film melodrama. In another Steven Spielberg film, *Close Encounters of the Third Kind* (1977), communication between humans and aliens takes place on a purely affective level—through five musical tones. *E.T.* moves somewhat beyond that primitive stage, to speech. But when words are used, as in the phrase "E.T. phone home!" they tend to be minimal and rudimentary—almost nonverbal. E.T.'s speech ignores established linguistic conventions and grammatical rules; he/it speaks directly from the heart. The expressiveness of these semiarticulate statements derives, in large part, from their childlike simplicity—from the inability of the alien to express in language the complex longings behind the phrase. This is melodramatic speech.

Spielberg's fascination with the melodramatic resurfaces with a vengeance in *A.I. Artificial Intelligence* (2001). At the heart of his story is a boy robot, David (Haley Joel Osment), who has been programmed to love. Adopted by a family whose child has been placed in suspended animation until a cure can be found for his terminal illness, David wins the love of his new mother, but, after her own child is restored to health, she abandons David in the woods. Neither he nor we ever quite recover from this traumatic moment. A figure of pure pathos, David then spends the remainder of the film looking for the Blue Fairy who, he has been told, can make him human and thus enable him to win back the love of his mother. As in *E.T.*, Spielberg invests the alien other—here the machine, David—with a capacity for feeling and emotion that exceeds that of any of the actual human beings in the film. In *A.I.*, the simulation of emotions becomes real emotion.

The popularity of melodrama as a form of theater for the middle classes during the nineteenth century and its ability to convey crucial dramatic information

High Melodrama for the new millennium: Monica (Frances O'Connor), the mother in *A.I. Artificial Intelligence,* abandons her unwanted cybernetic child, David (Haley Joel Osment) in the woods.

visually made it an ideal form for the silent cinema. Virtually every silent film—including the slapstick comedies of Charles Chaplin and Buster Keaton—was, on one level or another, a melodrama. During the 1910s and 1920s, the trade press routinely described the majority of films as melodramas. There were romantic melodramas, domestic melodramas, rural melodramas, Western melodramas, sociological melodramas, crime melodramas, society melodramas, mystery melodramas, underworld melodramas, and just plain melodramas. If the story or situation was not rooted in melodrama, then at least the acting or mise-en-scène was. It had to be, to communicate ideas and feelings without dialogue. Although the film melodrama successfully navigated the transition from silent to sound cinema in the late 1920s, silent melodrama, in many ways, represented the melodramatic impulse at its purest and most powerful.

TYPES OF MELODRAMA

The Melodramatic Mode

The melodrama, unlike the Western or the detective film, is a *modal* genre. But there is a genre called "the melodrama" which features conventional character types, such as heroes, heroines, and villains, as well as predictable plot elements, such as improbable reversals of fortune, accidents, and last-minute rescues. In terms of its predictable or formulaic plot patterns, a typical melodrama might begin with the disruption or disturbance of an idealized emotional paradise by some external force or act of villainy. A happy family in its home is threatened with eviction or its integrity is shattered by the abduction of one of its members; the blissful young lovers are separated or forced apart by those who would block their marriage. Subsequent action presents the struggle of the hero or heroine to restore this initial state of affairs by reuniting the family or removing obstacles that separate the lovers—goals that are accomplished by the end of the narrative. The plot of *Home Alone* (1990), for example, is essentially that of a melodrama: a child is accidentally separated from his parents; the home is threatened by burglars; the child successfully defends the home against outside attacks; and he is finally reunited with his parents.

However, the *mode* of *Home Alone* is more comic than melodramatic. The child is fairly well in control of things and actually enjoys his experience of being home alone. That is, the *treatment* of the situation is not overtly melodramatic; the filmmakers opted for comedy instead. As a mode, the melodrama—or, more accurately, the melodramatic is less concerned with specific plot and character types than with the creation of a certain mood and a powerful emotional response in the audience. In its status as a mode, melodrama resembles tragedy and comedy in that, though possessing a structure and identifiable motifs and character types, it crosses over from one genre to another. Thus, Westerns such as *Duel in the Sun* (1946), gangster films such as *The Godfather* (1972), action films such as *Spider–Man* (2002), and fantasy films such as the *Harry Potter* series (2001, 2002) are melodramatic. In other words, film melodrama exists primarily as an attitude or method of treatment—a melodrama is a film that features conventional character types and formulaic plot patterns presented in a *melodramatic* way.

A Moral Phenomenon

Like Westerns or gangster films, melodramas can also be defined in terms of their milieu. Much as Westerns are set in the West and gangster films in an urban criminal underworld, melodramas tend to take place in the domestic space of the family or in the private, intimate space of the romantic couple. At the core of melodrama, however, lies neither milieu nor plot but a certain mode of address to the spectator that is emotionalized by the use of melodramatic stylistic techniques. As a mode of address, the melodrama speaks to viewers in a way that is primarily emotional rather than logical. Indeed, one of the oppositions that characterizes traditional screen melodrama is that between emotion and reason. Characters in melodramas who are extremely articulate or presented as intellectuals are often exposed either as phonies or as emotional cripples who have lost touch with their feelings and need to be rescued from the paralyzing forces of rationality. The villain in *Terms of Endearment* (1983), for example, is predictably the college professor (Jeff Daniels), who cheats on his wife (Debra Winger) with one of his female graduate students. Glib men are just not to be trusted in melodramas.

In its attempt to deal with emotional or spiritual experience, the melodrama draws on the affective power of images and music to render the emotional dimensions of experience. That is, it attempts to depict those emotions that cannot be rendered in words. In attempting to say what cannot be said, the film melodrama traditionally relies on stylistic excess—on an extreme camera angle, an overstated set or costume design, a delirious camera movement, or an unusual color scheme—in an attempt to make visible that which is essentially invisible. The moral forces of good and evil that lie beneath the surface of experience are pressured to the surface by melodrama's excesses and put into relief. Melodrama reveals the structure of our experience of the world as a moral and emotional phenomenon, clarifying and working out in dramatic form the emotional and moral conflicts that take place within the individual. In this respect, it is an objective rendering of subjective inner experience.

Thus, in melodramas, children and animals often prove to be emotional touchstones—they are more capable of distinguishing good from bad and right from wrong than are their elders. In *E.T.,* the children intuitively understand the alien from another world and prove more adept than adults when it comes to communicating with it. Family and feelings are the common denominator to which all melodramas ultimately return. Melodrama is about the loss and recovery of feelings (*Awakenings,* 1990), about the restoration of the family unit (*Ransom,* 1996), about fathers and sons (*Affliction,* 1999), about mothers and daughters (*Thirteen,* 2003), about brothers (*Rain Man,* 1988), about sisters (*Little Women,* 1996), and about every other possible configuration of the family from those depicted in *Edward Scissorhands* (1990) and *The Prince of Tides* (1991) to those of *Batman Returns* (1992) and *American Beauty* (1999).

The melodrama and the melodramatic—whether in the form of a melodramatic situation, gesture, element of mise-en-scène, line of dialogue, or bar of music—have tended to be regarded by critics as second-rate forms of expression and clearly inferior to the more aristocratic forms such as tragedy and the tragic. One definition of melodrama describes it as "domestic tragedy." Tragedy was understood (by Aristotle and others) as a serious drama consisting of events and characters of considerable magnitude. In other words, classical tragedy from Aeschylus to Shakespeare dealt with kings, queens, princes, and other figures of social importance whose actions determined the fate of cities, principalities, kingdoms, and nations.

The realm of melodrama, by contrast, is limited to private as opposed to public spheres. It concerns more or less ordinary characters whose actions affect the fortunes of much smaller social units; it focuses on the fate of the couple, the family, and their immediate community. Although tragedy appealed to all classes, it emerged as the dramatic form par excellence of the nobility or social aristocracy in whose world it was situated. Melodrama, like certain forms of comedy, gives expression to the concerns of the lower ranks of society. It is the genre par excellence of the "historically voiceless" (to borrow David

Grimsted's term), and its popularity in the nineteenth century accompanied the emergence of a new social order to which it appealed—that of a middle-class mass society.

Democratic Virtue

Nineteenth-century melodrama brought with it a new vision of the universe and of the individual's place in it. Much as the French Revolution overthrew the traditional institutions of a supposedly divinely ordained, hierarchical society—the church and the monarchy—in favor of a more democratic social order, so the melodrama supplanted the elitist vision of the tragedy with a more democratic worldview. Classical tragedy, which died in the seventeenth century with Racine, could be seen as elitist largely through its concern for the fates of characters of a certain magnitude or social stature. But it was also aristocratic in its basic understanding of the essentially static relationship of individuals to the existing political and social order. The heroes and heroines of tragedy struggled to maintain the natural order of things or to repair that order when it had become unnatural. Thus, Oedipus in Sophocles' *Oedipus Rex* attempted to rid Thebes of the plague and restore it to health, much as Hamlet in Shakespeare's play concerned himself with purging the state of Denmark of something that was rotten. The heroes of tragedy sought to maintain or restore the order of the world, but that order and that world was *theirs*. For them, what was natural was necessarily a reflection of the value system of their particular social class. Both *Oedipus* and *Hamlet* ended with the imposition of a new order, but that new order was merely a more benign form of the dominant social order (i.e., monarchy) with which the drama began.

When characters in melodramas fought to maintain or repair the natural order of things, the values that informed their struggle were those of a different social class (i.e., the middle class). The stature of a character in a melodrama was a measure of his or her moral rather than social position. Virtue empowered its heroes and heroines; evil, its villains. Virtue was not the exclusive property of any one class but was equally obtainable by all. The commoner had as much access to the truth as the noble. Yet it was often easier for the lower classes to discover truth and to achieve virtue or moral wisdom because simple people were less burdened with artificial knowledge and distinctions than the nobility. But in tragedy, knowledge and truth tend to be the exclusive property of the aristocracy. As Grimsted argued, "the melodrama reflected and supported what is perhaps the key element in democratic psychology: the sense which individual men have of their ability to decide, and hence of their right to participate vitally in the wielding of power."

Dozens of stage melodramas (primarily those of European origin) cast the conflict between good and evil in social terms, presenting it as a class war in which the audience is encouraged to root for the underdog. Thus, the villain, frequently a landlord, routinely demanded the hand of his tenant's daughter when the rent was unpaid. Scores of other melodramas, especially those set in contemporary (nineteenth-century) America, staged moral conflicts in terms of geography. These works explored a basic opposition between nature and culture, between the innocence of those who lived in the world of nature—in small towns or on farms in the country—and the corruption and decadence of those who lived in the city. For example, D. W. Griffith's *Way Down East* (1920), an adaptation of a popular stage melodrama, traces the journey of its innocent heroine from the small town where she lives with her mother to the big city, where she is seduced and abandoned by a member of the social aristocracy. The film concludes with her return to life in the country, where she finds a job working on a farm, and with her recovery of innocence through her contact with the purifying world of nature.

A SOCIAL VISION

Melodrama as a Tool of Reform

Melodramas may work primarily on an emotional level, but they also deal with ideas and social problems. In this way, they speak to the fundamental interests of "the people." Grimsted observes that these dramas frequently deal with social and economic issues that concern the middle and lower classes—with "the hard lot of the poor, the corrupt practices of the rich, the social threat of rapid urbanization, the evil of slavery, the injury of bad family upbringing." Novels such as Harriet Beecher Stowe's antislavery narrative *Uncle Tom's Cabin,* which was adapted for the stage shortly after its publication in 1852 and became "the greatest success in the history of the American theatre," helped to transform the theater into a popular forum for the discussion of social issues.

Melodramas also serve as tools for social reform, describing the evils of middle- and lower-class vices such as gambling and alcohol. In one of Griffith's Biograph shorts, *A Drunkard's Reformation* (1909), the hero attends a play that dramatizes the disastrous consequences of drinking, and he vows never to touch alcohol again. Reformers praised melodramas because, as in *A Drunkard's Reformation,* they depicted the triumph of good over evil. Film in general (and film melodrama, in particular) was seen in the United States as a "grand social worker" in that it lured working-class men away from saloons and other forms of vice and promised, as Lary May points out, to teach "Anglo-Saxon ideals" to all, transforming all those who went to the movies into a "model citizenry."

Melodramas dramatized the fears of Victorian America about the toll that modernization and urbanization would take on the institution of the family. As Griffith suggested in the modern story of his four-story epic, *Intolerance* (1916), the anonymity of life in the city posed a danger to the traditional values of family and community; fatherless daughters and husbandless wives would be pursued by immoral men. Greedy factory owners were shown to be anything but paternalistic; they ruthlessly exploited their workers. In other films, the clichéd

Author's collection

Parodying a typical melodramatic situation, Mack Sennett (right) ties Mabel Normand to the railroad track in *Barney Oldfield's Race for Life* (1913).

image of a heroine tied to the railroad tracks gave voice to the particular concerns of a new social order—to the fears of an emerging lower- and middle-class society caught up in the onrush of fast-paced technological changes that threatened to overwhelm them. The average American was suddenly in danger of being crushed by the forces of industry, symbolized by the locomotive.

Though the melodrama was born in France, it adapted itself quite readily to the needs and demands of American audiences. Theatrical melodrama dominated the American stage in the late nineteenth century in the form of both European imports adapted for American audiences, such as Dion Boucicault's *The Poor of New York,* and domestic originals, such as *Uncle Tom's Cabin* or Augustin Daly's *Under the Gaslight.* Popular melodrama helped to shape American character, expressing the American temperament, preaching American ideologies, embodying American aesthetic principles. Daniel Gerould sees it as having been essentially egalitarian, "it was founded on a belief in opportunity for all, and dedicated to getting ahead and making money." [Unlike tragedy, melodrama is] "totally devoid of fatality and inevitability. Contingency rules; things can and will be otherwise. The individual can make of himself what he will. . . . Each human being has the chance in a society unfettered by Old World hierarchies of class and profession." In this way, melodramas embodied the American dream, offering success to anyone with the courage and strength to pursue it.

Politics and Melodrama

Given its associations with the French Revolution and its popular appeal in the United States, the melodrama was often identified as a tool of revolutionary change. Wylie Sypher argued that the genre conceived of things in terms of dialectical opposition—in terms of good and bad—and thus reflected the same worldview of inevitable class warfare and either/or ideology that informed Karl Marx's *Das Kapital.* Whether melodrama was a form of revolutionary consciousness or not, it nonetheless provided a way of looking at history that proved compelling to filmmakers who occupied vastly different positions on the political spectrum.

Griffith, for example, made melodramas that, on one hand, called for reform but that, on the other, also conveyed disturbing racial fears and a deep suspicion of radical change. Griffith's melodramatic polarization of society served as a weapon against blacks in *The Birth of a Nation* (1915) and against Bolsheviks (i.e., Communists) in *Orphans of the Storm* (1922). Griffith's melodrama was essentially populist in nature. It sought to restore an idealized, agrarian America that had been destroyed by big business, industrialization, and urbanization.

Approaching the genre in another way, the Soviet director Sergei Eisenstein infused his melodramas with a Marxist vision. His hero was the masses and his villains consisted primarily of the czar and counterrevolutionary forces in films such as *Potemkin* (1925) and *October* (1928). Though both Marxists such as Eisenstein and populists such as Griffith used melodrama to speak out on behalf of the plain people, Marxists spoke in the language of class conflict—the capitalist exploitation of the working classes. Populists spoke in the language of universal, heartfelt truths that all Americans supposedly understood and respected.

The politics of American melodrama remained steadfastly populist; they were driven by a desire for reform and never embraced the revolutionary spirit of Marxism. But populism was not monolithic; it encompassed a broad spectrum of various grassroots political positions. Rural populists, for example, consisted largely of farmers, farm workers, and residents of small towns. They tended to be Protestants whose families had lived in the United States for several generations. Urban populists were largely blue-collar laborers who worked in steel mills and factories, or wage earners with jobs in department and retail stores. Many were recent immigrants who retained strong ties to an ethnic community and tended to be non-Protestants, such as Catholics or Jews. Both wings of the populist camp supported social reform and shared a distrust of big business, industrialization, and the growth of impersonal corporations that threatened to swallow up the individual.

TWO FILM MELODRAMATISTS: GRIFFITH AND VIDOR

An Agrarian Past

Populism is neither monolithic nor static. It changes its point of view somewhat from decade to decade as the demographics of the American landscape change. It spoke, from the 1890s to 1920s, from the perspective of the agrarian majority. But in the 1920s, when the majority of Americans had moved from rural farms to live and work in the cities, populist rhetoric more and more frequently began to address the concerns of the urban working class. In particular, it attempted to deal with the problems posed to middle-class Americans by the shift that took place in American identity as it was slowly forced to confront its new foundation in urban and industrial culture. In the past, American identity had been tied to notions of individual success, which was understood to be directly related to one's character, energy, and enterprise. In the world of the 1920s postindustrial mass society, the ability of the individual to realize the American dream was seriously compromised by his or her powerlessness in the face of the growing industrialization and corporatization of modern life. This shift can best be illustrated by comparing the different visions of society and the individual's place in it in two silent film melodramas—Griffith's *The Birth of a Nation* (1915) and King Vidor's *The Crowd* (1928).

Griffith's silent melodramas spoke on behalf of nineteenth-century agrarianism. His films looked back to an earlier, more utopian, preindustrial past that was threatened by the forces of modernism. In *A Corner in Wheat* (1909), for example, the natural economy of the past is upset by the intervention of a greedy businessman. A farmer grows wheat out of which bread is made to feed the city's poor. But a middleman, in the form of a speculator in the grain market, interferes with this process. The speculator buys up all the wheat, then artificially drives up the price of flour to increase his profits, ignoring the plight of the urban poor who can no longer afford to buy a loaf of bread. Griffith's romanticized portrait of the farmer is heightened by the latter's heroic refusal to admit defeat at the hands of the stock manipulator. The film ends with the farmer's replanting his field, but it has become clear by now that his success rests not with his own efforts but in the hands of forces beyond his control.

A Corner in Wheat dealt with recent events—with the 1897–1898 attempt by a speculator to corner the wheat market on the Chicago Board of Trade (which provided, in turn, the basis for Frank Norris's novel *The Pit*, on which the Griffith film was partially based). *The Birth of a Nation* was made to celebrate the 50th anniversary of the end of the Civil War and was thus set in the much earlier era of the war itself (1861–1865) and Reconstruction (1865–1877). The world of the antebellum South, which provided the primary perspective from which Griffith viewed events, emerged as a paradise lost. In both the film and in popular mythology, the prewar agrarian South marked the final flowering of an old world (aristocratic) pastoral ideal before it fell victim to an unwanted industrialization externally imposed on it by the North.

History as Melodrama: *The Birth of a Nation*

The Birth of a Nation begins with an idyllic portrait of the southern Cameron family, whose happiness and tranquility is then disturbed by the war. Their attempts to restore this paradise lost after the war are thwarted by abolitionist politicians, northern carpetbaggers, mulattoes, and renegade blacks. Inspired by the traditions of his Anglo-Saxon (Scottish) heritage, Ben Cameron forms a modern-day clan—the Ku Klux Klan—to avenge the death of his sister and to protect southern womanhood from feared black rapists. After defeating the black militia and putting an end to black rule, the Klan restores a utopian social order. The film ends with a millennial vision in which Christ returns to earth, puts an end to war, and presides over a "heavenly throng" who celebrate the regeneration of mankind and the return to the ultimate populist paradise—a latter-day Garden of Eden.

Ben Cameron (Henry Walthall, right) refuses to shake hands with the mulatto lieutenant governor, Silas Lynch (George Seigmann) in *The Birth of a Nation* (1915).

The Birth of a Nation renders American history as melodrama. The Civil War takes the form of a family melodrama with the role of the villain(s) played by northern abolitionists, mulattoes, and blacks. The chief villain, however, proves to be the black race. For Griffith, the issue of slavery, introduced in the film's first shot of a slave market, leads to the outbreak of the war that then turns brother against brother. The northern Stonemans and the southern Camerons, once friends, are suddenly made unwilling enemies. The effects of the war are presented in melodramatic terms as well. Northern and southern families are forced to sacrifice their sons to the war effort—one Stoneman boy and two Camerons die in battle.

Given Griffith's racist scenario, the resolution of the conflict between North and South and the restitution of unity can only come through the reunification of the white race in the face of a common enemy—the black race. Near the conclusion of the film, the elder Camerons, their daughter, and the surviving Stoneman son take refuge from the black militia in the shack of two former Union veterans. An intertitle explains the obvious symbolism of the moment: "The former enemies of North and South are united again in common defence of their Aryan birthright."

The film's ultimate hero becomes the Ku Klux Klan, which rides to the rescue of the besieged whites. The film's ultimate solution becomes the transportation of blacks back to Africa. This action restores the purely white world that was disrupted at the beginning of the film when, as an intertitle claimed, "the bringing of the African to America planted the first seed of disunion." Indeed, historians note that the film originally ended with what Griffith described as "Lincoln's solution"—the deportation of blacks to Africa. This scene was apparently later cut from the final film. Griffith's melodramatic excess led to his distortion of historical reality. His depiction of blacks and his ending of the film were pure fantasy—the product of a melodramatic imagination that had put itself at the service of a racist agenda. The phenomenal success of the film suggests that it somehow spoke to the needs of a troubled America for a return to a simpler past and to a simplified notion of American identity based on racial purity. It also reveals the negative aspects of the populist mythology—its racism, its anti-intellectualism, its paranoia, its religious fundamentalism.

Everyman/No Man: *The Crowd*

The Crowd deals with a more contemporary historical reality—the transformation of 1920s America into an urbanized mass society. It follows its hero, John Sims (James Murray), from his birth in small-town America in 1900 to New York City, where he moves to live and work in the 1920s. The film shows his subsequent marriage, the birth of his children, and his raising of a family, and concludes more or less in the present (1928).

In the world of *The Birth of a Nation*, it was possible for its hero not only to control events around him but even to play a role in the shaping of history. Ben Cameron's life is spared by the intervention of Abraham Lincoln, "the Great

Courtesy of M-G-M

Everyman John Sims (James Murray) enjoys a day at the beach with his wife (Eleanor Boardman) and children in *The Crowd* (1928).

Heart," who pardons him when he is falsely charged with treason. And Cameron is, after all, the (fictionalized) founder of a powerful organization, the Ku Klux Klan. He possesses "agency," that is, he could do things that had consequence for others. The melodramatic action of *The Crowd* concerns the struggles of a character who has little or no control over his own destiny, much less that of the nation. John battles within a conformist culture to establish a unique identity, which is constantly threatened by the mundane realities of day-to-day existence. He tries to assert his own unique identity amid the drudgery of work in a large insurance office, the monotony of marriage, and the despair of failure as an employee, husband, and father.

Vidor's hero is an everyman—a man in and of the crowd. But as an everyman, he is also no man—a nobody whose identity, goals, and desires are given to him by others rather than stemming from his own inner needs. As a child, John is driven by his father's ambitions for him. When he and his boyhood friends tell each other what they want to be when they grow up, John proudly boasts, "My dad says I'm gonna be somebody big." Working for a large insurance company in New York, John becomes one of the crowd, behaving like everyone else. On a double date with his friend Bert and two girls, John watches Bert kiss his girl, then John kisses his date, Mary. On the subway ride home, John looks at a furniture ad that says "You furnish the girl; we'll furnish the home." He then turns to Mary, whom he has just met that night, and proposes to her.

Vidor presents John as the product of a world that lacks the romantic heroism of Ben Cameron's universe. In John's world, individual success is not tied to one's character, energy, or enterprise. Agency, the ability to shape one's own fate, is only an illusion. John is the product of the age of advertising; commercials shape John's desires and he becomes the perfect consumer in a mass society that is itself driven by the needs of a new, twentieth-century institution—mass consumption. In his spare time, John even writes copy for advertisements. Indeed, he achieves the greatest success in his life when he wins $500 for coming up with the catchy phrase: "Sleight o' Hand—The Magic Cleaner."

John's great fortune, however, is as unpredictable and uncontrollable as his misfortune, which mounts toward the end of the film. John does not distinguish himself from the crowd at work, remaining a mere clerk while his friend Bert is promoted. Later, one of his children dies in a traffic accident, he loses his job, his wife threatens to leave him, and he contemplates suicide. Through no fault of his own, John has not only failed to become "somebody big" but he has lost his identity—along with his job, his wife, and his family, who provided the only tangible signs of that identity for him. John's problems lay, in part, in his belief in the nineteenth-century notions of individualism and agency that Griffith celebrated in *The Birth of a Nation* and that John's father bequeathed to him on his birth. Vidor's film suggests that this ideology, or system of beliefs, no longer had any connection to contemporary social and economic reality. The film's hero is forced to recognize his own relative powerlessness as an individual and come to terms with his new status as one of the crowd. At the very end of the film, John recovers his identity as father, husband, and workingman and rejoins the crowd from which he earlier tried to remove himself. He discovers that a crucial aspect of his identity depends on his identification with the crowd—that he cannot exist apart from, but must be a part of, mass society.

ESCAPE AND TRANSCENDENCE

Home as "Seventh Heaven"

In *The Birth of a Nation*, Griffith implicitly rejected the modern in favor of a mythic past. In *The Crowd,* Vidor demonstrated the need for the creation of a new model for understanding the relation of the individual to the world of 1920s America. In general, the film melodrama conveyed either open hostility or profound ambivalence toward modern times. In films such as Frank Borzage's Academy Award–winning *Seventh Heaven* (1927), it became something to tran-

Courtesy of 20th Century-Fox

Diane (Janet Gaynor) and Chico (Charles Farrell) find a refuge from the outside world in their *Seventh Heaven* (1927).

scend. Borzage's hero and heroine defy the original sins of contemporary mass society—despair and cynicism. They overcome the anonymity and heartlessness of the city and create a refuge or "seventh heaven" within it. ("Seventh heaven" refers to their apartment, which is on the seventh [and top] floor of an apartment house in Paris, and thus closer to the heavens than the streets below where they are first introduced.)

They are subsequently separated by the world's first truly modern war—World War I. Both remain steadfastly loyal to one another, communicating through a quasi-spiritual ceremony they perform every day at 11 a.m. Even after the film's hero, Chico, (Charles Farrell), dies in combat, the heroine, Diane (Janet Gaynor), continues to be faithful to him, refusing a wealthy suitor. At the end of the film, Chico miraculously returns from the dead, and Diane, somehow sensing that he is still alive, rushes to him. The film's fairy-tale ending firmly plants it within the world of melodramatic wish fulfillment, which can overcome all the obstacles that mundane twentieth-century life places in the paths of young lovers.

The seventh heaven that the lovers create for themselves serves as a secular Garden of Eden amid the turmoil of modern times. It is an idealized space that virtually every melodrama—before and since—has sought to establish and protect from the outside world. The threats to this domestic space come, more often than not, from forces that are produced, in large part, by an increasingly impersonal and hostile urban mass society. In *A Man's Castle* (1933), a small wooden shack in a New York City "Hooverville," which has been built by those made homeless by the Great Depression, serves as a "safety zone" against economic despair. In *Since You Went Away* (1944), the home is described as the "fortress of the American family" and comes to symbolize the spirit of the home-front effort in World War II.

More recently, the home functions as a space that men have also begun to defend against urban corruption, crime, and violence. In *Fatal Attraction* (1987), Glenn Close repeatedly violates the space of the family as she attempts to win Michael Douglas away from his wife and child. Douglas first tries to prevent his family from learning of his affair with Close, then struggles to defend them against her increasingly violent attacks on the home (though it is only with the aid of his wife, played by Anne Archer, that he finally succeeds in warding off his demented stalker). And in *Ghost* (1990), Patrick Swayze comes back from the dead to protect his girlfriend, played by Demi Moore, from harm. At the end of the film, he quite literally defends their space as a couple, grappling with the film's treacherous villain who has invaded their newly renovated loft. The loft remains their space and clearly serves as a seventh heaven for the 1990s. More recently, in *Signs* (2002), Father Graham Hess (Mel Gibson) defends his home and family from invading aliens, taking refuge in the basement during a mass attack and then finishing off the random alien who remained behind after the others had left.

The Lure of the City: *Sunrise*

In F. W. Murnau's *Sunrise* (1927), a rural family (husband, wife, and child) is threatened by a woman who has journeyed from the city to the country and (apparently) seduced the husband. During a late-night rendezvous in the swamp with the man, she entices him with images of life in the city and then tries to encourage him to murder his wife, sell his farm, and come back with her to the city. This woman, a prototype for the Glenn Close character in *Fatal Attraction*, plays the role of villain, as does the city itself, which seems to be the source of her destructive power. She is also a product of the times—she is a "new woman." She has a short, mannish haircut; she smokes; she dresses like a flapper; she is sexually liberated; and she assumes an aggressive role in her relationships with men. The man's young wife, on the other hand, looks (although pretty) like an old-fashioned, nineteenth-century "old woman," in

Courtesy of 20th Century-Fox

The woman from the city (Margaret Livingston) seduces the husband (George O'Brien) in the swamp in *Sunrise* (1927).

other words, like a European hausfrau. She wears a peasant-style dress, and her hair, unlike that of the woman from the city, is long and blonde. Crosscutting between her with her child and the woman from the city embracing her husband emphasizes their status as moral opposites. The wife is associated with home and family; the woman from the city with the swamp and adultery.

However, the simple moral opposition between nature and culture, or the country and the city, is more complex than it initially appears. The woman from the city is associated with the country—in particular, with the swamp. The regeneration of the marriage between the husband and the wife takes place in the city, where they symbolically renew their marriage vows (at the marriage of another couple), formalize their relationship with a posed photograph, and celebrate their reunion with a peasant dance, which they perform before an audience of city dwellers.

Though Murnau's film seems to present a negative view of urbanization and industrialization, it undercuts its critique of the city with a suggestion that the experiences of its rural characters in the city provide a valuable perspective on their prior relationship that ultimately restores them to one another. Yet, the final reconciliation of the couple takes place in the country, in the domestic space of their bedroom, as the woman from the city returns to the city. In this way, *Sunrise* captures the ambivalence of an America that was negotiating a dramatic change in its identity from an agrarian to an urban base. The dramatic action of the film suggests that the innately natural values of the country can be renewed by contact with the city—that is, that the threats of an urbanized, industrialized America can be contained. Modernity will not destroy the values that inform American identity, but will test and prove their strength, guaranteeing the continuity of the experience of America as it evolved from an agrarian to an industrial society.

SOUND AND MELODRAMA

The coming of sound, which took place between 1926 and 1929, transformed the melodrama from *the* format or mode in which most films were made into one genre among many. Sound brought about changes in acting style, making it no longer necessary (or even desirable) to say everything with the body instead of the voice. In his first sound film, *Abraham Lincoln* (1930), Griffith attempted to stylize dialogue in order to suit it to the emotionalized atmosphere of the melodrama, much as he had earlier stylized his actors' performances. He hired the Pulitzer Prize–winning poet, Stephen Vincent Benét, to write the script and to turn the dialogue into poeticized speech. But Griffith's melodramatization of dialogue remains an isolated experiment in an industry that regarded sound as a crucial step forward in the medium's quest for greater and greater realism. In this context, that which was melodramatic was looked on as old-fashioned or, because of its overt interest in the world of emotion, as somehow appropriate only for women's pictures. Formerly a universal cinematic language, melodramatic style was suddenly demoted to an inferior dialect within a new, more realistic system of communication and signification.

Melodramas thrived during the sound era. Several of these "women's pictures," such as *Gone With the Wind* (1939) and *Rebecca* (1940), not only appealed to a general audience but also won Academy Awards, providing added prestige for the genre. The melodrama and the melodramatic continued to satisfy basic needs of audiences for certain kinds of characters, situations, and stories. But the sound melodrama necessarily distinguished itself from the silent melodrama, which was so closely identified with the silent film itself. The tradition of the theatrical melodrama, which began in France in the 1770s, dominated the nineteenth-century American stage, and provided an expressive language for early film directors such as Griffith, ended with the coming of sound. Although the theatrical melodrama died, its power to address human feelings lives on in the melodramatic, in an emotionalized way of telling stories that continues to move audiences, as the astounding success of *E.T.* at the box office demonstrates.

■ ■ ■ **SELECT FILMOGRAPHY**

A Corner in Wheat (1909)	*The Crowd* (1928)
A Drunkard's Reformation (1909)	*A Man's Castle* (1933)
The Birth of a Nation (1915)	*Gone With the Wind* (1939)
Intolerance (1916)	*Since You Went Away* (1944)
Broken Blossoms (1919)	*Mildred Pierce* (1945)
True Heart Susie (1919)	*Daisy Kenyon* (1947)
Way Down East (1920)	*E.T.: The Extra-Terrestrial* (1982)
Orphans of the Storm (1922)	*Terms of Endearment* (1983)
The Big Parade (1925)	*Home Alone* (1990)
Seventh Heaven (1927)	*A.I. Artificial Intelligence* (2001)
Sunrise (1927)	*Signs* (2002)

■ ■ ■ **SELECT BIBLIOGRAPHY**

BROOKS, PETER. *The Melodramatic Imagination: Balzac, Henry James, Melodrama, and the Mode of Excess.* New Haven, CT: Yale University Press, 1976.

GEROULD, DANIEL C. *American Melodrama.* New York: Performing Arts Journal Publications, 1983.

GLEDHILL, CHRISTINE, ed. *Home Is Where the Heart Is: Studies in Melodrama and the Woman's Film.* London: BFI 1987.

GRIMSTED, DAVID. "Melodrama as Echo of the Historically Voiceless," in Tamara K. Hareven, ed., *Anonymous Explorations in Nineteenth Century Social History.* Englewood Cliffs, NJ: Prentice-Hall, 1971.

LANDY, MARCIA. *Imitations of Life: A Reader on Film and Television Melodrama.* Detroit: Wayne State University Press, 1991.

LANG, ROBERT. *American Film Melodrama: Griffith, Vidor, Minnelli.* Princeton, NJ: Princeton University Press, 1989.

MAY, LARY. *Screening Out the Past: The Birth of Mass Culture and the Motion Picture Industry.* Chicago: University of Chicago Press, 1983.

MCKENNA, GEORGE, ed. *American Populism.* New York: Putnam, 1974.

WILLIAMS, ALAN. "Historical and Theoretical Issues in the Coming of Recorded Sound to the Cinema," in Rick Altman, ed., *Sound Theory/Sound Practice.* New York: Routledge, 1992.

CHAPTER 7

The Musical

FROM NARRATIVE TO MUSICAL NUMBER

Setting the Stage

In *Singin' in the Rain* (1952), when silent film star Don Lockwood (Gene Kelly) tries to tell Kathy Selden (Debbie Reynolds) how he feels about her, he is at a loss for words. Confessing that he's such a "ham" and needs "the proper setting," he takes her from a bright, sunlit exterior into a dark interior—a deserted motion picture stage. With the flick of a light switch, he paints "a beautiful sunset." Turning on a fog machine, he adds "mist from the distant mountains." With a bank of red lights, he conjures up "colored lights in the garden." Positioning his Juliet on a step ladder, he tells Kathy she is "standing on her balcony." Using a single floor lamp, he floods her with moonlight, then adds "500,000 kilowatts of stardust." Finally, he turns on a wind machine—"a soft summer breeze"—and he has the proper setting to speak (or rather sing) to her. The number is "You Were Meant for Me."

What Lockwood does here is what most musicals attempt in order to make a smooth transition from narrative action to musical number: they transform the setting or space from one that grounds the action from the more or less realistic world of the story (its fictional reality) into a different register. In this new world, new laws take hold; the characters are momentarily freed from the fictional reality of the narrative and surrender themselves to the fantasy of song and dance. In other words, the conventions of classic realist narration, in which characters do not normally break into song and dance, suddenly yield to the conventions of the musical number, in which they do.

The heart of the musical (what makes it a musical and not another kind of film) lies in its music and the characters who sing and dance to it. Characters in nonmusicals often sing, but their singing tends to be narratively motivated (and not very good). Cary Grant and Myrna Loy are connected as a couple in *Mr. Blandings Builds His Dream House* (1948) when they both sing "Home on the Range" in the shower. It's not unusual to sing in the shower: everyone does it. It's perfectly natural for a liberal politician such as Jay Bulworth (Warren Beatty) to try his hand at rapping in *Bulworth* (1998); it shows that he wants to be hip. And it's okay for *Legal Eagles* (1986) attorney Tom Logan (Robert Redford) to tap-dance in an attempt to cure his insomnia. These are all believable idiosyncratic practices; that is, they function as an extension of character.

Narrative Reality

The term "classic realist narration" should not be understood as meaning simple realism. It refers to a narrative world that is consistent and coherent; that world obeys a stated or unstated set of rules that give it credibility. That world may contain unrealistic elements, such as aliens (*Men in Black*, 1997) or portals into the brain of John Malkovich (*Being John Malkovich*, 1999), but as long as the characters in these films obey the laws of those worlds, audiences will summon the necessary willing suspension of disbelief to grant those characters and their world a certain verisimilitude; in effect, these films produce their own reality— a reality that is whatever those films want that reality to be—and, by adhering to that reality's laws, make it credible.

Musical Reality

Musicals, however, differ from classic realist narrations in that they have (at least) two sets of books. They operate according to two different laws—and they alternate back and forth between them. As Martin Rubin has written, musicals rupture the fabric of traditional narrative verisimilitude by suddenly shifting from narrative to musical spectacle—to song and dance—that the narrative fiction is unable to naturalize. This is precisely what makes a musical such as *Singin' in the Rain* or *Moulin Rouge* (2001) or *Chicago* (2002) different from a film with music, such as *In the Line of Fire* (1993, Clint Eastwood playing the piano) or *8 Mile* (2002, Eminem playing an aspiring rapper). In a musical,

In *Singin' in the Rain,* Don Lockwood (Gene Kelly) needs the proper setting—a studio sound stage—before he can tell Kathy Seldon (Debbie Reynolds) that "You were Meant for Me."

there's a shift from one level of reality to another that involves a rupture or break; in a film with music, the music is part of the narrative, a window that opens into the psychology of the character.

In the musical, this shift is what produces the lift or experience of ecstatic pleasure that we associate with most musical numbers; this lift involves a movement out of and away from the laws that govern the mundane world of the fiction. Musical sequences interrupt the linear flow of necessity—the narrative—and release the actors from their duties and responsibilities as credible identification figures for us, permitting them to perform for us, to display their exceptional talents as singers and dancers. We suddenly shift to a world of pure spectacle: in this fantasy world, Fred Astaire, Gene Kelly, and others drop the pretense, for a moment, that they are playing characters and perform for us simply as Astaire and Kelly.

Shifts in Register

Musicals operate on two different dramatic registers—that of the narrative and that of the spectacle. Their movement can be charted according to the shifts they make from one register to the other, that is, from narrative to song and back again. This movement is perhaps most obvious in what is considered to be Hollywood's first film musical, *The Jazz Singer* (1927), where the shifts from narrative to musical number are marked by shifts from silent footage (with orchestral accompaniment) to sound footage in which Al Jolson sings.

The example cited earlier from *Singin' in the Rain* deliberately foregrounds this shift in register, laying bare the dynamics of the musical itself. The fact that it takes place on a film stage and involves the machinery used to make films (lights; fog and wind machines) underscores its self-reflexive play with the essentially illusory foundations of the musical number.

Chicago

The transition from one register to another need not be slow or gradual. In a film such as *Chicago* (2002), a single cut will often serve to shift us back and forth from the real world to the musical number. As Roxie Hart (Renée Zellweger) listens in the holding pen of the Cook County jail to Big Mama Morton (Queen Latifa) giving her the instructions for new inmates, the lesson is intercut with an onstage musical number, "When You're Good to Mama," sung by Big Mama to a well-dressed audience in a crowded, fancy nightclub. *Chicago* opposes reality (the prison) and fantasy (the nightclub) through abrupt juxtapositions, but the editing also fuses the two worlds together. It's as if the prisoners somehow had access to the musical number through the cutaways. Other numbers in the film, such as "Funny Honey" and "Razzle Dazzle," play with a similar confusion between registers. In both these and other numbers, the film employs a variety of editing matches (eyeline matches, graphic matches, matches on action) to connect the narrative action to the musical number. Even when connected into an apparently seamless continuity, the narrative and the musical number depend on their essential difference from one another to produce the sense of ecstasy associated with the musical. "Ecstasy" (from the Greek word *ekstasis*) literally means "standing outside of oneself," and it depends on the sensation of displacement that is exactly the sense that *Chicago*'s staging of musical numbers attempts to achieve. Characters are there in their narrative bodies yet simultaneously outside of themselves singing and dancing in the same composite scene. Even when blurred, the distinction between registers remains perceptible, and our awareness of that distinction becomes the basis of the musical number's power to transport audiences.

The basic pattern for the musical numbers in *Chicago* involves an alternation between reality and fantasy within the numbers themselves. This tension is resolved in the final number ("I Move On"), when fantasy becomes reality. Roxie and Velma (Catherine Zeta-Jones) realize their individual dreams through a unique partnership: their collective notoriety is turned into the main attraction

Photofest

Fantasy becomes reality for Roxie (Renée Zellweger, right) and Velma (Catherine Zeta–Jones) in the final number of *Chicago* (2002).

at a big downtown Chicago theater, where they dance and sing for thousands of spectators. For the first time in the film, there are no cutaways to narrative action occurring elsewhere; the narrative action is here, on stage, in the performance of the number. The fundamental pattern of alternation between narrative and number that structures most musicals frequently moves toward an ecstatic resolution in the final musical number, but *Chicago* makes that pattern and process more explicit than do other works of the genre.

NARRATIVE AND MUSICAL NUMBER: DEGREES OF INTEGRATION

As Rubin points out, the history of the theatrical and film musical has traditionally been written in terms of this essential duality of the genre, in terms of the opposition between narrative and spectacle. Critics argue that, as a form, the musical evolves from disintegration to integration, from formats such as the revue to that of the book musical. The revue, which places self-contained musical numbers back to back with little or no narrative to connect them, enjoyed great popularity on stage in the *Ziegfeld Follies* of the 1920s and on film in all-star vehicles such as *Paramount on Parade* (1930), which featured 20 different numbers (seven of them in Technicolor) and boasted 13 different songwriters and 11 different directors. The book musical (so called because of the prominence of the story or book) attempts to integrate narrative and musical sequences, culminating in the supposedly seamless integration of story and music in stage musicals such as *Show Boat* (1927) and *Oklahoma!* (1943).

Rubin points out that the various forms of the musical (the revue, the operetta, the book musical) did not replace one another but continued to exist alongside each other. He argues that the movement toward integration, though clearly a dominant trend in the musical's evolution, had its limits. Total integration of story and number threatened to destroy the crucial gap that gives the musical number its affective power to enthrall audiences. Once the distinction between narrative and musical spectacle is erased, the energy that drives the musical will disappear, because there will be no lift, no ecstasy or movement out of one mode and into another, which is the musical's reason for being.

MUSICAL FORMS

The Backstage Musical

Every musical, then, exists in the tension between its narrative and its musical numbers. This tension is most strongly felt during the moments of transition from narrative to musical number. For the integrated musical, the musical that tries to cohere narrative and music, musical numbers emerge as something of a problem, which the narrative must somehow solve. Screenwriters attempt to solve these problems by providing motivation for the numbers or by constructing bridges from nonmusical to musical sections. The shifts can be motivated in a variety of ways. One way to naturalize song and dance within the realism of the narrative is to incorporate performance into the plot. The film's characters are identified as professional or amateur performers whose normal activity involves singing and dancing. In fact, one of the staples of the musical and one of its major subgenres is the backstage musical, in which various characters are brought together to put on a show. The film then becomes about the milieu of the theater, about performance; and the rehearsals and performances within it have a solid justification as necessary activities in this particular world.

Berkeley and *42nd Street*

Some of the more representative examples of the backstage musical can be found in a cycle of Warner Bros. films from the early 1930s, such as *42nd Street* and *Footlight Parade* (both 1933) and the *Gold Digger* films (1933, 1935, 1936), in which musical shows are cast, rehearsed, and finally staged in a succession of elaborate production numbers.

If the motivation for the numbers is realistic, the numbers themselves often defy conventional notions of realism. Berkeley's most famous production

In the title number from *42nd Street,* Peggy Sawyer (Ruby Keeler) dances her way to the top of the New York skyline—and to stardom.

numbers—such as "42nd Street" (*42nd Street*), "By a Waterfall" and "Shanghai Lil" (*Footlight Parade,* 1933), "Remember My Forgotten Man" (*Gold Diggers of 1933,* 1933), and "I Only Have Eyes for You" (*Dames,* 1934)—are all introduced as stage numbers being presented to a theater audience. But the numbers quickly modulate from the theatrical to the cinematic. The theater proscenium disappears, and the spectator becomes a transcendent eye swept along by a series of spectacular transformations that explode the original space of the theater stage into a fantasy space that is constantly reinventing itself in what Rubin describes as a seemingly endless succession of shifts of "scales, perspectives, locations, and dimensions." Berkeley's transformations range from simple shifts in perspective from eye-level to overhead shots—revealing geometrical compositions, in numbers such as "Young and Healthy" (*42nd Street*)—to complex shifts in location from stage to street to subway car to an abstract, illusory space (performers against a black background) in "I Only Have Eyes for You" (*Dames*). Clearly, Berkeley's realistic anchor in the backstage musical becomes the launching pad for the most unrealistic flights of fantasy.

Moulin Rouge

In *42nd Street,* every number is motivated as either a rehearsal or a performance on opening night. But not every backstage musical is quite as realistic in its motivation. *Moulin Rouge* (2002), for example, exhibits some of the basic plot elements of the typical backstage musical. Its narrative traces the development of the show from the writing of the script, to the search for a financial backer, to

In the "Diamonds are a Girl's Best Friend" number at the beginning of *Moulin Rouge,* Satine (Nicole Kidman) sings "The French are glad to die for love" but she prefers expensive jewels. At the end of the film, she dies for love.

preparing/rebuilding the theater, to rehearsals and the opening night performance. But many of its musical numbers have no realistic motivation. In the "Elephant Love Medley," when Christian (Ewan McGregor) and Satine (Nicole Kidman) sing love duets borrowed from popular songs by John Lennon ("All You Need is Love"), Paul McCartney ("Silly Love Songs"), Dolly Parton ("I Will Always Love You") and others, they are neither rehearsing nor performing in front of an audience. They are driven into song by a melodramatic intensification of feeling. The songs are deftly integrated into the dramatic action, but they also lift the lovers into a mutual rapture that slips them loose from all narrative bonds. The number celebrates an explosion of feeling, and it is this sort of pyrotechnics that lies at the heart of the musical.

Showpeople

Even if the central action around which the plot hinges is not the putting on of a show, the profession of the central character can often be that of a performer, thus motivating the presence of musical numbers. This is the case in a number of Astaire films, ranging from *Top Hat* (1935), *Swing Time* (1936), *Shall We Dance* (1937), and *Holiday Inn* (1942) to *Royal Wedding* (1951). Stories about professional entertainers can be based on famous personalities played by actors with unremarkable musical talents, as in *The Buddy Holly Story* (1978), with Gary Busey as Holly; *Coal Miner's Daughter* (1980), in which Sissey Spacek is country singer Loretta Lynn; and *La Bamba* (1987), in which Lou Diamond Phillips plays Ritchie Valens. Or they can be based on fictional performers played by exceptional talents—Frank Sinatra in *Pal Joey* (1957), Liza Minnelli in *New York, New York* (1977), or Julie Andrews in *Victor/Victoria* (1982).

Amateurs can also put on a show, as is the case for a number of Mickey Rooney/Judy Garland musicals, such as *Babes in Arms* (1939), *Strike Up the Band* (1940), and *Babes on Broadway* (1942). And amateurs can be elevated to the status of professionals in films such as *Dirty Dancing* (1987), in which Johnny Castle (Patrick Swayze) trains Baby Houseman (Jennifer Grey) to do a lift, to rhumba, and to lambada like a pro.

TRANSFORMATION OF SPACE: PERFORMER, PROPS, AUDIENCE

There was a time when song and dance were integral features of our culture's lived experience and the presence of musical numbers (in films set in that era) was motivated by that experience. A century ago, before the invention of radio or television, people entertained themselves at home. In *Meet Me in St. Louis*

© Everett Collection

Curtains, a stage, and an audience transform a family song-and-dance routine between little sister Tootie (Margaret O'Brien) and big sister Esther (Judy Garland) into a showstopping musical number in *Meet Me in St. Louis*.

(1944), set in 1903, Esther (Judy Garland) and Tootie (Margaret O'Brien) enter-tain party guests by performing a cakewalk together while singing "Under the Bamboo Tree"; later, their parents (Leon Ames and Mary Astor) sit at the up-right piano and sing "You and I," a song that draws a divided and despondent family back together again.

Performer

In the cakewalk number, the home is transformed momentarily into a theater. The performers emerge through a doorway from behind a pair of drapes resembling curtains. The room in which they perform becomes a stage; its walls resemble the proscenium of a theater; party guests become an audience. As illustrated here, the successful transition from a narrative situation to a musical sequence depends on the transformation of narrative space into performance space; ordinary settings are rearranged into a stage, lit differently, or shot differ-ently to suggest this transition. In "You and I," the setting is not theatricalized with curtains or props, but it is emotionalized, producing a sentimentalization of space that is just as transformative as the film's other musical numbers.

Props

Incidental props that are placed merely to create a realistic atmosphere are fre-quently appropriated by the performers in their numbers. Their initial status is transformed. What was once a mere coat rack suddenly becomes a dancing part-ner for Astaire in *Royal Wedding* (1951). Astaire and Kelly often whip up a dance in the least likely place, such as the boiler room of an ocean liner (Astaire in *Shall We Dance*, 1937), the Museum of Natural History (Kelly in *On the Town*, 1949), or a city street (Kelly in *It's Always Fair Weather*, 1955), and they incorporate the most unlikely props into these dances, from roller skates to garbage can lids.

The classic example of this sort of number in which narrative space is trans-formed into musical space occurs in *A Star Is Born* (1954) when Vicki Lester (Judy Garland) attempts to recreate a production number she has filmed earlier that day in the studio at home for her husband, Norman (James Mason). As Jane Feuer describes it, "she turns on the lamp ('lights'), positions a table ('camera') and beings the 'action.' She uses the elastic bands of a chair for a harp, a pillow for an accordion, a lampshade for a coolie's hat, a leopard-skin rug for an African costume [and] salt and pepper shakers for instruments in the Brazilian section."

The shift from narrative to music takes place almost magically before our eyes, providing a smooth transition that disguises the radical shift from one reality to another. But all these transformations involve the presence of another crucial ingredient: in addition to a performer, there must also be an audience. Part of the transformation from one register to another involves a metamorphosis of roles. Characters relate to one another in terms of performer (or coperformers) and audience. Passersby on the street stop, watch, and listen, acknowledging the performance. To fail to acknowledge the performance is to fail to mark the break it establishes between one register and another.

In *Love Me Tonight* , Maurice (Maurice Chevalier) measures Jeanette (Jeanette MacDonald) for a new riding habit, putting her measurements to music in a hummed reprise of "Isn't It Romantic?"

Rutgers Cinema Studies

Audience

Even though some musicals must have tried to pretend that no one noticed anything different going on when music and dance began, in so doing, such musicals undoubtedly diminished the affective power of the musical sequence. A performer needs an audience, even if it's only a horse, as in *Love Me Tonight* (1932) when Jeanette (Jeanette MacDonald) sings "Lover" to her horse. By definition, without an audience, there's no performance. A performance is always for someone. Of course, the performer is always performing for an unseen audience, for us; and a number of performances are directed straight at the camera, addressing us as the audience. Again, in *Love Me Tonight*, Maurice (Maurice Chevalier) looks right into the camera when he sings "Mimi," breaking one of the basic laws of classical cinema by returning the camera's look. Even so, Maurice is not just singing to us but to Jeanette as well, because she occupies the space of the camera in this shot.

STYLISTIC REGISTERS

From Black-and-White to Color

Other devices often used to mark a shift in register involve increased stylization or a change from one style to another. In a handful of films, shifts from black-and-white to color change the gears of the film's relations with its audience. In

Broadway Melody (1929), for example, the film goes from black and white to Technicolor for one musical number—the "Wedding of the Painted Doll" sequence. In a color film, the color palette might shift in the direction of greater saturation, as in the "You Were Meant for Me" number in *Singin' in the Rain,* when the action moves from a natural, sunlit exterior to the artificial, colored lights of a sound stage. *Dancer in the Dark* (2000) marks its musical numbers, such as "Cvalda" and "I've Seen It All," with subtle shifts in color saturation, most clearly seen in the change in Bjork's flesh tones from pale to flushed. However, this shift in color saturation does *not* occur in the final number—"The Last Song," when Bjork's character is executed; the number, which also lacks musical accompaniment, is anything but an ecstatic escape from the narrative.

From Noise to Music

This shift in register can also be achieved through other means. In the opening of *Love Me Tonight,* the editing imposes a rhythmic pattern on the shots of Paris as it awakens to a new day, giving a musical ordering to the various noises audible in the street (the tolling of church bells, a man swinging a pickax, the snores of a homeless man, the broom-sweeping of a concierge, the cry of a baby, the rasping of a saw, the hammering of a pair of cobblers, etc.). Editing transforms the noises of the city into music. Indeed, one definition of music is "organized noise." At any rate, this city "symphony" leads smoothly into the film's first musical number, Maurice Chevalier singing "The Song of Paree." Bjork's first number in *Dancer in the Dark,* "Cvalda," draws on a similar orchestration of machine noises in a factory to create musical rhythms as a prelude to song.

THE OPERETTA

The operetta, unlike the backstage musical, makes no attempt to motivate musical numbers realistically. Operettas tend to situate their characters in exotic nineteenth-century European settings—in the mythic land of Ruritania, for example (*The Love Parade,* 1929; *The Smiling Lieutenant,* 1931; *Love Me Tonight,* 1932; *The Merry Widow,* 1934). Looking back to the works of such composers as Johann Strauss, Franz Lehar, Victor Herbert, Rudolf Friml, and Sigmund Romberg, the light-opera music frequently demands classically trained voices, such as those of Jeanette MacDonald and Nelson Eddy (*Naughty Marietta,* 1935; *Maytime,* 1937), though it also accommodates the more popular style of Maurice Chevalier, a café and music-hall singer. The narratives of operettas borrow extensively from fairy tales and romantic melodramas. *Love Me Tonight,* for example, reworks the Sleeping Beauty story; Walt Disney's version of Snow White is cast in the form of an operetta. Operettas ranging from *The Love Parade* (1929) to *The Merry Widow* (1934), like certain forms of fairy tales, are populated with princes and princesses and kings and queens who live in faraway kingdoms where love overcomes all obstacles. *Moulin Rouge,* earlier described as a backstage musical, is an operetta as well. The backstage story of the film is just as fabulous as the story of the play-within-the-play in which a penniless sitar player falls in love with a beautiful courtesan who must sacrifice herself to an evil maharajah to save her country. In fact, Christian improvises this story based on the situation in which he finds himself: an impoverished writer who has fallen in love with a music hall star (Satine) who must sell herself to the Duke to further her career. Filming entirely in the interior of an Australian studio, director Baz Luhrmann constructs a fantasy version of Paris circa 1900 that sustains the dreamlike nature of a narrative that celebrates the romantic ideals of an artistic Bohemia. As the film's end title declares: "This story is about truth, beauty, freedom. But above all . . . love." As seen here in the recreation of a mythical Paris, the fairy-tale setting in which the narratives of operettas unfold is, by its very nature, removed from everyday reality. In this setting, song and dance become integral features of a different reality—that of musical fantasy.

In the operetta, the shift from narrative to musical number is often marked linguistically by stylization of the dialogue. Characters segue into the musical numbers by suddenly introducing a pronounced rhythm into the delivery of their lines; or their prose may suddenly turn into poetry. In *Love Me Tonight,* the intro to the Rodgers and Hart song "Isn't It Romantic?" begins with a conversation between Maurice (Maurice Chevalier), a tailor, and a customer who is trying on a new suit:

> Man: "Maurice, it's beautiful . . . the cloth . . . you make a work of art."
>
> Maurice: "The tailor's art for your sweetheart!"
>
> Man: "It's like poetry in a book! Oh, how beautiful I look!"
>
> Maurice: "The love song of the needle united with a thread . . . the romance of the scissors . . ."
>
> Man: "So Claire and I could wed. . . . You're a magician!"
>
> Maurice: "Isn't it romantic?"
>
> (Maurice then sings "Isn't It Romantic?")

When the dwarfs ask Snow White to tell them a story in *Snow White and the Seven Dwarfs* (1937), they engage in an exchange built around rhyming questions and answers:

> Snow White: "Once there was a princess . . ."
>
> Dwarf: "Was the princess you?"
>
> Snow White (nodding): "And she fell in love . . ."
>
> Dwarf: "Was it hard to do?" . . .
>
> Dwarfs: "Did he say he loved you? Did he steal a kiss?"
>
> Snow White (singing): "He was so romantic I could not resist."
>
> (She then begins singing "Some Day My Prince Will Come.")

THE ASTAIRE–ROGERS MUSICAL

The operetta failed to flourish after its heyday at Paramount and M-G-M in the 1930s, but another kind of musical (together with the backstage/performer musical) emerged as an important subgenre of the musical: the Astaire–Rogers films at RKO. As Rick Altman has suggested, these films might justifiably be called "screwball musicals" in that, like screwball comedies, they feature attractive romantic leads whose sexual desire for one another is displaced—not into slapstick comedy, but into song and dance. Like the screwball comedies, the scripts shine with verbal sophistication, wit, and urbane self-awareness like the Cole Porter lyrics the stars occasionally sing. Though remnants of vaudeville and the revue format surface from time to time (the "Bojangles of Harlem" number in *Swing Time,* 1936), for the most part, song and dance function as extensions of character and reflect stages in the couple's evolving relationship. Narrative complications throw up obstacles that the dance numbers easily overcome. It did not hurt that the numbers were written by the smartest song-writers on Broadway—Irving Berlin (*Top Hat,* 1935; *Follow the Fleet,* 1936; and *Carefree,* 1938), Cole Porter (*The Gay Divorcee,* 1934), George and Ira Gershwin

© Everett Collection

Ginger Rogers and Fred Astaire pick themselves up, dust themselves off, and start to dance all over again in *Swingtime.*

(*Shall We Dance*, 1937), and Jerome Kern and Dorothy Fields (*Swing Time*, 1936). These composers and lyricists engage in a verbal sparring, smart-set sophistication and sexual innuendo similar to that which distinguishes the work of screwball comedy's greatest screenwriters such as Charles Brackett and Billy Wilder (*Bluebeard's Eighth Wife*, (1938) and Preston Sturges (*Easy Living*, 1937).

The musical numbers in *Top Hat* (1935) range from partially to fully integrated. They include the staged public performance by famed dancer Jerry Travers (Astaire) at a London theater where he entertains the audience with a solo number, "Top Hat, White Tie, and Tails." But the film also contains numbers designed to convey character and plot information related to the romantic vicissitudes of the central couple, consisting of Jerry Travers and Dale Tremont (Ginger Rogers). In the "Isn't This a Lovely Day" number staged at a deserted gazebo in a park, Fred and Ginger engage in what Arlene Croce refers to as a "challenge dance (he does a step, she copies it, he does another, she tops it, and so on)." Their interaction perfectly captures the nature of their relationship as it evolves from a tentative effort at courtship initiated by Fred to a mutual romantic partnership as Ginger responds.

THE INTEGRATED MUSICAL

The Freed Unit

The development of the fully integrated musical is generally attributed to Arthur Freed, producer of a series of musicals at M-G-M from 1939 (*The Wizard of Oz*) to 1960 (*Bells Are Ringing*), including such classics as *Meet Me in St. Louis* (1944), *The Pirate* (1948), *On the Town* (1949), *An American in Paris* (1951), *Singin' in the Rain* (1952), *The Band Wagon* (1953), and *It's Always Fair Weather* (1955). What unites the Freed films is Freed's presence as producer and a small group of collaborators with whom he regularly worked. The "Freed Unit" consisted of performers such as Judy Garland, Mickey Rooney, Fred Astaire, Gene Kelly, Oscar Levant, Kay Thompson, and Cyd Charisse; directors such as Vincente Minnelli, Stanley Donen, Charles Walter, and Rouben Mamoulian; writers such as Betty Comden and Adolph Green; composers such as Alan Jay Lerner and André Previn; and musical arrangers such as Roger Edens.

The Astaire–Rogers films consist of numbers that alternate between partial and full integration. Freed's films tend toward a more fully integrated interplay between musical numbers and narratives. As Rubin explains, Freed Unit films "articulat[e] the tension" between narrative and numbers "in a particularly rich, vivid, and sophisticated manner." Narrative space opens up to incorporate musical space; musical space invades narrative space; distinctions between the two spaces become the subject of a sophisticated play with traditional notions of what is number and what is narrative. Essentially, the typical Freed number contains shifts back and forth *within* the number between its status as performance piece and narrative exposition.

In *Singin' in the Rain,* Don Lockwood (Gene Kelly) defies the dreary weather by singing and dancing in the rain.

Singin' in the Rain

The title number of *Singin' in the Rain* provides a clear example of this interaction. At the beginning and ending of the number, characters from the narrative space (the limo driver, a pedestrian, a policeman, and the man to whom Lockwood gives his umbrella) pass by him and stare at him incredulously as he sings and dances in his musical space; the two spaces acknowledge one another; yet characters in the narrative space remain unable to understand why the hero is singing and dancing in the rain. The number depends on this interplay for comic effect. Here, one register interacts with the other. The number explores the boundaries between the two and ultimately takes those boundaries as its subject.

In this interaction, it is possible to see exactly what makes the "Singin' in the Rain" number work. Lockwood and those around him respond differently to the same set of conditions. The rain dampens the spirits of the passersby, whose emotional states seem governed by the harsh weather. As the lyrics of the song make clear, the joy that Lockwood feels surfaces in defiance of the gloomy weather. Or, from another perspective, the stormy weather serves as a foil to magnify, through contrast, Lockwood's ecstatic transcendence of it. In this particular instance, the surrounding world does not shift to another register to permit song and dance; rather, the hero transforms that world through his responses to it. Puddles become a source of infantile pleasure for an overgrown kid to splash about in. Torrents of water cascading down a drainpipe drench Don's head, but the water only broadens the enormous smile on his face. His spirit is reborn in the baptismal font of musical rejuvenation, leaving him no alternative but to express his joy by singing and dancing in the rain.

IDEOLOGY AND THE MUSICAL

In an essay entitled "Entertainment and Utopia," Richard Dyer discusses the musical as an exemplary instance of entertainment. Like other forms of entertainment, the musical creates a utopian space in which the problems we regularly encounter in our lived experience in the world no longer exist. Instead of poverty, there is abundance; work-related exhaustion is replaced by limitless energy; the dreariness of everyday routine is exchanged for excitement and intensity; our actual isolation and alienation within mass culture is transformed into a heightened sense of our uniqueness as individuals within a close-knit community of unique individuals. For Dyer, the purpose of entertainments such as the musical is to manage the basic contradictions generated by the gaps and inadequacies of capitalism by creating a utopian version of a capitalist society. In this world, energy and initiative is recognized and rewarded. Men find, fall in love with, and win the women of their dreams, and women find their dream lovers in similar fashion.

Conservative musicals (e.g., *Grease* (1978)) effectively manage the contradictions inherent in capitalism, producing a utopian escape from an imperfect society. In the final sequence of *Grease,* Rydell High School is transformed into an amusement park where formerly alienated individuals become part of a community of carnival celebrants. And in the final number ("We Go Together"), Danny (John Travolta) and Sandy (Olivia Newton-John) ride a souped-up hot rod into heaven, leaving the trials and tribulations of typical teenage angst behind them. Progressive musicals tend to expose or undercut the utopian nature of the musical number. *Pennies From Heaven* (1981) is an adaptation of Dennis Potter's BBC miniseries about Depression-era characters trapped in unfulfilling lives who escape through the fantasy of song. But the film consistently qualifies the escapism of the musical numbers by making it quite clear that the performers, including Steve Martin and Bernadette Peters, are lip-synching to popular songs originally recorded by Bing Crosby, Connie Boswell, Fred Astaire, and others. The obvious lip-synching severely limits the extent of the hero's flight into another world; he can only escape his oppressive existence

Rutgers Cinema Studies

Arthur (Steve Martin) and Eileen (Bernadette Peters) re-enact a classic Fred Astaire and Ginger Rogers dance number in *Pennies From Heaven*.

through the popular recordings of his era. The resolution comes at the end of the film, in a fantasy sequence, when Steve Martin (as the hero, Arthur) sings the title song in his own voice. But this resolution, in which the real replaces the false, is undercut by the quality of the performance; Steve Martin's real voice is just not as good as the voices that he has been lip-synching. At the same time, his miraculous appearance, intact and alive after his supposed death by hanging, is exposed as obvious wish fulfillment in an otherwise exceedingly grim portrait of his noirish existence. Instead of transporting us into the never-never land of musical fantasy, the final number forces us to acknowledge our own kinship with Martin's unexceptional ordinariness.

THE END OF AN ERA

By the 1960s, the golden age of the American film musical had more or less come to a close. Big-budget musicals continued to enjoy success on Broadway, and these were then turned into popular motion pictures, but a number of them (denoted here with *) were based on 1950s stage musicals: for example, *Flower Drum Song** (1961); *West Side Story** (1961); *Gypsy** (1962); *The Music Man** (1962); *My Fair Lady** (1964); *The Sound of Music** (1965); *Camelot* (1967; opened on Broadway on December 3, 1960); *How to Succeed in Business without Really Trying* (1966);

A Funny Thing Happened on the Way to the Forum (1966); *Sweet Charity* (1968); *Half a Sixpence* (1968); and *On a Clear Day You Can See Forever* (1970).

From one perspective, the 1960s marked the high point of the film musical. In the 1950s, an unprecedented *two* musicals (*An American in Paris*, 1951; *Gigi*, 1958) had won Academy Awards for Best Picture. In the 1960s, *four* musicals— *West Side Story* (1961), *My Fair Lady* (1964), *The Sound of Music* (1965), and *Oliver!* (1968, a British production based on a 1960 London stage musical) won Academy Awards for Best Picture. However, *Oliver!* was the last film musical to win an Academy Award for Best Picture until *Chicago* (2002).

With the notable exception of two Julie Andrews vehicles, *Mary Poppins* (1964) and *Thoroughly Modern Millie* (1967), original (i.e., non-Broadway) film musicals tended to do poorly at the box office in the 1960s (e.g., *Doctor Doolittle*, 1967; *Star!*, 1968; *Chitty Chitty Bang Bang*, 1968), as did a number of adaptations of Broadway shows, including *My Fair Lady, Camelot, Hello, Dolly* (1969), and *Paint Your Wagon* (1969). Traditional musicals continued to lose money in the 1970s and 1980s (e.g., *Darling Lili*, 1970; *Lost Horizon*, 1973; *Mame*, 1974; *The Wiz*, 1978; *Xanadu*, 1980; *Pennies from Heaven*, 1981; *Victor/Victoria*, 1982; *The Cotton Club*, 1984; and *A Chorus Line*, 1985).

A NEW ERA BEGINS

However, a new generation of musicals appeared to address a new generation of audiences. Rock and roll was here to stay, seen in the success of a series of films starring Elvis Presley (*Love Me Tender*, 1956), two films featuring the Beatles (*A Hard Day's Night*, 1964, and *Help!*, 1965), *Woodstock* (1970), and two of the top-grossing musicals of all time—both starring John Travolta—*Saturay Night Fever* (1977) and *Grease* (1978), which was also a Broadway success before being made into a film.

More recently, the film musical has begun to stage a comeback. An even newer—and younger—generaton of audiences for the film musical was regularly being weaned on animated features as children, instilling in them a desire for more grown-up fare (*South Park: Bigger, Longer, Uncut*, 1999) as they got older. Thus, *The Little Mermaid* (1989), *Beauty and the Beast* (1991), *Aladdin* (1992), *The Lion King* (1994), *Pocahontas* (1995), and *Toy Story* (1995)—as well as decades of MTV—may very well have set the stage for the revival of the film musical in the new millennium with *Moulin Rouge* (2001) and *Chicago* (2002). Remakes of *Gentlemen Prefer Blondes* with Reese Witherspoon and *Guys and Dolls* with Nicole Kidman are currently in the works, as well as the musical version of *The Producers*. Whatever the reason may be for the return of the film musical, films such as *Moulin Rouge* and *Chicago* clearly pay homage to the traditions of the genre, evoking its most celebrated forms and dedicating themselves to its original social mission. Both films attempt to construct utopian solutions to real needs created by real social inadequacies within contemporary society. Their musical numbers lift us into a world of abundance, energy, intensity, and community. They satisfy our needs by managing our desires. In short, they entertain us.

■ ■ ■ SELECT FILMOGRAPHY

Broadway Melody (1929)
Love Me Tonight (1932)
42nd Street (1933)
Top Hat (1935)
Showboat (1936)
The Gang's All Here (1943)
Meet Me in St. Louis (1944)
An American in Paris (1951)
Singin' in the Rain (1952)
The Band Wagon (1953)

The Sound of Music (1965)
Cabaret (1972)
Saturday Night Fever (1977)
Grease (1978)
All That Jazz (1979)
Pennies From Heaven (1981)
Dirty Dancing (1987)
Everyone Says I Love You (1996)
Moulin Rouge (2001)
Chicago (2002)

■ ■ ■ SELECT BIBLIOGRAPHY

ALTMAN, RICK. *The American Film Musical.* Bloomington: Indiana University Press, 1987.

COLLINS, JAMES M. "The Musical," in Wes D. Gehring, ed. *Handbook of American Film Genres.* Westport, Greenwood Press, 1988.

CROCE, ARLENE. *The Fred Astaire & Ginger Rogers Book.* New York: Galahad Books, 1972.

DYER, RICHARD. "Entertainment and Utopia," *Movie* 24 (Spring 1977), 2–13.

FEUER, JANE. *The Hollywood Musical.* Bloomington: Indiana University Press, 1982.

RUBIN, MARTIN. *Showstoppers: Busby Berkeley and the Tradition of Spectacle.* New York: Columbia University Press, 1993.

CHAPTER **8**

American Comedy

LAUGHTER AND CULTURE

Comedy, Repression, and Cultural Dreamwork

For Sigmund Freud, jokes function, on an individual level, as a form of liberation; they provide those who laugh at them with a necessary, therapeutic release from the serious worries and cares that oppress the average human being. As a mass form, the genre of comedy works to release that which society as a whole tries to hold in check. In short, whatever a society represses frequently returns in the form of comedy to taunt it. This often occurs quite literally in the figure of the Shakespearean fool who tells a truth that others dare not utter. Only in a comedy does one seriously entertain the idea of throwing Mama from the train, shrinking the kids, or leaving small children home alone. Yet ambivalent feelings about family clearly lie beneath the surface of the modern American psyche, waiting to find expression in the form of comedy.

To study film comedy, then, is in part to look at the dream work of a culture's collective unconscious, to put it on the couch, and to make it speak of the forces that led to its production. Thus, if American film comedy plays with sexual, racial, ethnic, and class differences, it is because our culture as a whole denies their existence in the supposedly egalitarian democracy of contemporary America. And, because comedy is never taken seriously, American film comedy can often deal with these issues more openly than can other, more official genres, such as the historical film or the Western.

Silent comedy, for example, abounds in sight gags that play on racial and ethnic differences and give expression to a profound racism that crisscrosses the social structure. In *Seven Chances* (1925), Buster Keaton desperately searches for a woman to marry (before 7 o'clock on his 27th birthday) so that he can inherit $7 million. He spots several likely prospects on the street but does a double take and hurries away when one prospective bride turns out to be black and another, Jewish.

The Marx Brothers repeatedly made fun of Italian immigrants through the character of Chico, whose heavy accent and broken English become the source for extensive wordplay with Groucho; and in *Duck Soup* (1933), they parodied black musical and singing style, turning the traditional Negro spiritual "All God's Chillun" into a prowar production number entitled "All God's Chillun Got Guns." Wearing (as the script indicates) "watermelon grins" and swaying from side to side, they sang, "They got guns,/We got guns,/All God's chillun got guns./We gonna walk all o'er the battlefield/'Cause all God's chillun got guns." For the Marx Brothers, nothing was sacred.

Even in more recent times, racially insensitive ethnic comedy, which has all but disappeared from the big screen, continues to thrive on television. Archie Bunker's bigotry became a comic centerpiece of *All in the Family* (ca. 1971), in which the central character regularly referred to Jews as "hebes," Hispanics as "spics," blacks as "coons," and Italians as "dagoes." Archie's controversial racism got laughs not only from those who laughed with him, but also from those who laughed at him. During the mid-1970s, *Saturday Night Live* featured Czechoslovakian immigrants (Steve Martin's and Dan Ackroyd's "Two Wild and Crazy Guys") and the Japanese (John Belushi's "Samurai Warrior") as targets for running gags. *In Living Color* took deliberate tastelessness to a new level, transforming the unconscious racism of the past into a conscious racism. Comic sketches on this show explored the nooks and crannies of political incorrectness, making fun of blacks, whites, gays, and other minorities with equal abandon. As with *All in the Family,* the focus of its humor lay in exposing whatever hidden prejudice the audience might have, recasting it in a somewhat exaggerated form, and getting viewers to laugh at it.

From Racism to Social Integration

At the same time that it exploits our ethnic and racial diversity, American comedy deals with the processes by which differences are bridged and a (more or less) unified American society is constructed. As Northrop Frye suggests, "The theme of the comic is the integration of society, which usually takes the form of incorporating a central character into it." The theme of the comic includes not only the more general themes of the creation of couples through marriage (*The Wedding Singer,* 1998) and of communities through the absorption of individuals into larger groups (*The Majestic,* 2001), but also the more uniquely American theme of the immigrant experience, recounted in film comedies ranging from Charles Chaplin's *The Immigrant* (1917) to *My Big Fat Greek Wedding* (2002).

Immigrants: Chaplin to Depardieu

The richness of the theme of the immigrant experience emerged in the work of Chaplin, whose "Tramp" character embodied an essential ambivalence toward society. He sought its approval and acceptance yet repeatedly found himself unable to conform to its demands. Thus, Chaplin comedies often played against the genre's expectations, striking a note of pathos that qualified the comic thrust of the films as a whole. In films such as *The Circus* (1928) and *Modern Times* (1936), the Tramp reconciled himself to his outsider status and trudged off into the sunset (or sunrise) in search of a more utopian social system. Much of Chaplin's comedy stemmed from the tension that existed between the Tramp's conscious efforts to fit in and win the acceptance of others and his inherent resistance to authority and refusal to conform socially.

In Chaplin's films, it was the immigrant's desire for assimilation that became the source of comedy. In *My Big Fat Greek Wedding*, the desire for assimilation becomes a two-way street. The Greek-American heroine, Toula (Nia Vardalos), defies her family, who want her to marry a Greek American, and falls in love with a WASP, Ian Miller (John Corbett). Her desire for assimilation is again the source of comedy, as she transforms herself from hostess in her father's restaurant into a yuppie travel agent. But the film presents WASP culture, in the form of Miller's family, as ethnically sterile and uninteresting, especially in comparison with Toula's vibrant Greek American relatives and friends. In this way, the film implicitly calls her desire for assimilation into question. At the same time, the hero, Ian, tries to please Toula's family, and the source of much comedy comes from his misuse of Greek words and phrases taught to him by Toula's mischievous brothers. By the end of the film, Ian has become assimilated into the Greek American community. He and Toula live in a house just down the street from her parents and send their daughter to "Greek school" to learn Greek. The film becomes a celebration of Greek American ethnicity.

Integration and the Regeneration of Society

Though only a handful of American comedies deal explicitly with the immigrant experience, that experience can be seen as displaced and reworked in hundreds of other comedies in which an individual struggles to enter society. Through the theme of comic integration, American screen comedies demonstrate the flexibility of our democratic social structure in its ability to absorb

Toula's father (Michael Constantine) introduces his extended family to his future son-in-law, Ian Miller (John Corbett, right), and Ian's WASP parents, while Toula (Nia Vardolos, left) looks on in *My Big Fat Greek Wedding.*

new members and integrate them into a new social order whose unity and diversity exceed that of the old order. The typical resolution of a film comedy thus involves a marriage or other ritual celebration of the formation of a new community out of the old. In this way, it suggests a regeneration of the dying world that produced the disorder with which the comedy typically begins.

It Happened One Night (1934), for example, begins with a bad marriage between an heiress (Claudette Colbert) and a playboy-socialite. The film then spends the next 90 minutes explaining to both the heiress and the audience exactly why this marriage is wrong. It ends with the disruption of another false marriage—the public ceremony in which the heiress and the socialite are scheduled to renew their initial vows. And it then celebrates the "right" marriage: having fled the ceremony, Colbert returns to the middle-class newspaper reporter (Clark Gable) with whom she is really in love, and then marries him (after a hasty annulment of the initial, "wrong" marriage). This final marriage is right not only because Colbert and Gable really love one another but also because it heals the divisions in society, establishing a new order through the symbolic marriage of representatives of different social classes. Class difference is most often represented in terms of professional status. *Pretty Woman* (1990) brings together a corporate takeover specialist (Richard Gere) and a Hollywood hooker (Julia Roberts). In *While You Were Sleeping* (1995), a Chicago token clerk

(Sandra Bullock) falls in love with a wealthy lawyer (Peter Gallagher) and, when he falls into a coma, pretends to be his fiancée (though she winds up with his brother in the end). *As Good as It Gets* (1997) focuses on an unlikely romance between a cynical best-selling novelist (Jack Nicholson) and a waitress (Helen Hunt). In each case, the films rely on romantic comedy to unite different social classes.

Reforming the Workplace

The theme of integration often involves the outsiders' transformation of the very social system that they enter and regenerate from within. The film *9 to 5* (1980) celebrates the efforts of three secretaries (Jane Fonda, Dolly Parton, and Lily Tomlin) to reclaim their office from the male-chauvinist tyranny of corrupt boss Dabney Coleman and establish a new, more benign order. In *Working Girl* (1988), the traditional office hierarchy (the status quo) is upset when a lower-class secretary, Tess (Melanie Griffith), puts together a big deal without the knowledge of her upper-middle-class boss (Sigourney Weaver). Working outside the prescribed system, Tess pools her efforts with those of an upper-middle-class male executive from another company (Harrison Ford). Together they create an ideal business team, which functions more efficiently and effectively than any pairing within the existing system. This new order, which democratically combines members of different classes, ultimately triumphs over the old, more hierarchical, stratified system. Thus, the film celebrates the comic virtues of independence, innovation, and a willingness to break the rules.

Rites of Passage: Boys to Men

The comic aspects of the integration of the individual into society find perhaps their most improbable dramatization in *Big* (1988), in which a 12-year-old boy grows "big" overnight, becoming a 30-year-old man (Tom Hanks). Hanks flees to new York in search of an antidote to his magical growth, lands a job as an executive in a toy company, and gets his own apartment and a girl (Elizabeth Perkins). As an adult, he enjoys unqualified success, emerging as the boy wonder of his firm and the answer to his girlfriend's dreams for a more sensitive man to love. The comedy hinges on the efforts of Hanks (who remains a kid both in mind and spirit) to pass for and be accepted as an adult.

At the same time, it plays with his dual identity as boy and man. Though outwardly successful, Hanks discovers that he is unable (and unwilling) to give up his childhood and become an instant adult. Reversing his earlier, childish wish to become big, he learns to grow up—but in order to do so, he has to become a child again. At the end of the film, he gives up the pleasures and pains of being an adult. He sacrifices the rewards he has earned in the adult world—his career and his girlfriend—to come back to his own world, reverting to his original size and age and returning to his mother. Thus, *Big* features a double integration, focusing primarily on Hanks' trials and tribulations in becoming an adult but framing this in the anxieties surrounding the character's struggles with adolescence at the beginning and ending of the film.

Courtesy of Paramount

Groucho Marx turns the affairs of government into a song and dance act in Leo McCarey's 1933 classic *Duck Soup*.

Comic Disintegration and Disorder

Men to Boys: The Marx Brothers

Comedy remains risky business in more ways than one might imagine. On the most basic level, a film's gags and jokes may not always work, leaving the screenwriter or comedian in an embarrassing limbo. But comedy is even more dangerous when it does work. Comedy dares to disrupt the orderly processes of society by unleashing the forces of chaos and disorder. These, in turn, often get out of control. The Marx Brothers, for example, assaulted the very foundations of bourgeois society, mocking its repressive institutions. Groucho becomes president of a college in *Horse Feathers* (1932) and levels its time-honored traditions, cutting them down to the stuff of comedy. As the president of a small European country in *Duck Soup,* he literally reduces the operations of government to child's play (a game of jacks) and plunges the nation into war over an insult that never occurred. Once the genius of the Marx Brothers is uncorked, there is no putting it (or them) back into the bottle again; the brothers follow absurdist logic to its "logical" conclusion. Thus, Harpo, after parodying the midnight ride of Paul Revere in *Duck Soup,* winds up in bed with his horse, while the woman he has been pursuing in earlier sequences sleeps alone on a nearby cot. The Marx Brothers' anarchic brand of humor has no limits, pushing their best films, such as *Duck Soup,* to the point of nihilistic self-destruction.

The Release of the Repressed: Bringing Up Baby

Few comedies reach the riotous peaks hit by those of the Marx Brothers. More often than not, American comedy regulates and gives order to the forces of chaos. If the zany hero and heroine played by Cary Grant and Katharine Hepburn in *Bringing Up Baby* (1938) unleash a wild, man-eating leopard on the quiet Connecticut countryside, you can be sure that they will somehow get it back into its cage (or convenient jail cell) before the film is over.

Ironically, for comedy to achieve its goal of social cohesion, integration, and regeneration, it must first unleash the leopard. That is, comedy must acknowledge the elements of disorder or difference at work in the society it seeks to depict. Once exposed, these elements must then be either erased by being dissolved into a larger unity or subsumed within an all-encompassing system of checks and balances that neutralize them or, at the very least, hold them in place.

Bringing Up Baby, for example, is about attempts to control the irrational or disruptive elements of nature. Its hero, David (Grant), is a paleozoologist who is first seen assembling a dinosaur in a museum. His excessive control over nature (as represented by dead animals, fossils, and bones) is mirrored in his own sexual repression. His command over nature is merely an illusion. It was produced more by nature's passivity (the dinosaur is, after all, only the skeleton of a dead animal) than by his power. When he steps outside and encounters the living forces of nature—that is, Susan (Hepburn), Baby (a tame leopard), George (a dog), and the aforementioned wild leopard—his artificial control evaporates.

Hepburn's aggressive attempts to get Grant to notice her involve a harmonic collaboration with nature—she is assisted by Baby and George (who, following his canine instincts, steals and buries a precious dinosaur bone). Their adventures together result in bringing Grant back to life, as it were, and reviving those elements of nature within him that have become fossilized and dead. Nature, however, can be *too* natural. Baby and George, who are tame animals, represent the proper mixture of elements, balancing the forces of nature with those of civilization. The wild leopard represents nature in excess—it embodies the unruly aspects of nature that must be brought under control before the natural order of things can be restored. *Bringing Up Baby,* unlike a Marx Brothers comedy, carefully charts a course between dangerous extremes, never quite losing control of the forces of disturbance with which it plays. The wild leopard ends up back in a cage.

Containing Chaos

Capitalism Works: Trading Places

As *Bringing Up Baby* suggests, comedy functions as a kind of cultural safety valve; it lets off steam that would otherwise build up and explode, destroying the entire system. It is comedy's job to impose order on the disorderly and to

Courtesy of Paramount

In John Landis's *Trading Places* (1983), commodities broker Don Ameche becomes the target of street con man Eddie Murphy. In a classical comedy turnabout, Ameche then hires Murphy to run his company.

contain or harness the explosive elements that it awakens and that give it its power. Many comedies begin, for example, with a lack or deficiency that suggests the failure of society to resolve problems or differences. Poverty, for example, emerges as an implicit critique of society's ability to provide adequately for all of its citizens. Comedy liquidates that lack or solves that problem.

In *Trading Places* (1983), poverty and class differences vanish with the wave of a magic wand. In order to settle a bet about the various roles that environment and heredity play in the development of a person's character and skills, Mortimer and Randolph Duke, two wealthy commodity brokers played by Don Ameche and Ralph Bellamy, take a poor black con man named Billy Ray Valentine (Eddie Murphy) in off the street and elevate him to an executive position in their firm. At the same time, they not only fire but also throw in jail the white executive, Winthorp (Dan Ackroyd), whose position in the firm he takes.

With his reputation ruined, his bank account frozen, and his credit cards confiscated, Winthorp is forced into a life of poverty, ill health, and crime. The Dukes' initial disruption of the original status quo, which results in a reversal of fortunes, is not, of course, designed to eliminate poverty; indeed, the terms of their wager demand not only that Murphy take Ackroyd's place but also that Ackroyd take Murphy's.

However, The Dukes' scheme does inadvertently expose the source of poverty, which is seen to stem neither from environmental nor hereditary factors but rather from the whimsical nature of capitalism. Poverty emerges as the direct result of the Dukes' selfishness and comes from their willful abuse of their economic power and class privilege. Yet this potentially radical critique of capitalism gets deflected in Murphy's and Ackroyd's rush to get even with their meddlesome tormentors. Once impoverished, but now firmly entrenched (or so it seems by their dress and manner) in the upper-class, cutthroat, capitalist world of the Dukes, Murphy and Ackroyd defeat their former bosses on their own field of battle—the commodities exchange.

Their victory over the Dukes suggests that the system works; they, along with the film's other chief lackeys of capitalism—including a butler (Denholm Elliot) and a hooker (Jamie Lee Curtis)—become fabulously wealthy, at the expense of the now-impoverished Dukes. Basking in the sun on the beach of a tropic island, the film's victors enjoy the spoils of capitalism. At the same time, poverty, in the form of the Dukes, is banished from the screen, along with the class conflicts and economic extremes that characterize the urban jungle in which the film is earlier set.

Reforming Prostitution: **Pretty Woman**

In a similar way, *Pretty Woman* (1990) builds its comedy on potentially explosive material that it then, in turn, defuses by means of a tried-and-true, conventional comic resolution. The dynamite lies just beneath the surface of a supposed Cinderella-like plot line. Having come to Los Angeles for a week of business meetings, a high-powered executive (Richard Gere) hires a local prostitute (Julia Roberts) to act as his female companion. Though he initially has sex with her, he pays her several thousand dollars merely to escort him to a number of business-related social functions. Gere's business arrangement with Roberts tacitly acknowledges what many feminists insist is the actual status of women in a male-dominated society: they are commodities to be bought and sold— paid prostitutes whose beauty and talent primarily function within this system to enhance the stature of the men who possess them.

When Gere actually begins to fall in love with Roberts, the commercially exploitative nature of their initial relationship gradually disappears, replaced by a more genuine feeling. By falling in love with her and asking her to marry him, Gere snuffs the fuse on the dynamite. He redeems their relationship from the sordid realm of crass commercialism and rewrites its scandalous origins in the more proper language of middle-class morality. The disturbing disclosure of the real basis of sexual relations in contemporary society becomes buried beneath the film's happy ending, which showers Roberts with good fortune and bathes the audience in good feeling. Romantic fiction replaces the reality of class difference and bourgeois morality. At the end of the film, Gere climbs up to Roberts's balcony and proposes to her, explaining that "after all, this is Hollywood." In other words, although comedies tend to reveal cultural contradictions more clearly than do other genres, they also take great pains to resolve them, thereby undermining their status as radical works.

Comedy, Class and Democracy

American film comedy, like comedy in general, is the genre of the people. In Latin, it would be called *vulgus* (i.e., vulgar), signifying that it belongs to the crowd. In his book on realism and representation, *Mimesis,* Erich Auerbach distinguishes ancient tragedy, which concerns the affairs of nobles and the fate of kingdoms, from ancient comedy. Comedy is situated as often in the world of household slaves (as in the plays of Menander and Plautus) as in that of their masters, and, unlike tragedy, it tends to deal with everyday incidents in the lives of common citizens (as in the plays of Aristophanes).

American film comedy differs from that of other national cinemas. Its vitality depends on the egalitarian nature of American society (or at least on the common belief that America has no class system). American comedy not only celebrates the disempowered little guy—Chaplin's Tramp or Steve Martin's *The Jerk* (1979)—but also is the genre par excellence of upward social mobility, as can be seen by the rags-to-riches plot lines of *Trading Places, Pretty Woman,* and other films, such as *Brewster's Millions* (1985), *Working Girl* (1988), and *Forrest Gump* (1994).

The Discreet Charms of the Working Class

A similar populist spirit can be found in comedies in which the wealthy aristocracy is brought low by bad times and forced to join the working class. Depression audiences loved it when Claudette Colbert's heiress in *It Happened One Night* learned to live by her wits on the road. When she impersonated a lower-class plumber's daughter to escape detectives sent by her father, her upper-class reserve suddenly melted away and she actually seemed to enjoy the freedom of her new role. Her transformation into a regular girl was now complete.

In *Overboard* (1987), a contemporary reworking of Capra's classic comedy, obnoxious millionaire Joanne Stayton (Goldie Hawn) falls overboard, loses her memory, and is claimed by carpenter Dean Proffitt (Kurt Russell) as his wife. Like Capra's heiress, Joanna's dive overboard plunges her into the joys of working-class life. She becomes a caring wife and mother, complete with four rambunctious boys. Though she recovers her memory, she refuses to return to her old life, aligning herself with the have-nots who ironically have it all—or at least, everything that she wants.

Today's audiences find it amusing to watch stock market whiz kid Dan Ackroyd temporarily lose everything in *Trading Places,* especially when he hits bottom as a drunken Santa Claus who steals food at a company Christmas party. On occasion, bluebloods even willingly go slumming to see how the other half lives. Thus, Eddie Murphy's African prince in *Coming to America* learns about life in New York by taking a job as a busboy at McDonald's, where he discovers the simple joys and pleasures of the working class (while living on a rather generous allowance supplied by his father).

Celebrating Change

As a genre that is rooted in the popular and the vulgar, American comedy remains profoundly social. Not only do many comedies speak for those who have been disempowered by the social order, but the underlying celebration of *change* in the majority of film comedies presents an implicit threat to the status quo, as well. Change, of course, is a feature of all narratives. Narratives not only possess a structure which implies change—that is, they feature beginnings, middles and ends—but they also regularly begin with some literal change, with a disruption of events or with a disturbance of an equilibrium that is eventually restored.

Comedy undermines the status quo, and it also endorses change as a positive feature of history, unlike tragedy, which conceives of change negatively. But ultimately what is important in comedies is not so much the positive or negative aspects of change as the way in which characters respond to change. Essentially a subversive form, comedy celebrates change. It applauds flexibility—the ability of characterizes to adapt themselves to changing circumstances.

A SHORT HISTORY OF AMERICAN SCREEN COMEDY

Silent Comedy

Comic narratives, however, differ both from one another and from period to period in terms of the unique form which that change takes and in terms of the ways in which the films' characters respond to that change. In the 1920s, change took place on several levels in American screen comedies. On the most superficial level, silent comedy came of age as a format for feature-length films. Comedies expanded in length from two-reel (18–25 minutes) shorts to feature-length films, running from 45 to 85 minutes in length. The feature-length format transformed the nature of comic narratives, which became more elaborate and complex.

Slapstick

Two-reel comedies, such as those produced by Mack Sennett at Keystone, consisted of a series of gags, loosely strung together, that escalated from simple comic misunderstandings to physical roughhousing, such as pratfalls or the throwing of custard pies. This action, in turn, frequently led to an extended chase sequence, often featuring the Keystone Kops. This brand of broad physical comedy is known as "slapstick," a term that refers to the flat stick clowns used to strike one another in the more physical forms of theatrical pantomime. Slapstick, which was central to the humor of a number of comedians trained in the Sennett tradition, continued as a staple of many silent feature-length comedies. However, the major comic stars of the 1920s, such as Charles Chaplin, Buster Keaton, and Harold Lloyd, developed the art of slapstick into a form of self-expression, tailoring their comic routines to the unique nature of their screen characters.

In *The Circus* (1928), for example, Chaplin elegantly choreographed his slapstick; in one scene he rhythmically and repeatedly whacked his antagonist over the head with a billy club under the eyes of the policeman pursuing them both while each pretended to be a mechanical figure in an amusement park attraction. The sequence revealed a quasi-sadistic, yet charmingly childlike, aspect of the Tramp's persona: the little fellow discovered a safe way to strike back at a bully, protected from reprisals by his ingenious manipulation of the codes and conventions that govern other characters' behaviors in certain situations.

Keaton's slapstick similarly became an extension of his character. In *Sherlock Jr.* (1924), Keaton used the timeworn banana peel routine, carefully placing the peel to trip up his rival; the latter refused to be baited into the trap and it was Keaton himself who ultimately slipped on the peel. Much as Chaplin's slapstick was often aimed at others, Keaton's was just as frequently directed at himself.

Lloyd also made himself the butt of physical humor, serving as a tackling dummy for the college football team in *The Freshman* (1925); but unlike Keaton, who tended to be the unintended target of gags that inadvertently boomeranged back on him, Lloyd's comedy had a somewhat masochistic edge to it, complicating the audience's identification with him with a profound uneasiness.

Charles Chaplin

Chaplin's Tramp character was rooted in nineteenth-century values. Based on the archetypal American hobo (as described by Winston Churchill), "He was not so much an outcast from society as a rebel against it. He could not settle down, either in a home or a job. He hated the routine of regular employment and loved the changes and chances of the road. Behind his wanderings was something of the old adventurous urge that sent the covered wagons lumbering across the prairie towards the sunset." His character looked back to the defiant individualism found in Romanticism, yet retained the somewhat melodramatic, rigid moral outlook of Victorianism. The target of Chaplin's resistance was the modern world. His most memorable comic battles were with machines—whether in the form of a revolving door (*The Cure*, 1917), an escalator (*The Floorwalker*, 1916), or a folding Murphy bed (*One A.M.*, 1916).

In *Modern Times* (1936), Chaplin played a factory worker victimized by machines; in one scene, he served as a human guinea pig in an experiment involving a machine designed to feed workers automatically, which malfunctioned. In another, after working a shift tightening bolts on an automated assembly line, he went berserk with his wrenches, twisting everything in sight (from his foreman's nose to the buttons on a woman's dress). From Chaplin's quasi-populist perspective, urbanization and industrialization threaten the human spirit. Unable to defeat the machine, Chaplin took refuge from it by setting out on the road. At the end of the film, Chaplin and his girlfriend left the city, walking off together into the countryside, where they hope to find a pastoral paradise.

Courtesy of United Artists

Charlie gets caught up in the dehumanizing machinery of the Industrial Revolution in *Modern Times* (1936).

Buster Keaton

While Chaplin rejected the modern world, Keaton embraced it. More often than not, Keaton's comic costar was a machine. In *The General* (1926), it was a locomotive; in *The Navigator* (1924) and *Steamboat Bill, Jr.* (1928) it was an ocean liner and a steamboat, respectively; in *Sherlock Jr.* (1924), it was a movie projector; and in *The Cameraman* (1928), it was a motion picture newsreel camera. Buster's relationships with machines often proved more harmonious than those with human costars, especially his love interests, whom he could never quite understand as well as he understood the workings of his machines. If one of the most characteristic images of Chaplin is that of him caught up in the gears of a huge machine in *Modern Times*, then that of Keaton is of him mastering a machine—as in *Sherlock Jr.*, when he used the convertible top of his sinking automobile to transform the car into a sailboat.

Relying on the uniquely American virtues of common sense, ingenuity, and know-how, Buster overcame whatever human–made or natural obstacles were placed in his path. Unlike Chaplin's homeless Tramp, who resisted change and who was forever at odds with modernity, Keaton adroitly adapted himself to the ever-changing rules of the world around him, demonstrating a comic flexibility that enabled him to move to the pace of modern times.

While Chaplin's unskilled, working-class character was more often unemployed than not, Keaton played middle-class types who tended to be gainfully employed and who secured places for themselves in the power structure of contemporary society that were denied to Chaplin. In *Seven Chances*, for example, Keaton belonged to the profession par excellence of the 1920s: he was a stockbroker. Yet, whether Keaton was a millionaire (*The Navigator*) or a projectionist in a movie theater (*Sherlock Jr.*), he never seemed to become obsessed with his class status. Though he was internally driven to achieve goals (for example, to inherit $7 million in *Seven Chances*), he seemed less interested in enjoying the rewards that reaching the goal provide than in simply reaching the goal itself (for example, in getting married by 7 p.m. on his 27th birthday).

Harold Lloyd

Harold Lloyd, like Keaton, played middle-class (generally white-collar) workers. He was a clerk in *Girl Shy* (1924), a dry-goods salesman in *Safety Last* (1923), a shoe salesman in *Feet First* (1930), and an office worker in *Hot Water* (1924) and in *Mad Wednesday* (1947). Lloyd, however was consumed with middle-class values—with his status in the community, with impressing those around him, with making it.

As the anxiety-ridden Harold Lamb in *The Freshman* (1925), Lloyd riveted his desires on becoming popular in college, which he attempted to do by spending his money on lavish parties and winning a position on the football team. At the Freshman Frolic, his loosely-basted-together suit came undone, leaving him standing in front of his classmates in his shorts. Though he didn't quite make the football team, he mistakenly believed that he had when the coach permitted him to work as water boy (and tackling dummy). Exposed as the college boob, Harold refused to give up. When his teammates were all injured in the big game, the coach reluctantly put him in, and he miraculously scored a touchdown to win the game.

Lloyd's obsession with success found a perfect outlet in *Safety Last*, in the scaling of a skyscraper, a feat that became identified with him through his repetition of it in subsequent films. Fearful that his girl would discover that he was a failure, Harold concocted a scheme for making money by staging a publicity stunt for the department store in which he worked. He arranged for his friend, a professional "human fly," to attract crowds to the store by climbing the outside of the building. When, at the last minute, his friend was unable to go ahead with the stunt, Harold took his place. Each story of the building presented him with a different challenge; not only was it necessary for him to scale the building's surface but, along the way, he was forced to struggle with pigeons, a net, a dog, a mouse, a flagpole, a clock spring, and a weather vane. When he finally reached the top, Lloyd found his girlfriend waiting there to reward him for his ambition and courage. The moral of this and other Lloyd stories was clear: by overcoming his own fears and physical limitations, an average guy like Lloyd could prove himself worthy of success, living out the fantasy of upward mobility that preoccupied middle-class Americans of the 1920s.

The 1920s: Three Comic Visions

Chaplin, Keaton, and Lloyd translated into comic terms the social and economic upheavals of 1920s America, in which industrialization, urbanization, and the growth of a new, white-collar middle class transformed traditional social customs and behaviors. Chaplin looked back, somewhat nostalgically, to an earlier era of innocence before the idyllic world of the pastoral garden was disturbed by the machines of industry. Keaton delighted in the new machine age, using its tools to redefine his relationship with the world around him, which now included machines as well as nature. Lloyd captured the fear and uncertainty of the changes that took place in the social structure during this period, through the uniquely modern metaphor of the skyscraper, which epitomized the soaring ambitions of the 1920s as well as the economic structure that threatened (as in *The Crowd*) to make anonymous those who worked within it. Through his scaling of it, Lloyd demonstrated that this new world could be mastered, but only by means of a physiological and psychological ordeal that only a few were capable of withstanding. The machines of industry, which transformed modern America and gave birth to a new society based on mass production and mass consumption, also gave birth to the movies, which became the chief entertainment staple consumed by society. But by the end of the 1920s, the machines of the motion picture industry developed a new technology—sound—which, in turn, changed the nature of screen comedy.

Early Sound Comedy

The Clowns Speak

Although Chaplin, Keaton, and Lloyd continued to make pictures in the sound era, sound permanently altered the nature of film comedy. Realizing that his comic style, which was based on silent pantomime, would not translate easily to the sound film, Chaplin persisted in making silent (that is, nontalking) films until 1940. Mishandled by M-G-M during the transition to sound, Keaton's star fell quickly. Within a few years, he was playing supporting roles to Jimmy Durante; by 1934, he had returned to making shorts. Only Lloyd made a successful transition to sound, though his style of comedy remained more visual than verbal.

Sound ushered in a new generation of comedians, many of whom came from the stage. The clown tradition continued to flourish in the persons of W. C. Fields, Stan Laurel, and Oliver Hardy (all of whom had appeared in silent films); Mae West; the Marx Brothers; Joe E. Brown; Bert Wheeler and Robert Woolsey; and others. These performers combined slapstick with a unique, somewhat stylized verbal delivery of comic lines, which could be heard most clearly in the exaggerated speech patterns of Fields and West. The Marx Brothers provided perhaps the broadest range of comic speech styles, including not only Groucho's fast-talking urban spiel and Chico's immigrant dialect, but also Harpo's silence. Indeed, Harpo provided a bridge of sorts between the Chaplin-esque pantomime of the silent screen and the verbal slapstick perfected by Groucho's and Chico's misuse of language.

Romantic Comedies

Sound drew on other theatrical traditions as well. Romantic comedies, in which the central dramatic action involved the comic (as opposed to melodramatic) vicissitudes of a heterosexual love affair and which had been a staple of the silent screen, enjoyed a new lease on life in films that combined romance with the comedy of manners. These films tended to be set in the sophisticated world of the social aristocracy, to deal with the affairs and intrigues of the ladies and gentlemen who were privileged members of this world, and to make fun of the rules and conventions according to which they lived their lives.

The best examples of this hybrid form were films such as *The Smiling Lieutenant* (1931), *One Hour with You* (1932), and *Trouble in Paradise* (1932), which were directed by Ernst Lubitsch and written by Samson Raphaelson. Hollywood also adapted to musical comedies, such as *Glorifying the American Girl* (1929) and *Whoopee!* (1930), which were originally produced by Florenz Ziegfeld for the Broadway stage. Both of these films provided a format for a different form of humor—personified in the singing comedian with the banjo eyes, Eddie Cantor.

And, within a few years, Hollywood began to extend its own comic range, featuring comic performers from radio such as Jack Benny, Bob Hope, Edgar Bergen and Charlie McCarthy, George Burns and Gracie Allen, and others. At around the same time, the career of Will Rogers (the nationally known humorist who had already established himself in the motion pictures, radio, and weekly newspaper columns) reached new heights when the actor began to make sound comedies. Thus, Hollywood ransacked a variety of media for comic performers who brought with them the various styles and formats of different comic traditions, adding multiple and varied strains of popular comedy to the expanding field of comic styles that found a common home in 1930s American cinema.

Some of these different comic traditions had intersected in earlier screen comedies; romantic plots and subplots had provided the central dramatic situation for a number of slapstick comedians such as Keaton and Lloyd, whose films regularly concluded with winning the heroine's hand. In *The Gold Rush* (1925), Chaplin alternated between slapstick and romantic comedy but kept each sexually and geographically separate from the other: slapstick was the province of men, isolated and starving in the cabin in the wilderness. Romantic comedy was reserved for mixed company, taking place in the dance hall or in the cabin in the city. Though the three Marx Brothers steered clear of romantic entanglements, most of their comedies featured romantic subplots, which were built first around Zeppo Marx, and then around singer Allan Jones.

By and large, no matter how many comic styles an individual film incorporated, low slapstick routines remained carefully segregated from high romantic comedy. Though the hero might have thrown custard pies in one scene, played comedy of manners in another, and wooed the heroine in a third, leading ladies tended to be relegated to the more or less passive status of romantic objects to be won or lost by the hero; they rarely indulged in physical slapstick humor, which was considered unladylike.

Screwball Comedy

But in the 1930s, all of this began to change. High and low comedy were mixed together with greater and greater disregard for sexual difference. Various strains and styles of comedy found their way into a single hybrid form, known as the screwball comedy. The screwball comedy combined high comedy, such as romantic comedy and comedy of manners, with low slapstick comedy. It did not rely on clowns who looked funny, wore comic costumes, or possessed a recognizable comic persona. Instead, it took romantic leading men and women such as Irene Dunne, Katharine Hepburn, John Barrymore, and Cary Grant, who had established themselves in serious drama, and plunged them into the madcap world of vulgar slapstick routines.

Indeed, in *Twentieth Century* (1934), Barrymore—the "Great Profile" of the legitimate theater and the silent screen—even picked his nose, while removing putty from it. In *Bringing Up Baby,* Hepburn suffered indignities previously reserved for the lowest of low comedy—she became the butt of anal humor. As she angrily stalked off after a minor dispute with Grant in a fancy nightclub, she unknowingly tore her evening dress, losing the rear portion of her skirt and thus exposing her backside, which Grant attempted to cover as best he could with his top hat. Though Hawks handled this sexual vulgarity with characteristic good humor as a bit of good-natured fun, it was nonetheless a far cry for Hepburn from the propriety of *Little Women* (1933).

Under Restraints: Comedy and the Code

Not every screwball comedy indulged in such overt sexual play; indeed, most of them did not; but the majority of them tended to be covertly about sexual matters. In an essay entitled "Sex Comedy without the Sex," critic Andrew Sarris suggests that the screwball comedy was about the repression of sex, which then became the genre's chief subtext. Sarris argues that the genre was produced, in part, by the tightening of restrictions in the Production Code in July 1934.

Changes in the Code took place in response to a campaign by the Catholic Legion of Decency to ensure the "sanctity of the institution of marriage" by banning from the screen depictions of "adultery and illicit sex," "scenes of passion," "seduction or rape," "sex perversion," "white slavery," "miscegenation," "vulgarity," "obscenity," and other acts. This campaign was prompted, in part, by the increasing sexualization of film comedy (and other genres) that took

Courtesy of Columbia

In Frank Capra's Academy Award–winning film, *It Happened One Night* (1934), Clark Gable restores old-fashioned morality to the screen, erecting "the walls of Jericho," which serve to keep his desire for Claudette Colbert (and hers for him) in check.

place in the early 1930s; the chief target of the censors was, of course, Mae West, as well as Hollywood's original platinum blonde, Jean Harlow. Perhaps the most audacious of the pre-Code comedies was Lubitsch's *Design for Living* (1933), in which both Gary Cooper and Fredric March lived out of wedlock with Miriam Hopkins in the bohemian world of Paris.

When the Code outlawed presentation of such sexually illicit relationships in movies, a disconcerting tension was introduced into relationships between the sexes. Men and women still wanted one another, but their desire was denied. Perhaps the best example of what the Code did to the onscreen love life of Hollywood's heroes and heroines can be found in *It Happened One Night*. In this instance, one of the screen's sexiest male performers, Clark Gable, plays a character who seems to have internalized the Code—who censors his own sexual desires. In one particularly romantic moonlit scene, Gable has just fixed Claudette Colbert a bed of straw on the ground and fetched carrots for her to eat. They talk and almost kiss, but Gable holds back, recalling (perhaps) that she is a married woman.

When they share a motel room for the night, it is Gable who erects a curtain (which he calls "the walls of Jericho") that separates their beds. Capra underscores the sexual significance of the walls by showing them undressing on either side. The walls not only satisfy the Code, but also come to symbolize the moral barrier to the satisfaction of the couple's desires; Gable's refusal to topple them until the last scene, when the couple are (finally) legally man and wife, demonstrates his own sexual restraint and sets up a tension that can only be resolved by the consummation of their relationship, which, in accordance with the codes of comic modesty, takes place offscreen.

Since the Code forbade its onscreen representation, sexuality was driven underground. In many screwball comedies, it resurfaced in the form of physical slapstick. In *Holiday* (1938), Cary Grant's handsprings and backflips became a coded expression of his sexual liberation. In *Twentieth Century* and *His Girl Friday* (1940), the heroine's kicking of the hero served as a sign of sexual intimacy, which 1930s audiences learned to read as clearly as they had the cutaway from the lovers' kiss to the outside of the closed bedroom door, or the crisscrossed logs burning in a fireplace, or the familiar waterfall.

But, in screwball comedy, the cutaway that symbolized the consummation of a romantic relationship virtually never took place. Lovers remained in an uncomfortable limbo, which best translated itself into a kind of tension or conflict, as if the characters themselves were somehow aware that, because of the Code, any final union between them would be perpetually frustrated. In *Bringing Up Baby*, a psychiatrist explained that "the love impulse in man frequently reveals itself in terms of conflict."

Screwball Slapstick

Sexual desire in the screwball comedy followed a similarly Freudian path, revealing itself in terms not only of conflict but also of combat. As Ed Sikov has observed, lovers love inflicting pain on one another: in *The Mad Miss Manton* (1948), Barbara Stanwyck slaps Henry Fonda, who then slaps her back; Barrymore jabs Lombard with a pin to improve her stage scream in *Twentieth Century*; and Fredric March expresses his love for Carole Lombard in *Nothing Sacred* (1937) by socking her in the jaw. The violence in *Nothing Sacred* exceeded the bounds of even screwball comedy's good taste. Critics noted the vicious meanness of the scene in which March repeatedly hits Lombard, who tries without success to hit him back. But the Code was always more concerned with sex than with violence and did little to curb such behavior.

Though much of the lovemaking tended to take place in the form of male violence directed against women, women occasionally got their licks in as well. In *Mr. and Mrs. Smith* (1941), Lombard slams the door in Robert Montgomery's face, giving him a bloody nose; in *The Lady Eve* (1941), Stanwyck quite literally strikes up a relationship with Fonda in *The Lady Eve* (1941) by tripping him as he walks past her table. Screwball comedies gave a literal twist to the tried-and-true metaphor of comic sexual relations. The battle of the sexes became an unending succession of combat sequences that concluded with an uneasy truce.

Unlike romantic comedies, which traced the evolution of youthful heroes and heroines into harmonic couples and which tended to conclude with their blissful union or marriage, screwball comedies, rooted as they were in conflict, did not necessarily move toward the constitution of the couple or toward some other form of consummation. More often than not, they began with a couple already constituted, whose harmony was then shattered, disturbed by internal strife or conflict.

Love, War, and Unresolved Endings

Thus, *Mr. and Mrs. Smith* (1941), a screwball comedy of manners, opens with the Smiths (Robert Montgomery and Carole Lombard), locked in their bedroom, where they have vowed to remain until the argument that they began three days ago is settled. Once this dispute is finally resolved, their marriage picks up where it left off, only to come unraveled again when they discover that, owing to a legal technicality, they were never really married. For the remainder of the film, the couple continue to spar, waging both physical and psychological warfare with one another until the final scene when they achieve a stalemate of sorts, locked in a wrestling hold that doubles as a tentative sexual embrace.

If one of the themes of comedy is that of integration, then the screwball comedy genuinely played with that theme, looking at it from a variety of perspectives, including not only its inverse—disintegration—but also its variations, including quasi- or pseudo-integration. Films did not always conclude with the comic resolution of all of the problems which beset the couple. Much as screwball narratives often began with a couple on the verge of breaking up, so they just as frequently ended with a tenuous reconciliation.

By the end of *His Girl Friday,* nothing much really changes in the Cary Grant-Rosalind Russell relationship, except that he has forced her to see the absurdity of her proposed marriage to Albany insurance salesman Ralph Bellamy. The reasons that lead Russell to divorce Grant remain. However, after spending a day together trying to outwit one another, each realizes the worthiness of the other as an opponent. Russell decides that an unconventional and unstable life with Grant is better than the deadeningly conventional, dull, and ordinary marriage that awaits her with Bellamy.

Even in films such as *Bringing Up Baby,* in which a couple is created from scratch, as it were, courtship was far from harmonious and the final embrace far from idyllic. As Grant confesses to Hepburn, in moments of quiet he is strangely drawn to her, but "there haven't been any quiet moments . . . and [their] relationship has been a series of misadventures from beginning to end." In the final scene, after Hepburn has toppled his brontosaurus, Grant reflexively pulls her to safety and sits together with her on the top of a huge scaffold, but their misadventures as a couple are clearly not over. Hepburn's aggressive actions have, once again, left Grant speechless. When he puts his arms around her at the end, his hug is as much an acknowledgment of surrender as it is a declaration of love.

In *Twentieth Century,* Barrymore and Lombard go through romantic cycles—they become a couple, split, then reunite. Their relationship, which begins as a struggle for power in which Barrymore dominates her, evolves through a series of themes and variations on power, with Lombard defiantly asserting her own independence in response to each of his similar gestures. The squabbling with which the film ends becomes a form of romantic exchange, as each tries to respond in kind to the other, proving themselves equal to one another, and, through a screwball kind of logic, proving that they are thus made for each other.

The Politics of Screwball Comedies

Andrew Bergman argues that screwball comedies bridged class differences, solving the social problems of the Depression era. Capra comedies such as *It Happened One Night* and *You Can't Take It With You* (1938) fit this formula, as did one or two films written (*Easy Living,* 1937) and/or directed (*The Lady Eve,* 1941; *Palm Beach Story,* 1942) by Preston Sturges. But an equal number of screwball comedies, especially those directed by Howard Hawks (*Twentieth Century, Bringing Up Baby, His Girl Friday*) and Leo McCarey (*The Awful Truth,* 1937) or written by Sidney Buchman (*Theodora Goes Wild,* 1936) and Ben Hecht (*Nothing Sacred,* 1937) ignored Capra's populist rhetoric, subordinating overt political issues, such as class difference, to covert sexual issues, such as the threats posed to the male order by the sexually aggressive female, the instability of sexual relations, or simple sexual liberation.

Nonetheless, screwball comedies gave expression to the political and social concerns of the period. Bergman claims that the screwball comedy was politically conservative, if not reactionary. The anarchic comedies of the Marx Brothers assaulted the social order; the essential cohesiveness of the screwball comedy sought, in Bergman's view, to patch things up. But if screwball comedy is placed in the larger context of the development of screen comedy in the years between the two world wars, then it can be seen as marking a rebellious turn in the romantic comedy in response to anarchic comedy, such as that of the Marx Brothers or Wheeler and Woolsey.

Screwball comedy, like the anarchic comedian comedies, grew out of the social and economic turmoil of the stock market crash and the Depression. Much as the Marx Brothers exposed the arbitrariness of established institutions and the absurdity of traditional codes of social behavior, the screwball comedy revealed the essential artifice of the conventions that governed sexual relations, attacking the supposed stability of its chief institutions, such as marriage, and exposing the tensions beneath the traditional happy endings that concluded earlier romantic comedies. It reflected the reshuffling of the delicate balance of sexual power. Women already enjoyed the political enfranchisement granted them under the Nineteenth Amendment and a (limited) social equality, which found women doing traditionally male things such as smoking, drinking, and driving cars. But during the 1930s, women began to take a more aggressive role in economic affairs, becoming the breadwinners of the Depression-era family by working as unskilled help in low-paying jobs when their fathers and husbands were laid off or by pursuing white-collar careers as working women.

Though the screwball film did not, as Bergman insists, heal class difference, it did elevate class conflict onto a higher plane, admitting lower- and middle-class types, such as reporters and secretaries, to an upper-class milieu such as the sophisticated world of either the madcap heiress or the heir to the family business. In this upper stratum of society, class hostility found full expression as basic social conflicts, often cast in the form of sexual antagonism, played out in an inconclusive, Beckettesque fashion. The majority of the films tended to side with the lower- or middle-class protagonist, whose cynical critique of wealth and privilege echoed the democratic and populist attitudes of both the film's makers and its targeted audience.

Yet these attitudes also found acceptance among the upper-class characters against whom they were directed, who not only seemed to agree with their worst critics and to launch into their own self-criticism, but who also rewarded the messengers bringing them word of their own faults. Thus, in *It Happened One Night,* the newspaper reporter marries the poor little rich girl—with her father's blessing; and in *Easy Living, You Can't Take It With You,* and *The Lady Eve,* the socially inferior heroine proves to possess a spirit and integrity that reveals her to be superior to the upper class, which she joins through marriage to the business tycoon's son.

After the Screwball

Thesis Comedy

During the 1930s, Hollywood comedy developed a political consciousness. At one edge of the comic spectrum, Ernst Lubitsch's playful, apparently frivolous comedies of manners (*Trouble in Paradise,* 1932; *The Merry Widow,* 1934; *Angel,* 1937; *Ninotchka,* 1939; and *The Shop Around the Corner,* 1941) betrayed a greater and greater concern for social issues as the decade progressed and as his comic settings shifted from an upper-class (*Trouble in Paradise*) to a more middle-class (*Shop Around the Corner*) milieu. Chaplin and Capra pioneered the thesis comedy—comedy with an overt political message. *Modern Times* celebrated the common workingman and denounced the advent of automation and the machine age. *The Great Dictator* (1940) satirized fascism, in the persons of two dictators, Adenoid Hynkel (Chaplin) and Benzino Napolloni (Jack Oakie), who were undisguised caricatures of Adolph Hitler and Benito Mussolini, respectively; after the war, Chaplin continued his assault on militarism, the Cold War, and the impersonality of contemporary mass culture in *Monsieur Verdoux* (1947) and *A King in New York* (1957).

Frank Capra criticized the New Deal, intellectual pretension, and established culture in *Mr. Deeds Goes to Town* (1936); corruption in government in

Mr. Smith Goes to Washington (1939), and the protofascism of big business in *Meet John Doe* (1941). He sketched out his ideal plan for an agrarian, populist paradise, which he and novelist John Hilton called Shangri-La, in *Lost Horizon* (1937).

Chaplin's and Capra's politicization of comedy became, in turn, the target for another comedy by screenwriter and director, Preston Sturges. Sturges's central character in *Sullivan's Travels* (1941) is a Hollywood director who suddenly develops a social consciousness, abandons the making of escapist comedies (with names such as *Ants in Your Plants of 1939*), and sets off on a cross-country journey to research a prospective film (entitled *Oh Brother, Where Art Thou?*) about the poor, the unemployed, and the homeless. On his travels, Sullivan discovers that film comedy does have tremendous social value, providing a necessary release for audiences from intolerable misery and suffering, and he resumes his career as a director of escapist comedies.

War Comedies

Wartime comedies played a similarly crucial role in boosting morale. Abbott and Costello starred in a string of 15 comedies between 1941 and 1945, including the pre-Pearl Harbor service comedy, *Buck Privates* (1941). Bob Hope entertained the troops onscreen in films such as *Star Spangled Rhythm* (1942) and offscreen in his USO tours. In addition to his highly popular "road" pictures with Bing Crosby and Dorothy Lamour (*Singapore*, 1940); *Zanzibar*, 1941; *Morocco*, 1942; *Utopia*, 1945), Hope cringed his way through two war-related films, *Caught in the Draft* (1941) and *They Got Me Covered* (1943).

Home-front comedies provided comic relief for the more serious waging of the war, but often did so in somewhat perverse ways, getting comic mileage out of Hope's onscreen cowardice and out of problems at home, ranging from the housing shortages in Washington, DC (*The More the Merrier*, 1943) to the hypocrisy and corruption of small-town America (*Hail the Conquering Hero*, 1944). In the latter film, duplicity invades not only the private sphere of the family (a son pretends to his mother that he is serving in the Marines when he is really 4-F) and the couple (his girlfriend, though believing him to be fighting overseas, nonetheless dumps him for the mayor's son), but also the public sphere of politics (the major—the pawn of a political boss—endorses a self-serving civic policy of business as usual that undermines the town's efforts in support of the war).

As a home-front morale booster, the film was profoundly ambivalent. Although it mocked such American institutions as "momism" and the cult of the returning war hero, it reinscribed those same values. In the film, the virtues of the family and individual heroism are reinstated through the intervention of a squad of Marines, veterans of the Pacific war, who both believe in Mom and are genuine war heroes. The Marines make everything all right, proving that the same spirit that inspires the war effort, if brought home, can restore the traditional values of small-town America that the cynicism of the war years had permitted to deteriorate.

Sex and Neurosis: The Postwar Era

After the war, comedies continued to take on topical issues, such as the inter-marriage of American GIs with Europeans (*I Was A Male War Bride*, 1949), the movement of middle-class families to the suburbs (*Mr. Blandings Builds His Dream House*, 1948), and the development of radical new technologies that could transform the processes of nature (*Monkey Business*, 1952). Although the socio-historical situations were different, the sexual dynamics of these films looked back to those of the screwball comedies, which were built on a fundamental antagonism between the sexes. Slapstick comedy enjoyed a revival in the unlikely figure of Cary Grant, who excelled not only in Keaton-like physical stunts (*War Bride, Monkey Business*) but in rather sophisticated character comedy as well (as seen in *Blandings*, 1948, and *The Bachelor and the Bobby-Soxer* and *The Bishop's Wife*, both 1947).

As filmmakers began to test the limits of the Production Code, the restrictions of the Code began to relax somewhat. In turn, screen comedy became more and more overt in its treatment of sexual issues, giving rise to a new sub-genre—the sex comedy. Otto Preminger openly defied the Code in *The Moon Is Blue* (1953), which assaulted would-be censors not only in its open discussion of premarital sex but also in its use of previously taboo words such as "pregnant," "seduction," and "mistress," and the term "professional virgin" (a phrase coined by the film to describe the sexually teasing behavior of the film's heroine.)

Preminger successfully released the film without the required Production Code seal and, when it became one of the top-grossing films of the year, the rest of Hollywood took notice, and sex comedies grew racier and racier. Marilyn Monroe's screen character evolved from a sexually naive gold digger serving as the target of dumb blonde jokes (*Gentlemen Prefer Blondes* and *How to Marry a Millionaire*, 1953), into a figure of male sexual fantasy (*The Seven Year Itch*, 1955), and finally into a more worldly, sexually aware, but somewhat embittered romantic (*Some Like It Hot*, 1959). Sex comedy reached a new low in inspired vulgarity through the collaborative efforts of Jayne Mansfield and director Frank Tashlin. In *The Girl Can't Help It* (1956), Mansfield's sexual gyrations as she walks melt the iceman's ice, boil the milkman's milk, and shatter the eye-glasses of male onlookers. In *Will Success Spoil Rock Hunter?* (1957), her kiss pops popcorn in Tony Randall's pocket, a gag that Tashlin then followed with a seemingly unending string of phallic jokes.

Beneath the apparent complacency and conformism of 1950s America lurked the tell-tale twitches, involuntary spasms, split personalities, and deep-seated neuroses of Jerry Lewis, who gave expression to the anxieties character-izing that era of cold war politics and sexual repression. In *Artists and Models* (1955) and *Hollywood or Bust* (1956), Lewis caricatured the typical 1950s con-sumer, playing the part of an avid reader of horror comic books (and subscriber to their fantasy worlds) in the former film and a star-struck movie fan in the lat-ter. Dubbed "le roi du crazy" (the king of crazy) by French critics, Lewis's char-acter consumes mass culture so passionately that it drives him insane.

Marilyn Monroe emerges as the realization of Tom Ewell's sexual fantasies in Billy Wilder's wide-screen sex comedy, *The Seven Year Itch* (1955).

Courtesy of 20th Century-Fox

Comedy and Consumerism

Sex comedies of the 1950s also became the sites for a critique of contemporary mass culture. Wilder satirized paperback publishing in *Seven Year Itch*; Tashlin took the pop music industry over the coals in *Girl Can't Help It* and sent up movie stars, television, and the advertising industry in *Rock Hunter*. The latter film begins with a series of derisive television commercials, lampoons 1950s breast fetishism, laughs at rampant consumerism, derides grey-flannel dreams of success on Madison Avenue, exposes the dependence of corporate executives on alcohol and tranquilizers, mocks the faddish fascination with Freudian psychoanalysis, and holds the culture's fetishization of the bathroom up to ridicule.

A few years later, Billy Wilder's *The Apartment* (1960) takes a hard look at the relationship between sex and success in contemporary corporate America, casting the various members of the business community in the unflattering roles of pimps, prostitutes, and johns. The film's nebbishlike hero (Jack Lemmon) rises spectacularly through the bureaucratic hierarchy of a New York insurance company by letting his male superiors use his apartment for adulterous affairs with female employees. The film implicitly criticizes both the old-boy network of executives who take advantage of their positions to secure special favors for themselves and the ambitious young white-collar worker who learns how to play the game of office politics and who sells out to his superiors in exchange for promotion. It thus depicts a system dominated by corruption from top to bottom.

But the film concludes with a repudiation by those at the bottom of those at the top as Lemmon resigns from his much-coveted executive-level position, and an executive's much-abused mistress (elevator operator Shirley MacLaine) finally extricates herself from an adulterous relationship and joins Lemmon in his rebellion against the system.

Alienation and Self-Reflection: The 1960s and Beyond

Black Comedy of the 1960s

The bittersweet nihilism of Wilder in sex comedies such as *Irma la Douce* (1963) and *Kiss Me, Stupid* (1964) sets the mood for much of black comedy of the 1960s. "Black comedy" is a term used to describe comedies that make fun of dark subjects such as death (*The Loved One*, 1965), morbidity (*Harold and Maude, 1971*), and murder (*The Trouble with Harry,* 1955). The military becomes the source of dark humor in Stanley Kubrick's apocalyptic *Dr. Strangelove* (1964), which teaches us to laugh at (if not love) the bomb, in Joseph Heller's and Mike Nichols' World War II satire *Catch-22* (1970), in Robert Altman's Korean war farce *M*A*S*H* (1970), and in George Roy Hill's adaptation of Kurt Vonnegut's *Slaughterhouse Five* (1972). These critiques of the cold war, governmental bureaucracy, and American militarism found a receptive audience in the cynical college-age generation that led the antiwar movement in the late 1960s.

A similar critical sensibility informs Mike Nichols's direction of *The Graduate* (1967). This study of alienated youth suggests that no one over 30 can be trusted, that the older generation is obsessed with false, materialistic values, and that parents seek to use their children as a means of realizing their own ambitions. Comic shots, framed through fish tanks or diving masks, convey the alienation and entrapment of the younger generation in a social system that threatens to suffocate them.

At the same time, the commodification of culture that was taking place in the postwar era resulted in the proliferation of images of commercial products on television, in newspapers, and in magazines. In response to advertisements that encouraged us to consume, pop artists such as Andy Warhol appropriated those images, remade them, and sent them back (as well as sending them up) in a transformed state. Warhol's paintings of Brillo boxes or of Campbell's Soup cans pioneered the age of the put-on, send-up, and spoof, which conveyed the jaded skepticism of the young moviegoers who had been raised in the television era and who brought a new sophistication to their consumption of images.

Soup cans were not the only mass-produced products scrutinized by Warhol and others; the movies also provided subjects for parody. Warhol's own films, such as *Lonesome Cowboys* (1968), as well as several of those that he produced, such as *Frankenstein* and *Dracula* (both 1974), spoofed traditional Hollywood genres. At around the same time, mainstream humorists such as Mel Brooks took a critical look at familiar film genres (and at brand-name directors such as Alfred Hitchcock) in a series of highly popular, if not quite pop art, parodies of the Western (*Blazing Saddles*, 1974), the horror film (*Young Frankenstein*, 1974), the silent film (*Silent Movie*, 1976), the science-fiction film (*Spaceballs*, 1987), and the Hitchcock thriller (*High Anxiety*, 1977).

Woody Allen and the Art of Self-Reflection

Woody Allen's uniquely self-reflexive comic style has proved ideal for film parody. Allen not only makes fun of his own screen characters' hang-ups, fears, anxieties, and obsessions, but he also casts them in a series of familiar genre situations, ranging from the crime docudrama (*Take the Money and Run*, 1969) and the science-fiction thriller (*Sleeper*, 1973) to overt parodies of literary and film classics such as *Love and Death* (1975), which reworks Leo Tolstoy's *War and Peace*; *Play It Again, Sam* (1972), which pays tribute to *Casablanca* (1942); and *Stardust Memories* (1980), which serves as Allen's *8 1/2* (Fellini, 1963). With *Annie Hall* (1977) and *Manhattan* (1979), Allen made semiautobiographical melodramas that document the odyssey of a New York Jewish comedian beset by midlife crises and plagued with Bergmanesque self-doubt, who jokes his way through the contemporary wasteland of urban existence. The richness of experience that the Allen character seems to be seeking proves to lie in the past—in the escapist movies of the 1930s, which become the focus of *The Purple Rose of Cairo* (1985), in the postwar glory days of radio, which he celebrates in *Radio Days* (1987), in the Broadway theaters of the 1920s in *Bullets Over Broadway* (1994), and in the heyday of the 1930s film musical (*Everyone Says I Love You*, 1996). Yet Allen's comedy, like that of Brooks, proves too idiosyncratic and too ethnic for mass tastes.

From Animal Comedies to Ironic Romantic Comedies

The kinkier comedy of the original *Saturday Night Live* group (Chevy Chase, Bill Murray, John Belushi, Dan Ackroyd, Eddie Murphy, and Gilda Radner) played to a demographically broader, nonethnic audience in top-grossing films such as *Ghostbusters* (1984, 1989), *Beverly Hills Cop* (1984, 1987, 1994), *National Lampoon's Animal House* (1978), and *Coming to America* (1988). A frequent guest host on *Saturday Night Live*, Steve Martin single-handedly set out to restore the romantic comedy to preeminence in films such as *The Man With Two Brains* (1983), *All of Me* (1984), *Roxanne* (1987), *L.A. Story* (1991), and *Housesitter* (1991) as well as the family comedy in *Parenthood* (1989) and *Father of the Bride* (1991, 1995). Chevy Chase emerged as the father-knows-best of the 1980s as Clark Griswald in a series of National Lampoon *Vacation* films (1983, 1985, 1989). Yet the major contribution of this group proved to be the creation of a new comic subgenre— what William Paul refers to as the animal comedy—which began with *Animal House*, starring John Belushi, and continued in raunchy, exploitational teen-sex

There's Something About Mary
(Cameron Diaz).

comedies such as the *Porky's* films (1981, 1983, 1985), *Bachelor Party* (1984), *Fast Times at Ridgemont High* (1982), and *Revenge of the Nerds* (1984). What characterizes these comedies is an interest in adolescent sexuality (from masturbation to intercourse), a graphical grossness (from food fights and belching to lower bodily functions), and a comic celebration of vulgarity in general, which marks a new explicitness in screen comedy rivaling that found in recent horror films.

The unending cycle of generic development saw the animal comedy replaced in popularity in the late 1980s by more traditional family comedies, ranging from the somewhat crude *Problem Child* (1990, 1991) films which looked at the double-edged nature of child rearing for modern parents in the 1990s, to the more refined *3 Men and a Baby* (1987), *3 Men and a Little Lady* (1990), *Parenthood* (1989), *Look Who's Talking* (1989, 1990), and *Home Alone* (1990, 1992). In *Home Alone,* ambivalent attitudes toward children are submerged beneath a slapstick plot that celebrates cartoon–like violence directed toward outsiders who threaten the sanctity of the home. Audiences delight in Macauley Culkin's independence and ingenuity as an eight-year-old who is inadvertently left behind when his parents, brothers, and sisters fly to Paris for Christmas vacation. But beneath the surface of this contemporary comedy lies a deep-seated anxiety about the nuclear family in the 1990s, addressing, in particular, the unspoken guilt felt by working parents of latchkey children. But perhaps even more disturbing than its portrait of the preoccupied parents whose self-absorption results in the neglect of a child is the film's suggestion that the child can do quite well without his family—and that the most intense relationships in his life are with outsiders.

The traditional romantic comedy virtually disappeared in the 1970s and early 1980s, unable to hold its own against the decidedly nonromantic animal comedy. Frank Krutnik suggests that the new openness about sex that characterized the films of the 1960s through the 1980s led to the decline of the romantic comedy and to its replacement by sex comedies. The sexual revolution of the 1960s undermined traditional notions about romantic heterosexual relationships. For Krutnik, comedies of the 1990s sought to "reconcile old-fashioned romance with the erotic openness that is a legacy of the 1960s" *There's Something About Mary* (1998) thus combines elements of animal comedy (genitalia stuck in a zipper, ejaculate as hair mousse) with elements of romantic comedy (the innocence of the hero's love for Mary). Though the love felt by hero Ted (Ben Stiller) is pure, the film views that love ironically, through the device of a quasi-Brechtian narration (the singer who comments on the action) and the mirroring of the hero's love for Mary in the neurotic/obsessive behavior of her other suitors. The point is that we can never go back to the innocent love of *An Affair to Remember* (1957), but we can invoke that innocence in *Sleepless in Seattle* (1993) by knowingly referring to the earlier film and reworking its romantic relationship from the 1990s perspective of innocence lost.

From the childlike regression of the animal comedies of the 1970s and 1980s and the right of passage undertaken in the kid comedies of the 1990s to the rise of the ironic romantic comedy in the 1990s and the first decade of the new century, American screen comedy continues to document the growing pains of American culture. From Chaplin, Keaton, and Lloyd to Allen, Martin, Murphy, Murray, Myers and Carrey, comedians shape a comic vision of American life that reveals its unconscious. Freud noted that "only jokes that have a purpose run the risk of meeting with people who do not want to listen to them." Beneath its witty dialogue and behind its clever sight gags, American film comedy has a latent social agenda, addressing controversial issues in such a disarming way that they appear to lose all controversy. But it is possible to look through the laughter to catch sight of the underlying issues and social problems that give rise to comedy and see that American screen comedy is not always a laughing matter, that it contains serious questions that society can only address to itself in nonserious ways.

■■■ SELECT FILMOGRAPHY

The Immmigrant (1917)	*It Happened One Night* (1934)
Safety Last (1923)	*Twentieth Century* (1934)
Sherlock Jr. (1924)	*Modern Times* (1936)
The Freshman (1925)	*The Awful Truth* (1937)
Seven Chances (1925)	*Bringing Up Baby* (1938)
The General (1926)	*The Lady Eve* (1941)
The Circus (1928)	*Sullivan's Travels* (1941)
Design for Living (1933)	*Hail the Conquering Hero*
Duck Soup (1933)	(1944)

I Was A Male War Bride (1949)
The Seven Year Itch (1955)
Will Success Spoil Rock Hunter? (1957)
Some Like It Hot (1959)
The Apartment (1960)
The Graduate (1967)
M*A*S*H (1970)
Blazing Saddles (1974)
Annie Hall (1977)
National Lampoon's Animal House (1978)
Manhattan (1979)
Fast Times at Ridgemont High (1982)

Trading Places (1983)
Revenge of the Nerds (1984)
The Purple Rose of Cairo (1985)
Moonstruck (1987)
Coming to America (1988)
Working Girl (1988)
Big (1988)
Home Alone (1990)
Pretty Woman (1990)
Forrest Gump (1994)
As Good as It Gets (1997)
The Wedding Singer (1998)
There's Something About Mary (1998)
My Big Fat Greek Wedding (2002)

■■■ SELECT BIBLIOGRAPHY

AUERBACH, ERICH. *Mimesis: The Representation of Reality in Western Literature.* Garden City, NY: Anchor, 1957.

BERGMAN, ANDREW. *We're in the Money: Depression America and its Films.* New York: New York University Press, 1971

CAVELL, STANLEY. *Pursuits of Happiness: The Hollywood Comedy of Remarriage.* Cambridge, MA: Harvard University Press, 1981.

HORTON, ANDREW, ed. *Comedy/Cinema/Theory.* Berkeley: University of California Press, 1991.

KRUTNIK, FRANK. "Conforming Passions? Contemporary Romantic Comedy," in Steve Neale, ed., *Genre and Contemporary Hollywood.* London: BFI, 2002.

MAST, GERALD. *The Comic Mind.* Chicago: University of Chicago Press, 1979.

PAUL, WILLIAM. *Ernst Lubitsch's American Comedy.* New York: Columbia University Press, 1983.

————. *Laughing/Screaming.* New York: Columbia University Press, 1994.

SARRIS, ANDREW. "Sex Comedy without the Sex," *American Film* (March 1978), 8–15.

SIKOV, ED. *Screwball: Hollywood's Madcap Romantic Comedies.* New York: Crown, 1989.

CHAPTER **9**

War and Cinema

A WORLD OF EXTREMES

Film producer, writer, director, and World War II veteran Samuel Fuller, appearing as himself in Jean-Luc Godard's *Pierrot le fou* (1965), declares that "film is like a battleground: love, hate, action, violence, death . . . in a word, emotion." If film is like a battleground, then the war movie is potentially the ultimate form of the cinema, creating conditions in which extreme expressions of love, hate, action, violence, and death can find representation. If the cinema is, in part, a medium well-suited for the depiction of spectacle, the war film is uniquely capable of maximizing that spectacle: marshaling thousands of troops in battle formation; blowing up bridges, battleships, ammunition dumps, airfields, towns, and cities; and laying waste to not only individual armies but entire nations as well.

Much as the musical provides cathartic release from the mundane sphere of its narrative through escapist flight into a more fantastic world of song and dance, the war film has its own "production numbers" in the form of explosive action sequences, superhuman feats of bravery, and spectacular displays of mass destruction. But while characters in musicals leap into a more perfect, utopian world of harmony, energy, intensity, and abundance, characters in war films cautiously enter a hellish no-man's-land of violence and death in which life is not ideal. Rather, life in the state of war is, as Thomas Hobbes once wrote of life in the state of nature, "nasty, brutish, and short."

The war movie plunges its characters into a world of extremes where the slightest action (or even inaction) results in death—their own or that of their comrades. One of the images that best conveys the absolutist, either/or nature of human existence in the genre is that of the GI who inadvertently steps on an enemy land mine he knows will explode if he makes a move (see *Fixed Bayonets*, 1951; *The Boys in Company C*, 1978). His life, as well as that of the man standing next to him, depends on his self-control. He is forced to remain perfectly motionless while a comrade attempts to disarm the mine. Then he and his buddies carefully retrace their steps out of the minefield. Life (if you can call it that) is lived moment by moment. Each step becomes a nightmarish choice between life and death—a choice in which there is no real choice, only luck. Michael Cimino, the director of *The Deer Hunter* (1978), set forth a somewhat similar image, though one that proved to be more appropriate to the Vietnam War than the traditional us versus them concept of the GI in a minefield. For Cimino, the Vietnam War was intentionally self-destructive; it was like a game of Russian roulette.

BREAKING RULES

A Suspension of Morality

The battlefield is a world in which the laws, beliefs, behavior, and morality of civilization are suspended. It is not merely permitted for one man to kill another; it is imperative for him to do so. War rewrites civil and criminal law. To charge a soldier who kills the enemy with murder is, as Capt. Willard (Martin Sheen) reminds us in *Apocalypse Now* (1979), "like giving out speeding tickets at the Indy 500." There are, of course, rules of war, established by the Geneva Convention. And with the notable exception of *Saving Private Ryan* (1998), American soldiers in World War II films attempt, for the most part, to observe them. But, in the Vietnam war film, even those rules are honored as much in the breach as in the observance. Expediency governs morality; might makes right; the ends justify the means.

Although the difference between right and wrong is somewhat obscured and thus no longer absolute in the war film, relative moral distinctions remain. The good guys (usually us) fight fair and the bad guys (usually them) do not. Our enemies are shown not only torturing captured soldiers but also killing innocent civilians. In *The Heart of Humanity* (1918), Erich von Stroheim's Prussian officer, distracted from his attempted rape of a Red Cross nurse by the screams of an infant, picks the child up out of its cradle and tosses it out of a second-story window to its death. In *Bataan* (1943), the Japanese mutilate a Filipino soldier, fire on a Red Cross ambulance, and strafe a column of refugees, killing women and children. In *The North Star* (1943), a Nazi doctor first orders the children of a captured Ukrainian village to be fed, then forces them to give blood transfusions for German wounded; one child dies when too much blood is drained out of his body.

Even the good guys break the rules on occasion, though they are generally seen as motivated by either moral outrage, expediency, or compassion. And their violations of official codes of conduct generally take place in the Korean and Vietnam wars in which America's moral status is not as clearly delineated as it was in World War II. In *The Steel Helmet* (1951), an American sergeant deliberately shoots a North Korean prisoner of war in retaliation for his callous response to the death of a young Korean boy. In *Apocalypse Now,* Willard shoots a dying Vietnamese girl rather than let his hypocritical comrades, who originally wounded her, delay his mission by taking her to a place where she might obtain medical assistance. At the end of *Full Metal Jacket* (1987), a Marine known as "Joker" complies with the pleas of a wounded female Vietcong sniper, who is writhing on the floor in pain, and kills her.

The fact that soldiers commanded by Capt. Miller (Tom Hanks) in *Saving Private Ryan* repeatedly shoot surrendering German soldiers marks the film as a post-Vietnam, revisionist account of Allied behavior in the Second World War. Much as the film acknowledges in grisly detail the incredible violence of combat, it also depicts the immediate aftermath of combat as a moral lacuna in which the laws of war are put on hiatus and men traumatized by the experience of combat seek catharsis in brutal acts of retribution against the enemy.

Deviant Narratives: From Individual to Group Goals

As an ultimate form of the cinema, the war film is empowered to suspend even the laws of classical narrative construction. Traditional Hollywood films center on the individual, whose goals and desires drive the story line and whose psychological complexity becomes the focus of narrative exposition. In war films, the needs of the individual frequently give way to those of the group. The exceptional circumstances of the battlefield force individuals to place their own needs beneath those of the platoon, squadron, division, battalion, fleet, army, and nation.

Air Force (1943) details the transformation of assorted individual characters into a cohesive fighting unit whose own identities are subsumed in the larger identity of "Mary Ann," the B-17 bomber on which they serve during the first few days of World War II. *Twelve O'Clock High* (1949) tells a similar story of a flight commander who transforms a ragged collection of bomber pilots, navigators, bombardiers, and gunners into a precision fighting unit of 21 B-17s, which are drilled to fly together in tight formation, drop bombs in unison on their

Courtesy of Warner Bros.

The crew in *Air Force* (1943) functions as a multicultural group: the Polish Winocki (John Garfield, left), the WASP crew chief (Harry Carey), the Jewish Weinstein (George Tobias), and the Swedish Peterson (Ward Wood).

target, and protect one another from attacking enemy fighters. In *Saving Private Ryan*, the chaotic slaughter of American troops on Omaha Beach is presented in terms of a series of vignettes in which individual soldiers are randomly maimed or killed. It is only when Capt. Miller gathers the survivors together and forms a combat *team* that the men fight as a unit, destroy an enemy pillbox, make a hole in the Germans' defenses, and win the day. From a somewhat different perspective, the theme of *Black Hawk Down* (2002), a film about the American humanitarian mission in Somalia in 1993, is "leave no man behind." The mission on which the men are sent may not exactly make sense, but the Army Rangers and Delta Force specialists know what they're fighting for: "It's about the men next to you. That's all it is." The group becomes all-important.

Indeed, individual heroism is often represented in the war film as a form of self-indulgence, and thus as counterproductive to the accomplishment of the collective goals of the group. Tension between the desires of the individual and the needs of the group is regularly worked out through an educational process during which the individual (such as John Garfield's Winocki in *Air Force*) learns how crucial his cooperation is to the survival of the team. Or it is resolved through the individualistic outsider's ritualistic, sacrificial death.

In both *The War Lover* and *Hell is for Heroes* (1962), Steve McQueen played alienated loners whose heroic actions come in direct violation of orders.

Unwilling or unable to function as a member of a combat team, the loner's recklessness endangers his comrades. He ultimately harnesses his heroism in the form of a self-destructive energy. He then uses this energy to save his crew or to transform himself into a suicidal weapon, which he then directs against the enemy. Thus, in the former film, the loner holds his damaged plane on course, sacrificing himself so that his crew can have time to bail out. In the latter film, he straps himself with explosives, charges an enemy pillbox, and blows himself up in an attempt to destroy it. He does all of this in order to put an end to the battle that continues, however, to be waged after his death.

Even in a film such as *Sergeant York* (1941), which celebrates the individual real-life exploits of one of World War I's most famous combat heroes, Alvin York (Gary Cooper) attributes his killing of 25 German soldiers and his single-handed capture of 132 others to a desire to protect his buddies, who are pinned down by enemy machine-gun fire. The only place for individual heroism in war films is in service to the larger needs of the group.

SEXUAL COMBAT: MASCULINITY IN THE WAR FILM

Oedipal Battles

Typical Hollywood plots hinge on love triangles, trace the vicissitudes of star-crossed lovers, and conclude with the last-minute embrace of the hero and heroine. In war films, the absence of women—and even their marginal presence—results in an entirely different set of sexual dynamics. Headstrong recruits engage in oedipal romance or warfare (or in both, as in *Platoon*, 1986) with their top sergeants. Oedipal rivalry becomes a means of proving their courage and manhood to these older, more experienced, father figures.

In *Sands of Iwo Jima* (1949), a sensitive young Marine comes to terms with his dead father through an oedipal conflict with a tough, no-nonsense sergeant (John Wayne), who served with and idolized the boy's father. In *Apocalypse Now*, Willard's similarly oedipal relationship with Col. Kurtz (Marlon Brando) is crystallized for us on a figurative level when he finds the letter Kurtz wrote to his son in Kurtz's dossier and reads it, implicitly identifying, as its reader, with the person to whom it is addressed. It is finalized for us literally when, at the end, the would-be son kills Kurtz and takes his place. Willard becomes Kurtz's emissary to the world, bringing the latter's knowledge of the horror of war back with him to explain to Kurtz's son and to all others who need to understand the essential nature of war in general and that of the Vietnam War in particular.

Conventional Homoeroticism

When women enter this predominantly male world, they are often the shared objects of desire of two or more soldiers, who compete with one another for their affection. This romantic rivalry provides the chief dramatic structure for both versions of *What Price Glory?* (1926, remade in 1952), the World War I comedy in which Capt. Flagg battles Sgt. Quirt over the affections of a French innkeeper's daughter, Charmaine. The reappearance of this motif in *Hot Shots!* (1991), in which the hero (Charlie Sheen) and his nemesis both court the same girl, testifies to its status as a timeworn genre convention.

In enjoying sexual relations with the same women, the men enjoy what psychoanalysts describe as a displaced homoerotic or homosocial relationship with one another in which their rivalry becomes a form not of sexual competition but of exchange. The abduction and gang rape of a Vietnamese girl by several members of an American army patrol in *Casualties of War* (1989) provides a more brutal example of the rather complex way in which the male relationships in war films are bound up with notions of homosexual desire. Here, as in so many other instances of gang rape, the rape victim serves as a means of sexual exchange among men—as a bond that they all share and that solidifies their ties to one another.

A Midnight Clear (1992), set in World War II, conceives of male camaraderie in similarly homoerotic terms. The film's buddies not only all sleep with the same young girl on their last leave together, but when one of the comrades dies, they also take off their clothes and ritualistically bathe him, conducting a sexualized communion of sorts.

Masculine/Feminine

Women pose a variety of threats to men in war films. The mere appearance of a wife on screen introduces an emotional element that is often realized in terms of the man's essential vulnerability. Thus, in *Thirty Seconds Over Tokyo* (1944), the syrupy scenes between Capt. Ted Lawson (Van Johnson) and his wife (Phyllis Thaxter) presage his injury and the subsequent amputation of his leg. At the beginning of *Air Force*, the farewell scene between Capt. Quincannon (John Ridgely) and his wife introduces an emotional vulnerability in the hero that ultimately makes him one of the most likely candidates among the crew to die before the film reaches its conclusion. The pervasive familiarity of the convention is brought home in *Hot Shots!* when one of its scenes parodies an airman's farewell to his wife just before his comic crash. The implicit message of this motif is that relations with a woman suggest a vulnerability in the hero to that which lies outside the masculine world of war—to the feminine—and this vulnerability will eventually destroy him.

If every human psyche consists of masculine and feminine elements, the psyche of the male soldier must be reshaped to repress the feminine—to transform him into a ruthless, unemotional, fighting machine. In every war film, masculinity is put in crisis, as it were; the toughness of the hero becomes an issue crucial to both his survival and that of his fellow soldiers. Drill sergeants in Marine boot camps repeatedly refer to young recruits as "ladies" (*Boys in Company C*, 1978; *Full Metal Jacket*, 1987; *Heartbreak Ridge*, 1986). Sgt. Zack in

Courtesy of Warner Bros.

The drill instructor (Lee Ermey) turns basic training into a course in masculinity in *Full Metal Jacket* (1987).

Steel Helmet draws on a similar tactic, referring to his untested troops as "ballerinas." This explicit challenge to the manhood of the recruits is designed to force them to overcome that which is considered weak or feminine in their nature and become hardened Marines—that is, to become men.

In *Full Metal Jacket,* boot camp becomes a course of instruction in masculinity, including a series of exercises in which the men are forced to train while holding onto their own genitals, as if monitoring the development of their own manhood. Director Stanley Kubrick's broadly satirical gesture in *Jacket* emerges as a purely physical rendering of a process of masculinization that takes place on a more emotional level in other war films. In *Twelve O'Clock High,* Gen. Savage (Gregory Peck) represses all emotion in his handling of his airmen, arguing that his predecessor has made them emotionally dependent on him by treating them as children rather than as men. When he collapses before a mission and the entire squadron successfully carries it off without him, the fliers finally prove to him that they have grown from children into men.

The archetypal Hollywood combat soldier is a caricature of masculinity; his cartoonlike toughness is epitomized in Sylvester Stallone's Rambo. This character is itself a compilation of action heroes found in comic books such as *Terry and the Pirates, G.I. Joe, G.I. Combat, Sgt. Rock, Steve Canyon,* and *The 'Nam,* as well as *Captain America, Wonder Woman,* and other comic book series which feature quasi-militaristic action figures who began their careers fighting Nazis in World

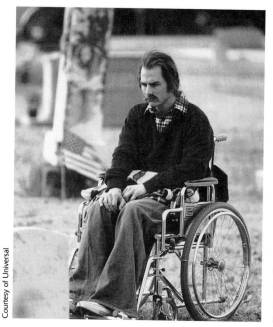

Courtesy of Universal

Crippled by war, returning Vietnam veteran Ron Kovic (Tom Cruise) visits the grave of the victim of his friendly fire in *Born on the Fourth of July* (1989).

War II but have rarely, if ever, worn a uniform. Though this notion of machismo is presented as essential to the success of a soldier on the battlefield, it is often revealed as out of place in the more domestic sphere of traditional sexual relationships. In *Heartbreak Ridge,* as Tania Modleski points out, Clint Eastwood's Sgt. Tom Highway, whose wife divorced him because "marriage and the Marine Corps weren't too compatible," reads women's magazines in an attempt to regain a sensitivity that his Marine training has deliberately repressed. He also seems to realize that if he is to have any kind of normal relationship with women, he needs to learn to speak their language instead of his own.

Back from the Front

In the war film, the normal world—the world of family, wives, and children—remains an alien world that both the soldier and the returning war veteran have difficulty reentering. Willard tells us that when he went home, he wanted to be back in Vietnam and that he hardly said a word to his wife until he said yes to a divorce. The difficulty of the adjustment of veterans to the peacetime world of wives and children has become a familiar motif in films that deal with returning veterans. For veterans of World War II, like those in *The Best Years of Our Lives* (1946), reintegration, though difficult, is at least possible. But for those vets returning from Vietnam, as seen in *Rolling Thunder* (1977), *Coming Home* (1978), *First Blood* (1982), and *Born on the Fourth of July* (1989), homecoming is decidedly more traumatic and assimilation less successful. War's overmasculinization of the men (in this latter group of films, at least) has made them unfit for the traditional social order; that is, they have become masculine in excess, uncontrollable in their potential for rage or violence.

Successful reentry into society demands that they undergo a process of demasculinization. In certain instances (*Coming Home, Fourth of July*), the returning soldier is presented as a cripple, who has been feminized or made passive in combat and who must come to terms with his paralysis through a psychic healing process in which his initial rage at his misfortune is channeled into socially acceptable behavior. He evolves from embittered warrior into participant in the peace movement. In other instances (*Thunder, First Blood*), returning veterans refuse to accept the passive status imposed on them and direct their bottled-up violence toward domestic enemies, recreating battle situations at home. If the veterans resist feminization, their excessive masculinity either destroys them or forces them to become outlaws or social outcasts, as in the case of Rambo in *First Blood*.

CROSSOVERS: WAR AND GENRE

The bizarre sexual dynamics found in the war film reflect its status as a genre that occupies the extreme edges of the familiar terrain of classical Hollywood cinema. In other words, the excesses of the war film function to define, through a process of transgression, the norms of conventional cinema. The war film, however, is not entirely the loose cannon of all Hollywood genres that the above description of the combat film might lead us to suspect. The all-male world of the combat film with its wall-to-wall battle and action sequences is not the sum total of the war film. It merely stands at one end of a spectrum that includes a broad variety of perspectives on war. Much as war permeates every aspect of a society engaged in it, so the war film crosses over other genres. There are war comedies such as Charlie Chaplin's *Shoulder Arms* (1918), in which Charlie mocks the authoritarian discipline of boot camp and the conditions of trench warfare at the front before capturing the Kaiser. Or *M*A*S*H* (1970), in which wisecracking battlefield surgeons engage in comic repartee in an attempt to cope with the bleak futility of war and the tragic waste of human life that accompanies it.

There are even war musicals (of a sort), ranging from loosely basted together narratives dealing with the entertainment of the troops, such as *Stage Door Canteen* (1943) and *For the Boys* (1991), to love stories with wartime settings, such as *South Pacific* (1958) and *The Sound of Music* (1965).

The existence of war comedies and war musicals has forced critics to reconsider any narrow definition of the war film. The genre has tended to be identified as a whole with one of its subgenres, the combat film; with a single historical period, the twentieth century; and with a handful of global conflicts—

Courtesy of Warner Bros.

At the end of *Casablanca*, Rick Blaine (Humphrey Bogart, right) and Capt. Louis Renault (Claude Raines) walk off together to join the Free French forces at Brazzaville.

World War I, World War II, Korea, Vietnam, and the 1991 Gulf War. But the war film extends beyond the precise borders of the combat film, and it looks both backward and forward in time to eras other than our own. To a certain extent, every film that depicts or refers to war, as well as every film made during a war, functions as a war film.

From this perspective, the musical melodrama *Meet Me in St. Louis* (1944), set in turn-of-the-twentieth-century America, can even be seen as a war film, celebrating home and family—traditional values for which World War II was being fought. *Casablanca* (1942), based on an unproduced play set in North Africa prior to the Japanese attack on Pearl Harbor and American involvement in the Second World War, functions as a metaphor for American isolationism and the need to take sides in this new global conflict. Filmed in the spring of 1942, the story focuses on Rick Blaine (Humphrey Bogart), an expatriate American who is described by Capt. Renault (Claude Rains) as "completely neutral about everything . . . including women." When an acquaintance of his, Ugate (Peter Lorre), is fleeing from the Vichy police and appeals to him for help, Rick does nothing, explaining, "I stick my neck out for nobody." But by the end of the film, Rick does take sides, joining the Free French to continue the fight against the German Third Reich.

More explicitly, Westerns made during the Vietnam war, such as *Ulzana's Raid* (1972), are war films, refiguring the Vietcong as Indians. However, the war film could be more usefully defined as a representation of war from the points of view of those whose lives it touches. At the heart of this definition lies the combat film, which focuses primarily on men in war, and in which combat sequences occupy a large percentage of the overall running time of the film itself, as is the case with films such as *Bataan* (1943) and *Battleground* (1949). The war film genre, however, also includes films about the military in which combat occupies only a small fraction of the story line, as in *From Here to Eternity* (1953), *The Wings of Eagles* (1957), *Born on the Fourth of July* (1989), and *Dances With Wolves* (1990), as well as films set outside the narrow world of the military in which there is no combat at all and war provides a background against which certain war-related dramatic conflicts are set.

Films in which involvement in a war is debated, such as *Casablanca* (1942), *To Have and Have Not* (1944), *Alice's Restaurant* (1969), and *Hair* (1979), serve as one parameter of the genre, whereas films that celebrate the efforts of those left behind to maintain the home front, such as *Since You Went Away* (1944), *Hail the Conquering Hero* (1944), and *Swing Shift* (1984), serve as another.

War can be seen not only from the perspective of civilians and the American or Allied fighting forces, but also from that of the enemy, as in *All Quiet on the Western Front* (1930) or *A Time to Love and a Time to Die* (1958). On occasion, it can even be seen from both sides of a conflict, as in the case of *Tora! Tora! Tora!* (1970), a Japanese-and-American coproduction that tells the story of the attack on Pearl Harbor from both points of view.

THE BATTLE FOR PUBLIC OPINION: PROPAGANDA AND THE COMBAT FILM

Preaching War and Peace

The nature of its subject matter has made the war film a crucial weapon in the shaping of public opinion about individual wars and war in general. The genre has become a battleground on which different political factions have fought with one another over the hearts and minds of American moviegoers. One of the first war films, *Tearing Down the Spanish Flag* (1897), which consisted of a single shot of a hand ("the hand of righteous destiny") tearing down a Spanish flag, mobilized audiences in support of the recently declared war on Spain.

Antiwar films manipulated isolationist sentiment to keep America out of World War I. Thomas Ince's *Civilization* (1914), for example, argued for the inhumanity of war through an allegorical story in which the hero, a submarine commander, refuses to fire on an ocean liner, sinks his own ship, dies, and is resurrected by Christ, who sends him forth to preach for peace on earth.

Shortly after the sinking of the *Lusitania* in May 1915, J. Stuart Blackton led the prowar, anti-German cause with *Battle Cry of Peace* (1915), in which American advocates of national disarmament and peace are revealed to be dupes of foreign spies who mastermind an invasion of New York City that leaves it in ruins. Finally, in April 1917, after the sinking of four American merchant ships by German submarines, Woodrow Wilson, recently reelected on the basis of the slogan, "He Kept Us Out of War," asked Congress to declare war on Germany, prompting a stream of prowar films and terminating isolationist filmmaking activities.

Prowar feeling was so predominant that one pacifist film producer, Robert Goldstein, was sentenced to 10 years in jail for making an anti-British film, *The Spirit of '76* (1917), which was released just prior to America's entry into the war on the British side. Anti-German sentiment dominated *The Kaiser, Beast of Berlin* and *To Hell with the Kaiser* (both 1917); in the latter, the Kaiser is presented as a tool of Satan, who encourages the German emperor to sink unarmed passenger ships, engage in chemical warfare, and blow up Red Cross hospitals. Even D. W. Griffith, whose *The Birth of a Nation* (1915) and *Intolerance* (1916) depict the horrors of war and end with heavenly images of world peace, joined the prowar bandwagon (at the request of the British government), directing *Hearts of the World* (1918), a war melodrama in which the Huns play the villains.

After the war, Hollywood reverted to the pacifist neutrality to which it subscribed during peacetime. *The Big Parade* (1925), *What Price Glory?* (1926), and other films dramatize the costs of war in human life and in the spirit of those who survived.

Mass Conversion: The Politics of *Sergeant York*

American sentiment regarding the war in Europe remained more or less isolationist until the bombing of Pearl Harbor on December 7, 1941. Prior to that date, members of Congress carefully scrutinized Hollywood productions, suspecting certain films such as *Confessions of a Nazi Spy* (1939), *The Great Dictator* (1941), and *The Mortal Storm* (1940) to be prowar propaganda (while apparently missing the antifascist metaphorical implications of *The Sea Hawk* (1940), in which the English defeat of the Spanish Armada in 1588 is geared to arouse sympathy for a beleaguered England). The aviator Charles Lindbergh and other members of the America First organization campaigned to maintain American neutrality.

But as world events slowly converted America to a wartime mentality, Hollywood served as a tool of antifascist filmmakers and the Roosevelt administration for the reeducation of an isolationist and pacifist populace into reluctant warriors. The conversion that takes place in *Sergeant York* (1941)—of the born-again Christian Alvin York from a conscientious objector into a patriotic soldier—serves as apt metaphor for the film industry's project during the months immediately preceding American entry into the war; Americans were, like York, uncertain about war. After World War I, Americans resumed their predominantly isolationist stance. Though events in Europe in the 1930s prompted certain segments of society (including the president, Franklin Delano Roosevelt) to call for American intervention, many others, like York, needed to be shown their larger responsibility to the world community.

York's education takes place in two interrelated stages. Struck by lightning while raising hell outside the local church in the backwoods of Tennessee, he undergoes a miraculous religious conversion and discovers the truth of what

Courtesy of Warner Bros.

Pacifist Alvin York (Gary Cooper) is issued a gun by the Army in *Sergeant York* (1941).

his pastor told him earlier—that an individual, like a tree, cannot stand alone, that "a fellow's got to have his roots in something outside his own self." Torn between his newfound religious faith, which teaches him "Thou shalt not kill," and his duty as a soldier, York reconciles his obligations to both of these demands on his loyalty through a rationalization inspired by a passage in the Bible: he will render unto Caesar that which is Caesar's and unto God that which is God's. He'll obey his duty to the state and observe, as far as possible, his religious faith.

In this way, York (and Americans) could uphold, without rupturing them, the basic isolationist principles that underpinned his (their) identity while realizing his (their) obligations to things outside himself (themselves). Retaining its inherent distaste for European entanglements and war, America could, at the same time, give itself over to the larger historical (and moral) necessity of fighting fascism.

The logic that underscores the World War II war film is that of the reluctant warrior who hates war but fights nonetheless; in this way, the American war film (unlike those produced by the British, for example) was undermined with an antiwar sentiment that justified America's apparent about-face from isolationism to interventionism. British war films, such as *In Which We Serve* (1942), took popular support of the war for granted. *Of course* the Nazis, who had declared their intention of ultimately invading England, needed to be both fought and destroyed.

Why We Fight: Education and the War Film

The conversion process that lies at the center of *Sergeant York* reappears in dozens of combat films in the form of an educational process. This instructive aspect of the war film aligns it with the agitational and propagandistic cinema of certain state-produced foreign films such as *Battleship Potemkin* (1925) or *Triumph of the Will* (1935), as well as with America's own series of propaganda films, *Why We Fight* (1942–1945), which were produced by Frank Capra for the Army. But the propagandistic function of the American combat film is mediated somewhat by its overt *narrativization* of the educational process. Unlike Soviet and Nazi propaganda, the Hollywood war film acknowledged its status as a didactic tool, filtering its polemical arguments through characters in the narrative rather than presenting them directly. In this way, the American war film disarmed potential objections to it as blatant propaganda.

However, shortly after Pearl Harbor, Hollywood was commandeered by the government to contribute to the war effort. The recently created Office of War Information (OWI) set up shop in Los Angeles, where its Bureau of Motion Pictures served as a watchful eye over war-related productions. Its civilian members reviewed scripts, sat in on script conferences, and made suggestions about the content of finished films. The OWI's relationship with the studios remained purely advisory, serving in a capacity similar to that of the Production Code administration of the Hays office. Both the OWI and the studios dismissed any notion that the government was involved in censoring the movies, but the industry's voluntary cooperation with the Bureau of Motion Pictures undoubtedly played a role in determining the final content of a number of films made during the war.

The war film was a school for soldiers. The common soldier, whose inherent resistance to killing and to war (as well as to military discipline) was broken down in boot camp, was trained to fight and to obey (*Sands of Iwo Jima*, 1949; *Battle Cry*, 1955; *The Boys in Company C*, 1978). Having graduated from boot camp, he continued to learn—through combat—not only how to fight but why he was fighting; contact with the enemy revealed the latter's essential villainy and taught him just how necessary the war was (*Guadalcanal Diary*, 1943; *Gung Ho!* 1944; *The Green Berets*, 1968).

Combat convinces Ens. Torre (Brandon de Wilde) in *In Harm's Way* (1965) that what he initially refers to as "Mr. Roosevelt's war" is not merely a politically expedient plan to advance the personal interests of the president (and the Democratic party) but a just war to which he finds himself committed as well. The conscientious objector in *Steel Helmet* discovers that philosophical objections to war in general have no place on the battlefield; he picks up a gun and begins to shoot at North Korean soldiers.

A similar educational process took place for civilians and other neutral observers. In Alfred Hitchcock's *Lifeboat* (1944), the survivors of a torpedoed ocean liner rescue the captain of the German U-boat that attacked them. The Nazi then betrays their trust, stealing more than his fair share of food and water and piloting them into enemy territory. When the others learn of what he has done, they denounce the fascist philosophy that inspires his actions, and kill him.

Naive war correspondents, such as Huntley Haverstock (Joel McCrea) in *Foreign Correspondent* (1940), discover the treacherous nature of the enemy through their aggressive investigative reporting. Cynical newspaper correspondents, such as Williams (Henry Hull) in *Objective Burma* (1945), accompany soldiers in the field and, through their participation in combat, come to understand the true nature of the enemy. On seeing the mutilated bodies of the men in his patrol, Williams loses his objectivity and bursts into a racist diatribe against the Japanese: "I thought I'd seen or read about everything one man can do to another, from the torture chambers of the Middle Ages to the gang wars and lynchings of today. But this—this is different. This was done in cold blood by people who claim to be civilized. Civilized! They're degenerate, immoral idiots. Stinking little savages. Wipe them out, I say. Wipe them off the face of the earth."

Perhaps the most famous conversion takes place in *The Green Berets* (1968), in which a liberal antiwar reporter (David Janssen) joins John Wayne's Green Beret unit in Vietnam to see for himself what the war is like. The war correspondent's skepticism colors his coverage of the war until he witnesses Vietcong atrocities. "This is what the war is all about," a soldier tells him. "Are you gonna stand there and referee or are you gonna help us?" In an abrupt about-face, the journalist picks up a gun and helps the American forces defend themselves against an enemy attack.

The Vietnam Reversal

The educational process that took place in the classic war film illustrated "why we fight" and rationalized the necessity of war. In terms of this and other issues, *The Green Berets* emerged as one of the most representative of war films. Yet it was also unique in that practically every other film about the Vietnam war reversed this traditional educational process. In Vietnam, the soldier learned to question the simplistic, cold war rhetoric about the nature of the enemy and the justness of the American cause which had been the cornerstones of the lessons taught in high school history classes and in basic training.

The experience of Vietnam taught that American involvement in the war made little or no sense. U.S. fighting forces not only learned from past example that war in general is hell but some also discovered for themselves that this particular war was wrong; some soldiers became pacifists or antiwar activists, as in *Getting Straight* (1970) and *Coming Home.* In *Born on the Fourth of July*, paraplegic Vietnam veteran Ron Kovic (Tom Cruise) reviews his participation in the war from the perspective of a rat-infested VA hospital in the Bronx and is radicalized, becoming a leader of the antiwar movement.

The *Boys in Company C* discover that all that matters in Vietnam is the delivery of luxury items to the general for his personal amusement and the securing of good body counts for the reports sent back to headquarters. War becomes a game, like the soccer match they play against the South Vietnamese at the end of the film, a game they realize they are expected to lose. Finally, Army Pvt. Eriksson (Michael J. Fox) in *Casualties of War* (1989) learns about the nature of the American presence in Vietnam when he is confronted with the moral corruption of other members of his squad who have abducted, raped, and killed a Vietnamese girl; he first tries to prevent them from harming her and, having failed, eventually blows the whistle on them, a gesture that figuratively represents his rejection of American behavior in the war itself.

RACE, ETHNICITY, AND THE WAR FILM

Earlier war films celebrated American intervention overseas, using the occasion to present an idealized portrait of American democracy. American identity was at risk in World War II, and it was the particular virtues of that identity—democratic equality—that would win it. Thus, the combat films celebrated group teamwork, as we have seen earlier in our examination of *Air Force* and other films. The group was shown as consisting of various ethnic and social types, imitating the melting-pot ideal of American culture. As Jeanine Basinger points out, in war films the tough career sergeant regularly has under his command a rich kid from the suburbs, a poor kid from the inner-city ghetto, a lower-middle-class cab driver from Brooklyn, a Jew, a Hispanic, an Italian American, a Polish American, and an African American.

By cooperating with one another, they win the war and also demonstrate that the idea of America really works. Unfortunately, history tells us something different. For example, though blacks are occasionally depicted as serving together with whites, as in *Crash Dive, Sahara* (1943) and *Bataan* (1943), the armed forces were not integrated until 1948, when President Truman officially ended segregation in the military. Though blacks served valiantly in World War II, they did so, much as they had in World War I and in the Civil War (see *Glory,* 1989), in segregated units commanded by white officers.

The reality of domestic racial tension was exemplified by race riots in Detroit and other cities in 1943; by the call, within the black community, for a "Double V"—a victory over the Axis in Europe and Jim Crow at home; and by a 1942 survey reporting that 49 percent of Harlem blacks believed they would be no worse off if Japan were to win the war. Domestic racism remained in place. For example, public fear of a Mexican American crime wave led to the racially motivated police harassment of Mexican American teenagers ("zoot suiters" who wore oversize sport coats and peg-top pants) in Los Angeles in 1942–1943. Wartime racism surfaced in continuing discrimination against blacks, Mexican Americans, and other minorities such as Native Americans.

The demonization of the enemy: a Japanese officer (Richard Loo) looms over his American prisoners of war in this publicity material for *The Purple Heart* (1944).

Courtesy of 20th Century-Fox

Perhaps the most scandalous act of racism was the internment of thousands of Japanese Americans in detention camps during the war and the confiscation of their property during the war—a policy the Office of War Information attempted to justify in a documentary newsreel, *Japanese Relocation,* which was released at the end of 1942. It wasn't until after the war, however, that Hollywood took a more critical stance toward relocation, treating it as an embarrassing moment in American history, in films such as *Go for Broke!* (1951), *Bad Day at Black Rock* (1955), *Hell to Eternity* (1960), and, more recently, *Come See The Paradise* (1990).

But all of this wartime racial tension was rewritten into onscreen racial harmony, which is a more expedient reality. Any notion of segregation or racism in the armed forces would clearly undermine the ideal of equality for which America was supposedly fighting. Racism at home was, therefore, suppressed, or rather, displaced onto a race that it was permissible to hate: the U.S. enemy, the Japanese—who, once the Japanese Americans had been eliminated from view, could become visible signs of difference, of racial otherness against which animosity could be directed. Hollywood did this in *Across the Pacific* (1942), *Air Force* (1943), *Objective Burma* (1945), *The Purple Heart* (1944), and dozens of other films.

CONFLICTED: THE PSYCHIC VIOLENCE OF WAR

The Enemy Is Us

During peacetime, Hollywood was free to produce war films to express anti-war sentiment exposing the hypocrisy, incompetence, and insanity of the military establishment, as in *Paths of Glory* (1957), *Anzio* (1968), *Dr. Strangelove* (1964), and *M*A*S*H* (1970); the corruption and cowardice of officers (*Attack!* 1956; *Bitter Victory,* 1957); and the futility and senselessness of war (*Hell is for Heroes,* 1962; *The Victors,* 1963; *Johnny Got His Gun,* 1971; *A Bridge Too Far,* 1977). With the exception of *The Green Berets,* which was the only film about the Vietnam War made during the war itself, virtually every other film about the Vietnam War took an antiwar stance that was critical either of U.S. political policy that led to involvement in the war or of the physical, emotional, and psychological damage incurred by servicemen in Vietnam.

Vietnam War films tend to undermine the traditional values celebrated in films about World War II and other wars by reversing or obscuring the clear-cut distinctions drawn in earlier war films between "us" and the enemy. Indeed, in many of the major films that deal with the Vietnam War, "we" become the enemy. In *Company C,* the black sergeant Tyrone Washington (Stan Shaw) attempts to shoot his own commanding officer, whose ineptness has resulted in the deaths of several comrades. *Deer Hunter* reduces the war to a game of Russian roulette in which Americans are driven first by torture and then by psychic trauma to shoot themselves.

In the opening sequence of *Apocalypse Now,* Willard smashes his own image in the mirror; the central action of the film involves his mission, which has as its objective the termination of an American officer rather than the killing of the enemy, who, for the most part, remain unseen. The film concludes with Willard's ritualistic slaughter of Kurtz, with whom he identifies and whom he resembles in several ways.

Platoon dramatizes the internal division of America over the war through the ideological conflict between two platoon sergeants (Tom Berenger and Willem Dafoe). One American (Berenger) kills another (Dafoe) only to be slain, in turn, by a third (Charlie Sheen). *Fourth of July* depicts the war as a struggle in which Americans kill one another by accident, through friendly fire, a tragic phenomenon that resurfaces in Gulf War films such as *Courage Under Fire* (1996).

The Aftermath

The metaphorical representation of Vietnam as a self-destructive conflict extends into postwar representations of the aftermath of the war, seen in the betrayal narratives of a series of films involving war veterans. Thus, in *Good Guys Wear Black* (1977), an American politician who has originally conspired with the

Courtesy of Orion

Vietnam is seen as America at war with itself in *Platoon* (1986): the innocent Chris (Charlie Sheen, left) poses with the ruthless and violent Sgt. Barnes (Tom Berenger, center) and the more moderate and rational Sgt. Elias (Willem Dafoe).

enemy to betray a crack American special forces unit proves to be responsible for their methodical assassination after the war.

The enemy in the POW/MIA rescue mission drama *Rambo: First Blood Part II* (1985) is as much the CIA, which tries to ensure that Rambo's mission fails, as the North Vietnamese, who continue to hold American prisoners of war. The difficult adjustment of Vietnam veterans to postwar America is frequently cast in terms of conflict between them and those who stayed behind. In *Rolling Thunder* (1977), a veteran looks on helplessly as his wife and child are slain by a gang of thieves, intent on finding the silver dollars given to him by local residents on his return home. He subsequently tracks down the robbers and, with the help of another veteran, kills them in a military-style assault. Other veterans become vigilantes (*Slaughter*, 1972; *Gordon's War*, 1973; *Magnum Force*, 1973; *Taxi Driver*, 1976) or are portrayed as criminals capable of insane acts that threaten domestic stability (*Black Sunday* and *Twilight's Last Gleaming*, 1977; *Betrayed* and *Distant Thunder*, 1988).

Though the veterans of other wars are occasionally depicted as having difficulty in adjusting to civilian life, as seen in *Pride of the Marines* (1945), *The Best Years of Our Lives* (1946), and *Till the End of Time* (1946), their problems remain contained within the family or the workplace; they rarely result in acts of civil disorder or criminal violence.

The scars of the Vietnam War, however, extended much deeper into the American psyche, producing veterans whose violence reaches from the confines of the family into the public sphere. The clear sense of victory (and of closure or completion) that characterized World War II produced a cinema that was itself untroubled in its representation of war. The sense of defeat (and lack of closure) that characterized the Vietnam war led to a cinema that continually sought explanations for the war's outcome and attempted to rewrite our defeat in Vietnam as a postwar victory. Thus, Vietnam veterans return to Southeast Asia to rescue prisoners of war (*Uncommon Valor*, 1983; *Missing in Action*, 1984; *Rambo: First Blood Part II*, 1985). Or the larger loss of the war is restaged as a smaller, domestic battle that could be won (*Gordon's War*, 1973; *Slaughter*, 1976; *Rolling Thunder*, 1977; *Good Guys Wear Black* and *A Force of One*, 1979; *Forced Vengeance*, 1982; and *Eye of the Tiger*, 1986).

THE 1991 GULF WAR AND WORLD WAR II REDUX

The Gulf War

Contemporary war films are shaped by the American experience in Vietnam. One film about a fictional incident in Yemen, *Rules of Engagement* (1999), actually begins in Vietnam where the film's central character, Marine officer Terry Childers (Samuel L. Jackson) rescues fellow officer Hays Hodges (Tommy Lee Jones) during an attack. *Courage Under Fire* focuses on another Vietnam veteran, Lt. Col. Nathaniel Serling (Denzel Washington), and his experiences in the Gulf War. It also features a former Ranger who fought in Vietnam, Tony Gartner (Scott Glenn), now a reporter for the *Washington Post,* who befriends Serling while conducting an investigation of his conduct during the war. However, it is not these literal links to Vietnam that connect these films to earlier films about Vietnam.

More importantly, it is these films' approach to combat as a source of personal trauma that links them to films about the Vietnam War. As Michael Hammond points out, both films take the form of investigations into traumatic combat experiences in an attempt to find out what actually happened. Both films sift through the testimony of trustworthy and untrustworthy eyewitnesses in a cathartic process that enables the central characters ultimately to come to terms with the trauma of combat. In *Rules of Engagement*, Childers orders his men to fire on an angry mob of anti-American demonstrators outside the American embassy in Yemen, killing 63 supposedly unarmed civilians, in order to rescue the ambassador and his family. In *Courage Under Fire*, Serling fires on his own troops in the heat and confusion of a tank battle, killing his best friend. He is subsequently assigned to investigate a military action to ascertain whether the female officer who led it, Capt. Karen Walden (Meg Ryan) should be posthumously awarded the Medal of Honor.

Both films treat instances of combat as initially unknowable, opaque events that overwhelm consciousness. Through a process of methodical investigation, their truth can be ascertained, providing some small measure of uneasy closure on the event for those involved.

World War II

Saving Private Ryan

Courage Under Fire deals with memory and trauma as contemporary facts of war. The opening and closing of Spielberg's *Saving Private Ryan*, like those of *Schindler's List* (1993), occur at public memorials for the dead, where their memory is not only kept alive but ritualistically passed on to successive generations who owe their own lives to the sacrifices made by these who went before them. An 80-year-old man visits a military graveyard on the cliffs above Omaha Beach in Normandy, stands at the foot of the grave, and remembers D-Day, the Allied landing on Omaha Beach on June 6, 1944. It's not until the end of the film that the audience realizes that the flashback it has been watching was not that of the 80-year-old man standing at the foot of a grave but that of the soldier, Capt. John Miller, buried in that grave. Just before he dies, Miller (Tom Hanks) tells the object of his costly rescue mission, Pvt. Ryan (Matt Damon), to "earn it." He means that Ryan should try to become worthy of the many lives that saving him cost. Spielberg's framing sequences give no indication of Ryan's worthiness, aside from the evidence of the supportive family (loving wife, son, and daughters) accompanying him. The assumption is that Ryan's worthiness consists in his dutiful role as the bearer of Miller's traumatic memories of combat, as the vehicle through whom those memories will be passed to future generations (as suggested by the mise-en-scène of Ryan's family members). An 80-year-old Ryan has come to Normandy for closure prior to his own death. In reliving Miller's story (in taking on Miller's memory), Ryan assumes the pain and suffering of his rescuers while remaining unabsolved of his own feelings of guilt for having survived. It is precisely this relationship to memory that Spielberg wishes to convey to audiences watching the film. He wants the audience to experience it as trauma and thus to burn it into their own memories.

The Thin Red Line

"There's only a thin red line between the sane and the mad."
James Jones

The flashback that structures *Saving Private Ryan* proves to be not just the memory of Miller but the collective memory of the entire platoon. The only flashbacks in *The Thin Red Line* are those of Pvt. Witt (Jim Caviezel) and Pvt. Bell (Ben Chaplin), and they are memories of idyllic moments away from the theater

Dream Works/Photofest

Capt. Miller (Tom Hanks, right) lands at Omaha Beach in Normandy with his platoon in *Saving Private Ryan.*

of war—Witt's fond recollections of the natural paradise he discovered when he went AWOL among the Melanesian Islanders at the beginning of the film and Bell's of intimate moments with his wife back home. *Red Line* refuses the narrative strategies which give unity and coherence to *Ryan.* War in *Red Line* is incoherent. The film's characters search for some kind of coherence or meaning in it. Thus, Bell reverts to memories (which seem mixed with fantasies) about his wife; Pvt. Witt meditates on Nature, War, Evil, and the possibility that humanity has one big soul; Sgt. Welsh (Sean Penn), thinking perhaps of Witt, imagines "find[ing] something that's his" and "mak[ing] an island for himself"; and Lt. Col. Tall (Nick Nolte) focuses his thoughts on career advancement. If Spielberg's narration is unified and collective, Malick's is fragmentary and subjective. *Red Line* is narrated by as many as eight different voices, ranging from the central characters mentioned above to quite minor characters such as the dead (or dying) Japanese soldier, his face half-buried in the dirt, who asks his slayer, "Are you righteous? Kind? Does your confidence lie in this?"

Not only does each voice reflect a different perspective on the events depicted in the film, but the voiceovers reflect a similar fragmentation. They repeatedly return to the notion of a duality that structures both nature and human experience. The film begins with Witt's voice wondering why Nature "contends with itself." And it ends with Witt's final thoughts: "Darkness and light, strife and love—are they the workings of one mind? Features of the same face?"

Pvt. Witt (Jim Caviezel) experiences the first part of the battle for Guadalcanal as a medic in *The Thin Red Line*.

Rutgers Cinema Studies

The soldiers in *Red Line,* unlike those in *Ryan,* almost never fight as a team. With the exception of Capt. Gaff's assault on a Japanese pillbox, combat scenes feature confused individuals incapable of seeing the larger picture into which they presumably fit, or of seeing the chaos and pointlessness of war. Malick's soldiers, unlike Spielberg's, form no bonds of brotherhood over the course of the film. They remain isolated individuals. The film's central character is a habitual deserter, wandering off on his own instead of becoming part of a team. Though he ultimately sacrifices himself at the end to save others, his death prompts a final flashback of him swimming blissfully under water with Melanesian children on his beloved island paradise. His death is less a sacrifice than an escape to another world, one that is not "blowing itself to hell." Even within the chain of command, divisiveness rules. Capt. Staros (Elias Koteas) refuses a direct order from Lt. Col. Tall to lead his men on a frontal assault of Japanese positions.

Nominally, in *Ryan,* "the mission is the man;" the group is sacrificed to rescue a single individual. But Pvt. Ryan must earn this. In other words, Ryan is forced into an economy of debt in which he owes everything to the men who died on his behalf. He gives value to their lives by giving value to his own. The film is a perfect illustration of an idealized, democratic reciprocity whereby the individual exists by and for the community to which he belongs. *Red Line* questions the moral economy that *Ryan* upholds. As one of the film's voiceovers notes, "War does not ennoble men; it turns them into dogs. It makes them small, mean, ferocious. It poisons the soul." Unlike *Ryan*, Malick's film provides no answers. It only asks questions: "Does our ruin benefit the earth? Does it help the grass to grow? The sun to shine?"

MEDIATION AND REPRESENTATION

The war film mediates our relationship to war, helping to prepare us for it, reconcile us to victory or defeat, and adjust us to its aftermath. The conventions of the war film continue to shape our understanding of real wars—to inspire us, on one hand, to fight in them and, on the other, to protest against them. Though wars continue to be fought and won or lost on the battlefield, they also continue to be fought and won or lost through their representation on the movie or television screen. Images of war explain why we fight; they stage and restage war's battles; and they attempt to explain why we won or lost.

In other words, all contemporary wars are waged on two fronts—on the battlefield and on the screen. Hollywood's job has been to make sure not that we always win but that we are always right—that our victories are informed by an inherent pacifism and distaste for war that redeems us from the sins of our conscienceless enemies, and that our single defeat (in Vietnam) is the product not of our consciencelessness but of our heightened conscience, which sets us against ourselves and provides the basis for the recasting of our defeat as a victory in Hollywood's various epilogues to the war. Whether we win or lose the battle, the movies are there to enable us to win the war.

■ ■ ■ SELECT FILMOGRAPHY

Hearts of the World (1918)	*Sands of Iwo Jima* (1949)
The Great Dictator (1940)	*Fixed Bayonets* (1951)
Sergeant York (1941)	*The Steel Helmet* (1951)
Casablanca (1942)	*Battle Cry* (1955)
Air Force (1943)	*The Longest Day* (1962)
Bataan (1943)	*The Dirty Dozen* (1967)
Guadalcanal Diary (1943)	*The Green Berets* (1968)
Since You Went Away (1944)	*Rolling Thunder* (1977)
The Story of G.I. Joe (1945)	*The Boys in Company C* (1978)
The Best Years of Our Lives (1946)	*Coming Home* (1978)

The Deer Hunter (1978)	*The Hunt for Red October* (1990)
Go Tell the Spartans (1978)	*Schindler's List* (1993)
Apocalypse Now (1979)	*Courage Under Fire* (1996)
Rambo: First Blood Part II (1985)	*Paradise Road* (1997)
	Saving Private Ryan (1998)
Heartbreak Ridge (1986)	*The Thin Red Line* (1998)
Platoon (1986)	*Rules of Engagement* (1999)
Full Metal Jacket (1987)	*Three Kings* (1999)
Born on the Fourth of July (1989)	*Pearl Harbor* (2001)
Casualties of War (1989)	*Black Hawk Down* (2002)

■ ■ ■ SELECT BIBLIOGRAPHY

BASINGER, JEANINE. *The World War II Combat Film: Anatomy of a Genre.* New York: Columbia University Press, 1986.

DICK, BERNARD. *The Star-Spangled Screen: The American World War II Film.* Lexington: University Press of Kentucky, 1985.

DOHERTY, THOMAS. *Projections of War: Hollywood and American Culture, 1941–1945.* New York: Columbia University Press, 1999.

FUSSELL, PAUL. *Wartime: Understanding and Behavior in the Second World War.* New York: Oxford University Press, 1989.

HAMMOND, MICHAEL. "Some Smothering Dreams: The Combat Film in Contemporary Hollywood," in Steve Neale, ed., *Genre and Contemporary Hollywood.* London: BFI, 2002.

JEFFORDS, SUSAN. "Friendly Civilians: Images of Women and the Feminization of the Audience in Vietnam Films," *Wide Angle* **7**, no. 4 (1985): 13–22.

KOPPES, CLAYTON, AND GREGORY BLACK. *Hollywood Goes to War: How Politics, Profits, and Propaganda Shaped World War II Movies.* New York: Free Press, 1987.

MODLESKI, TANIA. "A Father Is Being Beaten: Male Feminism and the War Film," in *Feminism without Women: Culture and Criticism in a "Postfeminist" Age.* New York: Routledge, 1991.

SHINDLER, COLIN. *Hollywood Goes to War: Films and American Society, 1939–1952.* London: Routledge and Kegan Paul, 1979.

SUID, LAWRENCE. *Guts and Glory: Great American War Movies.* Reading, MA: Addison-Wesley, 1978.

CHAPTER **10**

Film Noir: Somewhere in the Night

MADE IN THE USA

Film noir—literally "black film"—is a French phrase, but it refers to an American phenomenon made in Hollywood, USA. Though several of the directors associated with film noir, such as Billy Wilder, Fritz Lang, Otto Preminger, and Edgar G. Ulmer, were foreign-born, the majority of those who explored the darker reaches of the noir experience were American, born and bred. They have included, among others, Orson Welles, John Huston, Nicholas Ray, Samuel Fuller, Joseph H. Lewis, Anthony Mann, Raoul Walsh, Joseph Mankiewicz, Don Siegel, Phil Karlson, Tay Garnett, Frank Tuttle, Edward Dmytryk, Henry Hathaway, and Jacques Tourneur who, though born in Paris (1904), grew up in Hollywood (from 1914).

Even more important, the source material for the bulk of noir narratives came from the underworld of American pulp fiction. For example, nearly 20 percent of the films noirs made between 1941 and 1948 were adaptations of hard-boiled novels written by American authors such as Dashiell Hammett, Raymond Chandler, James M. Cain, Horace McCoy, Cornell Woolrich, and others. An even greater percentage of films noirs were written by American screenwriters whose original scripts were heavily influenced by the hard-boiled style of these proletarian, tough-guy writers of the 1930s and 1940s. And, as we shall see, film noir deals with a uniquely American experience of wartime and postwar despair and alienation as a disoriented America readjusts to a new social and political reality.

There is a French connection, however. Film noir was discovered and christened in postwar France. On August 26, 1944, the Allies liberated Paris. During the Nazi occupation, which began in the summer of 1940, the Germans had banned the exhibition of American films in French theaters. Finally, in 1945, an enormous backlog of American films, which had been made during the war but had not been seen in Nazi-controlled territories, reached French screens.

French audiences were overwhelmed by a flood of American films, and critics were startled by the changes that had taken place in American film production during the war. The prewar classical Hollywood cinema, which was dominated by the rationality, symmetry, and order of their favorite directors such as William Wyler, John Ford, and Frank Capra, had given way to a subversive strain of behavioral deviance in American films, which were now dominated by crime, corruption, cruelty, and an apparently unhealthy interest in the erotic. American film had suddenly—from the French perspective, at least—turned grimmer, bleaker, and blacker.

During a short period from mid-July to the end of August, 1946, a succession of extremely downbeat films opened in Paris. The cycle began with a Hammett detective yarn, *The Maltese Falcon* (Huston, 1941). It was followed by *Laura* (Preminger, 1944), an *amor fou* in which a police detective falls in love with a murder victim by looking at her portrait. Then there were a Raymond Chandler–Philip Marlowe mystery, *Murder, My Sweet* (Dmytryk, 1944); James Cain's study of corruption, distrust, and betrayal, *Double Indemnity* (Wilder, 1944); and the nightmarish *Woman in the Window* (Lang, 1944). Several months later, a second wave of similarly dark American motion pictures hit the French capital, including *This Gun for Hire* (Tuttle, 1942), *The Killers* (Siodmak, 1946), *The Lady in the Lake* (Montgomery, 1946), *Gilda* (Vidor, 1946), and *The Big Sleep* (Hawks, 1946).

French critics were quick to recognize that many of these films possessed similar stylistic elements and settings, common character and narrative traits, and recurrent thematic concerns. They pointed out that these features resembled, in a number of ways, certain characteristics found in prewar American pulp fiction. In fact, most of these first 10 films were adaptations of hard-boiled novels. Dozens of such novels had recently been translated into French and published as a group in a series edited by Marcel Duhamel at Gallimard Press, which marketed them under the generic title of *Serie Noire* or "Black Series."

The term "film noir" was coined by two French critics in an attempt to describe these movies. The adjective "noir" aptly conveys not only the films'

Photofest

In *Laura,* homicide detective Mark McPherson (Dana Andrews) falls in love with the dead woman in the portrait.

antecedents in the *romans noirs* (black novels) of Dashiell Hammett, Raymond Chandler, James M. Cain, Horace McCoy, Cornell Woolrich, Graham Greene, and others but also the essential nature of the *experience* that audiences have in watching the films. These films unsettled audiences. Through their violation of the traditional narrative and stylistic practices of classical Hollywood cinema that oriented and stabilized spectators, these films created an uncomfortable and disturbing malaise or anxiety in their viewers.

FILM NOIR: GENRE, SERIES, OR MODE?

Noir as Genre: A Set of Conventions

Though most critics and historians regard noir as a mode of film practice whose identity resides chiefly in its ability to make audiences uneasy, there is considerable disagreement over what *exactly* film noir is. A number of recent scholars treat film noir as a *genre,* discussing it in terms of its iconography (dark city streets glistening at night with fresh rain), fixed character types (proletarian, tough-guy, antiheroes ensnared by treacherous femmes fatales), and predictable narrative patterns (murder plots and criminal investigations in which the hero's moral fallibility leads to his victimization and/or defeat at the hands of his enemies and often results in his death or in an otherwise unhappy ending).

For those who view it as a genre, film noir (like the Western, gangster film, and musical) relies on a well-defined system of conventions and expectations. Yet these critics also acknowledge film noir's distinctive *style*—it is *dark*. Low-key lighting becomes the norm, replacing the pre–noir norm of cheerful, high-key lighting setups. But style is a feature that rarely, if ever, figures in the definition of a genre.

Noir as Series: A Certain Style

Others insist that film noir is not a genre but a *series* or cycle, and view it as an aesthetic movement, somewhat as German Expressionism was in the 1920s. Though certain characters, narrative situations, and thematic concerns appear again and again in film noir, these elements tend to resist conventionalization and play against expectations. In addition, critics of the genre argument note that film noir lacked the institutional status of traditional genres. Producers, directors, and screenwriters of 1940s and 1950s films noirs, unlike those of Westerns, musicals, or gangster films, did not deliberately set out to make films noirs. There was no body of noir conventions for them to follow. Nor did audiences who saw films noirs view them as they did conventional genre pictures. That is, they did not look at them in relation to a fixed system of prior expectations.

At the same time, a number of critics contend that film noir cannot be a genre because it crosses over traditional genre boundaries; there are noir westerns (*Pursued*, 1947; *Duel in the Sun*, 1946), gangster films (*White Heat*, 1949), melodramas (*Mildred Pierce* and *Leave Her to Heaven*, 1945), costume pictures (*Hangover Square*, 1945; *Reign of Terror*, 1949), sequences in musicals ("The Girl Hunt Ballet" in *The Band Wagon*, 1953), and even comedies (*Arsenic and Old Lace*, 1944; *M. Verdoux*, 1947).

Yet both the pro and con positions concerning noir's status as a genre have a certain validity. Like genre films, every film noir does rely, to some extent, on identifiable character types and conventionalized narrative patterns. The detective hero falls into the clutches of the spider woman, extricating himself from danger only by repressing those passions that drew him to her in the first place and by "sending her over" (i.e., giving her over to the police). Yet, it is just as clear that that which is *generic* in film noir is precisely that which is *not* noir. There is nothing in the above outline of the typical detective story that is necessarily eery, disorienting, or anxiety-producing for the audience.

The problem of film noir's status lies in its essentially schizophrenic nature: film noir is not a genre, but every film noir is also a genre film. In other words, the conventions and systems of expectations that can be found in films noirs are those of the various genres to which these films belong—those of the detective film, the melodrama, or the Western. But what makes these films noir is the similar, transgeneric attitude they take toward their particular genre—the twist they give to conventional genre types, forms, and patterns. Thus, films noirs are all genre films; yet the genre to which they belong is not that of film noir but that of the detective film, the crime film, the Western, the melodrama, or some other genre.

Noir as Mode: An Uneasy Feeling

Another way of understanding the relationship of film noir to the question of genre is to return to the notion of noir as a specific emotional reaction produced by certain films in an audience. In this respect, film noir can be seen as a purely affective phenomenon; that is, it produces certain emotional reponses in people. Given this definition of noir, not every film noir needs to be noir from start to finish; it needs only to be noir for a moment or two. It requires only a single character, situation, or scene that is noir to produce the disturbance or disorientation that is necessary to give the audience an unsettling twist or distressing jolt.

"Noir" thus emerges as an adjectival attribute or characteristic, functioning much as the terms "tragic," "comic," or "melodramatic" do in relation to the genres of tragedy, comedy, and melodrama; "noir" becomes a description of tone, attitude, or mood. In other words, noir, like the "melodramatic," which also crosses over generic boundaries, is not so much a genre as a *mode*—a particular way in which genre information is conveyed.

Traditional modes, however, do not have any temporal boundaries; they are just the way certain stories are told. Although that way of telling stories changes slightly from year to year, in general, it remains fairly consistent over extended lengths of time. Melodramatic historical pictures, for example, continue to be made from period to period, ranging from *The Birth of a Nation* (1915) and *Gone With the Wind* (1939) to *JFK* (1991), *Malcolm X* (1992), *Nixon* (1995), and *Seabiscuit* (2003). Melodramatic Westerns flourished back in the 1940s (*Duel in the Sun, Pursued*) as well as in the 1980s (*Lonesome Dove*) and 1990s (*Lone Star*, 1996; *The Hi-Lo Country*, 1999).

If film noir is a mode, should it not also transcend time? If so, then *Fatal Attraction* (1987) would be as much a film noir as earlier films such as *Leave Her to Heaven* (1945) or *Angel Face* (1953) in which demonic women wreak their vengeance on men. Similarly, *L.A. Confidential* (1997) resembles classic noir films such as *The Big Heat* (1953), in which a rogue cop battles crime on the street and corruption in the police department. But neither *Fatal Attraction* nor *L.A. Confidential* are really noir; they are only pseudo–noir.

By the same token, contemporary remakes of postwar films noirs—*Body Heat* (a 1981 reworking of *Double Indemnity*), *Against All Odds* (a 1984 remake of *Out of the Past*), *Farewell, My Lovely* (a 1975 remake of *Murder, My Sweet*) or *Underneath* (a 1995 remake of *Criss Cross*)—are frequently mistaken as films noirs. A number of critics, especially those who view film noir as a genre, insist that these recent works are films noirs. However, others, especially Paul Schrader, contend that they are not, arguing that film noir, as a cycle, came to an end in the late 1950s. Indeed, Schrader, whose own projects as a screenwriter (*Taxi Driver*, 1976) and director (*Cat People*, 1982) have clearly been heavily influenced by film noir, refuses to describe his own work or even noirish contemporary detective films such as *Chinatown* (1974) as films noirs. For Schrader, film noir belongs to a specific historical era lasting roughly from 1941 (*The Maltese Falcon*) to 1958 (*Touch of Evil*).

NOIR AESTHETICS, THEMES, AND CHARACTER TYPES

For Schrader, film noir as a mode (rather than a genre) was an aesthetic movement. Like the more familiar, European aesthetic movements of German Expressionism or Italian Neorealism, film noir emerged as a cycle or series of films. It consists of a finite group of motion pictures made during a specific historical period that share certain aesthetic traits and thematic concerns.

Aesthetically, noir relies heavily on shadowy, low-key lighting; deep-focus cinematography; distorting, wide-angle lenses; sequence shots; disorienting mise-en-scène; tension-inducing, oblique, and vertical compositional lines; jarring juxtapositions between shots involving extreme changes in camera angle or screen size; claustrophobic framing; romantic voiceover narration; and a complex narrative structure, characterized by flashbacks and/or a convoluted temporal sequencing of events.

Thematically, film noir grapples, as Robert Porfirio suggests, with existential issues such as the futility of individual action; the alienation, loneliness, and isolation of the individual in industrialized, mass society; the problematic choice between being and nothingness; the absurdity, meaninglessness, and purposelessness of life; and the arbitrariness of social justice, which results in individual despair, leading to chaos, violence, and paranoia.

Typical noir heroes do not need to be detectives, though the social alienation of figures in that profession makes them archetypal noir protagonists. Often, they are merely antisocial loners—tramps or drifters as in *Detour* (1945) and *The Postman Always Rings Twice* (1946). But even the gainfully employed—such as insurance salesman Walter Neff in *Double Indemnity* (1944) or cashier Chris Cross in *Scarlet Street* (1945)—can be subject to a certain deadpan, existential angst, especially given their relatively faceless anonymity in a larger, dehumanizing work environment.

But perhaps the most existential of all noir heroes is the amnesiac. In *Somewhere in the Night* (1946), he is an ex-Marine (played by John Hodiak) who possesses only two enigmatic clues to his identity and is plunged into a sinister underworld of crime as he follows these leads in an attempt to figure out who he is. A similar mystery centered around an amnesiac became the central focus

Courtesy of 20th Century-Fox

Amnesiac and returning war veteran George Taylor (John Hodiak) searches for clues to his real identity in *Somewhere in the Night* (1946).

of Alfred Hitchcock's *Spellbound* (1945), in which Gregory Peck is cured of his amnesia by a psychiatrist (played by Ingrid Bergman) with whom he has fallen in love. The amnesiac reappeared in Robert Florey's *The Crooked Way* (1949), which tells the story of another shell-shocked veteran who becomes involved with racketeers as he investigates his own past. These amnesiacs epitomize the social estrangement and psychological confusion that had settled in the formerly healthy American psyche after the war. Audiences established a troubled identification with these heroes who had become cut off from their own pasts and whose identity crises mirrored those of the nation as a whole.

As both a style and a bundle of thematic concerns, film noir initially seems to be a phenomenon that could appear at any moment in time. But, as an aesthetic movement, it is necessarily grounded in a particular historical period—that of wartime and postwar America. To what extent is it a style or (thematic) content? To what extent is it a unique feature of American film history? Clearly, noir is a combination of all of its various identities. It is part genre, part series, part mode.

Certain stylistic elements and thematic concerns associated with film noir look back to 1920s German Expressionism and 1930s French Poetic Realism. They also look forward to certain American films of the 1970s and 1980s that appropriated noir stylistics in an attempt to capture the apocalyptic mood of an era disillusioned by the Watergate cover-up and psychically scarred by the Vietnam War. But they finally belong to only one period and place—to 1940s and early 1950s America.

Neither the German Expressionist *The Cabinet of Dr. Caligari* (1919) nor the French Poetic Realist *La Bête Humaine* (1938) have ever been described as films noirs. However, Hollywood's reworking of the former (*Strange Illusion*, 1945) and remake of the latter (*Human Desire*, 1954) have. Why? And why is it that Schrader and others have not accepted contemporary remakes of postwar films noirs, ranging from *Farewell, My Lovely* (1975) and *The Big Sleep* (1978) to *Body Heat* (1981) and *Against All Odds* (1984), as films noirs? The answers to these questions return us to the moment of the discovery of film noir in postwar France and to the notion that film noir's identity is somehow bound up with its ability to disturb audiences.

NOIR STYLISTICS: A SHIFT IN PERSPECTIVE

American Expressionism

What struck French critics about film noir was its essential difference from earlier American films. The narrative linearity of 1930s classical cinema had suddenly given way to narrative disjunction, fragmentation, and disorientation, as seen in the flashback-within-flashback-within-flashback structure of *The Locket* (1946). *Citizen Kane* (1941) had blazed the trail for complex narrative structure, and dozens of films noirs, even including marginal, low-budget efforts such as *Raw Deal* (1948) and *Ruthless* (1948), modeled themselves on Welles's masterpiece. *Kane* served as a source for much of noir's subsequent stylistic and narrative practice, though it lacks one ingredient crucial to most definitions of noir: its narrative is not concerned with crime nor are its characters situated in a criminal milieu.

The soft, evenly distributed, high-key lighting style of the 1930s, which functioned to direct the audience's attention and to glamorize stars, yielded virtually overnight to the harsh, low-key lighting of the 1940s, which obscured the action, deglamorized the star, and reduced the actors to shadowy formal elements embedded in the overall design of the composition. The carefully constructed sense of space found in classical cinema, which worked to maintain the spatial orientation of the spectator, disappeared and was replaced by wide-angle cinematography, which, as in films such as Welles's *Touch of Evil* (1958), distorted space and disoriented the spectator.

Conventional eye-level camera positions gave way, in films such as *Kiss Me Deadly* (Aldrich, 1955), to extreme low- and high-angle perspectives. Welles and Aldrich frequently cut from one extreme angle to another to heighten the assault on the spectator's sense of complacency. With every violation of the norm, film noir stylistics marked an intrusive intervention between the spectator and the straightforward exposition of the story, foregrounding narrative form and thus making it visible.

From the perspective of French and presumably American audiences as well, film noir could be understood as the same old familiar classical Hollywood cinema possessed by a new, recognizably alien spirit, which incorporates aesthetic elements and thematic concerns previously found only in foreign art films. Expressionistic devices such as highly subjective, voiceover narration (*Detour,* 1945) or hallucinatory sequences (*Murder, My Sweet,* 1944) suddenly replaced more conventional, less visible narrative practices. It was all right for foreign films, such as *Caligari,* to be a bit odd. American audiences expected that. But when American films began to adopt—even for only a moment—a foreign tongue, the disquieting forces of fear and paranoia crept into what used to be, for most American audiences at least, the stabilizing and reassuring experience of going to the movies.

From Disturbing Conventions to Conventional Disturbances

If foreign elements had appeared in American films that had more overt artistic pretensions, they might have been understood as justified by the artistic nature of the film itself, as in the case of *Citizen Kane.* But they cropped up in the least likely places—in sleazy detective films, low-budget crime pictures, and run-of-the-mill melodramas. No wonder audiences became uneasy. The staple of the industry and the films most frequently identified with everyday motion picture entertainment—genre films—had developed psychotic tendencies. Something had clearly gone wrong somewhere. In other words, these films were noir in the context of the more conventional body of Hollywood cinema that preceded them. They were noir for audiences seeing them for the first time in the 1940s and 1950s. And, though they continue to appear noir in relation to earlier films for subsequent audiences, we tend to be less disturbed by them today than our grandparents must have been in the postwar era. Subsequent American cinema—itself influenced by film noir—has hardened us to its unsettling power.

This is clearly not the case for the derivative films noirs of the 1970s, 1980s, and 1990s, which look back stylistically and thematically to the authentic films noirs of the 1940s and 1950s. Following the publication of Schrader's "Notes on Film Noir" in 1972, screenwriters and directors deliberately set out to make films noirs, transforming the disruptive stylistic strategies and disturbing thematic obsessions of postwar film noir into a system of expectations and conventions. As they watched *The Long Goodbye* (1973), *Chinatown* (1974), or even the science-fiction film, *Blade Runner* (1982), audiences recalled the private-eye films of the 1940s to which these works allude. Directors in the 1970s quoted film noir stylistic devices in an attempt to reconstruct the postwar period in which their films are set.

In these instances, film noir has been transformed from an aesthetic movement into a genre. Stylistic elements that, in the 1940s and 1950s, were part of a strategy to disorient spectators have been refashioned, in the 1970s and later, into a systematic, carefully tailored look designed to trigger a conventional acknowledgment on the part of viewers who identify that look with films of the late 1940s. The overall effect of these allusions to earlier films noirs on contemporary audiences is more reassuring than unsettling. The noir films of the 1970s and later are not noir. They are pseudo–noir.

NOIR AND THE PRODUCTION CODE

Forbidden Subjects; Twisted Treatments

The Production Code—the body of censorship regulations governing what Hollywood was permitted to show on the screen—played a crucial role in making films of the 1940s and early 1950s noir. Subsequent changes in this Code resulted in the production of films that were decidedly less noir. Prior to 1968, when the Production Code instituted in the 1930s was abandoned for a version of the present film-rating system, certain subject matter was prohibited from the screen. Taboo subjects ranged from the depiction of nudity, homosexuality, interracial sexual activity, incest, rape, and abortion to excessive violence or brutality, profanity, the detailed depiction of criminal acts, and the use of drugs.

American films of the mid- to late 1930s rarely dealt with these subjects, but film noir frequently did, often resulting in amazing displays of narrative contortion as the films alluded to prohibited material without directly violating the Code. Acts of sadism and violence, such as the scalding of an individual's face with a pot of boiling hot coffee in *The Big Heat* (1953), regularly took place off-screen. Their intensity was amplified by violent or otherwise disjunctive editing or offscreen sound effects. Homosexuality figured prominently in the motivation of the plots of several original novels later made into films noirs; but on the screen this motivation was concealed, disguised, or recast in another form. It was desexualized and displaced—occasionally in ways that laid bare deep cultural fears about homosexuality with an astounding clarity. Thus, the homophobia that prompts the central murder in Richard Brooks's novel, *The Brick Foxhole*, was transformed by Hollywood self-censorship into anti-Semitism in Edward Dmytryk's screen adaptation of the book, *Crossfire* (1947).

In other instances, the presence of sexual abnormality and the use of drugs in novels were repressed altogether in their film adaptations, resulting in narrative incoherence, as in *The Big Sleep* (1946). Indeed, the centrality of drugs and sex to the Chandler novel on which the Hawks film was based forced its producers to resort to the most obscure sorts of subterfuges in an attempt to adapt the original plot to the screen. These gymnastics resulted in a final product that, although directed by one of the most obsessive practitioners of narrative logic—Howard Hawks—was almost incomprehensible to anyone who had not read the original Chandler novel.

© S. S. Archives/Shooting Star

In *The Big Sleep* Marlowe (Humphrey Bogart) find's his client's daughter, Carmen (Martha Vickers), drugged and incoherent in a blackmailer's apartment with the body of a dead man at her feet.

The End of Censorship; the End of Noir?

The relaxation of the Production Code in the late 1950s, along with the advent of the ratings system in the late 1960s, prepared the way for a new era of explicitness in the 1970s. By that time, films dealt more or less openly with adultery (*Body Heat* and *The Postman Always Rings Twice,* 1981), rape (*Straw Dogs,* 1971; *Frenzy,* 1972), incest (*Chinatown,* 1974), drugs (*The French Connection* I and II, 1971, 1975; *Farewell, My Lovely,* 1975), extreme violence (*Dirty Harry,* 1971; *Taxi Driver,* 1976), prostitution (*Hustle,* 1975; *Taxi Driver,* 1976), and, last but not least, nudity and sexual intercourse (see all of the above films and a large percentage of all 1970s films).

Michael Winner's remake of *The Big Sleep* (1978) was free to include everything that had been outlawed by censors in the 1940s, and it did so with a vengeance. But its graphicness doomed it as a film noir. No stylistic or narrational contortions were necessary to get it past the censors. Its subject matter may have been sensational (though in the context of 1970s movies, it was pretty tame), but the way in which this material was presented was neither disturbed nor disturbing. It was as classically direct as any film from Hollywood in the 1930s. The matter-of-factness with which previously taboo material was dealt in the sexually liberated climate of the 1970s is what distinguishes the earlier, authentic films noirs of the 1940s and 1950s from the pseudo–films noirs of the 1970s and later.

INNOCENCE LOST: THE LITERARY ORIGINS OF FILM NOIR

In examining film noir as an affective phenomenon—as an uncomfortable experience for spectators—we have tended so far to define it negatively by stating what it is not and what is not it: it is not a genre, and films of the 1970s and later that appropriate the style and themes of earlier films noirs are not necessarily noir. But it is also possible to define film noir more positively in terms of the various negative forces that helped bring it into being. For instance, the outbreak of war in Europe, American entry into World War II, and postwar efforts to return to normal set the agenda for a more downbeat brand of cinema than audiences had encountered in the 1930s.

The immediate postwar era, in particular, seems to have been guided by the mistaken belief that the relatively simple world of prewar America for which returning servicemen had fought and for which they nostalgically longed could be magically recreated. The general realization that this was a delusion clearly influenced both the world-weary cynicism of film noir and the sense of frustration and experience of disempowerment that stood at its center. American innocence could not be easily recaptured.

In fact, film noir suggested that American innocence had been lost long before the war. It became clearer and clearer that something more than money and jobs was lost during the Great Depression. The spirit of noir traces its origins back to certain thematic and stylistic antecedents that it shares with American popular fiction of the 1920s and 1930s.

Hard-Boiled Fiction

In both content and style, American hard-boiled novels introduced a new tradition of realism to the genre of detective fiction. This realism was characterized by a revolutionary shift in both the class and the technique of the detective, the milieu in which the detective worked, and the language that he or she spoke. Unlike English detective fiction, which was dominated by aristocratic dabblers in detection, armchair experts in the art of deduction, or dotty old women armed with upper- or middle-class sensibilities, the novels of Hammett, Cain, McCoy, Chandler, and others featured a proletarian tough guy who lived on the fringe of the criminal world.

As Ross Macdonald, the creator of Lew Archer, explains, the protagonist of these works was "the classless, restless man [sic] of American democracy, who spoke the language of the street." As Macdonald's own language suggests, American hard-boiled detectives were almost by definition, male. While the relative gentility of the world in which English detectives functioned permitted female sleuths, the "mean streets" down which the hard-boiled detective walked were not safe for women.

The private eye's milieu was characterized not by garden parties, teas, masked balls, and other ceremonies of the well-to-do but by dark city streets, back alleys, grungy offices (with a pint of booze in the desk drawer), desolate hotel rooms, sleazy bars, pool halls, gambling dens, houses of prostitution, and other attractions in the neon-lit, red-light districts that dominated the wrong side of town. Hammett's Personville (pronounced "Poisonville") and Chandler's Bay City epitomized the corrupt metropolises the typical hard-boiled detective haunted. As Steven Marcus suggests, this was a Hobbesian world in which life was nasty, brutish, and short—a world characterized by universal warfare, anarchy, and mistrust.

For the majority of these Depression-era novelists, contemporary America was an urban, industrialized landscape peopled by characters caught in the grip of passion, lust, greed, jealousy, and other naturalistic drives. The "boys in the back room," as Edmund Wilson called the "Black Mask" school of writers of pulp detective fiction, looked back for inspiration neither to Wilkie Collins, the Dickensian author of *The Moonstone* and *The Woman in White*, nor to Sir Arthur Conan Doyle, but to Émile Zola and other nineteenth-century naturalists, whose matter-of-fact depiction of decadence and corruption caught their imagination.

The Detective Hero

Unlike their European predecessors, Edgar Allan Poe's Dupin or Conan Doyle's Sherlock Holmes, the hard-boiled detectives did not rely on the powers of deductive reasoning, acute observation, or scientific method to solve their cases but rather on dogged perseverance, animal cunning, physical stamina, and brute force. Noir heroes, whether detectives or not, were similarly weak as intellects. In *Double Indemnity*, when insurance investigator Barton Keyes asks Walter Neff to give up his sales job to work behind a desk with him, Walter refuses. After noting that he has always considered Walter "a shade less dumb" than the other salesmen, Keyes sarcastically quips that Walter isn't really smarter than the others; he is just a bit taller.

In matching wits with Phyllis, the film's femme fatale, Walter comes in second. She successfully manipulates him into helping her do away with her husband and then, when he begins to suspect her of treachery at the end, she outmaneuvers him, countering his plot against her with a plot of her own against him. About all he can do is arrange to die last (i.e., after she has died), enjoying the fate that lies in store for most noir heroes.

Though the brawny, proletarian tough guy of American detective fiction might have lacked the mental powers of his brainy predecessors, he, like his successors in film noir, attempted to make up for his failings as a man of intellect with his verbal wit. Both the writer of detective fiction and the detective hero controlled their worlds by controlling language. They had style—verbal style. Hammett's sparse, highly verbal, prose style and straightforward syntactical style established a no-nonsense world in which the monosyllabic directness and the dogged, one-fact-or-clue-after-another, linear logic of the detective hero effectively cut through the web of lies spun by everyone he encounted, from the Fat Man and his gunsel to Joel Cairo and the femme fatale.

At the other end of the stylistic spectrum, Chandler's complex syntactical style, colorful metaphors, and descriptive excesses established a narrative voice that valued the ability to turn a phrase. The prowess of his private eye was measured by his control of language, especially witty repartee which enables him to enjoy an edge over his opponents in the verbal arena, even though they may have been able to dominate him physically. In *Farewell, My Lovely*, Marlowe even dubbed one of his flat-footed, slow-witted antagonists "Hemingway." Here Chandler, through his detective hero, took a jab at the impoverished verbal style that informs a number of Hemingway-influenced American mystery writers and confirmed the privileged status, in his work at least, of verbal wit over linguistic directness.

Noir and Verbal Wit

In Chandler's reworking for the screen of Cain's *Double Indemnity*, the first encounter between Fred MacMurray's Walter Neff and Barbara Stanwyck's Phyllis Dietrichson provides the chief example of hard-boiled repartee used as a mode of playful combat. Always the glib insurance salesman trying to make a sale, Neff attempts to talk his client's wife into bed with him while she coyly counters his advances. Their conversation concludes with the following exchange:

> PHYLLIS: There's a speed limit in this state, Mr. Neff. Forty-five miles per hour.
>
> WALTER: How fast was I going, officer?
>
> PHYLLIS: I'd say around 90.
>
> WALTER: Suppose you get down off your motorcycle and give me a ticket?
>
> PHYLLIS: Suppose I let you off with a warning this time?
>
> WALTER: Suppose it doesn't take?
>
> PHYLLIS: Suppose I have to whack you over the knuckles?
>
> WALTER: Suppose I bust out crying and put my head on your shoulder?
>
> PHYLLIS: Suppose you try putting it on my husband's shoulder?
>
> WALTER: That tears it! [*pause*] Eight-thirty tomorrow evening then?
>
> PHYLLIS: That's what I suggested.
>
> WALTER: Will you be here too?
>
> PHYLLIS: I guess so. I usually am.
>
> WALTER: Same chair, same perfume, same anklet?
>
> PHYLLIS: I wonder if I know what you mean?
>
> WALTER: I wonder if you wonder?

Insurance salesman Walter Neff (Fred MacMurray) spars with his client's wife (Barbara Stanwyck) in *Double Indemnity* (1944).

Double Indemnity's double entendres about "speeding," and "traffic tickets" not only introduce the couple's relationship in terms of crime and punishment, but also establish their basic sexual antagonism. This initial, seemingly harmless, sexual banter serves to structure the implicit sexual hostility that governs their relationship during the remainder of the film and prepares the groundwork for their last, nonverbal exchange, when they finally stop talking and shoot one another.

WOMEN IN FILM NOIR

The origins of film noir in pulp fiction help explain its distinctive attitude toward the representation of women. The proletarian tough guy achieves his toughness by repressing all signs of weakness in himself—and all weakness, for him, is associated with the feminine. At the end of *The Maltese Falcon*, Humphrey Bogart's Sam Spade deliberates between his feelings (a "feminine" virtue) for Brigid O'Shaughnessy (Mary Astor) and his loyalty to professional codes (a "male" virtue), which requires him to avenge the murder of his former partner. Spade sticks by the male codes of the detective and, by resisting Brigid's final appeals and turning her over to the police, rejects his feminine side.

Women as Social Menace

The threat that women and the feminine posed to the noir hero presented itself on two different fronts—the socioeconomic and the psychoanalytic. On the socioeconomic front, as Sylvia Harvey shows, the changing status of American women during the war and postwar period challenged male dominance. The entry of women into the workforce and their taking over of traditional male roles violated the fundamental order of sexual relations. Previously, middle-class women were confined to the home, where they took care of the domestic needs of the family, while men were able to move back and forth freely between the home and the workplace. In the 1940s, women took jobs in factories, replacing men who had gone into the service (see *The Life and Times of Rosie the Riveter*, 1980). They worked on assembly lines in defense plants, making tanks or airplanes (see *Swing Shift Maisie*, 1943, or *Swing Shift*, 1984).

These changes posed a threat to traditional values, which were seen as centered in the institution of the family. Film noir registered the antifeminist backlash by providing a picture of a postwar America in which there is no family or in which the family exists chiefly as a negative phenomenon. In noir, the family was either nonexistent or negative. It was characterized either as a claustrophobic, emasculating trap (snaring the henpecked husband, Chris Cross, in *Scarlet Street*) or as a bankrupt system of perfunctory relationships, featuring murderous wives (*Double Indemnity*) and corrupt children (*Mildred Pierce*). In leaving the private sphere of home and family to enter the public sphere of work, women (such as Mildred Pierce), it was assumed, had abandoned—or at least neglected—the domestic needs of their sweethearts, husbands, and children. Film noir dramatized the consequences of this neglect, transforming women into willful creatures intent on destroying both their mates and the sacred institution of the family.

Classical Hollywood cinema had taken great efforts to shield the family from the world of crime. Traditional genre films routinely opposed the sacred space of the family to that of the world outside. Even gangster films sought to contrast the bonds of family with those of the gang. Crime films centered dramatic conflict around the struggle of each institution with the other over the possession of the identity or soul of the gangster hero, a process illustrated in *Public Enemy* (1931) through the (ineffectual) efforts of Tom Powers's family to keep him from a life of crime. In film noir, the world of crime and that of the family overlap. Crime had moved from outside the family to within it, and the impetus for crime came as often from women as from men.

Typical film noir families consisted of wives who killed their husbands (*Double Indemnity, The Postman Always Rings Twice*), husbands who killed or tried to kill their wives (*Gaslight, The Two Mrs. Carrolls*), children who killed or tried to kill their parents or stepparents (*The Strange Love of Martha Ivers, Angel Face*), uncles who tried to kill their nieces (*Shadow of a Doubt*), aunts who killed their nephews (*Leave Her to Heaven*), and lovers who killed one another (*Out of the Past, Gun Crazy*).

Women as Psychological Terror

The psychoanalytic front reflected women in film noir who presented a psychic threat to the typically insecure noir hero. Laura Mulvey, following Freud, argues that the image of women on the screen functioned to recall, for the male spectator, the castration anxiety he experienced on first perceiving sexual difference as a child. As an institution that supported male dominance and patriarchy, classical Hollywood cinema attempted to alleviate this anxiety through a process known as disavowal in which the female's castrated status was denied. This denial could be achieved either through her fetishization or through her devaluation, or both.

In fetishization, the image of the woman was *overvalued*, often through the use of lingering close-ups, glamorous costumes, or other techniques that transformed her into a spectacle. In becoming pure spectacle, the lack that she signified was thus filled in, replaced by her objectification. Marlene Dietrich, for example, was routinely fetishized by Josef von Sternberg in films such as *The Blue Angel* and *Morocco* (1930) and *Shanghai Express* (1932), in which close-ups of her legs or her face turned her into an object of both male desire and male fantasy.

Through a process of *devaluation*, woman was seen as guilty object—her "castration" serving as the symbol of her punishment. Thus, Alfred Hitchcock, in films such as *Notorious* (1946) or *Vertigo* (1958), presented guilty women who were the objects of male investigations into the original source of their guilt. The heroine in the former film is a "fallen woman"—the daughter of a Nazi spy, an alcoholic, and a playmate of wealthy men; the heroine in the latter film is a paid accomplice to a murder. These women are first punished and then later, having revealed their guilty secrets, rescued (or, in the case of *Vertigo*, not rescued) by the heroes. A similar logic motivated the representation of women in film noir. As Mulvey explains, female sexuality was routinely devalued by the male protagonists, who felt threatened by it.

Thus, women in film noir tended to be characterized as femmes fatales, intent on castrating or otherwise destroying the male hero. This role was played with nightmarish fidelity by Jean Simmons in *Angel Face* (1953), Barbara Stanwyck in *Double Indemnity*, Joan Bennett in *Scarlet Street*, and a host of other spider women.

Often noir women were both fetishized and devalued, constructed as spectacular objects of male sexual fantasy who then turned on those whose desires initially empowered them. Thus, Stanwyck first appears in *Double Indemnity* standing at the top of the stairs, dressed only in a bath towel. Moments later, her body is fetishized through close-ups of her ankle as she descends the stairs. Yet her initial appearance as spectacle is subsequently revealed to have been staged; it is all part of her seduction and subsequent entrapment of the hero, whom she then manipulates into killing her husband.

The femme fatale in *Out of the Past* (1947) romantically materializes before the detective hero in the exotic setting of Mexico, emerging first out of the

The iconography of film noir: In *Out of the Past* (1947), the treacherous femme fatale (played by Jane Greer, left) holds a smoking gun, while the vulnerable male hero (Robert Mitchum) smokes a cigarette.

sunlight, then out of the moonlight, as he sits in a small cantina in Acapulco. By the end of the film, her path has been strewn with the bodies of an apparently endless succession of dead men, culminating with that of the hapless hero (Robert Mitchum), whom she shoots in the groin.

A CRITIQUE OF POPULISM

New Culture, Old Myths

The destabilization of sexual relationships found in film noir is symptomatic of a larger social disorder. Prior to World War II, American society had been held together by various myths that structured its identity as a nation. These myths rested, in large part, on the principles of Jeffersonian democracy, which assumed a fundamental equality based on the universal ownership of property. More specifically, Jeffersonian democracy was based on the agrarian ideal of the yeoman farmer, whose self-sufficiency was rooted in his ability to grow enough food for himself as well as additional produce to sell to his neighbors. In other words, notions of democratic equality were founded on the universal ownership of property. This equality-through-universal-ownership concept provided the fundamental principle for a mythology that drove nineteenth-century American expansionist ideology. The democratic promise of cheap or free land to those who settled the frontier thus served as the motivation for western settlement, which became, in turn, a realization of America's manifest destiny.

But the closing of the frontier, the exhaustion of free land, and the rapid industrialization of America in the latter part of the nineteenth century began a slow process of social change. The agrarian ideal gave way to an industrialized mass society. By 1920, for the first time in American history, more people lived in urban than in rural areas. The old middle class consisting of shopkeepers, farmers, and other property owners gave way to a new middle class dominated by hourly wage earners, who owned neither land nor houses.

Though millions of laborers and white-collar workers lived this new reality, they continued to subscribe to the old, preindustrial-era myths. It was only after the Depression that the power of these myths began to waver. Film noir reflects a transitional stage in American ideology as American identity shifted from nineteenth-century, preindustrial, agrarian prototypes to twentieth-century models that acknowledged the nation's transformation into a mass consumer society and an industrialized, corporate state.

Double Indemnity's Walter Neff, for example, works for a large, anonymous, consumer-based corporation—the Pacific All-Risk Insurance Co. He is a product of postwar consumer society. He lives alone in an efficiency apartment, goes bowling for fun and relaxation, has clandestine rendezvous with married women among shelves of mass-produced baby food and other mass-market products at the local supermarket, and drinks beer in his car at a drive-in restaurant. Film noir captured the emptiness of Neff's world. As a movement, it reflected the chaotic period in which old myths began to crumble and no new myths were there to take their place—the period in which national identity was in crisis.

Capra and Film Noir

The best examples of these old myths appear in the work of Frank Capra, whose films epitomize the classicism and order of pre–noir Hollywood cinema. Capra's vision of America was set forth in a series of films made in the late 1930s, culminating in *Mr. Deeds Goes to Town* (1936) and *Mr. Smith Goes to Washington* (1939), which articulated a populist ideology. These films celebrated nineteenth-century agrarian values such as hard work, frugality, honesty, good neighborliness, self-sufficiency, egalitarianism, common sense, personal authenticity (as opposed to phoniness), and moral sincerity. Through the heroic efforts of their stalwart protagonists, they attacked the twentieth-century evils of industrialism, big business, special interest groups, commercialism, political

George Bailey (James Stewart, left) finds his beloved Bedford Falls transformed into a noirish Pottersville in *It's a Wonderful Life.*

machines, urban corruption, cynicism, and intellectualism—all of which threatened the populist spirit that had animated small-town America.

The threat to this idyllic world was presented most powerfully in Capra's postwar celebration of small-town American values—*It's a Wonderful Life* (1946). Here George Bailey (James Stewart), through his building and loan company, holds off the efforts of corrupt, greedy capitalists such as Mr. Potter (Lionel Barrymore) to transform the city of Bedford Falls into an ugly, modern American metropolis. George Bailey, having sacrificed his own desires and needs in the service of his family, friends, and the larger community, believes that his life has been a failure and, like the existential noir hero, is driven to contemplate suicide. But his guardian angel rescues him from his own self-destructive efforts and reveals to him what Bedford Falls would have been like if he had never lived.

Like the alienated hero of film noir, George wanders through Bedford Falls, which has now become "Pottersville," in search of someone who would confirm his identity and the fact of his prior existence. In a reversal of certain earlier noir films such as *Somewhere in the Night* (1946), it is the town, not George, that has developed amnesia. Yet, the experience for George remains as weird and alienating as that which any of his shell-shocked predecessors had undergone. The Pottersville sequence reverses the populist ideal of small-town America, displaying no families, homes, or small businesses. All of these have apparently been destroyed by the forces of big business and industrialization identified with Potter, who reduces proud homeowners to tenants in slum dwellings.

For a few minutes, the corrupt nature of contemporary corporate America that this and Capra's earlier 1930s films had struggled so hard to combat and, through their heroes' ultimate triumphs, to deny, surfaces. It is a world in which the individual has no stake in society and thus no power or place in a social system that is suddenly revealed to be nondemocratic (i.e., not based on an equal ownership of property). Capra, however, quickly patches up this crack in American populist ideology, relegating the Pottersville sequence to the status of a bad dream and restoring George to his family, friends, and community.

Yet, the presence of this nightmarish inversion of Capra's ideal American community in the film brilliantly illustrates film noir's subversive relationship to classical Hollywood cinema, which attempted to repress the very forces to which film noir gave voice. Film noir, as a phenomenon of the 1940s, grew out of the horrifying realization that the populist myth that had given comfort and order to American identity in the past was just that—only a myth—and that a new reality—that of Pottersville—had taken its place. It was a realization that, coupled with the trauma of war and the disillusionment of the postwar period, served to smash the utopian fantasy world of 1930s ideology. In other words, film noir represents a remarkable epistemological shift in America's self-conceptualization. Capra's utopian, small-town America didn't exist anymore—except in Capra pictures.

FILM NOIR: AN UNDERCURRENT IN THE MAINSTREAM

Film noir, however, did not entirely dismantle American myth and American identity in the 1940s; it proved to be only one major current in (and clearly beneath) a flood of films that reaffirmed traditional American values and identity. With the exception of certain downbeat items such as *The Best Years of Our Lives* (1946), and *Duel in the Sun* (1946), the box-office champs of the postwar era tended to be films that were decidedly not noir—films such as *Meet Me in St. Louis* (1944), *National Velvet* (1944), *The Bells of St. Mary's* (1945), *The Jolson Story* (1946), *Life With Father* (1947), *The Road to Rio* (1947), *Easter Parade* (1948), *Jolson Sings Again* (1949), *Samson and Delilah* (1949), *David and Bathsheba* (1951), *Show Boat* (1951), *An American in Paris* (1951), *Quo Vadis?* (1951), and *Ivanhoe* (1952).

By the late 1950s, the advent of television virtually destroyed the low-budget, B-film industry that provided the bulk of films noirs. The mood of the country began to reflect a newfound, postwar prosperity (indeed, economic historians began to refer to the United States as "the affluent society"); and, at the end of the decade, the promise of John F. Kennedy's "New Frontier" turned Americans from potentially depressing thoughts of the technological blight produced by industrialization to utopian visions of a machine-age paradise filled with labor-saving devices. The trauma of the Depression and the shell shock of the war years, which destabilized American identity briefly in the postwar era, had supposedly been treated and cured. The films noirs that were noir "for us" no longer spoke to the needs some Americans felt for films that addressed their own existential malaise.

But the scar on the American psyche that film noir represented remains visible today for all of us to see. It was brought back to the surface of the American psyche by another war—that in Vietnam. And film noir's ability to convey a sense of paranoia and betrayal made it the ideal form for capturing the spirit of post-Watergate America. Americans rediscovered film noir in the 1970s because it provided a way of looking at experience that not only reflected that experience but also finally made sense. Film noir of the 1940s and 1950s became the source material that prompted a new understanding of postwar American reality. In rediscovering it, Americans located a more modern body of myths through which they might come to terms with contemporary American experience.

■ ■ ■ SELECT FILMOGRAPHY

Citizen Kane (1941)
The Maltese Falcon (1941)
This Gun for Hire (1942)
Double Indemnity (1944)
Murder, My Sweet (1944)
Detour (1945)
Hangover Square (1945)
Leave Her to Heaven (1945)
Mildred Pierce (1945)
My Name is Julia Ross (1945)
Scarlet Street (1945)
The Killers (1946)
The Locket (1946)
Somewhere in the Night (1946)
The Spiral Staircase (1946)
The Strange Love of Martha Ivers
    (1946)
Crossfire (1947)
M. Verdoux (1947)
Out of the Past (1947)
Pursued (1947)
The Lady From Shanghai (1948)
Moonrise (1948)
The Naked City (1948)
Ruthless (1948)
Gun Crazy (1949)

Sunset Blvd. (1950)
Macao (1952)
Angel Face (1953)
The Big Heat (1953)
The Big Combo (1955)
Kiss Me Deadly (1955)
Touch of Evil (1958)
Pseudo–noirs
The Long Goodbye (1973)
Chinatown (1974)
Night Moves (1975)
Farewell, My Lovely (1975)
The Big Sleep (1978)
Body Heat (1981)
The Postman Always Rings Twice
    (1981)
Blood Simple (1984)
Against All Odds (1984)
Miller's Crossing (1990)
The Grifters (1990)
Cape Fear (1991)
Red Rock West (1993)
Underneath (1995)
Devil in a Blue Dress (1995)
Bound (1996)
L.A. Confidential (1997)

■ ■ ■ SELECT BIBLIOGRAPHY

BORDE, RAYMOND, AND ETIENNE CHAUMETON. *Panorama du Film Noir Americain.* Paris: Editions du Minuit, 1955.

CAMERON, IAN, ed. *The Book of Film Noir.* New York: Continuum, 1993.

COPJEC, JOAN, ed. *Shades of Noir.* London: Verso, 1993.

HARVEY, SYLVIA. "Woman's Place: The Absent Family of Film Noir," in E. Ann Kaplan, ed., *Women in Film Noir.* London: BFI, 1978.

HIRSCH, FOSTER. *The Dark Side of the Screen: Film Noir.* San Diego: Barnes, 1981.

KAPLAN, E. ANN, ed. *Women in Film Noir.* London: BFI, 1980.

KRUTNIK, FRANK. *In a Lonely Street: Film Noir, Genre, Masculinity.* London: Routledge, 1991.

MARCUS, STEVEN. "Introduction," in *The Continental Op,* by Dashiell Hammett. New York: Vintage, 1975.

MULVEY, LAURA. "Visual Pleasure and Narrative Cinema," *Screen* 16, no. 3 (Autumn 1975).

NAREMORE, JAMES. *More Than Night: Film Noir in its Contexts.* Berkeley: University of California Press, 1998.

PLACE, JANEY. "Women in Film Noir," in E. Ann Kaplan, ed., *Women in Film Noir.* London: BFI, 1978.

PORFIRIO, ROBERT G. "No Way Out: Existential Motifs in the Film Noir," *Sight and Sound* 45, no. 4 (Autumn 1976), 212–217.

SCHRADER, PAUL. "Notes on Film Noir," *Film Comment* 8 (Spring 1972), 8–13.

SILVER, ALAIN, AND JAMES URSINI, eds. *Film Noir Reader.* New York: Limelight Editions, 1996.

———— AND ELIZABETH WARD, eds. *Film Noir: An Encyclopedic Reference to the American Style.* Woodstock, NY: Overlook Press, 1979.

TELOTTE, J. P. *Voices in the Dark: The Narrative Patterns of Film Noir.* Urbana: University of Illinois Press, 1989.

CHAPTER 11

The Making of the West

THE AMERICAN FILM GENRE PAR EXCELLENCE

For over 40 years, from 1926 to 1967, Hollywood produced more Westerns than any other kind of film. During these years, roughly one-quarter of all Hollywood films were Westerns and, though no statistics exist for the years prior to 1926, Westerns similarly dominated American silent film production. The popularity of the silent Western began with *The Great Train Robbery* (1903), which reenacted a famous robbery by Butch Cassidy and the Wild Bunch that had occurred only a few years earlier. The genre's appeal increased with "Broncho Billy" Anderson, Thomas Ince, and D. W. Griffith Westerns. And it culminated in the box-office success of films featuring Dustin Farnum, William S. Hart, and Tom Mix. The screen personae of these Western stars captivated audiences from the mid-1910s through the late 1920s.

Though a sizable proportion of the total number of Westerns made in Hollywood undoubtedly included many B films, the sheer quantity of Westerns produced—whether classified as A, B, or Z pictures—testifies to the overwhelming popularity of the genre. Other genres, most notably the gangster film, remained uniquely American in origin, but the Western became the American film genre par excellence, not only in terms of the quantity and quality of films made but also in terms of its longevity as a genre.

Though almost all the great Western stars of the postwar era, such as Gary Cooper, Randolph Scott, Joel McCrea, and John Wayne, are now dead and the genre itself has been repeatedly proclaimed dead (by Pauline Kael and others), rumors of the death of the Western have, as Mark Twain might have said, been somewhat exaggerated, as recent revivals of the genre in the late 1980s and 1990s, such as the television mini-series *Lonesome Dove* (1989), *Dances With Wolves* (1990), *Back to the Future Part III* (1990), *City Slickers* (1991), *Unforgiven* (1992), *Last of the Mohicans* (1992), *Tombstone* (1993), *The Ballad of Little Jo* (1993), *Posse* (1993), *Maverick* (1994), *Legends of the Fall* (1994), *Wyatt Earp* (1994), *Dead Man* (1995), *The Quick and the Dead* (1995), *Lone Star* (1996), *The Mark of Zorro* (1998), and *The Hi-Lo Country* (1999) suggest.

A century after *The Great Train Robbery* (1903), Westerns continue to be made. Kevin Costner's *Open Range* (2003), a revisionist revenge Western, pits a pair of old West open-range cattlemen (Robert Duvall and Kevin Costner) against a new West rancher (Michael Gambon) who engages in old West brutality to oppose the open range and to claim it as private property. Ron Howard's *The Missing* (2003), a New Age reworking of *The Searchers* (1956), focuses on the attempts to rescue a white girl (actually six white women and one Native American woman) abducted by a multicultural band of former army Indian scouts and renegade white men. The searchers consist of the white girl's estranged grandfather (Tommy Lee Jones) who abandoned his family to live with Native Americans, as well as her strong-willed mother (Cate Blanchett) and her equally determined little sister (Jenna Boyd)—both of whom refuse, in an un-Fordian gesture, to wait at home while the hero accomplishes the mission on his own. The sexual and racial dynamics of the Western may have changed over the years, but the genre survives.

And even if the film Western were to disappear entirely, the power of the myth of the West that gives film Westerns much of their vitality would, in all likelihood, continue to flourish in the everyday world of modern America. We would still be listening to country-and-western music performed by singers and musicians in Western dress. We would still pay premium prices for "sweated" Stetsons and jeans, broken in for us by real cowboys out West. Those of us with a bit less money would still buy new Wrangler jeans off the rack. And we would still be eating fast food at Roy's (Roy Rogers restaurants, that is), smoking Marlboro cigarettes, and driving cars named Thunderbird, Mustang, Colt, Bronco, Pinto, Cougar, Sundance, and Cimarron.

If nineteenth-century western myth has become so powerful in twentieth-century America, what accounts for that power? If the Western has become *the* American genre, in what way(s) is it uniquely American? How does it address American concerns, what is its relationship to American culture, and what role does it play in the construction of an American identity? How does the genre change from period to period and what accounts for the fluctuations in its popularity, which reached an all-time high in the 1950s, then suddenly dropped in the 1960s and continued to fall in the 1970s and later? The study of the phenomenon of the Western that follows attempts to answer these and other questions.

FRONTIERS: HISTORY AND CINEMA

Frederick Jackson Turner and the 1890s

The birth of the Western film was inextricably bound up with the death of the West; more specifically, with the closing of the frontier. In Chicago, at a meeting of the American Historical Association on July 12, 1893, Frederick Jackson Turner presented a paper, "The Significance of the Frontier in American History," that revolutionized traditional thinking about American history. Turner's thesis began with a declaration that the frontier, according to the U.S. Census Report of 1890, no longer existed. He argued that the existence of the frontier had played a crucial role both in American expansion during the nineteenth century and in the shaping of American character as well.

Turner maintained, "The peculiarity of American institutions is the fact that they have been compelled to adapt themselves to the changes of an expanding people—to the changes involved in crossing a continent, in winning a wilderness, and in developing at each area of this progress out of the primitive economic and political conditions of the frontier into the complexity of city life." For Turner, the closing of the frontier marked an end not only to the first period of American history, but also to the influence of the frontier on the development of American identity.

Turner, however, failed to reckon with the movies (and with other popular forms of entertainment in which the old West survives) that have recreated the frontier and, with it, an experience (by proxy) of the frontier for subsequent generations of Americans. In other words, at around the time when the frontier began to disappear, the Western began to replace the West, continuing, albeit in a purely mythic way, to shape American character. Subsequent historians have called Turner's frontier thesis into question, pointing out that the development of the West (and of American identity) cannot fully be explained by looking solely at the question of the frontier.

". . . Print the Legend"

Although Turner's frontier thesis may not be entirely accurate as history, it is nonetheless compelling as myth, providing a scenario of the role the West plays in American history, which Western films and literature have told over and over again until it seems to be true. In other words, at Turner's frontier, not only does East meet West, but fact also meets fiction. Indeed, fiction is ultimately what the West is about. It is a site for the telling of the story of American identity. As the newspaper editor explains it in *The Man Who Shot Liberty Valance* (1962), "This is the West. . . . when the legend becomes fact, print the legend."

Early in May of 1893, Thomas Edison publicly demonstrated his latest invention, the Kinetoscope, to a gathering of engineers and scientists in Brooklyn. Within a year, Edison began to record on film various attractions, including stunts from Buffalo Bill Cody's Wild West Show featuring Cody, Annie Oakley, a group of Sioux Indians, and other performers. In addition to these early actualities of 1894, in 1898 Edison filmed two fictional scenes, *Cripple Creek Bar-Room* and *Poker at Dawson City*. With these few flickering images, which lasted, in toto, less than five minutes of screen time, the film Western was born. It recreated for mass consumption one of the most dramatic periods of American development—a period that had just come to an end and had just become the stuff of legends.

The fact that the first representations of the West on motion picture film were images of a Wild West show and that the first blockbuster Western, *The Great Train Robbery*, was an updated reworking of a Wild West show staple— "The Attack (by outlaws or Indians) on the Deadwood Stage"—is not insignificant. Nor was it an accident that Tomas Ince's popular Bison 101 series arose, in 1911, out of a partnership between the movies and the Miller Brothers' 101 Ranch Wild West Show or that Western stars such as Will Rogers, Tom Mix, and Tim McCoy entered the movies from the world of rodeos and Wild West shows.

Buffalo Bill's Wild West Show, which began as a Fourth of July celebration organized by Cody in North Platte, Nebraska, in 1882, celebrated a West that was rapidly disappearing or, as some historians of the West might contend, never actually existed. It involved a transformation of history into theater and of actuality into myth. By 1895, when Cody added Sitting Bull to his list of attractions, it had become clear that the strategy of the Wild West show was to turn the real old West into a spectacle for the entertainment of the new West, the East, and Europe. The popularity of Cody's show was astounding. During the 1885–1886 season, more than 1 million people attended its performances in Madison Square Garden and over 6 million spectators saw it, over a six-month period, at the Chicago World's Fair. By 1901, Cody's show employed over 500 people and he earned more than $1 million a year for his efforts.

What Cody had begun, Hollywood appropriated and adapted to suit its own needs. The movies not only continued but also expanded on Cody's commercialization and commodification of the West by mass-producing the Wild West show and reworking its thrills and chills into an ever-increasing number of different narrative situations. Robert Altman's *Buffalo Bill and the Indians, or Sitting Bull's History Lesson* (1976), which was based on Arthur Kopit's play *Indians,* provides a satiric portrait of the essential phoniness of this tradition, debunking Cody and calling into question the way in which American history has been turned into the stuff of show business. Clint Eastwood's *Bronco Billy* (1980), on the other hand, reaffirmed the values of that tradition, presenting the Wild West show and the myths of the old West, which it celebrates, as a means of personal redemption in a modern-day world corrupted by selfishness and greed.

Buffalo Bill (Paul Newman) serves as star and master of ceremonies of his own Wild West show in *Buffalo Bill and the Indians, or Sitting Bull's History Lesson* (1976).

Courtesy of United Artists

THE LITERARY WEST

Dime Novels and Pulp Magazines

The commercialization of the West did not begin with the advent of the movies or the Wild West show but dates back to the 1860s, when Erastus Beadle published the first dime novel—Ann Stephens's *Malaeska: The Indian Wife of the White Hunter* (1860). Indeed, Buffalo Bill himself owed his fame and fortune to the dime novels. An obscure cavalry scout and buffalo hunter for the Union Pacific Railroad's construction crews, Cody was discovered in 1869 by dime novelist Ned Buntline, who retold (and greatly embellished) Cody's story in a newspaper serial entitled "Buffalo Bill, the King of the Border Men." The dime novels similarly conferred celebrity status on Wild Bill Hickok, Calamity Jane, Billy the Kid, Jesse James, and others.

Inexpensively printed and sold at prices from 5 to 25 cents, dime novels were mass-produced in runs of 60,000 copies and enjoyed wide circulation in the Civil War and post–Civil War era. In 1860, Beadle issued one of the most popular and profitable Western stories—Edward Ellis's *Seth Jones: Or the Captives of the Frontier,* which sold more than 600,000 copies. Between 1860 and 1865, Beadle sold more than 5 million dime novels and, over the course of his career, published more than 3,100 different titles in 33 separate series.

Later, when publishers began to explore the mass distribution of popular literature through the mails, dime novels gave way to magazines, which, in 1879, Congress permitted to be sent quite cheaply through the postal service to subscribers. After that, western stories began to serve as a staple of pulp magazines, including *Argosy* (founded in 1882) and *Western Story Magazine* (founded in 1919).

From Natty Bumppo to Shane

Dime novels and pulp Westerns looked back, as did every story or film about the West, to the *Leatherstocking Tales,* written by James Fenimore Cooper in the 1820s. The adventures of Cooper's fictional hero, Natty Bumppo, were based, in part, on the exploits of the real-life Daniel Boone, who died in 1820. Their sagas epitomized the contradictory nature of American experience. They both lived in a space that stands between two not only different but also opposed cultures, and both Boone and Bumppo repeatedly moved back and forth between those worlds. That space was the frontier, and it defined the nature of their characters. They not only occupied the frontier but also embodied it, serving as sites where the two worlds met.

Both Boone and Bumppo were torn between the naturalness of the wilderness and the artifice of civilization, between savagery and humanity, between the freedom of nature and the constraints of culture. Like Boone, who reportedly pulled up stakes and moved further west whenever he could see the chimney smoke of his nearest neighbor, Cooper's hero also fled before the advance of civilization. But also like Boone, Bumppo's flight into the wilderness resulted only in the blazing of a trail for others to follow, leading to the further encroachment of civilization on the wilds of nature.

Cooper's frontiersman provided the archetype for the western hero that we find in dime novels and films. According to Henry Nash Smith, "of seventy-nine dime novels selected as a sample of those dealing with the West between 1860 and 1893, forty contain one or more hunters or trappers whose age, costume, weapons, and general functions entitle them to be considered lineal descendants" of Cooper's Leatherstocking. Natty Bumppo, also known as Deerslayer and Pathfinder, literally survived in the dozen or more film adaptations of Cooper's novels.

But he also served as a more general model for the heroes featured in scores of other films, ranging from the Boone-like backwoods hunters in *The Big Sky* (1952) to the alienated antiheroes of *Stagecoach* (1939), *Shane* (1953), and *The Searchers* (1956). This figure also provided the central focus for the James Stewart–Anthony Mann and Randolph Scott–Budd Boetticher Westerns of the 1950s; for Clint Eastwood's man with no name in Sergio Leone's Italian-made "spaghetti" Westerns; and for Eastwood (again) in his own directorial efforts in the genre, *High Plains Drifter* (1972), *Pale Rider* (1985), and *Unforgiven* (1992).

In *Shane* and *The Searchers*, for example, the hero is a social outcast who rides in from the wilderness, enters the frontier community, leads it in its struggle to civilize the frontier, helps defeat the hired guns or Indians who stand in the way of progress, and then returns to the wilderness. In emerging from and retreating to the wilderness, the hero remains identified with the natural landscape and functions as a force of nature in purging that landscape of corruption.

The western hero's conflict with Indians, however, represented a significant exception to this rule in that the Indians were not associated with corruption but rather with an unruly force of nature that, in the eyes of white culture, resisted the natural development of the West into an agrarian paradise. In both instances, the hero was quite frequently identified with the violent world against which he was pitted. Thus, Shane (Alan Ladd) and Ethan Edwards (John Wayne) fight the gunfighter Wilson and the Comanche war-chief Scar, their alter egos; that is, men like themselves. In slaying the enemies of society, who often resemble him in appearance or character, the western hero symbolically destroys himself. Having brought peace to the community through the use of his superior strength and unique skills, this western hero is unable to enter the community because it can no longer tolerate the excessive violence with which he, like his former enemy, remains identified.

Bundles of Oppositions

Turner's mythology of the West provides the foundation for Jim Kitses's structural analysis of the Western. Drawing on the structural anthropology of Claude Levi-Strauss, Kitses sees the thematic concerns of the Western in terms of the following pairs of opposed concepts:

THE WILDERNESS	CIVILIZATION
The Individual	*The Community*
freedom	restriction
honor	institutions
self-knowledge	illusion
integrity	compromise
self-interest	social responsibility
solipsism	democracy
Nature	*Culture*
purity	corruption
experience	knowledge
empiricism	legalism
pragmatism	idealism
brutalization	refinement
savagery	humanity

The West	*The East*
America	Europe
the frontier	America
equality	class
agrarianism	industrialism
tradition	change
the past	the future

For Kitses, it is possible to understand all Westerns as articulating a national mythology; the deep structure that informs that mythology—seen above in his series of antinomies—reveals basic contradictions that lie at the core of the American psyche.

ADAPTATION: WHEN EAST MEETS WEST

Bowlers to Buckskins

The western hero was forged amidst the conflicting forces that characterized the formation of the frontier. At the frontier, nature and culture met, an encounter that transformed both. To survive, the pioneer from the East had to adopt the ways of the West; the colonist put aside his or her European dress and behavior, put on buckskin and moccasins, built the log houses of the Iroquois, and learned, like the Indian, to hunt, to fish, and to read the signs of nature. Struggle for survival in the natural landscape westernized the easterner. Extreme instances of this can be found in *Broken Arrow* (1950), *Run of the Arrow* (1957), *A Man Called Horse* (1970), *Little Big Man* (1970), and *Dances With Wolves* (1990), in which Easterners (and in one case, an English lord) abandon their own culture for that of the Indian tribes with which they live.

More typically, the Easterner adapted to the West, while retaining certain eastern traits. The eastern tenderfoot played by Robert Young in *Western Union* (1941) exchanges his city clothes for western boots, chaps, vest, and hat, a ritualistic ceremony that appears in countless Westerns and is parodied in *City Slickers* when the three heroes comically outfit themselves for the trail drive that follows. As in the latter film, this purely superficial transformation precedes Young's more thorough westernization, which takes place under the tutelage of a western mentor (played by Randolph Scott in *Western Union* and Jack Palance in *City Slickers*), against the background of a hostile natural landscape (and, in the former film, skirmishes with renegade Indians).

Feminine Transformations

Often, the process of westernization is dramatized through the transformation of eastern women into frontierswomen. As Turner points out, from the days of the Revolutionary War until the closing of the frontier, the East was never quite able to understand the West. Easterners tended to view the frontier as a rough and uncivilized region inhabited by rude, semiliterate, semibarbaric backwoodsmen. Like many other Westerns, *Drums Along the Mohawk* (1939) plays with this prejudice. The film begins with the wedding of the hero, Gil (Henry Fonda), to Lana (Claudette Colbert), the genteel daughter of a well-to-do Albany family, who leaves behind the elegant houses and fancy gowns of the city for the wilderness of west central New York (ca. 1776).

On her arrival in the Mohawk Valley, the heroine becomes hysterical at the sight of Blueback (Chief John Big Tree), a friendly Indian, and is dismayed to discover that her new home is a crude one-room log cabin. Her fine eastern furniture is destroyed, along with their cabin, in an Indian attack, and the couple are forced to become tenant farmers for a local widow. Gradually, the heroine's fear of the wilderness gives way to an appreciation of the self-sufficiency, courage, good neighborliness, and generosity of the frontier community, and she willingly takes her place in it.

In *The Virginian* (1929), Molly (Mary Brian), a schoolteacher from Vermont, is shocked when she discovers that the Virginian (Gary Cooper) has lynched his best friend, Steve (Richard Arlen), for cattle rustling. Vowing to return East, she declares that western justice is nothing other than cold-blooded murder. Rebuked by a homespun Wyoming frontierswoman who explains the pragmatic necessity of the codes of the West to her, Molly learns to accept the ways of the western community, stays on as the schoolmarm, and ultimately marries the Virginian. The education of the heroine in these films provides one of the genre's most familiar dramatic patterns—a scenario that perhaps finds its fullest treatment in *High Noon* (1952), in which the hero's Quaker bride (Grace Kelly) discovers that her religious principles have little or no currency in the West, and, in the final sequence, shoots a man in the back to save her husband's life.

Or the westernization of the eastern heroine can take other forms, ranging from cross-dressing to packing six-guns (see Joan Crawford as Vienna, who does both in *Johnny Guitar,* 1954). Inspired by a true story, *The Ballad of Little Jo* (1993) documents the saga of an eastern aristocrat, disowned by her wealthy family for having an illegitimate child, who journeys west. To avoid sexual harassment, she cuts her hair, slashes her face to acquire a "masculine" scar, puts on men's clothes, and changes her name from Josephine to Jo. She successfully passes for a man, becoming a leader in the local community's battle with corporate cattlemen. It is only on her death that her neighbors discover she was a woman. Sam Raimi's *The Quick and the Dead* (1995) casts Sharon Stone as an Eastwood-like woman with no name. Wearing a cowboy hat, Leonesque serape, chaps, and boots, Stone plays a gunfighter intent on avenging her father's murder. Like the Eastwood character in Leone's films, Stone rides off into the wilderness at the end, suggesting that men have no exclusive copyright on the Leatherstocking role.

Teaching a Tenderfoot

An educational process similar to that of the eastern woman takes place in a number of Westerns in which a feminized male character, often a youth or a

Courtesy of Paramount

Tom Doniphon (John Wayne) teaches tenderfoot Ranse Stoddard (James Stewart) to shoot in *The Man Who Shot Liberty Valance* (1962).

tenderfoot from the East, is instructed in the codes of the West by a tough representative of the masculine frontier society. One of the most familiar sequences in Westerns is the shooting lesson, in which the experienced gunfighter attempts to teach a novice how to draw his six-shooter quickly and hit a target. John Wayne frequently finds himself in this role, instructing the young Matthew Garth to outdraw his opponent by watching his eyes in *Red River* (1948); sharing his expertise about Indians with his "nephew," Martin Pauley (Jeffrey Hunter), in *The Searchers* (1956); showing the green lawyer from the East, Ranse Stoddard (James Stewart), how to squeeze the trigger in *The Man Who Shot Liberty Valance* (1962); and retraining knife-fighter Mississippi (James Caan) to use a sawed-off shotgun in *El Dorado* (1966). In most of these instances, the encounter between mentor and apprentice functions (as in many war films) as a stage in an elaborate rite of passage through which the younger hero is forced to repress the feminine elements of his character and, as a result, to become a more masculine, more westernized figure.

Women, Civilization, and Nature

The status of women in the Western remained somewhat conventional and secondary, even when they had learned the codes of the West. More often than not, women represented the forces of civilization; they embodied the values of family, community, education, domestication, and cultivation that informed the male hero's transformation of the wilderness into a garden. In short, women served as the agents of easternization. If a woman was westernized through her encounter with the landscape, then her presence also served to easternize it.

In *My Darling Clementine* (1946), the Boston-bred heroine gradually enters the western community, a process that begins by her dancing with its nominal leader, Wyatt Earp, at the church dedication ceremony. Her westernization is symbolized by her subsequent abandonment of eastern for western dress (her dark, constricting, formal-looking suits give way to white blouses and flowing skirts). By the end of the film, she has become Tombstone's first schoolmarm. Following her instruction by others in the ways of the West, she begins to educate it in the ways of the East—by teaching a new generation of westerners reading, writing, and arithmetic.

Women in Westerns did not always represent eastern values. In a number of films, they symbolized the West itself and functioned as contested sites for the playing out of struggles between the forces of East and West or of old West and new West. *Duel in the Sun* (1946), a virtual allegorization of the dilemma that lay the heart of the Western genre, linked the identity crisis (and ultimate fate) of its central character, Pearl, to the larger identity crisis of the American nation as it settled the West. The product of an English (eastern) father and a western Mexican-Indian mother, the mestiza Pearl is, quite literally, the meeting place between East and West.

Forced to choose between two brothers—Jesse, who represents law, order, and the progressive domestication of the new West, and Lewt, who is tied to the

The mestiza Pearl (Jennifer Jones, left) views herself through both the racist perspective of Senator McCanles (Lionel Barrymore) and the nurturing encouragement of Mrs. McCanles (Lillian Gish) in *Duel in the Sun* (1946).

lawlessness and violence of the old West—Pearl first submits herself to Jesse's civilizing but repressive guidance and then to Lewt's unbridled passion. Unable to repress her own sexual desires (i.e., the forces of nature) she yields to Lewt; but, aware that Lewt and what he represents must be destroyed, she kills him and is killed herself in the process. This action paves the way for the emergence of an unconflicted (that is, not internally torn between two identities as she is) new order in the West.

In a similar way, Hallie (Vera Miles) in *The Man Who Shot Liberty Valance* (1962) represented a West that gradually passed from the hands of the old West (John Wayne's Tom Doniphon) to that of the new (James Stewart's Ranse Stoddard). Stoddard wins Hallie, in part, by teaching her to read and write and by instilling in her his belief in law and order and his dreams of the future. Alongside the wild cactus rose given to her by Doniphon, Stoddard plants the vision of a real (i.e., eastern, carefully cultivated) rose, the product of dams and irrigation projects that will transform the wilderness into a garden.

Though this transformation is necessary and inevitable, Hallie, as symbol of the West, both embraces and resists it. She marries the easterner, Stoddard, but is unable to forget her feeling for the westerner, Doniphon, on whose coffin she places a wild cactus rose. Though Hallie, unlike Pearl in *Duel*, survives the implicit battle of the film's two heroes over the possession of her, something in her dies. She has lost her former energy, passion, and fiery temper. The very qualities that draw the eastern hero to her and to the West are destroyed through her easternization.

ON NATIVE GROUND: LANDSCAPE AND CONFLICT

A Struggle for National Identity

The easternization of the West is played out not only across the bodies of western heroines but also across the body of the West itself—across the landscape that provides the very basis of the genre. The Western, as its name suggests, is defined, in large part, in terms of its setting. (The genre, of course, is also historically defined; the dramatic action of A Westerns is set in the time period of, roughly, 1865 to 1890; that of low-budget B Westerns, on the other hand, is frequently pushed into the twentieth century, with heroes and villains often trading horses for cars, jeeps, and airplanes and relying on telephones and shortwave radios instead of the telegraph.)

Much as the traditional space of the melodrama is the home, that of the Western is the landscape of the West. It is in this landscape that the struggle for a national identity took place; the West was where that which was eastern, European, or old world engaged in a process of continual self-redefinition, repeatedly reborn with each step taken farther toward the West.

The journey in *Stagecoach* (1939), for example, takes its passengers from the easternized West of Tonto, where the Ladies' Law and Order League purges the town of its undesirable elements, to the wild West of Lordsburg, where gambling, prostitution, and violence such as the climactic shoot-out in the street still prevail. From here, the tarnished hero (the outlaw Ringo, played by John Wayne) and heroine (the prostitute Dallas, played by Claire Trevor) push further west (actually, to Mexico) toward rejuvenation in the wilderness. They are saved, as we are told by those who oversee their departure, from "the blessings of civilization."

Though Ringo and Dallas flee the advance of civilization in search of a less oppressive existence in nature, the very stagecoach that brings them to the edge of the frontier represents the forces of progress that eventually transformed the landscape. As the frontier pushed farther and farther to the West, forests were cleared, the range was fenced off, farms and towns were built, and stagecoach routes and railroad tracks began to crisscross formerly uncharted territory. The stagecoach and the train came to symbolize the taming of the wilderness and the linking of the West to the East.

From Wilderness to Garden

The building of the transcontinental railroad, celebrated in *The Iron Horse* (1924), *Union Pacific* (1939), *Kansas Pacific* (1953), and other films, remained closely identified with the evolution of the West. Attacks on trains, featured in films as diverse as *The Great Train Robbery* and *Jesse James* (1939), *Duel in the Sun* (1946), and *Butch Cassidy and the Sundance Kid* (1969), were figured as defiant gestures against the inevitable progression of the West into the twentieth century. In a handful of films, such as *The Professionals* (1966) and *Once Upon a Time in the West* (1968), the railroads represented rampant eastern capitalism, which rode roughshod over all obstacles in its path.

As Leo Marx showed (in *The Machine in the Garden*), American fiction from Nathaniel Hawthorne to F. Scott Fitzgerald concerned itself with the uniquely American experience of a pastoral ideal destroyed by the intrusion of technology. The Western's ambivalent attitude toward progress in general and toward trains in particular situates it firmly within this larger tradition and reveals deep-seated tensions that underlie the Western's account of the West's transformation from a wilderness into a garden.

At the frontier, the wilderness met civilization and, as a consequence of this encounter, the wilderness disappeared and was replaced by a frontier society that combined elements of both the wilderness and civilization. As Turner described it, "Gradually this society lost its primitive conditions, and assimilated itself to the type of the older social conditions of the East; but it bore within it enduring and distinguishing survivals of its frontier experience. Decade after decade, West after West, this rebirth of American society had gone on," transforming America from a European colony into an autonomous nation whose character was determined not by borrowing from or imitation of Old World culture but its own unique experience of the New World.

According to Turner, successive waves of western immigration resulted in a series of encounters at the frontier between distinct cultures or societies. The various conflicts that characterize the different kinds of Westerns correspond, in large part, to the successive stages of western development from a wilderness into a garden. In each instance, the old(er) West resisted the coming of the new(er) West, but the new West ultimately triumphed. All of these subgenres of the Western not only provide convincing evidence that the Western is *about* the frontier, but they also provide an attempted rationalization of history. They present the historical movement from one period to the next as inevitable and thus suggest that the product of this Darwinian process of natural selection— twentieth-century America—is itself natural and right. In this way, the Western justifies the present and reaffirms our identity as a nation, an identity that has slowly been constructed during this process.

A Clash of Cultures: Cowboys and Indians

The first major period of Westerns focuses primarily on the hero's struggle for survival in a natural landscape (as in *Jeremiah Johnson,* 1972) or recounts the adventures of a Daniel Boone-like character in the wilderness (see the hunter/ trapper films cited above). In these films, the chief conflict lies between culture and nature. The next stage/subgenre of the Western concerns conflicts not between culture and nature but between two distinct cultures—that of whites and Native Americans. This comprises one of the largest of the Western's several subgenres, which is the cowboy/cavalry and Indian pictures. These films dominated the genre from its inception until its demise, running from *The Battle at Elderbush Gulch* (1913) to *Ulzana's Raid* (1972), *Dances With Wolves* (1990), and *The Last of the Mohicans* (1992).

In many of these films, Native Americans are stereotypically portrayed as violent savages. In fact, only a handful of Westerns portray them as fully developed, individual characters or display any sensitivity, beyond a superficial concern for accuracy in costume and artifacts, to the particulars of Indian culture. Even in the films that are most sympathetic to them, Indians are not presented as Indians, but as romantic, Rousseauesque noble savages living in implicit defiance of a decadent European civilization. This idealized image of the Native American dominates recent revisionist Westerns such as *A Man Called Horse* (1970), *Return of a Man Called Horse* (1976), and *Dances With Wolves* (1990). The portrayal of the Indian as nightmarish devil (as seen in the characters of Scar in *The Searchers* and Silvaje in *Stalking Moon,* 1969) or as victimized saint (seen in the persons of Broken Lance in *Devil's Doorway* and Cochise in *Broken Arrow,* both 1950) betrays his or her status more as a figment of the imagination of white culture than as an authentic inhabitant of the frontier.

The majority of the Indians who achieve recognition as heroic symbols or as figures of empowerment on the screen are played primarily by white actors as in *Apache* (1954) (Burt Lancaster), *Taza, Son of Cochise* (1954) (Rock Hudson), and *The Searchers* (1956) (Henry Brandon). The Native Americans to achieve prominence as actors within the film industry are few and far between. Chief Thundercloud starred in *Ramona* (1936), enjoyed the lead in Monogram's *Trail Blazers* serials, and played character parts in Westerns for over 20 years. Chief Yowlachie, who steals scenes from Walter Brennan in Howard Hawks's *Red River* (1948), worked in movies from the mid-1920s until his death in 1960.

Jay Silverheels won renown as Tonto in the *Lone Ranger* television series and played Geronimo in *Broken Arrow* (1950). Chief John Big Tree acted in motion pictures from 1915 to 1950 and appeared in such classic Ford Westerns as *Stagecoach* (1939), *Drums Along the Mohawk* (1939), and *She Wore a Yellow Ribbon* (1949), where he plays Pony That Walks, the Christian Indian who wants to spend his time smoking and getting drunk with John Wayne's Nathan Brittles. Chief Dan George won national acclaim for his role as Old Lodge Skins in *Little Big Man* (1970).

Dances With Wolves brought Graham Greene, a member of the Oneida tribe, to national prominence. He had earlier appeared in a film about Native Americans in the contemporary West in *Powwow Highway* (1989); subsequently, as a Sioux sheriff, he would befriend the part-Indian FBI agent played by Val Kilmer in *Thunderheart* (1992). *Powwow Highway* also featured Gary Farmer, a native of the Cayuga Nation. Farmer then starred in *Dead Man* (1995) as Nobody, in *Smoke Signals* (1998) as the dead man Arnold Joseph, and in *Skins* (2002) as Verdell Weasel Tail. Eric Schweig, a part-Inuit, part-German actor, played Uncas in *The Last of the Mohicans* (1992), Eperow in *Squanto: A Warrior's Tale* (1994), Rudy Yellow Lodge in *Skins* and the shaman Chiden in *The Missing* (2003). Cherokee Wes Studi rose from playing a savage Pawnee in *Dances With Wolves* and Magua in *The Last of the Mohicans* to Geronimo in Walter Hill's *Geronimo: An American Legend* (1993). Studi also plays the role of Joe Leaphorn in television adaptations of Tony Hillerman's Navaho detective novels (*Skinwalkers*, 2002; *A Thief of Time*, 2003; and *Coyote Waits*, 2003).

Native Images, White Values

The majority of speaking parts in Westerns went to white actors. This phenomenon tends to confirm the suspicion that Indians in Westerns function largely as psychic projections of the fears and desires of the white frontier community and have little or no connection with the Native Americans who originally inhabited the West. Even in films supposedly sympathetic to the plight of Native Americans, such as *Dances With Wolves*, stereotypical attitudes toward Indian savagery persist. Here, nobler, more advanced tribes—the Lakota Sioux—fight against their deadly enemy, the primitive Pawnee, who savagely murder whites and Sioux alike.

Certain contemporary Native Americans criticize *A Man Called Horse* (1970) for its suggestions of Indian brutality in its depiction of the Ceremony of the Sun (or Sundance) initiation ritual (in which Horse [Richard Harris] is tortured

Courtesy of Orion

In *Dances With Wolves* (1990), Lt. John Dunbar (Kevin Costner) comes to recognize the value of Kicking Bird's (Graham Greene's) Native American lifestyle.

by having wooden pins inserted under the skin of his chest and being hoisted by these pins to the rafters of a lodge house). One could similarly fault the positive image of the Sioux in *Dances With Wolves* for its reliance on a spectrum of values that depend on negative images of the Pawnee. At the same time, in its treatment of conflict between whites and Native Americans, the Sioux again emerge as more civilized against a background of white violence and irrationality. At any rate, the depiction of the Sioux in *Dances With Wolves* merely continued the pattern of conflict between new and more civilized versus old and less civilized cultures that underlies the genre as a whole.

Out-of-Time Antiheroes

A handful of Westerns, made in the 1960s and early 1970s and set in the period after the closing of the frontier, look back nostalgically to the old West and feature legendary characters who have outlived the heroic gold, silver and bronze ages of the West and are regarded as either curiosities or unwanted embarrassments by an indifferent or openly hostile twentieth-century society. The values of the world around these old West character types has become corrupted by the forces of corporate capitalism, such as railroads, banks, mining interests, or

Courtesy of Dino De Laurentis

J. B. Books (John Wayne) confirms his suspicion that he has cancer when he visits Dr. Hostetler (James Stewart) in *The Shootist* (1976).

trusts. These institutions play an increasingly significant role in the rooting out of these defiant individualists who have fallen out of step with the advancing parade of modern times.

The suicidal resistance of these western antiheroes to the values of modernity lies at the heart of several Sam Peckinpah Westerns, including *Ride the High Country* (1962) and *The Wild Bunch* (1969), whose outlaw heroes are pursued by an ignoble assortment of bounty hunters in the employ of the railroads. This spirit also provides the dramatic core of nontraditional, late Westerns such as *McCabe and Mrs. Miller* (1971), in which the hero, who refuses to sell out to a mining conglomerate, is gunned down by its henchmen.

Whether lawmen, gunfighters, or outlaws, these antiheroes lived by a set of frontier codes that became antiquated in the twentieth century. This notion of the Western hero as a dying breed is, perhaps, best exemplified in *The Shootist* (1976), in which aging gunslinger J. B. Books (John Wayne) is literally dying of cancer (as was Wayne himself when the film was being made). Books rides into Carson City in January 1901, the very day on which the local newspaper headlines Queen Victoria's death. This news item not only foreshadows his own death but also symbolizes the passing of the values of the previous century, most particularly, of a certain moral integrity with which he is identified.

The townspeople of Carson City, concerned more with their own material well-being than with their loyalty to the abstract ideals of individualism and community, are driven by a set of values that might best be described as post-Victorian. Books' chief relationships are with those who seek to profit from his death by selling his horse, his life story, or clippings of his hair. Refusing to die passively in bed, Books stages a confrontation (on his birthday) with three local troublemakers who fancy themselves good with a gun. This gunfight takes on the dynamics of a last hurrah, in which the authenticity of the old (movie) West, symbolized by legendary Western film star Wayne, emerges and defeats derivative western types in the form of television Western stars Hugh O'Brien and Richard Boone. Though he rides to the gunfight on a streetcar, Books nonetheless recaptures, through his display of traditional western courage and skill, the heroic stature of a bygone era.

CONTEMPORARY VISIONS, ENDURING MYTHS

Throughout its history, the Western has played a crucial role in dramatizing and recreating for successive generations of Americans the original experience of the frontier, which shaped (and which continues, through each new cycle of Westerns, to reshape) American character. At the same time, the Western becomes a site for the working out of problems that plague contemporary American society. In certain instances, the Western's role is fairly overt. During the Korean War, films such as *Rio Grande* (1950) acted out national frustration in being unable to pursue the enemy beyond the 48th parallel in Korea by sending a cavalry troop across the Mexican border to rescue children who have been abducted by Indians. During the Vietnam War, in the aftermath of the My Lai massacre, Westerns such as *Soldier Blue* and *Little Big Man* (both 1970) vividly portrayed the massacres of Indians at Sand Creek and Washita River by U.S. forces. *Ulzana's Raid* (1972) doubled as an allegory for America's misguided involvement in Southeast Asia, and *Jeremiah Johnson* and *Bad Company* (both 1972) played on antiwar sentiment.

In Vietnam, U.S. troops referred to territories occupied by the Vietcong as "Indian country." John Wayne's war epic, *The Green Berets* (1968), reworks Western motifs to transform the Vietnam War into the language of the Western. The film dubs the jungle outpost of U.S. forces "Dodge City." And the climactic action of the film is a restaging of the story of the Alamo (earlier depicted in a movie of the same name, a Western directed by Wayne in 1960) in which the camp is surrounded and besieged by the enemy. However, instead of a fight to the death in which American forces nobly sacrifice themselves, the special forces in *The Green Berets* actually win the battle, providing an ideologically correct, upbeat ending to a downbeat Western myth.

Lyn Tan suggests that the decrease in the production of Westerns in the late 1970s was answered, in part, by a Westernization of the Vietnam War film. Western motifs can be found, for example, in films such as *Apocalypse Now* (1979) in Lt. Col. Kilgore's (Robert Duval's) costuming (a western-style cavalry hat) and in the mustering of his air cavalry, which flies off to battle accompanied by a bugle call. In *Rambo: First Blood, Part II* (1985), the hero John Rambo (Sylvester Stallone) adopts the weapons and tactics of Native Americans in his hand-to-hand jungle combat with the Vietcong. Drawing on Richard Slotkin's study of the Western, Tan argues that the jungles of Vietnam function as a frontier wilderness where the hero undergoes "regeneration through violence." In Oliver Stone's *Platoon* (1986), the young hero Chris (Charlie Sheen) undergoes a violent rite of passage in Vietnam and "returns to civilization as a resurrected frontier hero."

In general, however, the Western was both a barometer of contemporary history and a site for the production and perpetuation of myths that are crucial to the larger ideological demand of sustaining a nineteenth-century American identity that was repeatedly under attack in the twentieth century. The Western celebrated the values of a preindustrialized, rural, agrarian America in which an individual's contact with nature became a source of perpetual rejuvenation and in which the pastoral ideal of the yeoman farmer that informed Jeffersonian democracy still flourished.

Back to the Garden

Set, for the most part, in a period prior to the closing of the frontier in 1890, the Western looks forward to the continued development of a populist paradise. Made in an increasingly industrialized and urbanized society, the Western looks backward from the vantage point of a fallen culture to a Garden of Eden from which it has been expelled by its own progress and development. Thus, the representation of history and progress remains profoundly ambivalent in most Westerns; the passing of the old West and its transformation into the new West necessarily involves tremendous loss. A-level Westerns set in the twentieth century tend to feature heroes who resist modernity and struggle against its machines, whether they be trains, planes, or automobiles, or modern methods of mining, manufacture, and merchandising. (In B Westerns, however, history plays a more neutral role: contemporary technology becomes a tool that is appropriated by both good guys and bad guys; the past has little or no nostalgic value.)

Three Amigos! (1986) and *City Slickers* (1991) present characters in flight from a contemporary, mechanized, depersonalized, urban America who discover an exciting world of adventure out West. The modern world (1920s Hollywood and 1990s New York, respectively) not only has turned them into alienated individuals whose contact with any larger community has been severed but also has rendered their existence artificial or in some way dishonest. The Three Amigos, for example, have lost touch with modern-day reality and believe instead in the fictions of their own Hollywood movies. The three city slickers lead lives of quiet desperation in a modern metropolis from which they periodically escape through fantasy vacations to exotic, faraway places. The West enables both groups of middle-aged men to recover a lost authenticity.

Though set in a more traditionally western period, *Dances With Wolves* reveals a similar rejection of the insanity of the decadent white culture that would win the West in favor of the more natural and authentic Native American culture that was losing it.

In all three Westerns, the West functioned as a paradise lost, as a world in which utopian communities reaffirmed the value of the individual and provided a stable identity for that individual within it. This world no longer exists in modern mass society, in which traditional notions of the individual's relationship to the community and ability to shape or control events and history have been replaced by a pervasive sense of social alienation and powerlessness. Ever since the closing of the frontier and the disappearance of the old West, contemporary American audiences have needed the Western to provide them with a mythical, quasi-utopian past in which they are empowered as individuals and become members of a society whose values and beliefs are rooted in the stable realities of the land itself.

Unforgiven

These utopian visions of the West are subject to qualification, if not downright repudiation, in the two major Westerns of the 1990s, *Unforgiven* (1992) and *Dead Man* (1995). *Unforgiven* explores the myths of the old West, debunking them with one hand and reconstituting them with the other. It exposes the hypocrisy and cowardice of dime-novel gunslinger English Bob (Richard Harris) and

Courtesy of Warner Bros.

The sheriff of Big Whiskey, Little Bill Daggett (Gene Hackman), instructs outlaw Will Munny (Clint Eastwood) on the fine points of frontier law in *Unforgiven* (1992).

traces the restoration to the status of legend of the infamous killer William Munny (Clint Eastwood). Introduced as a widower, father of two, and mud-spattered pig-farmer, Munny has reformed, having promised his dead wife Claudia to give up strong drink and wickedness. When reminded of his violent past, he repeatedly insists, "I ain't like that no more."

Conscience-stricken and guilt-ridden, Munny may regret his past, but he easily rationalizes (in the name of woman) the killing of two cowboys. These cowboys "cut up a woman" and, as his former partner Ned (Morgan Freeman) says, "I guess they got it coming." Munny is introduced under the sign of the woman—he tends his dead wife's grave—and is identified as a feminized figure, remaining more or less passive for most of the film.

Jane Tompkins argues that the feminization of the United States in the East, after the Civil War, drove men west in search of a site in which their masculinity could be rejuvenated. In *Unforgiven*, the new West has undergone a similar feminization. Both Munny and Ned are initially seen as emasculated, as former outlaws reformed by their women. Munny's emasculation is completed at the hands of Little Bill (Gene Hackman), the sheriff of Big Whiskey, who mercilessly beats him up and watches as he crawls across the floor of the saloon and out the door.

Nursed back to health by the "cut-up whore" whose external scars mirror Munny's internally-scarred psyche, Munny avenges his own humiliation and the brutal death of his partner Ned. Acting like a character out of a dime novel, Munny rides back into town and kills Little Bill and four of his men in a shoot-out that reenacts the legendary ones in famous dime novels.

The violence of the film is both irrational and part of a rational moral economy in which one act of violence is answered by another. When the cowboy cuts up Delilah, Little Bill attempts to mete out punishment by whipping the criminal. Skinny, owner of the whorehouse, invokes the principle of property and insists that Delilah is now damaged goods; her disfigurement must be compensated for in some way. Alice, as leader of the women designated as property, objects and, together with the other prostitutes, posts a thousand-dollar reward for the death of the cowboys. At the end of the film, just before Little Bill dies, he protests, "I don't deserve this." Munny tersely replies, "Deserve's got nothing to do with it." But it does. In the larger economy of the film, Little Bill has failed to distinguish between the rights of property and moral rights. In avenging the death of Ned and the disfigurement of Delilah, Munny asserts the priority of moral economy over an economy based solely on property.

Munny's earlier moral uncertainty has become, by the end of the film, an unswerving moral clarity. Munny knows what he must do and, with that knowledge, he becomes the agent of a larger moral economy that shatters the ambiguity governing actions earlier in the film. Although much of the film explores the nonheroic passivity and doubt of the hero and the crisis of masculinity in the late West, it finally reaffirms traditional myth, transforming Munny into a larger-than-life western hero.

Rutgers Cinema Studies

William Blake (Johnny Depp) completes his journey to the afterworld by canoe in *Dead Man.*

Dead Man

Unlike Will Munny, William Blake (Johnny Depp), the hero of Jim Jarmusch's
Dead Man, is a figure of innocence—a blank slate on which the film imposes a
series of false identities that he then becomes. Metalworks owner John Dickinson labels him a killer, hires three bounty hunters to track him down, and plas-
ters every tree in the West with "Wanted" posters for him. Though Blake did kill
Dickinson's son, Charlie (Gabriel Byrne), he did so in self-defense, only after
Charlie had killed the woman Blake was with and shot Blake himself. But, by
the end of the film, Blake has become a notorious outlaw, having killed six men.

An outcast Indian named Nobody (Gary Farmer) mistakes Blake for the
English poet William Blake, noting, "It's strange that you don't remember anything of your poetry." Later, Nobody tells Blake that his six-shooter "will replace [his] tongue. [He] will learn to speak through it and [his] poetry will now
be written with blood." A few scenes later, two lawmen named Lee and Marvin
(Jarmusch's tribute to Western star Lee Marvin) point their guns at him and
ask, "Are you William Blake?" Blake replies, "Yes. Do you know my poetry?"
Then he shoots one lawman, whose rifle goes off, killing the other. William
Blake has become "William Blake," writing poetry with a gun.

Blake's journey, like his namesake's poetry, takes him from innocence to
experience, from anonymity to notoriety, from passive spectatorship (his journey West by train; his walk through the town of Machine to the metalworks) to
active participation (his brief career as a gunfighter), from life to death, and

from death to salvation. When Nobody finds him at the end of Act One, Blake is already a dead man. The remainder of the film functions as Blake's metaphysical journey through a landscape of Native American spirituality (Nobody's peyote visions) and beliefs about Christian salvation (from Sally Jenko's scriptures to the religious maxims of the man who runs the trading post). In Jarmusch's film, the white man's West is a living hell—epitomized in the industrial landscape of Machine, the mercenary (and cannibalistic) bounty hunters, and the predatory fur trappers—through which the hero must pass on his way to "the place where all the spirits come from . . . and where all the spirits return." However, Blake himself, as what Nobody's refers to as "a stupid white man," has no understanding of the spiritual implications of his journey. When Nobody tells him it is time to go back where he came from, he replies, "You mean Cleveland?" Then again, when Nobody gives him tobacco for his voyage, Blake, unaware of the ceremonial significance of tobacco in Native American culture, answers, "I don't smoke." In spite of his epic odyssey across the landscape of the West, Blake has learned nothing.

For Jarmusch, the West is not a site of rejuvenation but of death. White culture is associated with senseless killing, moral decadence, dehumanizing industrialization, religious fanaticism, and cannibalism. If white culture is dysfunctional and alienated, Native American culture, in the figure of Nobody, is not much better. Nobody functions as Blake's spiritual guide in his journey to the next world, but Nobody is himself an outcast—a man, like Blake, without a place in either the world of the white man or that of the Native American. For Jarmusch, the West offers nothing but death. There is no job, family, or community that might provide his characters a place in it. The only option is to keep moving, and the only advice for those who set out on this journey to nowhere is that of Henri Michaux, quoted at the outset of the film: "It is preferable not to travel with a dead man."

Periods of Popularity

Americans have needed the Western more in certain periods of their history than in others. The Western flowered as a film genre in the 1950s, when over 800 were made. Its popularity gradually withered in the 1960s, when less than 200 Westerns were released, and the genre virtually disappeared in the late 1970s and 1980s. Fluctuations in its popularity reflect the genre's changing status as a means for audiences to come to terms with the modern world. It is possible to locate the origins of the Western in the disturbance of an agrarian-pastoral order introduced by the Industrial Revolution, technological innovation and urbanization, and in the transformation of small-town America into a modern mass society. Given this origin, the proliferation of A Westerns in the years 1946–1958, a period in which explosive developments took place in the sciences, could be seen as a response to the anxiety of society as a whole over the increasingly important role that technology played in shaping human consciousness and in increasing international instability (through the nuclear arms race and the cold war).

Of course, the postwar concern for the bomb hardly explains prewar fascination with the Western, which led to over 1,300 (mostly B) films made in the 1920s and over 1,000 oaters released in each of the next two decades. In these instances, the genre's celebration of agrarianism is less clearly a response to an increasing fear of nuclear war than it is a conservative reaction to a growing dependence on technology and to the impersonality of the consumer-oriented mass culture that accompanied the modernization of America in the 1920s and later. Thus, William S. Hart appealed, as a western hero, to the codes of a pre-industrial, largely Protestant, nineteenth-century small-town society, representing the forces of a Victorian moral order that opposed the corruption of a world which had become decadent. In *Hell's Hinges* (1916), Hart plays a good-bad man who is redeemed by the love of the virtuous sister of a minister. Wreaking an Old Testament vengeance on those sinners who have burned down the town church, Hart corners them in the saloon and sets both it and the rest of the town of Hell's Hinges afire, purging the town of its criminal element before he and the film's heroine set off on a new life together.

Ambivalence: Land, Technology, and Utopia

Epic A Westerns of the 1920s, such as *The Covered Wagon* (1923) and *The Iron Horse* (1924), embraced the expansionist optimism and go-getter ethos of the 1920s through a celebration of the principles of Manifest Destiny. The dramatic westward expansion of the United States in the nineteenth century, which many believed was justified by God and geography, became a metaphor for the legitimation of American enterprise and the unrestrained development of the business economy in the 1920s.

Ironically, in John Ford's *Iron Horse*, an industrial technology—the first transcontinental railroad—serves as the device that links the past with the present and symbolizes the growth of America into a corporate giant. John Ford's utopian conception of the railroad persisted into the 1930s, in spite of the Great Depression and the resulting cynicism it produced regarding the excesses of unregulated rugged individualism. Bankers (such as the self-serving embezzler Gatewood in *Stagecoach*) took the brunt of the criticism for the nation's ills, but the railroads continued to represent the promise of a corporate capitalism that might rescue America from the contemporary cycle of hard times. Thus, by the end of Roosevelt's second term of office, *Union Pacific* (1939), which recounts the building of the first transcontinental railroad, epitomized (in this particular case) the conservative concerns of the A Western: through heroic efforts, Americans could overcome all obstacles and rebuild the greatness of the past.

B Westerns reinforced this affirmation of capitalist enterprise through an unending series of films whose plots were based on the conflict over property; films about range wars, cattle rustling, claim jumping, or disputes over land boundaries and water rights tended to come down on the side of those whose moral (if not legal) rights to property needed protection by the benevolent, intervening force of the government or its agents. Though the superficial look of the Western changed from year to year (along with its variations in plot types), its underlying principles and beliefs remained constant, planted firmly in the terrain of American populist ideology.

Westerns echoed populism's dream of an agrarian utopia, populated by farmers whose stake in democratic society is assured by their ownership of land that they work themselves, which makes them economically self-sufficient and gives them equal footing with others in their community. The traditional enemies of these small farmers proved to be those of Depression audiences as well—bankers and big business.

Though the railroads, as the symbol of big business in the West, also became targets of populist attack, the building of the first transcontinental railroads depicted in *The Iron Horse* and *Union Pacific* functioned less as a symbol of big business than of a national unity achieved through the labor of the working class. *Union Pacific* even exposes the corruption of the robber barons and corporate trusts that sought to divert government funds allocated for the construction of the railroads. The railroad consists largely of populist individuals—an incorruptible troubleshooter (played by Joel McCrea) and a scrappy Irish postmistress (Barbara Stanwyck)—who join forces to fight off the agents of big business who try to delay construction of the railroad for their own personal profit.

But beneath this celebration of individual effort lay deep misgivings about the modern technology on which these enterprising individuals relied. The benefits of industrial America did not always outweigh the drawbacks that accompanied it. Thus, the progress achieved in another "utilities" Western, *Western Union* (1941), comes at considerable cost; telegraph lines may have been strung, but they stretch over the graves of an earlier generation of pioneering westerners (such as Randolph Scott) who gave their lives for this new technology that spawned a revolution in the fledgling communications industry.

The Western enjoyed unprecedented popularity in the 1950s because it enabled audiences to retreat to a world in which technology posed more promise than threat. In this respect, Westerns reflected, albeit quite indirectly, a deep-rooted uneasiness on the part of postwar America in regard to technological advancement. This uneasiness was strikingly similar to that found in 1950s science-fiction films, which dramatized the darker side of scientific development in the form of alien invasions, mutations produced by atomic explosions, and apocalyptic visions at the end of the world triggered by a rampant technology that had run amuck.

SPACE: THE FINAL FRONTIER

The popularity of the Western endured just so long as it continued to address the basic concerns of a technophobic American populace. It began to fade just at the point that America attempted to reconcile itself to certain realities that underlie its status as a highly industrialized mass society. In the 1890s, Turner

Courtesy of 20th Century-Fox

The Western hero resurfaced in the science-fiction film: Han Solo (Harrison Ford) functions as a futuristic cowboy in *Star Wars* (1977).

and others noted the closing of the western frontier. In the 1960s, John F. Kennedy proclaimed a "New Frontier," which, in addition to new domestic policies—including tax reform, federal aid to education, medicare, civil rights, and the Peace Corps—dramatically increased spending for the space program. Responding in part to the initiative taken by Eisenhower shortly after the Soviets launched the first satellite into space in 1958, Americans made science and mathematics a new priority in both primary and secondary educational instruction. Within a decade, there emerged a new generation of young Americans (of moviegoing age) who no longer shared their parents' deep-seated anxiety toward science and technology.

With Kennedy and Johnson, the conquest of outer space became a central goal around which the American pioneering spirit, engineering know-how, and technology were marshaled. With the advent of the space program, popular attitudes toward science and technology slowly began to change. Although no one event can be said to have determined the demise of the Western, by the 1970s, the West and the genre of the Western were no longer the most powerful sites for the definition of a contemporary American identity. Outer space and the "space" opera or science-fiction film replaced the West and the horse opera in the popular imagination. No longer were Americans to be defined by the primal contact between culture and nature, but by that between culture and advanced technology.

Steven Spielberg's *Close Encounters of the Third Kind* (1977) and *E.T.: The Extra-Terrestrial* (1982) rewrote the technophobia of the 1950s as technophilia in the 1970s. Spielberg reimagined the future brought about by technological change as utopian, and reconfigured technologically advanced alien cultures (which had been regarded as threatening in the 1950s) as benign. The Western's fearful retreat to a preindustrialized past gradually gave way, in popularity, to the science-fiction film's wholehearted adoption of a technological future. Westerns, of course, have continued to be made, as have technophobic science-fiction films. *Star Wars* (1977), for example, proved both technophilic—in its humanization of technology in the form of anthropomorphic robots C3PO and R2D2, and technophobic—in its adoption of the medieval codes of the Jedi knights and its endorsement of human intuition over science (in the film's finale, Luke Skywalker [Mark Hamill] turns off his computerized gun sight and learns to "reach out with [his] feelings" in the attack on the Death Star).

Though opposed in their attitudes toward technology, the Western and the science-fiction film remain remarkably similar in their celebration of the frontier experience. Indeed, as the power of the Western faded, the science-fiction film snatched up the body of its themes, situations, icons, and motifs. *Star Wars* borrowed extensively from *The Searchers*, reworking its basic plot involving the abduction and rescue of the hero's niece/sister and reusing one of its most powerful images (the hero's discovery of a burned-out ranch house containing the bodies of his dead relatives). It even includes a western saloon sequence in which first Obi-Won Kenobi (Alec Guinness) uses his light sabre to defend Luke from an alien bully and then Han Solo (Harrison Ford), dressed like a western hero, shoots it out with an alien bounty hunter sent by Jabba the Hut.

Close Encounters, another reworking of *The Searchers* plotline, focuses on the attempts to retrieve an abducted child (Carey Guffey) from (benign) alien captors. Its search leads to the western landscape of the Badlands and to the Devils Tower, a site sacred to Native Americans. Devils Tower functions as a space-age frontier where the old world has a close encounter with the new.

The survival of the Western in the new form of the science fiction film is amply evident in two films of the early 1980s. The low-budget *Battle Beyond the Stars* (1980) remade the story of *The Magnificent Seven* (1960), which, in turn, was a remake of Kurosawa's *Seven Samurai* (1954). In the film, helpless farmers on a small planet (named "Akira," for Kurosawa) hire seven mercenaries, including Robert Vaughn, who reprises his role from *Magnificent Seven*, and a character called "Space Cowboy" (George Peppard) to defend them from a galactic warlord and his band of mutants, who have threatened to destroy them. *Outland* (1981), another space opera, starred Sean Connery as a marshal overseeing law and order at a mining site on a volcanic moon of Jupiter, reworking the plot of *High Noon* (1952), although it lacked the final shoot-out between hero and villain that concluded the earlier film.

Western iconography abounds in science-fiction films. It is present in the use of rugged western landscapes, as in the *Star Wars* films, *Close Encounters*, and *Starship Troopers* (1997); and it resurfaces in certain items of costuming, such as the full-length black duster that Neo (Keanu Reeves) wears to do battle in *The Matrix* (1999). Like a lawman or bounty hunter in an Antony Mann or Budd Boetticher Western, Air Force Capt. Steven Hiller (Will Smith) drags by its parachute rope a captured alien, across "the burning desert" back to the "fort" in Area 51, in *Independence Day* (1996). And in *Starship Troopers,* there's a classic Western scene in which the troopers defend their fort against thousands of savage warrior bugs.

In 1983, *The Right Stuff* represented Chuck Yeager (Sam Shepard) as a Western hero—a cowboy on horseback who looks on as the lone-wolf test pilots of his generation are replaced by corporate team players. In *Space Cowboys* (2000), a film inspired by Sen. John Glenn's geriatric return to space in 1998, four aging Chuck Yeager types join forces to prevent a Soviet communications satellite from crashing to Earth. Three of the four astronauts are played by former Western stars (Clint Eastwood, Tommy Lee Jones, James Garner) and one of these (Jones) is introduced wearing cowboy boots. Proving themselves more courageous and resourceful than the new generation of NASA astronauts, the four old-timers possess what Ed Buscombe describes as "cowboy values."

Science fiction and the Western meet face to face in *Wild Wild West* (1999), a film set in the 1870s West that features giant iron tarantulas driven by steam engines and deadly, flying magnetic discs. Based on a 1960s television series, *Wild Wild West* is an example of "steam punk," a subgenre of science fiction in which radical technological advances take place early in the industrial era. The Western literally becomes a science-fiction film, complete with elaborate special effects and computer generated imagery.

In a handful of science-fiction films, the narrative situations, motifs, and iconography of the Western function as a way of providing audiences with familiar signposts to guide them through the unfamiliar and unknown landscape of an alien space. The otherness of outer space is transformed into the more familiar world of the West. We will conquer outer space as we have conquered other alien spaces in the past. It is nothing more than a new, albeit "final," frontier.

■ ■ ■ SELECT FILMOGRAPHY

Hell's Hinges (1916)
The Iron Horse (1924)
The Virginian (1929)
Stagecoach (1939)
The Outlaw (1943)
Duel in the Sun (1946)
My Darling Clementine (1946)
Pursued (1947)
Fort Apache (1948)
Red River (1948)
She Wore a Yellow Ribbon
  (1949)

Broken Arrow (1950)
Devil's Doorway (1950)
High Noon (1952)
The Naked Spur (1952)
Shane (1953)
Apache (1954)
Johnny Guitar (1954)
The Man from Laramie (1955)
The Searchers (1956)
The Day of the Outlaw (1959)
Ride Lonesome (1959)
Rio Bravo (1959)

The Man Who Shot Liberty Valance
  (1962)
Ride the High Country (1962)
El Dorado (1966)
The Wild Bunch (1969)
Little Big Man (1970)
McCabe and Mrs. Miller (1971)
High Plains Drifter (1972)
Ulzana's Raid (1972)
Buffalo Bill and the Indians, or
  Sitting Bull's History Lesson
  (1976)
The Outlaw Josey Wales (1976)
The Shootist (1976)
Pale Rider (1985)
Dances With Wolves (1990)

Unforgiven (1992)
The Last of the Mohicans
  (1992)
The Ballad of Little Jo (1993)
Posse (1993)
Geronimo: An American Legend
  (1993)
Maverick (1994)
Wyatt Earp (1994)
Tombstone (1994)
The Quick and the Dead (1995)
Dead Man (1995)
Lone Star (1996)
Wild Wild West (1999)
The Hi-Lo Country (1999)
The Missing (2003)

■ ■ ■ SELECT BIBLIOGRAPHY

BUSCOMBE, ED, ed. *The BFI Companion to the Western.* London: Andre Deutsch, 1988.

CAWELTI, JOHN. *The Six-Gun Mystique Sequel.* Bowling Green, OH: Bowling Green State University Popular Press, 1999.

KILPATRICK, JACQUELYN. *Celluloid Indians: Native Americans and Film.* Lincoln: University of Nebraska Press, 1999.

KITSES, JIM. *Horizons West.* Bloomington: Indiana University Press, 1969.

MARX, LEO. *The Machine in the Garden: Technology and the Pastoral Ideal in America.* New York: Oxford University Press, 1964.

ROSENBAUM, JONATHAN. *Dead Man.* London: BFI, 2000.

SLOTKIN, RICHARD. *Gunfighter Nation: The Myth of the Frontier in Twentieth Century America.* New York: Atheneum, 1992.

SMITH, HENRY NASH. *Virgin Land: The American West as Symbol and Myth.* Cambridge: Harvard University Press, 1950.

TAN, LYN. "Gunfighter Gaps: Discourses of the Frontier in Hollywood Movies of the 1930s and 1970s." Ph.D. Dissertation, Sheffield Hallam University, 1998.

TOMKINS, JANE. *West of Everything: The Inner Life of the Westerns.* New York: Oxford University Press, 1992.

WRIGHT, WILL. *Sixguns & Society: A Structural Study of the Western.* Berkeley: University of California, 1975.

PART **THREE**

A Postwar History

The institutional base for classical Hollywood cinema was established in the second decade of the twentieth century with the vertical integration of the film industry—that is, when studios became involved in the fields of distribution and exhibition, and exhibitors entered the production and distribution arena. This industrial base remained more or less intact for almost 40 years—until 1948, when the United States Department of Justice and the Supreme Court declared the present structure of the film industry to be in violation of the Sherman Antitrust Act and ordered the studios to divest themselves of their theater holdings. Over the next decade, the studios gradually sold off their theaters. And, over the course of succeeding decades, the role of the studios gradually evolved from that of producers and distributors of motion pictures to primarily that of distributors of films that had been independently produced.

The structure of the film industry changed in response not only to court-imposed orders but also to profound changes that took place in the area of leisure-time entertainment. Postwar audiences differed dramatically from their prewar counterparts. As a result of demographic changes, which involved the shift of a significant part of the moviegoing audience from the cities to the suburbs, the traditional (habitual) movie audience gave way to a new breed of infrequent moviegoers, who could be lured out of their houses and away from their television sets only by exceptional films—by big-budget blockbusters or special-event films.

The chapters that follow chart the postwar transformation of Hollywood from its status as a semistable institution, which had been established in the first few decades of this century, to an industry that has become increasingly flexible in its structure. Indeed, during this time period, Hollywood was forced to respond to a succession of challenges that threatened its economic survival. These ranged from government intervention (forced divestiture in 1948, the House Un-American Activities Committee hearings in 1947 and 1953) and the competition of television in the 1950s to the advent of cable TV, the VCR and videotape in the 1980s and the distractive lure of video games and the Internet in the 1990s, as well as DVDs and satellite and digital television as the new millennium began.

A review of these changes shows how variations within the larger cultural profile of the United States resulted in significant alterations in the kinds of films that are now being made. As the industry adapted itself to a constantly changing set of economic, social, political, and cultural demands, it gradually became a different kind of cinema. Many of the features of traditional classical Hollywood cinema survive, especially the narrative patterns and stylistic forms it perfected during the heyday of the studio system. And it continues to perform a similar cultural function, representing the experience of postwar America.

But the movies no longer speak to the entire population in the way that prewar cinema did; older generations of Americans rarely go to the movies; the great majority of moviegoers grow younger and younger over the years. The largest percentage of today's audience is between 12 and 20 years of age. The following history of postwar Hollywood cinema is designed to provide an account of the forces that transformed the old classical Hollywood cinema into the new classical Hollywood cinema, and to provide a portrait of the latter as an institution.

CHAPTER **12**

Hollywood and the Cold War

ORIGINS: COMMUNISM, HOLLYWOOD, AND THE AMERICAN WAY

Revolution and Repercussion

Unofficially, the cold war began in 1917, when the Communist Bolsheviks came to power in Russia, after unseating the more moderate Mensheviks who ran the country after the overthrow of the czar. The cold war officially ended more than 70 years later, in 1991, when the Soviet Union began to unravel. America responded to the Russian Revolution with a Red scare that was triggered in 1919 by labor unrest, strikes, and the growing unionization of the work force. Even the Boston police force formed a union and went on strike, leaving the city defenseless and forcing officials to call out the state guard. The official responsible for breaking this strike, Governor Calvin Coolidge, parlayed his antiunion stance into a probusiness platform that later won him a nomination for vice president in 1920. When President Warren Harding died in 1923, Coolidge found himself president.

In 1919, anarchists, Bolsheviks, and other radical groups were suspected of sending a series of bombs through the mail to prominent political leaders and industrialists, terrorizing government officials and capitalists. In 1920, five socialists were elected to the New York State Assembly, then expelled by that body because, as socialists, they were members of "a disloyal organization composed exclusively of perpetual traitors." To many, it seemed as if the forces of revolution had spread beyond the borders of Russia, and the Communist goal of worldwide revolution was threatening the United States as well. Blaming the postwar strikes by steel workers and coal miners on "the Red menace," the U.S. Attorney General ordered that all Communists be rounded up and deported. Over 6,000 men were arrested, and more than 500 were deported as undesirable aliens.

At the same time, Hollywood produced a number of anti-Communist films, including *Bolshevism on Trial* (1919), which was based on a novel by Thomas Dixon, the author of D. W. Griffith's *The Birth of a Nation* (1915). Playing on popular fears of worldwide revolution, publicity for the film asked, "Shall [Bolshevism] travel to America, gathering in its net Western peoples and Democratic organizations?" *The Right to Happiness* (ca. 1919) sought from its viewers the answer to a similar question: "Which would you rather have in this country—destruction under the Red flag or construction and co-operation under the American Flag?" Griffith's *Orphans of the Storm* (1922), which ostensibly dealt with the French Revolution, warned its audiences in an opening intertitle of the dangers of "Anarchy and Bolshevism," suggesting that the film be seen as a lesson in history. "The lesson: the French Revolution RIGHTLY overthrew a BAD government. But we in America should be careful lest we with a GOOD government mistake fanatics for leaders and exchange our decent law and order for Anarchy and Bolshevism."

The Red scare of the early 1920s also led to the arrest of two Italian immigrants and suspected anarchists, Nicola Sacco and Bartolomeo Vanzetti, for the murder of a payroll clerk. Their controversial trial and subsequent execution in 1927 made them internationally famous, focusing unwanted attention on the American legal system and the country's treatment of radicals. Fear of potential Reds spread to the motion picture industry. In 1922, the FBI opened a file on Charlie Chaplin after he entertained a leader of the American Communist Party in his home. They continued to document his supposedly subversive activities and associations until 1952, when Chaplin left the United States and his reentry permit was revoked by the State Department.

A similar fate befell actor-singer Paul Robeson (a Phi Beta Kappa Rutgers graduate and the son of a runaway slave), whose denunciation of American racism was linked to his sympathy for the Soviet Union, thus branding him a Communist. His last Hollywood film was *Show Boat* (1936); after that, his controversial political statements resulted in his being blacklisted, forcing him to go abroad for employment. In 1950, his passport was revoked, effectively end-

"Are you now or have you ever been a Communist?" Responding to the Red scare of the 1950s, Robert Walker swears to his mother (Helen Hayes) on the Bible that he is not a Communist, in *My Son John* (1952).

Courtesy of Paramount

ing his career as a concert performer who earned the bulk of his income from his work overseas.

The threat of worldwide revolution in the wake of the 1917 Russian Revolution began to seem a bit less likely when postwar leftist movements in Germany, Hungary, and other European countries failed to succeed in establishing Communist or socialist governments. As a result, concern about domestic radicals gradually subsided in the United States. At the same time, the prosperity of the American economy in the 1920s appeared to undermine Communist critiques of capitalism—that is, until the stock market crash in 1929.

In the Red: The Depression Era

Hollywood had never attempted to glamorize bankers, industrialists, and stock speculators. After the crash, these capitalist figures tended to be regularly identified with the fiscal mismanagement that had brought about the Great Depression, but their villainy was more often seen in terms of individual greed than of class oppression. Decades later, during the Communist witch-hunts of the late 1940s and early 1950s, right-wing novelist Ayn Rand, author of *The Fountainhead,* would read these characterizations of the business community as Communist-inspired. In her booklet *Screen Guide for Americans,* Rand warned Hollywood filmmakers, "Don't Smear Industrialists," "Don't Smear the Free Enterprise System," and "Don't Smear Success." Rand also advised screenwriters, "Don't give your character—as a sign of villainy, as a damning characteristic—the desire to make money."

But the depiction of capitalists in 1930s Hollywood films, ranging from Chaplin's *City Lights* (1931) to Frank Capra's *You Can't Take It With You* (1938), was inspired more by the reactionary spirit of populism, which seeks reform, than by the radical spirit of Communism, which preaches revolution. In other words, the system works, though it often needs watching. Indeed, for every bad capitalist or millionaire, these movies suggest that there is a good capitalist who might make things right.

However, the films depicting Communists continued to portray them negatively. In Depression-era comedies, Bolsheviks not only behave like deranged lunatics but—even worse—they have no sense of humor, style, or wit. Thus, the Bolshevik in Ernst Lubitsch's *Trouble in Paradise* (1932) denounced the heroine (Kay Francis), a wealthy cosmetics manufacturer, and lectures to her that "any woman who spends a fortune in times like these for a handbag—phooey, phooey, phooey!" In topical melodramas such as *Heroes for Sale* (1933) and *Little Man, What Now* (1934), Communists were exposed as essentially selfish phonies who are unconcerned with the genuine poverty and hardship of others.

In *Heroes,* for example, the European inventor is a Bolshevik who is described by another character as "kinda cracked." He quotes Lenin, speaks of "class servitude," denounces "dirty capitalists," and refers to the workers as "sheep." But he abruptly changes his tune when his invention turns him into a millionaire, describing the poor and the needy as "a cancer on civilization." When the hero objects, saying, "I thought you hated all employers and capitalists," the former radical replies: "I despise them, I spit on them. But I'm willing to get rich with them." The film carefully distinguishes the unemployed "heroes" referred to in its title from foreign subversives. When vigilante groups force an army of homeless and jobless men to board a train that will get rid of them by shipping them across the state line, they refer to the men as "Reds." But the hero quickly corrects them, declaring, "We're not Reds; we're ex-servicemen!"

Although studios such as Warner Bros. openly supported much of the social reform proposed by Franklin Roosevelt's New Deal, Hollywood drew the line when it came to more radical politics. In 1934, muckraking author and millionaire-socialist Upton Sinclair campaigned for the office of governor of California, promising to "End Poverty in California." Working together with the conservative press, the studios launched a negative publicity campaign against Sinclair, describing him as a "dangerous Bolshevik beast." M-G-M produced fake newsreels depicting hordes of tramps besieging little old ladies on their porches, and newspapers reproduced photographs of hoboes and criminals aboard trains bound for California, intent on taking advantage of Sinclair's promise. The photos were later identified as stills (featuring professional actors) from a Warner Bros. movie about homeless teenagers, *Wild Boys of the Road* (1933). Needless to say, Sinclair lost the election.

Anti–Fascists, Populists, and "Dupes"

During the Spanish Civil War, Hollywood's anti-Communism was tempered somewhat by its anti–fascism. The specter of yet another Fascist dictatorship in Spain, supported by those already in place in Hitler's Germany and Mussolini's Italy, prompted many liberals to support the Communist-backed Loyalists in their fight against Generalissimo Francisco Franco's Fascists. Screenwriter Dorothy Parker and playwright Lillian Hellman organized a group of Loyalist supporters in Hollywood into the Motion Picture Artists Committee to Aid Republican Spain. Members included writers Dashiell Hammett, Dudley Nichols, and Julius and Philip Epstein; directors John Ford and Lewis Milestone; and actors Louise Rainer, Melvyn Douglas, Fredric March, Paul Muni, and John Garfield. Ford donated an ambulance to the American Abraham Lincoln Brigade, which fought on the side of the Loyalists.

Producer Walter Wanger, together with screenwriter John Howard Lawson, made a film about the Spanish Civil War, *Blockade* (1938), which was released by United Artists. However, pressure from the Hays Office and the Roosevelt administration, which were nervous about taking sides in the conflict, undermined the project, which had been designed as a warning about the dangers of the spread of fascism in Europe. As a result, the film became a simple love story about an idealistic farmer (Henry Fonda), whose political affiliation is never stated, and a beautiful spy (Madeleine Carroll) who works for the other side. The Loyalists and the fascists were never identified by name, and viewers had difficulty knowing whether Fonda was a Loyalist or merely a humble advocate for the universal rights of people.

While Hollywood could not quite come out in favor of the left-wing Loyalists in *Blockade*, it could still make fun of Communists in *Ninotchka* (1939) and *Comrade X* (1940). In the former film, for example, Greta Garbo's dogmatic Soviet official is easily seduced away from the party line by the luxuries of capitalism—in particular, by a frivolous hat that she sees in a store window.

Populist films that exposed the predicament of the working class took pains to make it clear that the support of labor was not to be confused with Communist propaganda. Ford's adaptation of John Steinbeck's *The Grapes of Wrath* (1940) explores the ways in which migrant farm workers were exploited, but it carefully distances itself from anything that might be considered un-American. Thus, Tom Joad (Henry Fonda), though radicalized by his experiences at the hands of farm owners and their company police, remains ignorant of the larger political debates that surround the plight of labor in the film. Someone mentions to him that Reds are suspected of causing trouble by organizing the workers, and he responds by asking, "Who are these Reds, anyway?"

By the late 1930s, the government had begun to take greater and greater interest in Hollywood's anti–fascism, which was considered to be Communist-inspired. In 1938, Representative Martin Dies, the first chair of the House Un-American Activities Committee (HUAC), declared that those members of the industry who had joined the Hollywood Anti-Nazi League (whose list of sponsors included moguls Carl Laemmle, Jack Warner, and Dore Schary) were "Communist dupes." In 1940, Dies opened hearings to investigate the presence of Communists in Hollywood, naming actors Fredric March, Humphrey Bogart, and James Cagney, and screenwriter Philip Dunne, as suspected Reds. All four successfully cleared themselves in testimony given to the Dies Committee, but a precedent had been set. Witch-hunters such as Dies discovered that they could generate enormous publicity by using Hollywood as the target of their investigations.

World War II and Government Policy

During World War II, the government put a hold on its inquiries into Communism in Hollywood. Industry personnel had been suspected of being Communists largely because of their participation in anti–fascist causes and organizations. With American entry into the war, anti–fascism suddenly became national policy, and, with the exception of a brief period during which the Soviet Union and Germany had signed and observed a nonaggression pact (1939–1941), Russia was an ally in America's fight against Germany, Italy, and Japan. For the time being, HUAC kept a low profile.

However, right-wing elements in the Hollywood community continued the anti-Communist campaign that the Dies Committee had begun. In February 1944, they organized themselves into the Motion Picture Alliance for the Preservation of American Ideals, which dedicated itself to purging the industry of "Communists, radicals, and crackpots." Members of the Alliance included

Actor Adolphe Menjou of the Motion Picture Alliance for the Preservation of American Ideals testifies before the House Un-American Activities Committee about subversives in Hollywood.

director Sam Wood; producer Walt Disney; actors Robert Taylor, Barbara Stan-wyck, Adolphe Menjou, Gary Cooper, Clark Gable, John Wayne, and Ward Bond; writers Ayn Rand and Borden Chase; labor representative Roy Brewer of IATSE (the International Alliance of Theatrical Stage Employees); and Lela Rogers, the mother of actress Ginger Rogers.

During the war, the Alliance issued statements calling on patriotic elements in the film industry to combat "totalitarian-minded groups working within the industry for the dissemination of un-American ideas and beliefs." In response, Dies and his committee returned to Hollywood to investigate the Alliance's charges. In 1945, HUAC, which had originally been a temporary committee, was made permanent, partially in response to the publicity it and the Alliance generated by investigating radicals in Hollywood.

During the war, Hollywood produced a number of films designed to give support to American allies. Thus, in addition to celebrating England in *Mrs. Miniver* (1942) and *The White Cliffs of Dover* (1944), the major studios produced several pro-Soviet films, including *Song of Russia* (1943) and *Mission to Moscow* (1943). These works were commissioned, in part, by the U.S. government, which sought to familiarize Americans with the plight of our allies. But these productions would come back to haunt Hollywood in the postwar years, when any support of the Soviet Union was deemed traitorous.

INQUISITION: HUAC, MCCARTHY, AND THE HOLLYWOOD TEN

Friends and Foes

Immediately after the war, the long-time tensions that had existed between the United States and the Soviet Union were renewed. In March 1946, former British Prime Minister Winston Churchill gave voice to the concerns of the West in response to the threat of Soviet postwar expansion. After observing the fate of Eastern Europe after its "liberation" by Russia, Churchill declared that "from Stettin in the Baltic to Trieste in the Adriatic, an Iron Curtain has descended across the continent," identifying the spread of Communism with the imprisonment of innocent nations behind an "Iron Curtain." Churchill's phrase succinctly conveyed the fears of the West that it was also in danger of being swallowed up behind the ever-expanding walls of totalitarian oppression. At the same time, Communism began to play a greater and greater role in the postwar political landscape of the Far East, especially in North Korea, China, and Indochina.

In the United States, business feared that labor unions would be taken over by Communists in a somewhat similar way. In 1945, the Conference of Studio Unions (CSU; those unions not represented by IATSE) began a strike against the studios, which lasted for over eight months. Warner Bros. relied on scabs, fire hoses, tear gas, and other violent means to disperse union pickets and break the strike. During the fall of 1946, another industrywide strike by the CSU resulted in charges, from opponents of the strike, that the unions represented by the CSU had become infiltrated by Communists.

Meanwhile, a nationwide strike by coal miners, which began in April 1946, was followed by a national strike of railway workers in May. These strikes were resolved only after President Harry Truman threatened to draft striking workers into the armed forces.

The elections of 1946 witnessed a number of races in which Republican candidates accused the Democratic opponents and the Democratic New Deal administration of Communist sympathies. Both Richard Nixon and Joseph McCarthy relied on Red-baiting to gain their seats in Congress. In 1947, President Truman, in an attempt to demonstrate his administration's own anti-Communist bias, officially declared a "cold war" against the Soviet Union that was designed to contain the spread of Communism abroad. Funds were allocated to assist anti-Communist forces in Greece and Turkey in their struggle against armed minorities in their own countries. At the same time, Truman initiated a series of domestic loyalty probes to root out Communist infiltration of government and labor in the United States. As a result of Truman's loyalty review program, between March 1947 and December 1952 more than 6.6 million people were investigated, and more than 500 were dismissed because their loyalty was in question.

"Are You Now or Have You Ever Been . . . ?"

It was in this atmosphere of governmental distrust and suspicion that the House Un-American Activities Committee renewed its investigation of subversives in the film industry. Preliminary closed-door hearings were held in May 1947 by new Committee Chair J. Parnell Thomas. After hearing testimony from members of the Motion Picture Alliance for the Preservation of American Ideals and others, Thomas announced that Hollywood filmmakers had "employed subtle techniques in pictures in glorifying the Communist system and degrading our own system of Government and Institutions." Later that year, in October, Thomas conducted public hearings in Washington, D.C., during which his committee interviewed 24 "friendly" and 11 "unfriendly" witnesses (18 had been called, but only 11 testified). The friendly witnesses—including actors Robert Taylor, Robert Montgomery, Adolphe Menjou, Ronald Reagan, and Gary Cooper; director Sam Wood; and producer Walt Disney—complained about the subversive activities of Communists in the film industry and identified as many of them as they could by name.

The "unfriendly" witnesses, many of whom had been named as Communists, attended the hearings but refused to cooperate with the Committee, contending that its investigation was illegal and in violation of their rights under the First Amendment of the Constitution. These witnesses included German playwright Bertolt Brecht, who testified that he had never been a member of the Communist Party and then fled from the United States on the following day (thus, this eleventh witness avoided making the "Hollywood Ten" the "Hollywood Eleven").

The Hollywood Ten (and their lawyers), January 1948:

Top row (left to right for all rows): Ring Lardner, Jr., Edward Dmytryk, Adrian Scott
Middle row: Dalton Trumbo, John Howard Lawson, Alvah Bessie, Samuel Ornitz
Front row: Herbert Biberman, attorney Martin Popper, attorney Robert Kenny, Albert Maltz, Lester Cole

The remaining 10 "unfriendly" witnesses were subsequently known as the Hollywood Ten. They included writer Alvah Bessie (drama critic for *New Masses* and coscreenwriter of *Objective Burma*, 1945); director Herbert Biberman (*Meet Nero Wolfe*, 1936); writer Lester Cole (*Objective Burma*); director Edward Dmytryk (*Crossfire*, 1947); screenwriter Ring Lardner, Jr. (*Woman of the Year*, 1942); founder and first president of the Screen Writers Guild, John Howard Lawson (*Action in the North Atlantic*, 1943); writer Albert Maltz (*Pride of the Marines*, 1945); writer Sam Ornitz; writer-producer Adrian Scott (*Murder, My Sweet*, 1944; *Crossfire*, 1947); and writer Dalton Trumbo (*Thirty Seconds Over Tokyo*, 1944).

They were accompanied to the hearings by an independent group of famous Hollywood celebrities such as Edward G. Robinson, Humphrey Bogart, Lauren Bacall, Danny Kaye, John Garfield, Gregory Peck, John Huston, and others (such as writer Philip Dunne) who had become members of the Committee for the First Amendment. During the hearings, these celebrities participated in a radio broadcast from Washington that denounced HUAC and supported the First Amendment but gave no direct support to any individual "unfriendly" witnesses with whose confrontational tactics they disagreed.

The Hollywood Ten initially sought to use the hearings as a platform for exposing the dangers of anti-Communism and for protesting the way in which the Committee threatened their rights under the First Amendment of the Constitution (although none of the Ten chose to invoke the First Amendment, preferring instead to answer the Committee in their own words). Each came with a prepared statement to read, but only one, Albert Maltz, was permitted to present it. They were all asked by members of HUAC, "Are you now or have you ever been a member of the Communist Party?" Because they all refused to answer, they were cited with contempt of Congress, were tried and convicted, and, sentenced to from six months to one year in jail. After exhausting their appeals (and after the U.S. Supreme Court refused to hear their cases), they began serving their sentences in 1950.

Blacklisting

Shortly after the October hearings, more than 50 studio executives, members of the Motion Pictures Producers Association, met secretly at the Waldorf-Astoria Hotel in New York to discuss steps that the industry might take to protect itself from the fallout from the hearings. In particular, the producers feared threatened boycotts of their films organized by the Hearst newspapers, the American Legion, and other patriotic national organizations. Much as the industry had earlier adopted self-censorship, through the agency of the Hays Office in order to prevent the creation of external censorship review boards, here it adopted a policy of self-regulation that was coupled with the institution of blacklisting.

Issuing what would be known as "the Waldorf Statement," the studio heads agreed to suspend the Hollywood Ten without pay, to deny employment to anyone who did not cooperate with HUAC's investigations, and to refuse to hire Communists. In this way, the industry effectively instituted a blacklist of unemployable talent. The numbers of those blacklisted ultimately extended beyond the Hollywood Ten and those who refused to testify before the Committee at subsequent hearings to include any employees who were suspected of Communist sympathies and who were unable to clear themselves to the satisfaction of the studios. By the mid-1950s, more than 200 suspected Communists had been blacklisted by the Hollywood studios. The blacklist remained unchallenged from 1947 until 1960, when screenwriter Dalton Trumbo, one of the original Hollywood Ten, worked openly in the industry and received screen credit for his work on producer-director Otto Preminger's *Exodus* (1960) and actor-producer Kirk Douglas's *Spartacus* (1960). However, the blacklist did not begin to give way until the mid-1960s, and it remained in effect for a number of artists well into the 1970s.

Alger Hiss, the Rosenbergs, and Senator McCarthy

A second round of HUAC hearings on Hollywood took place in 1951. In the interim, the cold war had dramatically escalated. A Communist coup had taken place in Czechoslovakia in 1948. In July 1948, a federal grand jury indicted (and subsequently convicted) 11 leaders of the American Communist Party with conspiracy to overthrow the United States government. In 1949, Mao Tse-tung defeated the forces of Chiang Kai-shek and China became a Communist nation. That same year, the Soviets exploded their first nuclear weapon, launching an arms race that would continue for over four decades. In January 1950, former New Deal official Alger Hiss was convicted of perjury charges stemming from a 1948 accusation by admitted former Communist Whittaker Chambers, a senior editor at *Time* magazine, that Hiss had sold government documents to the Soviets in the 1930s when he worked in the State Department. Hiss's apparent guilt enabled Republicans to portray the Roosevelt administration as thoroughly infiltrated by Communists, a notion that would subsequently be exploited by Senator Joseph McCarthy in his attack on Communists in government. (The release of secret Soviet records in 1992 ultimately cleared Hiss of any association with Communist espionage.)

In February, the British arrested Dr. Klaus Fuchs, an atomic scientist who had worked with the Americans on the A-bomb at Los Alamos, charging that he had spied for the Soviets. The arrest of Fuchs led to the subsequent arrest and conviction of his supposed accomplices, Americans Harry Gold, Morton Sobell, and Julius and Ethel Rosenberg. (The Rosenbergs were executed for espionage in 1953.) Several days after the highly publicized arrest of Fuchs, Senator McCarthy launched a witch-hunt for Communists working in government. Speaking in Wheeling, West Virginia, he declared that he had a list of 205 names of Communists who were knowingly employed by the State Department.

Even though McCarthy's charges were investigated and proved false by a special committee of the Senate, the press continued to publish his accusations and headline the threat of the Red menace until the Army-McCarthy hearings, which were held from April through June 1954. The televised hearings exposed the senator as a bully and a self-serving demagogue who would do anything to advance his own career. Later that year, in December, the Senate voted to censure McCarthy, whose credibility as a force in national politics quickly crumbled.

Naming Names

During the 1951 HUAC hearings, dozens of former Communists and suspected Communists chose to cooperate with the Committee in an attempt to clear themselves. Unlike the Hollywood Ten, they chose to identify other supposed Communists by name. In April of 1951, Edward Dmytryk, one of the Hollywood Ten, reappeared before HUAC in a carefully orchestrated attempt to clear himself and regain employment in Hollywood. He answered the committee's questions and identified 24 former Communists. Within a matter of weeks, he was back at work, directing a low-budget film for the King Brothers. The following year, he returned to work at the major studios.

Dozens of other Hollywood artists cooperated with the Committee and chose to name names, although most of them held out for several months or even years before doing so. Screenwriter Martin Berkeley, director Robert Rossen, director Frank Tuttle, actor Lee J. Cobb, writer Budd Schulberg, actor Larry Parks, director Elia Kazan, composer David Raksin, actor Sterling Hayden, and writer Clifford Odets all named names. The victims of this round of testimony included writers Dashiell Hammett, Paul Jarrico, Michael Wilson, and Carl Foreman; actors Mady Christians, Canada Lee, John Garfield, Larry Parks, Howard da Silva, Paul Robeson, and Gale Sondergaard; and directors Abraham Polonsky, Joseph Losey, and Jules Dassin.

Actor Lionel Stander, who is known to audiences today for his role as the chauffeur in the TV series *Hart to Hart*, was blacklisted for perhaps the longest period—from the late 1940s until 1965. Stander's 1951 testimony provided one of the few lighter moments in the saga of the blacklist. When questioned by HUAC, he offered to cooperate with them in exposing "subversive action." Stander declared, "I know of a group of fanatics who are desperately trying to undermine the Constitution of the United States by depriving artists and others of Life, Liberty, and the Pursuit of Happiness without due process of law. . . . I can tell names and cite instances and I am one of the first victims of it. And if you are interested in that and also a group of ex-fascists and America-Firsters and anti-Semites, people who hate everybody including Negroes, minority groups and most likely themselves . . . and these people are engaged in a conspiracy outside all the legal processes to undermine the very fundamental American concepts upon which our entire system of democracy exists." Stander was referring, of course, to HUAC itself.

The hearings produced very little evidence of Communist influence on the motion picture industry. One witness recalled that Stander had once whistled the Communist anthem, "The Internationale," in a film while waiting for an elevator. Another noted that screenwriter Lester Cole had inserted lines from a famous pro-Loyalist speech by La Pasionaria about it being "better to die on your feet than to live on your knees" into a pep talk delivered by a football coach.

THE COLD WAR ON SCREEN

Pro-Soviet Wartime Films

Chief targets of HUAC investigators were a handful of pro-Soviet films, such as *The North Star* (RKO, 1943), *Song of Russia* (M-G-M, 1943), *Days of Glory* (RKO, 1944), and *Mission in Moscow* (Warner Bros., 1943), which had been made during the war by major studios as part of the war effort. *The North Star*, which celebrates the resistance of a small Russian village to the Nazis when they invade it, was written by Lillian Hellman and directed by Lewis Milestone, both of whom were subsequently investigated by HUAC. *Mission to Moscow*, which was based on the autobiography of Joseph Davies, the U.S. Ambassador to the Soviet Union, was supposedly made at the request of Franklin Delano Roosevelt in order "to show American mothers and fathers that . . . the Russians are worthy

Courtesy of M-G-M

An American in Russia: Symphony conductor Robert Taylor (a friendly witness for HUAC) falls in love with Soviet musician Susan Peters in *Song of Russia* (1943).

allies." This piece of obvious pro-Soviet propaganda demonstrated the virtues of our new allies and whitewashed, in the process, their faults, including Stalin's infamous purge trials of the late 1930s.

HUAC focused on this film in particular in an attempt to suggest that the Roosevelt administration was pro-Communist and that Hollywood had served as FDR's unwitting tool, producing pro-Soviet propaganda. But it was difficult to fault Hollywood for its support of an acknowledged American ally in its war against Germany. Indeed, in a 1947 statement delivered to HUAC in defense of the film, producer Jack Warner argued that "if making *Mission to Moscow* in 1942 was a subversive activity, then the American Liberty ships which carried food and guns to Russian allies and the American naval vessels which convoyed them were likewise engaged in subversive activities." In his testimony, Warner "protected" FDR, denying that the President played any role in encouraging the studio to make the film.

However, Warner later named the film's screenwriter, Howard Koch, as a Communist, insisting that whatever pro-Soviet sentiments anyone could find in the film had been slipped into it by Koch. Koch, who had coauthored such patriotic scripts as *Sergeant York* (1941) and *Casablanca* (1942), became—as a result of Warner's desperate need for a fall guy on whom to pin responsibility for the film's obvious sympathy for the Soviet Union—yet another victim of the blacklist, remaining out of work for over 10 years.

The Anti-Commie Cycle

Ironically, Hollywood produced more films with subversive messages after HUAC began its investigations than it did before them. For every anti-Communist picture released in the wake of the first HUAC hearings of 1947, there was another film that attacked the scapegoating and witch-hunting tactics of HUAC and the anti-Communist far right. With films such as *The Iron Curtain* (1948), *The Red Menace* (1949), *The Woman on Pier 13* (a.k.a. *I Married a Communist*, 1949), *I Was a Communist for the FBI* (1951), *The Whip Hand* (1951), *Walk East on Beacon* (1952), *My Son John* (1952), *Big Jim McLain* (1952), and *Pickup on South Street* (1953), Hollywood openly condemned Communists, associating them with espionage and with plots involving the violent overthrow of the American government.

The *Iron Curtain*, which was based on the confessions of a real-life Russian defector, exposes the operations of a Soviet spy ring in Canada. In *The Red Menace*, a disillusioned war veteran falls victim to Communist propaganda, which the film's narrator describes as "Marxian hatred . . . intent upon spreading world dissension and treason." In *Big Jim McLain*, John Wayne plays an FBI agent who tracks down Communist spies in Hawaii for HUAC; the film's end credits even thank the members of the Committee, who—"undaunted by the vicious campaign against them"—continue to fight against Communist subversion. *Pickup on South Street* portrays Communists as more treacherous and corrupt than common criminals, who at least observe the codes of the underworld. The film's hero, a small-time pickpocket, is no patriot, but he learns that you can't "play footsie" with the "Commies," who are even less trustworthy than police stool pigeons and prostitutes.

Us versus Them: Science Fiction and Paranoia

Few of these blatantly anti-Communist works made a profit at the box office, but virtually every studio made them in order to demonstrate their anti-Communist zeal. Films dealing with the Korean war, such as *The Steel Helmet* (1950), and *Fixed Bayonets* (1951), or with the war in Indochina, such as *China Gate* (1957), provided a more traditional formula for the expression of anti-Communism by moving the conflict between "us" and "them" from within the borders of America itself to foreign shores. These movies tended to fare somewhat better with audiences. Even more successful than these overtly anti-Communist films were the covert war films—science-fiction films. These works captured the decade's greatest fears—fear of the bomb and fear of a Communist takeover—but did so without the crude tactics of the more flagrantly political films that merely restaged the HUAC hearings in a somewhat more dramatic form or simply reworked recent events that had taken place in Korea.

In *Them!* (1954), gigantic ants (which appear to be mutations produced by nuclear testing) attack Los Angeles, while in *The Incredible Shrinking Man* (1957), a radiation shower serves as the source for human mutation. But instead of producing giant insects, fallout from the bomb actually diminishes the size of the film's hero, who then struggles to survive in a world in which the everyday (in the form of household pets and spiders in the basement) threatens his very existence. Cold war tensions also find expression in films in which invaders from outer space threaten to take over the Earth. In *The Thing* (1951), a creature from outer space that feeds on the blood of its victims and plants seeds that will

Communism as an alien invasion: In *Invasion of the Body Snatchers* (1956), King Donovan (left), Kevin McCarthy, and Dana Wynter look at a "pod" that has duplicated Donovan's features.

enable it to reproduce, gives monstrous form to contemporary fears about the spread of Communism.

Invaders From Mars (1953) and *Invasion of the Body Snatchers* (1956) exploited the association of Communism with brainwashing, which had developed in the aftermath of the Korean war when American prisoners of war were said to have been indoctrinated with Communist ideology. In *Invaders*, Martians implant crystals in the brains of local citizens, transforming them into slaves who do their bidding. In *Invasion*, aliens take over the bodies of the local residents by placing "seed pods" in their houses. The pods copy their features while they sleep, taking them over "cell by cell." Once they have been taken over by the pods, the film's characters lack individuality, feeling, and emotion; they have, in short, become Communist dupes.

God and Country

Even biblical epics took up the issues of the cold war. In *The Ten Commandments* (1956), right-wing director Cecil B. DeMille provided a prologue to the movie in which he asks "whether men are to be ruled by God's law—or whether they are to be ruled by the whims of a dictator." He stresses the relevance of these issues by then asking, "Are men the property of the state? Or are they free souls under God?" And he finally links these issues to the current cold war by observing that "the same battle continues throughout the world today."

Yet, it is in this same genre that the radical left was able to make a case for the Hollywood Ten and the evils of repressive government. The original script of the first CinemaScope blockbuster, *The Robe* (Fox, 1953), for example, was (according to Philip Dunne who rewrote it and received sole screen credit for the film) written by a blacklisted writer. (The most recent generation of prints of *The Robe* has restored this blacklisted writer's name to the credits; he was Albert Maltz.) It cast Caligula as a witch-hunting, McCarthyesque figure and the Christians as persecuted victims of his demonic attempts to purge the Roman empire of potential subversives—that is, of Christians. The hero, Marcellus, is converted to Christianity and publicly tried for treason at the end of the film. The film's Christians meet in underground caverns (i.e., cells) and resist the fascism of the Roman state. Similarly, the pagan villain in *Prince Valiant* (Fox, 1954) captures Prince Valiant and refuses to release him unless he betrays his Christian comrades. The villain literally asks the hero to name names, demanding that the prince "confirm this list—your father named them all." Needless to say, the prince stoically refuses, remaining silent in spite of being tortured.

Subversions

Subversive messages also surfaced in the Western. Because he was ultimately blacklisted, Carl Foreman's script for the critically acclaimed box-office success *High Noon* (1952) emerges as an obvious example of resistance within the industry to outside investigators such as HUAC. The film's hero, ironically played by a real-life friendly witness, Gary Cooper, is threatened by a gang of cutthroats (HUAC) who are on their way to town (Hollywood). The sheriff-hero is unable to find allies to help him in the (Hollywood) community. He nonetheless confronts and defeats them, waging a battle alone that the townspeople ought to have fought with him.

A few years earlier, hard on the heels of being blacklisted as one of the original Hollywood Ten, Alvah Bessie wrote the screenplay for *Broken Arrow* (1950), which proved to be one of the highest-grossing films of the year. Bessie was able to accomplish this by using a "front," another screenwriter (Michael Blankfort) who pretended to be the author of the script and received screen credit for it. (In 1976, Woody Allen starred in a film called *The Front* that dealt with this method of outwitting the blacklist.) The *Broken Arrow* story, which later served as the basis for a highly popular television series of the same name in the mid-1950s, involved the unusual friendship between a white man, Tom Jeffords (James Stewart), and an Apache, Cochise (Jeff Chandler). In befriending the Indians, Jeffords is regarded as a traitor to his own people, who attempt to lynch him. Jeffords, however, is rescued by the Army. He subsequently marries an Indian girl and plays the role of peacemaker between the Apaches and the whites, but the leading citizens of a nearby town attack the Indian camp, killing Jefford's wife in the process.

In Bessie's scenario, Jefford's friendship with the Indians and his campaign for peaceful coexistence between reds and whites marks him as a traitor (a Communist or Communist sympathizer) in the eyes of his own community. The

The anti-HUAC Western: Joan Crawford and Sterling Hayden portray innocent victims of witch-hunting vigilantes in *Johnny Guitar* (1954).

townspeople emerge as barely disguised Communist witch-hunters. The film's sympathies clearly lie with Jeffords, who, like the blacklisted writer, is not only rejected by society but also becomes the target of its violence and anger.

A similar scenario crops up in *Johnny Guitar* (1954), which was written by Philip Yordan and directed by one of Hollywood's young rebels, Nicholas Ray. The film's plot reworks the HUAC confrontations between suspected subversives and local vigilantes in terms of a typical Western. Again, the community is seen to be intolerant of those in it who are not like themselves. And the unconventional, nonconformist hero and heroine are forced to defend themselves against the false accusations of society. The casting of the film makes its allegorical status as an anti-HUAC vehicle even clearer. The hero, whom the town suspects of having robbed the bank, is played by confessed former Communist Sterling Hayden. One of the chief leaders of the vigilantes is played by Ward Bond, a member of Hollywood's most vocal anti-Communist group, the Motion Picture Alliance for the Preservation of American Ideals. The final shoot-out dramatizes the central battle between the forces of conformity and those of nonconformity. However, it does not take place between the two former cold warriors, Bond and Hayden, but between two women who, in the form of the neurotic and sexually repressive Emma (Mercedes McCambridge) and the former prostitute Vienna (Joan Crawford), reconfigure the political extremes of the film in sexual terms. Though carefully disguised, the anti-HUAC and antiauthoritarian sentiments of the film clearly encourage audiences to root for Hayden and Crawford as the victims of social oppression.

As in the case of Alvah Bessie, blacklisted writers continued to work secretly in Hollywood and were often drawn to projects that provided a platform for the expression of liberal ideas. On more than one occasion, blacklisted writers even won Academy Awards for their work. In 1956, the (unclaimed) Academy Award for best story went to *The Brave One*, which was written by "Robert Rich," one of Dalton Trumbo's aliases. The story deals with the efforts of a Mexican peasant boy to rescue his bull from slaughter in the arena. The next year, the Academy Award for best screenplay went to *The Bridge on the River Kwai* (1957), which explores life in a Japanese prisoner-of-war camp, questions blind obedience to authority, and takes a critical stance toward those who collaborate with the enemy. The script for this box-office blockbuster was signed by Pierre Boulle, author of the original novel on which the film was based. Boulle, however, did not speak a word of English; the script was actually written by two blacklisted writers, Carl Foreman and Michael Wilson.

The secret work of blacklisted writers tended to fare better at the box office than did the one or two projects that directly attacked the system. In 1954, a group of blacklisted filmmakers, including Herbert Biberman, Michael Wilson, and Paul Jarrico, worked on an independently made feature, *Salt of the Earth*, which was a prolabor film dealing with the 1951–1952 strike by Mexican American zinc miners. The film exposed a double standard whereby minority workers were paid less than their white coworkers and were forced to work under hazardous conditions. In addition, it celebrated the efforts of the miners' wives in winning the strike. Its feminist narrative perspective, unique for the 1950s, provided a model for Barbara Kopple's *Harlan County, U.S.A.* (1977), a documentary about a strike by Kentucky coal miners.

American immigration officials attempted to halt production of *Salt of the Earth* by deporting its Mexican star as an illegal alien before the film was completed. Laboratory technicians and projectionists, members of the anti-Communist IATSE union, refused to process prints of the film or to project them in theaters. And right-wing organizations such as the American Legion threatened to organize boycotts if exhibitors attempted to show the film. As a result, the film played in only a limited number of situations in the United States.

Chaplin in Exile

The most overt attack on HUAC came from Charles Chaplin, whose prior association with "known Communists" such as composer Hanns Eisler and writer

Bertolt Brecht put him under suspicion as a Communist sympathizer. In 1952, Chaplin's apolitical, semiautobiographical drama about a music hall comic, *Limelight,* became the target of a nationwide boycott organized by the American Legion. Chaplin, who had never become an American citizen, had embarked on a worldwide tour to promote the film, after first securing a permit from the State Department to reenter the United States on his return. In September, 1952, shortly after Chaplin left the country, the U.S. Attorney General suddenly revoked Chaplin's reentry permit on the grounds that Chaplin was an "unsavory" character. The Attorney General insisted that Chaplin answer questions about his political beliefs before he would be granted permission to reenter the United States.

A few weeks later, the American Legion denounced Chaplin as a Communist "fellow traveler" and launched a boycott of *Limelight,* vowing to sustain their protest until Chaplin returned to the United States to answer questions about his political sympathies. Refusing to submit himself to the ordeal undergone by other members of the Hollywood community who had been forced to testify before HUAC, Chaplin gave up his residence in the United States and moved to Switzerland, where he lived until his death in 1977. Chaplin did not return to the United States until 1972—20 years later—when he journeyed to New York City, where he was honored by the Film Society of Lincoln Center in a special tribute, and then to Los Angeles to receive an honorary Oscar from the Academy of Motion Picture Arts and Sciences.

During the period of his European exile in the mid-1950s, Chaplin wrote, starred in, and directed *A King in New York* (1957) which was a bitter denunciation of American McCarthyism, in general, and HUAC, in particular. Chaplin, however, did not release the film in the United States until 1973. In the film, Chaplin plays the dethroned king of a fictional European country who flees to the United States. There he meets and befriends a young boy, whose parents are Communists who have been called to testify before HUAC. The boy, played by Chaplin's son, Michael, denounces the government for its totalitarian behavior, including acts similar to Chaplin's own experiences, such as being deprived of a passport to travel. Chaplin's king shields the boy from HUAC, which has subpoenaed him to testify about his parents' political beliefs and loyalties. The FBI eventually tracks the boy down, takes him into custody, and forces him to name names to secure the release of his parents.

Because he has helped the boy, the king is called to appear before HUAC to explain his actions and to give testimony about his political sympathies. On his way to the hearings, the king's finger becomes accidentally caught in the nozzle of a fire hose, which he is forced to bring into the hearing room with him. The water is turned on and the king inadvertently ends up dousing the members of HUAC with a stream of water. In spite of this mishap, the Committee clears the king of the charges that he is a subversive. He is, after all, a monarch and thus, by profession, an anti-Communist. However, at the end of the film, Chaplin's king decides to return to Europe rather than live in a society dominated by the forces of fear and political repression.

In Defense of the Informers: *On the Waterfront*

Perhaps the most curious film to be inspired by the HUAC hearings, however, was *On the Waterfront* (1954), which was written by Budd Schulberg and directed by Elia Kazan. Both Schulberg and Kazan were friendly witnesses who had named names when they testified before HUAC. Voted Best Picture of the Year by the Academy, *Waterfront* functioned as a cleverly disguised defense of those members of the Hollywood community who informed on their colleagues. In the film, ex-prizefighter Terry Malloy (Marlon Brando) is a union (read "Communist") "dupe" who slowly discovers just how corrupt and vicious the local longshoremen's union actually is. The union leadership, which is dominated by mobsters, is seen to be responsible for the death of a potential stool pigeon who threatens to inform on them. It also exploits the very workers it claims to protect. Near the end of the film, union boss Johnny Friendly orders the murder of Terry's protective brother Charley (Rod Steiger), and Terry then testifies against the union in hearings held by the Waterfront Crime Commission. The film concludes with Terry's return to the docks, where he openly confronts the union's hired thugs, who beat him up. Terry's defiance of the union, however, wins him the support of the other workers, who join him in his repudiation of the union leadership. The message of the film was clear: it's not only okay to inform, but those who do are the real heroes.

AFTERMATH

The Fight Continues

By the late 1950s, the political power of HUAC and Senator McCarthy had declined. In 1953, the Soviet Union's hard-line premier, Joseph Stalin, died and the Korean war came to a conclusion. At the end of 1954, the Senate voted to condemn McCarthy for his verbal abuse of fellow senators and for his contempt for the Senate itself. McCarthy's influence quickly faded, and he died three years later. During the early 1960s, Hollywood slowly began to abandon the blacklist, openly acknowledging the work of Trumbo (*Exodus, Spartacus*) and other blacklisted individuals.

However, Hollywood continued to fight the cold war, though the hysterical anti-Communism of the 1950s quickly gave way to a cooler, more calculated manipulation of cold war fears for dramatic effect rather than for political propaganda. In other words, Communists began to function more as traditional villains than as real-life threats to our national security. The paranoid vision of *The Manchurian Candidate* (1962) suggests that brainwashed Korean prisoners of war have been programmed to assassinate American political candidates. Yet, the film also condemns a McCarthyite politician who is, ironically, revealed to be an unwitting pawn in the larger game plan the Communists have devised to take over the United States.

Rabid anti-Communism and nuclear anxiety were still strong enough in the mid-1960s—The Barry Goldwater era—to provide the stuff of black humor in Stanley Kubrick's *Dr. Strangelove* (1964), which explores the political fallout after a fanatical anti-Communist in the American military deliberately launches a nuclear attack on the Soviets. In the 1970s, Dalton Trumbo's adaptation of Henri Charriere's novel about unjust imprisonment in a French Guiana penal colony, *Papillon* (1973), includes a sequence in which the hero (played by Steve McQueen) refuses to betray the name of a friend, and it concludes with a comparison of McQueen's defiance of authority with costar Dustin Hoffman's complicit resignation to it.

John Wayne's *The Green Berets* (1968) took a hard line against those who opposed the war in Vietnam, suggesting that they were the unfortunate victims of Communist propaganda. *Rambo: First Blood Part II* (1985) attempted to keep the cold war alive by mixing old-fashioned, us-versus-them anti-Communism with a new ingredient—the revelation of treachery from within. As a result, Rambo takes on not only the Vietcong and its Russian military advisers, but also the American CIA and the political establishment, which attempt to undermine Rambo's mission to rescue POWs. Sylvester Stallone successfully manipulates anti-Communist sentiment again that same year in *Rocky IV* (1985), which pits Rocky against a Soviet boxer who is responsible for the ring death of Rocky's old friend, Apollo Creed.

Red Dawn (1984), a right-wing fantasy written and directed by John Milius, imagined what it would be like if the Cubans and the Soviets invaded the United States, transforming rural Colorado into a battleground in which American teenagers wage a guerrilla war with the Communist invaders. Cold war tensions also fueled *Top Gun* (1986), in which Navy pilots test their mettle against Soviet MiGs, and *No Way Out* (1987), in which Russian agents are found working in the Pentagon. The fact that the latter film was a remake of an apolitical film noir, *The Big Clock* (1948), further illustrates the way in which the cold war had been reduced to the status of a timely convention which could be plugged into virtually any traditional narrative formula.

Mikhail Gorbachev's rise to power in the Soviet Union in 1985 and the advent of the era of *glasnost* served to undermine further the viability of cold war rhetoric in American films. *Rambo III* (1988) attempted to prolong the anti-Soviet sentiments that had helped to make *Rambo II* a box-office hit by sending Rambo to Soviet-occupied Afghanistan to fight Russians, but the film did not do well commercially, putting an end to the highly successful *Rambo* series. By 1990, the relaxation of the U.S./Soviet tensions could be dramatically seen in the adaptation of Tom Clancy's 1984 cold war novel, *The Hunt for Red October*, into a suspense melodrama in which Sean Connery's Soviet submarine commander emerges as the film's hero, successfully outwitting both his Soviet superiors and his American counterparts.

The end of the cold war: Soviet submarine commander Marko Ramius (Sean Connery) plots to defect to the Americans in *The Hunt for Red October* (1990).

Courtesy of Paramount

Win, Lose, or Draw?

From the vantage point of the 1990s, the cold war, the HUAC hearings in Hollywood, and the blacklist emerge as nightmarish aberrations that properly belong to another time, another place, and another generation. Recent attempts to recreate this world, such as *Guilty by Suspicion* (1991) in which Robert De Niro plays a director forced to give testimony to HUAC, have failed to connect with contemporary filmgoers, who find little in these dramatic situations with which they can identify. Even before the cold war officially concluded, Hollywood discovered that audiences could not care less about the supposed Red menace threatening from without and within. If then-President Ronald Reagan, an old cold warrior from the 1950s, could come to terms with the "evil empire" of the Soviet Union, then so could the rest of us.

Subsequent attempts to address the cold war era at home have experienced similar disappointments at the box office. Matt Dillon starred in *Golden Gate* (1993) as a Communist-hunting FBI agent in San Francisco who comes to regret his role in persecuting an innocent Chinese American. In *The Majestic* (2001),

Hollywood screenwriter Peter Appleton (Jim Carrey) is blacklisted for attending a political meeting to try to pick up a woman who had leftist leanings. After a bout of amnesia and a Capraesque idyll in small-town America, Peter returns to confront his accusers, invoking the Bill of Rights and the First Amendment. Both pictures failed to connect with post–cold war America.

During the presidential campaign of 1992, George Bush insisted that the United States had won the cold war, forcing the collapse of Communism. What is more likely is that both the United States and the USSR lost it by spending themselves into a state of economic disaster, characterized by rampant inflation, recessions, and escalating deficits. Day by day, the cold war is emerging as a common enemy of the peoples of both the United States and the Soviet Union. At any rate, this appears to be the message that Hollywood is sending in films such as *The Hunt for Red October,* in which lower-echelon officers in the Soviet navy, such as nuclear submarine commander Marko Ramius (Sean Connery), and in the American CIA, such as analyst Jack Ryan (Alec Baldwin), join forces to outwit the doomsday scenario being written by their political superiors and to establish the grounds for a post–cold war alliance of Soviet and American peoples.

Set shortly before Gorbachev came to power, the film documents the attempts of Ramius and his fellow officers to defect from the Soviet Union and the political and military responses of both the United States and the Soviet Union. In the final scenes, American and Soviet officers collaborate, jointly serving as the crew of the Soviet Typhoon-class submarine, Red October, as it evades destruction by cold war forces that emanate both from within (a KGB saboteur) and from without (an overzealous Soviet submarine commander). Unconventional naval tactics, including the cooperation of an American submarine, result in the self-destruction of the Soviet Union's representative of cold war philosophy, the promise of a healthy revolution in the Soviet Union itself, and the suggestion of peaceful coexistence between the two countries in the future.

HUAC remained in existence until 1975 and the cold war finally came to an end in the 1990s, but its conclusion is owed not to politicians or governments but to those who were most often subjected to its tensions—its victims.

■ ■ ■ SELECT FILMOGRAPHY

Bolshevism on Trial (1919)
Orphans of the Storm
 (1922)
Trouble in Paradise (1932)
Heroes for Sale (1933)
Blockade (1938)

Ninotchka (1939)
The Grapes of Wrath (1940)
Mission to Moscow (1943)
The North Star (1943)
The Iron Curtain (1948)
The Red Menace (1949)

The Woman on Pier 13 (a.k.a.
  I Married a Communist, 1949)
Broken Arrow (1950)
The Steel Helmet (1950)
Fixed Bayonets (1951)
I Was a Communist for the FBI
  (1951)
Big Jim McLain (1952)
High Noon (1952)
My Son John (1952)
Walk East on Beacon (1952)
Invaders From Mars (1953)
Pickup on South Street (1953)
Johnny Guitar (1954)
On the Waterfront (1954)

Them! (1954)
Invasion of the Body Snatchers
  (1956)
China Gate (1957)
The Incredible Shrinking Man
  (1957)
A King in New York (1957)
The Manchurian Candidate
  (1962)
The Green Berets (1968)
Red Dawn (1984)
Rambo: First Blood Part II (1985)
The Hunt for Red October (1990)
Golden Gate (1993)
The Majestic (2001)

■ ■ ■ SELECT BIBLIOGRAPHY

ALLEN, FREDERICK LEWIS. *Only Yesterday: An Informal History of the 1920s*. New York: Harper & Row, 1931.

BENTLEY, ERIC, ed. *Thirty Years of Treason: Excerpts from the Hearings before the House Committee on Un-American Activities, 1938–1968*. New York: Viking, 1971.

CAMPBELL, RUSSELL. "Warners, the Depression, and FDR: Wellman's *Heroes for Sale*," *The Velvet Light Trap*, No. 4 (Spring 1972), 34–38.

CEPLAIR, LARRY, AND STEVEN ENGLUND. *The Inquisition in Hollywood: Politics in the Film Community, 1930–1960*. Berkeley: University of California Press, 1983.

COGLEY, JOHN. "HUAC: The Mass Hearings," in Tino Balio, ed., *The American Film Industry*, rev. ed. Madison: University of Wisconsin Press, 1985.

DICK, BERNARD. *Radical Innocence: A Critical Study of the Hollywood Ten*. Lexington: University Press of Kentucky, 1989.

DOWDY, ANDREW. *Movies Are Better Than Ever: The Films of the Fifties*. New York: Morrow, 1973.

DUNNE, PHILIP. *Take Two: A Life in Movies and Politics*. New York: McGraw-Hill, 1980.

MALAND, CHARLES. *Chaplin and American Culture: The Evolution of a Star Image*. Princeton, NJ: Princeton University Press, 1989.

McGILLIGAN, PATRICK, AND PAUL BUHLE. *Tender Comrades: A Backstory of the Hollywood Blacklist*. New York: St. Martins Press, 1997.

NAVASKY, VICTOR. *Naming Names.* New York: Viking, 1980.

NORMAN, BARRY. *Talking Pictures: The Story of Hollywood.* London: BBC Books, 1987.

SAYRE, NORA. *Running Time: Films of the Cold War.* New York: Dial Press, 1982.

WHITFIELD, STEPHEN J. *The Culture of the Cold War.* Baltimore: Johns Hopkins, 1991.

CHAPTER **13**

Hollywood in the Age of Television

THE BIG DECLINE: HOLLYWOOD LOSES ITS AUDIENCE

Something strange happened to American audiences in the postwar era: their 20-year romance with the movies began to fade. Weekly motion picture attendance, which hit a high of 95 million in 1929, had averaged 85 million during the war years and climbed to 90 million in the immediate postwar period of 1945–1948. But attendance fell off dramatically thereafter, sinking to 60 million per week in 1950 and then to 46 million in 1953. During the late 1960s and early 1970s, weekly attendance fell below the 20 million mark, reaching a low of 15.8 million in 1971. By the end of the 1970s, attendance had slowly climbed back to the 20 million mark, where it remained until 1988. By 2002, it had risen to over 30 million. But, over a span of a mere 20 years, between 1948 and 1968, Hollywood had lost three-quarters of its audience and the nature of moviegoing in America had evolved from the status of ingrained habit to infrequent diversion.

The reasons for the decline in the popularity of motion pictures were complex, and Hollywood's response to this decrease in attendance is itself quite fascinating. Its attempts to recoup this lost audience inaugurated a new era in the cinema—an era of big-budget, widescreen blockbusters that began in the early 1950s and continues, although in a somewhat less spectacular form, to the present. Contemporary attitudes toward motion pictures from the 1980s to the present look back, in part, to this period of readjustment in the 1950s when the industry began to respond, for the first time, to changing conditions in postwar lifestyle and to shifting patterns in leisure-time amusements. American cinema, which had enjoyed the status of *the* mass entertainment medium par excellence for almost 40 years, gradually redefined itself, during the 1950s, as a specialized form of participatory activity in a larger field of recreational endeavors. The George Lucas and Steven Spielberg productions that dominated the motion picture marketplace from the late 1970s to the 1990s had their origin in the special-event widescreen spectacles that brought audiences (albeit in limited numbers) back to the movie theaters in the 1950s.

AT LEISURE: RECREATION IN POSTWAR AMERICA

The Role of Television

Historians have traditionally assumed that the postwar decline in motion picture attendance was directly related to the advent of television, which provided audiences with entertainment that was both free and readily available in the home. Statistics, however, do not quite bear this out. In 1949–1950, average weekly motion picture attendance decreased by one-third, from 90 to 60 million. This was the largest drop-off to date in the history of moviegoing, which did not plunge as precipitously again until 1965–1967, when it fell by over 50 percent (from 44 to 17.8 million). During 1949–1950, there were only a handful of television stations and relatively few families owned television sets. In 1948, the Federal Communications Commission had placed a freeze on the issuance of licenses for new television stations that lasted until 1952. As a result, there were only 50 stations in operation, and most of these were situated in urban areas. (This number increased to 108 by 1952, as stations that were under construction in 1948 and thus not subject to the freeze were completed and went on the air.)

The number of television sets did increase significantly during this period, from 940,000 (1949) to 3.875 million, but this growth remained modest in comparison to subsequent increases that saw the number of sets jump to 10.3 million in 1951, to 20.4 million in 1953, and to 34.9 million in 1956. By the end of the decade, 90 percent of American homes had television sets. The expansion of television in the 1950s was due, in part, to the termination of the freeze on new stations and to the completion, in 1951, of a network of coaxial cable and microwave links that permitted coast-to-coast hookups and expanded the broadcast range of television transmission to include suburban and rural areas, thus enabling TV networks to reach 40 percent of all American homes. Television undoubtedly played a crucial role, during the period from 1950 to 1956, in the motion picture industry's redefinition of itself, but it cannot be blamed for the demise of the movies, which had begun several years earlier. Television was merely a highly visible, superficial symptom of a much more profound change in postwar entertainment patterns rather than the direct cause of the movies' downfall; the source of the problem lay elsewhere—in the economic and sociocultural transformation of blue- and white-collar Americans during the postwar period into the "leisured masses."

Do Something! Passive Entertainment versus Action

During the war years, approximately 25 percent of all money spent on consumer recreation went for tickets to the movies. By the 1980s, this percentage had fallen to roughly 2.5. Though expenditures for recreation increased (as did ticket prices), less and less of each dollar spent on recreation was paid for admission to the movies. Americans had not just stopped going to the movies; they had begun doing something else instead. After the war, Americans grew disenchanted with passive entertainment and took a greater and greater interest in participatory recreation—in gardening, golfing, bowling, hunting, fishing, and boating. The workweek dropped from a wartime high of 48 hours to 40 hours in the postwar era and, for the first time in our nation's history, employers began to offer workers one- and two-week paid vacations. Indeed, the length of the average vacation doubled between 1941 and 1953. At the same time, wages increased: disposable personal income rose from $76.1 billion in 1940 to $207.1 billion in 1950, and then to $350 billion in 1960.

With more money to spend and more leisure time in which to spend it, middle- and working-class Americans could devote larger blocks of time to recreation than had ever been possible before. The traditional six-day workweek encouraged the careful budgeting of leisure time, making an evening at the movies an ideal solution to consumers' short-term needs for inexpensive entertainment. However, the new five-day workweek and multiweek paid-vacation plans permitted people to spend weeks on vacation camping in the nation's public parks; to spend weekends hunting, fishing, and boating; to pass the day golfing, gardening, or puttering around the house, working on do-it-yourself home-repair projects. According to one magazine survey, more than 30 million Americans took up gardening in the postwar era. The sale of power tools for use in home workshops increased by almost 700 percent; over $175 million was being spent by golfers each year for greens fees, $21 million for hunting and fishing licenses, $800 million for sporting goods, and $200 million for musical instruments.

Although television was clearly a passive rather than an active entertainment medium, it proved to be remarkably well-suited to the new active lifestyle of most Americans. TV made continuous live and prerecorded programs available to busy homemakers during the day and to breadwinners in the evening on demand; that is, it could satisfy the needs of an increasingly diverse at-home viewership for a form of spectatorial activity that fit more readily into their daily schedules than did an evening at the movies. In other words, a continuing demand for some passive entertainment persisted in this new era of active involvement, and television ultimately proved to be better tailored to the filling in of short-term leisure-time needs than the movies.

The House, the Car . . .

The decline of the movies was tied, in many ways, to the increasing affluence of the average American, whose newfound wealth enabled him or her to buy into a radically new lifestyle. The combination of wartime shortages, accumulated savings, and increased earnings led to a postwar spending boom, during which many Americans both literally and figuratively bought their way into a new world. Indeed, the very things that Americans bought took them further and further away from the movies. Through their most important purchases—cars and houses—consumers left urban areas and the downtown/neighborhood motion picture theaters for the wide-open spaces of the suburbs, where inexpensive housing developments, good schools, shopping centers, and freeways back to the city sprang up to service an increasingly young and mobile middle-class population.

New car sales skyrocketed from 69,500 in 1945 to 5.1 million in 1949, 6.7 million in 1950, and 7.9 million in 1955. VA/FHA mortgages and GI loans enabled an unprecedented number of young married couples to purchase houses in the suburbs. These houses were being mass-produced for as little as $8,000 per unit by construction entrepreneurs such as William J. Levitt on sites near the large metropolitan areas of New York City and Philadelphia. During the 1950s, more than 1.5 million New Yorkers moved out of the city into the surrounding suburbs. Of the 13 million new homes built between 1948 and 1958, 11 million were located in the suburbs.

. . . The Drive-In

The motion picture industry was caught by surprise by this rapid population shift. Motion picture theaters had been concentrated in large urban areas, which traditionally generated the lion's share of box-office revenues. First-run theaters in large urban areas typically accounted for 70 to 80 percent of a film's box-office receipts. Only a handful of theaters were located in the suburbs, and it would take time and money to build new theaters in these areas.

An antitrust suit against the majors, known as the Paramount Case, had recently forced the studios to sign a consent decree whereby they agreed to divorce their production and distribution operations from their exhibition chains. At the same time, these chains, which tended to have the most capital for investment in and expansion to new suburban sites, were prevented by the terms of the consent decree from acquiring new theaters. Although several formerly independent theater chains were free to buy or build new theaters, only a

The drive-in: The movies followed their vanishing audience to the suburbs.

handful of chains could afford to expand, especially given declining attendance figures, reduced cash flow, minimal cash reserves, and rampant theater closings.

The quickest and cheapest solution to the problem of theater construction in the suburbs was the drive-in, which involved, in comparison with the construction of indoor theaters, only a modest outlay of capital for land acquisition and development and construction of a screen, projection booth, and sound system. As a result, drive-ins popped up all over the map, increasing in number from 554 in 1947 to 4,700 in 1958.

Drive-ins adapted themselves as much as possible to the needs of the postwar generation. Instead of hiring a babysitter, dressing up, driving into town, and hunting for a parking space (or paying to put the car in a parking lot), couples with young children took the kids along with them to the drive-in (usually at no extra cost). Many drive-ins provided playgrounds for children to amuse themselves in until the picture started. Parking was, of course, readily available and, since films were viewed from the semiprivacy of one's own car, there was no need to dress up. A number of drive-ins furnished laundry facilities so that families could spend an evening out and complete unfinished household chores at the same time.

While drive-ins flourished, urban theaters closed at the rate of roughly two a day, with more than 5000 theaters going out of business between 1946 and 1953.

FEWER, BIGGER, WIDER, DEEPER

This Is Cinerama

The response of the motion picture industry to its sudden loss of a regular mass audience was characteristically cautious. The studios made fewer but more expensive films, hoping to lure audiences back to the theater with quality product—lavish biblical spectacles such as *Samson and Delilah* (1949) and *David and Bathsheba* (1951), as well as remakes of tried-and-true historical spectacles such as *Quo Vadis?* (1951). It was not so much the Hollywood establishment, however, as the independent producers who engineered a technological revolution that would draw audiences back to first-run, downtown theaters. On September 30, 1952, *This Is Cinerama* opened at the Broadway Theater in New York, launching a widescreen revolution that would permanently alter the shape of the motion picture screen, which had resolutely remained more or less square for over 60 years, from 1889 to 1952–1953. Less than two months later, another independent effort, the 3-D exploitation picture *Bwana Devil*, premiered in Los Angeles, and audiences stood in lines stretching around the block to catch a glimpse of this new sensation that made lions appear to leap from the screen into the laps of spectators sitting in the theater.

Both Cinerama and 3-D produced enhanced illusions of depth that filmmakers manipulated to provide thrills and chills previously unavailable to filmgoers. Cinerama used three cameras mounted alongside of and set at 48-degree angles to one another to film panoramic vistas. Together, these three cameras covered an angle of view of 146 by 55 degrees, which closely approximates that of human vision, which is 160 by 60 degrees. When these three images were projected in the theater by three synchronized projectors onto a deeply curved screen that extended across the full width of most movie palaces, they engulfed audiences, producing a powerful illusion of depth by filling the spectator's field of view, including peripheral vision. Multitrack stereophonic sound, which originated from five speakers situated behind the screen and from a battery of surround speakers placed to the sides of and behind the audience, reinforced the spectators' illusion of engulfment, which was described in the press as audience "participation."

The Cinerama experience began with a roller coaster ride that put spectators into the first car of the Atom Smasher Roller Coaster at the Rockaways Playland amusement park; it ended with a hair-raising air tour of Bryce Canyon, Yosemite, the Grand Canyon, and Zion Canyon (in Zion National Park) in which the camera, mounted in the nose of a B-25 bomber, transformed the audience into barnstorming daredevils, hedgehopping through and over sheer canyon walls. World War II flying ace General James Doolittle reportedly clutched his

A sketch of the Cinerama system:
The Cinerama camera (*bottom*)
recorded a panoramic image on
three strips of film (*center*), which
were then projected, from three
separate booths in the theater,
onto a deeply curved screen (*top*).

chair during the stunt-flying sequences, and local drugstores made a fortune
selling Dramamine to spectators who became airsick during the film.

The 3-D Assault

Whereas Cinerama engulfed audiences, pulling them into the action depicted
on the screen, 3-D assaulted audiences—hurling spears, shooting arrows, firing
guns, and throwing knives at spectators sitting peacefully in their theater seats.
The technology of 3-D (unlike that of Cinerama, which exploited the phenomenon of peripheral vision) was rooted in the basic principles of binocular vision.

By bolting two cameras together so that their lenses were spaced as far apart as human eyes, angling them slightly toward one another, and filming in synchronization, one camera could record action as seen by the right eye and the other as seen by the left. Projected simultaneously through separate polarizing filters, the right and left eye records could be directed toward the right and left eyes of spectators wearing 3-D glasses. The polarized filters in the glasses permitted the spectators' right eyes to receive only right-eye information and the left to see only left-eye information. Synthesizing the two different views, the spectators' brains interpreted the information three-dimensionally.

This Is Cinerama, which played for more than two years at one theater in New York City and enjoyed similarly lengthy runs in Los Angeles, Detroit, Chicago, and two or three other cities, grossed more than $20 million and spawned a string of highly successful Cinerama travelogue-adventures, such as *Cinerama Holiday* (1955), *Seven Wonders of the World* (1956), *Search for Paradise* (1957), and *Cinerama South Seas Adventure* (1958), before the first two Cinerama fiction films—*The Wonderful World of the Brothers Grimm* and *How the West Was Won*—were finally released in 1962. By March of 1953, *Bwana Devil* (1952), which was filmed in 3-D in Natural Vision, had grossed over $5 million. Within three weeks of its highly publicized release in April of 1953, *House of Wax*, the first big-budget Natural Vision effort, had grossed over $1 million and, by the end of its run, had pulled in $3.2 million at the box office. Shortly after the successful opening of *Wax*, a string of cheaply made exploitation pictures were issued in 3-D in 1953, including *Sangaree, It Came From Outer Space, Fort Ti, The Maze,* and *Charge at Feather River.*

The technology required for 3-D production and exhibition, unlike that for Cinerama, was fairly inexpensive, facilitating a boom in the 3-D marketplace. Within a matter of months after the initial release of *Bwana Devil*, more than 4,900 theaters were converted to 3-D, and, during the next two years, 46 films were shot in the process. But for every quality 3-D production such as *Kiss Me Kate* (1953) or *Dial M for Murder* (1954), there were a half-dozen low-budget B pictures in 3-D, ranging from *Man in the Dark* and *Robot Monster* (1953) to *The Creature from the Black Lagoon* and *Gorilla at Large* (1954).

By late 1953, the 3-D craze had begun to wane, beset by technological problems that produced eye strain and headaches in spectators, a growing resistance on the part of moviegoers to wearing special 3-D glasses, and the negative association of the process in the public's mind with poorly made exploitation films. As a result, major 1954 3-D productions, such as *Kate* and *Dial M*, were exhibited primarily in flat (non–3-D) versions. By the end of 1953, 3-D had given way to Cinerama-like widescreen filmmaking, in particular to CinemaScope, which had been developed by 20th Century-Fox to duplicate the effect of Cinerama without incurring the tremendous costs associated with that technology.

CinemaScope

Shortly after the premier of *This Is Cinerama* in New York, Fox executives put their research and development employees to work, charging them with finding

Author's collection

The 3-D craze: Spectators must wear special polarized glasses in order for the system to produce an illusion of depth.

a technology that would reproduce the participation effects of Cinerama in a way that would be suitable for adoption by the film industry as a whole (which had refrained from adopting Cinerama because it was designed for use only in a handful of theaters of appropriate size and location). Fox engineers combined anamorphic lens technology, which had been developed in the 1920s by French scientist Henri Chretien, with multitrack stereo magnetic sound, which had been pioneered by the Cinerama system, and with a highly reflective, slightly curved motion picture screen, which Fox had perfected for its theater television system. Chretien's anamorphic lens squeezed a Cinerama-like image possessing an extremely wide angle of view onto a standard strip of 35mm film. Four magnetic soundtracks, placed on the same strip of film that held the image, provided stereo magnetic sound. And, although CinemaScope lacked the compelling illusion of depth provided by Cinerama, its huge, 64-by-24-foot curved screen generated a modest sense of engulfment—so much so that certain roller-coaster-type effects, such as the shooting-the-rapids sequence in *River of No Return* (1954), produced pronounced discomfort in audiences.

Between the premier of *This Is Cinerama* in the fall of 1952 and the release of the first CinemaScope feature, *The Robe*, in September of 1953, the film industry flip-flopped back and forth between 3-D and nonanamorphic widescreen formats, which ranged in their aspect ratios (or ratio of width to height) from

Author's collection

The Robe (1953) in CinemaScope: A single projector (lower right) used 35mm film and an anamorphic lens to project a widescreen image onto a slightly curved screen.

1.66:1 to 1.85:1. These ratios were achieved by cropping the tops and bottoms of 35mm images in projection. Though the 3-D revolution begun by *Bwana Devil* failed, the widescreen revolution launched by Cinerama and completed by CinemaScope succeeded. Since 1953, every film produced and exhibited in the United States has been shot in one widescreen process or another. Within a matter of one or two years, every country in the world (except for Japan) had abandoned the old Academy aspect ratio of 1.37:1 for one or more of the new widescreen formats. By the end of the 1950s, the dominant aspect ratio for 35mm projection in the United States were standardized at 1.85:1 (for flat, nonanamorphic films) and 2.35:1 (for CinemaScope, Panavision, and other anamorphic features), while European standards were fixed at 1.66:1 and 2.35:1, respectively. Today, only television retains the old, narrow-screen aspect ratio of 1.33:1 (which is slightly smaller than the official Academy ratio of 1.37:1).

The projection of widescreen films in color and in stereo sound on theater screens as wide as 55 to 65 feet and as tall as 24 to 27 feet was undoubtedly meant to provide spectators with a viewing experience dramatically superior to that available at home on narrow, 13- to 19-inch, black-and-white television screens possessing low-fidelity, monaural sound. But the marketing of widescreen cinema to the public proved to be less concerned with comparisons of widescreen to television than it was with the similarities of the widescreen experience to other, highly participatory forms of leisure-time entertainment.

Todd-AO and the Theatrical Experience

If the Cinerama experience resembled an amusement park ride, the Cinema-Scope experience was likened to the legitimate theater, where spectators and performers shared the same space. The credits for *The Robe* appeared against a dark red theater curtain, which then opened to reveal the panoramic spectacle of ancient Rome. During the credits of the second CinemaScope feature, *How to Marry a Millionaire* (1953), theater curtains parted to disclose the 20th Century-Fox studio orchestra playing an overture to introduce the stage-based comedy that follows. Advertisements for CinemaScope (as well as for 3-D, Cinerama, and Todd-AO) regularly depicted audiences watching the onscreen spectacle, as if both spectator and spectacle shared the same space, as in the theater. In describing CinemaScope's participation effect, publicists repeatedly likened the format's broad image to the oblong *skene* (or stage) of the ancient Greek theater and pointed to the heightened sense of presence whereby the spectators felt that they were actually there, in the midst of the onscreen action.

The appeal to theatrical experience can be seen most clearly in the market-ing of the Todd-AO process, which was introduced with the premiere of the motion picture adaptation of Rodgers and Hammerstein's long-running Broad-way musical, *Oklahoma!*, in October 1955. Advertisements proclaimed, "You're in the show with Todd-AO," and boasted of the enhanced illusion of presence provided by the system, declaring "Suddenly you're there . . . in the land that is grand, in the surrey, on the prairie! You live it, you're a part of it. . . . you're in *Oklahoma!*" Todd-AO productions were exhibited, like Cinerama productions, in select urban theaters at premium prices on a roadshow basis; that is, reserved seat tickets were sold in advance for specific matinee or evening performances on specific days. In other words, *Oklahoma!* in Todd-AO was presented to the public in much the same way that the stage version of *Oklahoma!* had been. Films in Todd-AO were not mere movies, they were semi-legitimate shows which appealed to the cinema's carriage trade or moviegoing elite.

Todd-AO technology ushered in the first commercially successful wide-film format and, though somewhat ahead of its time, it looked forward to the presentation of motion pictures in 70mm and Dolby stereo that became a com-monplace of film exhibition practice from the 1960s through the 1980s. A spe-cially built Todd-AO camera outfitted with a series of nonanamorphic, wide-angle lenses (including a bug-eye lens that took in an angle of view of 128 degrees) re-corded panoramic action on 65mm (instead of 35mm) film. For exhibition, a 70mm format was used; the 65mm image was accompanied by the six stereo magnetic soundtracks that occupied the additional 5mm on the release print. The widescreen image was projected onto a deeply curved theater screen, which provided audiences with a sense of engulfment in the image similar to that experienced with Cinerama. *Oklahoma!* exploited this participation effect in its opening sequence when Curly (Gordon MacRae) rides through a field of corn "as high as an elephant's eye" and later, when Laurey (Shirley Jones) trapped on a roller-coaster-like runaway buckboard. However, these thrills and chills gradually gave way, after the second Todd-AO extravaganza, *Around the*

Courtesy of the Academy of Motion Picture Arts and Sciences

Oklahoma! (1955) in Todd-AO: A single projector (A) produced a widescreen image (without the use of an anamorphic lens) by projecting 70mm film onto a deeply curved screen.

World in 80 Days (1956), to less sensational and less obvious participation techniques in subsequent Todd-AO theatrically based shows such as *South Pacific* (1958), *Porgy and Bess* (1959), *Can-Can* (1960), and *The Sound of Music* (1965).

The success of Todd-AO spawned a number of other wide-film processes, including M-G-M Camera 65 (*Raintree County*, 1957; *Ben-Hur*, 1959), Super Panavision 70 (*The Big Fisherman*, 1959; *Lawrence of Arabia*, 1962), Ultra Panavision 70 (*Mutiny on the Bounty*, 1962; *It's a Mad Mad Mad Mad World*, 1963), and Super Technirama 70 (*Spartacus*, 1960; *El Cid*, 1961; *King of Kings*, 1961). Twentieth Century-Fox eventually secured ownership of the Todd-AO process in 1958 after Mike Todd's death and used it for the studio's big-budget films (*Can-Can*, 1960; *Cleopatra*, 1963; *The Agony and the Ecstasy*, 1965; *The Sound of Music*, 1965), relegating CinemaScope to second-class status as a format. By 1960, Panavision had replaced CinemaScope as the reigning 35mm anamorphic process—a status it continues to hold today.

WAR WITH TELEVISION, PEACE WITH ITS REVENUES

From Villain to Partner

Throughout the 1950s, Hollywood fought a phony war against television, identifying it as the enemy in a conflict that was essentially less with television than with other forms of leisure-time entertainment. Film comedies—ranging from the prewidescreen, black-and-white, code-breaking *The Moon Is Blue* (1953) to the Deluxe color, CinemaScope send-up of the advertising game, *Will Success Spoil Rock Hunter?* (1957)—poked fun at television commercials. In *Happy Anniversary* (1959), David Niven expresses his outrage at TV by kicking in the screens of one television set after another. In film melodramas as disparate as *All That Heaven Allows* (1955) and *Bigger Than Life* (1956), the presence of television sets functions as an indicator of the stultifying nature of a bourgeois, middle-class lifestyle.

But by the mid-1950s, Hollywood's battle with television for an audience had given way to an unspoken truce. In 1954, Disney contracted with ABC to produce a weekly TV show called *Disneyland*, used to promote Disney's theatrical films as well as the Disneyland theme park, which opened in 1955. In 1955, General Teleradio, which had recently acquired the assets of RKO, sold that studio's library of feature films and shorts to television. In 1956, Columbia, Warner Bros., Fox, and M-G-M sold or leased their pre-1948 features to television; and, in 1958, Paramount sold its backlog of old feature films to MCA for television broadcast. At around the same time, Hollywood studios began to produce weekly programs such as *Warner Bros. Presents, M-G-M Parade*, and *Twentieth Century-Fox Theatre* for television, and entered into negotiations with the major craft guilds (the Screen Actors Guild, the Screen Directors Guild, the Writers Guild of America, and so on) to secure royalty agreements that would enable the studios to release more recent (post-1948) feature films to television. Shortly after an agreement was reached between the producers and the guilds, an era of prime-time broadcast of recent feature films was inaugurated, beginning with NBC's *Saturday Night at the Movies* broadcast of *How to Marry a Millionaire* in September 1961.

Panning and Scanning: Making CinemaScope Fit on TV

Ironically, the first contemporary feature film sold to television had originally been filmed in CinemaScope, which was designed, in part, to provide theatrical viewers with something they could not get at home on television—that is, a widescreen image (and stereo sound). To prepare this film for television broadcast, it had to be drastically cropped so that it could fit on the narrow, 1.33:1 television screen. Even more ironically, 20th Century-Fox, which had received an Oscar in 1954 for its development of the CinemaScope process, received another Oscar in 1962 for perfecting a technique of panning and scanning the original widescreen image so that it could be recomposed for television.

Courtesy of the Museum of Modern Art

Widescreen films on TV: To make a widescreen image (above) of Marilyn Monroe in *How to Marry a Millionaire* (1953) fit the narrow TV screen, the techniques of panning and scanning were used to crop the image (left). Marilyn not only lost her legs, but much of her luxurious apartment as well.

Much as money had driven the original invention, innovation, and diffusion of widescreen processes like CinemaScope, money also drove the dismantling of those processes. The growing reliance of the film industry on television (and later video) as a subsidiary market for its motion picture product made panning and scanning both necessary and profitable. NBC had paid Fox $25 million to air *Millionaire* and a package of 30 other Fox features—a financial windfall for Fox, which was in severe financial straits at the time.

As other networks bargained with other studios for films to air in prime time, the average price per film rose from $180,000 in 1961 to $800,000 by the end of the decade. Recent box-office hits commanded hefty sums; in 1966, ABC paid Columbia $2 million for *The Bridge on the River Kwai* (CinemaScope, 1957); shortly thereafter, ABC bought *Cleopatra* (Todd-AO, 1963) from Fox for $5 million. Though a number of the pricey prime-time features, such as *The Wizard of Oz* (1939) and *Gone With the Wind* (1939), had been made before the widescreen revolution and posed little problem for TV broadcasters (once the networks had converted to color), widescreen films could not be shown on television without either cropping the sides of the image or showing the tops and bottoms of an image that was supposed to have been cropped in projection in the theater.

For decades, Hollywood producers accommodated television broadcasters by providing them with cropped versions of widescreen films that had to be formatted to fit the narrow television screen. Often, this resulted in absurd compositions, such as the diner scene in David Lynch's *Blue Velvet* (Panavision, 1986) in which Laura Dern's nose listens attentively to Kyle MacLachlan's explanation of what he discovered in Isabella Rossellini's apartment. Because Lynch's original composition was too wide for television, the rest of Dern's face ended up on the cropping-room floor.

The distribution of movies on videocassette, which began in the mid-1980s, has done nothing to alleviate this problem. Though a number of major film directors and cinematographers have complained that their work is butchered when it is cropped for video or television broadcast, distributors insist that consumers want movies to fill their TV screens and would be reluctant to watch letterboxed versions of the film that preserve the widescreen composition of the original, theatrical version. Letterboxing reduces the size of the image so that its full width can be seen on the TV screen; blue or black masking is used above and below the image, giving the final image the appearance of a slot or rectangular letterbox within the overall square of the TV screen.

DVDs and Widescreen TV

Consumers in the know prefer letterboxed versions of films and chose to watch movies in widescreen laser disc editions on high-end home theater equipment. The advent of DVDs (digital video discs) and widescreen television in the late 1990s has finally solved the problem of seeing widescreen films on television. DVDs routinely employ letterboxing (and/or anamorphic compression for 16×9 display on a widescreen TV). Though some DVD titles come in full-screen (i.e., cropped) versions, educated consumers now prefer to see widescreen films in the widescreen DVD format. Widescreen TV has reformatted the shape of the TV screen to fit the shape of most widescreen films. The experience of watching widescreen TV instead of standard TV is comparable to that of watching a CinemaScope motion picture rather than pre-widescreen films. Widescreen television has finally brought the widescreen revolution of the 1950s home.

Since the mid-1980s, home entertainment has become an increasingly important factor in the overall economics of the motion picture industry. Between 1985 and 2002, the VCR became a standard feature in the American home; more than 91 percent of households owned one or more VCRs. The growth of the DVD marketplace from 1997, when the technology was introduced, to the present has been even more phenomenal. In just five years the number of DVD players sold jumped from 320,000 (1997) to 25,100,000 (2002), and the titles available increased from 600 to 20,000. By 2002, over 35 percent of U.S. households had DVD players. Theatrical box office receipts hit an all-time high of $9.5 billion in 2002, but revenues from the sale and rental of videotapes and DVDs more than doubled that, reaching $22 billion.

Home entertainment consists of more than movies on video. In 1975, Home Box Office (which began its operations in 1972) started to transmit recent

1.33   1.66

1.85   2.21 (70mm)

2.35 (scope)

2.55 (50's Fox scope)

Theatrical aspect ratios from 1.33:1 (top) to 2.55:1 (bottom).

motion pictures and other entertainment programs via satellite to cable subscribers. HBO thus introduced a "premium" service that augmented the
"basic" cable service, which for several decades had enjoyed a marginal existence by supplying network programming to customers with poor reception in
out-of-the-way places.

In 1977, Ted Turner followed HBO's example, relying upon satellite transmission to expand the audience for his "superstation," TBS, which broadcast
older movies, sporting events, and other shows. Shortly thereafter, Showtime
(1978) and The Movie Channel (1979) entering the home movie channel marketplace, joining forces in 1983.

Today, there are more than 72 million cable households (i.e., two-thirds of all
U.S. households), half of which subscribe to premium cable channels showing

Hollywood movies and made-for-cable movies by Showtime, HBO, and others. HBO, for example, has made over 100 TV movies, a number of which (such as *Real Women Have Curves* and *American Splendor*) have been released theatrically. Though theatrical attendance remains strong, more and more film spectators have become *video* spectators, watching new and old releases in the comfort of their own homes.

Movie-"Going"

The advent of the home audience transformed traditional theatrical exhibition in three significant ways. It effectively eliminated second-run theaters, repertory cinemas, and porno houses. After a film's initial release, it no longer played a subsequent run in cheaper, neighborhood theaters but went directly into video distribution, finding its next audience on premium cable channels and in video rental outlets. Revival houses were unable to compete with video stores, which made older films available to home viewers virtually whenever they wanted to see them. Meanwhile, the porno industry converted almost entirely to tape, providing X-rated films that customers could view in the privacy of their own homes—that is, in a more congenial atmosphere than ever before.

Even for theatrical audiences, the experience of going to the movies became less and less distinct from watching them at home on television. The size of movie theaters and of movie screens, especially in multiplexes and mall cinemas, grew smaller and smaller. Audiences, shaped by the conditions of the home viewing experience, began more and more frequently to talk during movies, providing the sort of play-by-play commentary on the onscreen action characteristic of television sports announcers. Ironically, movie-"going" in the 1990s recalls that of the 1890s, when members of the audience watched films individually on the minuscule, peep-show screen of Edison's Kinetoscope, as well as that of the nickelodeon era (ca. 1905), when spectators looked at movies in small, storefront theaters which were about the size of some of today's smaller multiplexes. Of course, contemporary multiplexes tend to provide better, cleaner surroundings than did storefront nickelodeons (as well as state of the art digital sound systems) but they lack the sense of showmanship associated with the neighborhood theaters of the 1930s, 1940s, and 1950s. The days of the movie palace, when going to the movies was as much of a unique experience as the movie itself, are clearly over.

For better or worse, the future of the movies lies with video. Today, more and more films are shot using high definition television (HDTV) cameras or digital cameras, which many engineers insist produce images equivalent to those of 35mm motion picture cameras.

Much as the advent of the movies did not destroy the theater and that of television did not destroy the movies, the rise of home video has not killed off the movies. Indeed, industry analysts note that more Americans are watching movies today than they have since the 1950s—largely because home video has extended the potential audience for movies and now reaches those viewers who lost the movie-going habit in the postwar era. In spite of new, at-home video technologies ranging from the VCR and cable to the DVD and high-definition widescreen TVs, the movies—that is, motion pictures projected on a screen for mass audiences in theaters—have continued to survive as a popular, entertainment experience. There is ultimately no substitute for seeing 35mm motion pictures projected on an enormous, 40–50 foot screen in a well-maintained movie theater with six-channel digital sound.

BLOCKBUSTERS

Big Event Pictures

The heyday of the widescreen blockbuster extended from the mid-1950s to the mid-1960s and included films such as *War and Peace* (VistaVision, 1956), *Around the World in 80 Days* (Todd-AO, 1956), *The Ten Commandments* (VistaVision, 1956), *South Pacific* (Todd-AO, 1958), *Ben-Hur* (M-G-M Camera 65, 1959), *Spartacus* (Technirama-70, 1960), *Exodus* (Panavision-70, 1960), *El Cid* (Technirama-70, 1961), *Mutiny on the Bounty* (Panavision-70, 1962), *Lawrence of Arabia* (Panavision-70, 1962), *Cleopatra* (Todd-AO, 1963), and *The Sound of Music* (Todd-AO, 1965).

However, spiraling production costs and a string of box-office disasters such as *Dr. Dolittle* (1967), *Star!* (1968), *Hello, Dolly* (1969), *Paint Your Wagon* (1969), *Darling Lili* (1970), and *Tora! Tora! Tora!* (1970) heralded the end of the big-budget widescreen spectacle. In 1963, Cinerama abandoned its original three-strip system for a single-strip 70mm format, losing much of earlier Cinerama's powerful illusion of engulfment and participation in the process. Though the trade name "Cinerama" continued to serve as a draw at the box office, and certain Cinerama productions such as *2001: A Space Odyssey* (1968) proved to be both critical and commercial successes, Cinerama ultimately became virtually indistinguishable from other super-70mm processes.

At around the same time (ca. 1963), Panavision developed a laboratory process that enabled producers to blow 35mm anamorphic prints up to 70mm without significant loss in quality. This technology, which was introduced with Otto Preminger's *The Cardinal* (1963), permitted producers to film in the less expensive 35mm format and to release films in 70mm, if their estimation of the box-office potential of the finished film warranted it. In permitting any film to become a potential 70mm blockbuster, the 70mm blowup tended to undermine the very notion of the widescreen blockbuster.

The long-standing association of the blockbuster with extravagance, costly sets and costumes, high-priced stars, and lavish production values gave way to a decidedly less exclusive product that included both big and small pictures. At one end stood David Lean spectacles such as *Doctor Zhivago* (1965) and costume pictures such as *Becket* (1964) and *Camelot* (1967), and at the other were more or less standard genre pictures, ranging from musicals (*Bye Bye Birdie*, 1963, and *Sweet Charity*, 1969) to Westerns (*The Professionals*, 1966; *The Wild Bunch*, 1969; *Two Mules for Sister Sara*, 1970; and *Wild Rovers*, 1971).

Since the early 1990s and the advent of digital sound, 70mm film has virtually disappeared. The audience's love affair with 70mm and Dolby Stereo, which began in earnest with the release of *Star Wars* in 1977, proved to be more an affair with six-channel stereo sound than with the spectacular image quality provided by 70mm film. Digital sound technology, in the form of DTS (Digital Theater Systems) and Dolby Digital, made it possible for distributors to provide audiences with six-track stereo sound, using conventional 35mm prints with none of the additional costs involved with 70mm prints and stereo magnetic sound tracks. The added attraction of 70mm was soon forgotten, effectively signaling the end of Hollywood's association with big-screen entertainment. But 70mm film remains the basis for the big-screen attraction of Imax, which used the format to project images as big as 80 feet high and 100 feet wide in specially-designed theaters.

The redefinition of the nature of the motion picture experience that took place in the 1950s succeeded in the short term but failed over the long haul. Dwindling audiences did return to theaters, but the appeal to participation did little to halt the slow erosion of the traditional, prewidescreen motion picture audience. As those habitual moviegoers disappeared, Hollywood attempted to shore up its losses by instituting a new kind of entertainment and a new pattern of moviegoing, both of which resembled, to a certain extent, the content and form of the legitimate theater. This pattern of infrequent moviegoing could only sustain the industry in an era of blockbusters—an era in which each film became a special event that drew the sometime spectator away from other leisure-time activities and back into the movie theater. However, over the years, widescreen cinema has lost its impact; it has become the norm for all production and thus no longer enjoys any status as a revolutionary new technology.

Narrowing Expectations

Though certain contemporary films, especially those of Steven Spielberg and George Lucas, continue to revive the notion of participation by presenting themselves as events, the notion of participation has become degraded, descending to a fairly primitive experience in which spectators respond in a programmatic way to predictable stimuli. Participation has gradually become more and more passive. The infrequent consumption of motion pictures has become automatic and habitual, especially in today's small-screen theaters and multiplexes, which are only a fraction of the size of and provide only a fraction of the experience of yesterday's movie palaces. In the age of television, we have narrowed both our sights and our expectations, reconciling ourselves to a postrevolutionary cinema that holds few if any surprises, thrills, or chills as a medium. Of course, the current craze for special effects has restored, in part, the special status of the medium to overwhelm the spectator with the sort of attractions that lured spectators to it at the turn of the century. Though we continue to be excited by the content of the movies, their basic format, which has remained unchanged for the past 30 years, has lost much of its power to engage us as participants in a dramatically new audiovisual sensory experience.

■ ■ ■ SELECT FILMOGRAPHY

Bwana Devil (3-D, 1952)

This Is Cinerama (Cinerama, 1952)

House of Wax (3-D, 1953)

Kiss Me Kate (3-D, 1953)

The Robe (CinemaScope, 1953)

Dial M for Murder (3-D, 1954)

River of No Return (CinemaScope, 1954)

White Christmas (VistaVision, 1954)

Oklahoma! (Todd-AO, 1955)

Around the World in 80 Days (Todd-AO, 1956)

The Searchers (VistaVision, 1956)

The Ten Commandments (VistaVision, 1956)

Will Success Spoil Rock Hunter? (CinemaScope, 1957)

South Pacific (Todd-AO, 1958)

Ben-Hur (M-G-M Camera 65, 1959)

Exodus (Panavision-70, 1960)

Spartacus (Technirama-70, 1960)

El Cid (Technirama-70, 1961)

Lawrence of Arabia (Panavision-70, 1962)

Mutiny on the Bounty (Panavision-70, 1962)

Cleopatra (Todd-AO, 1963)

The Sound of Music (Todd-AO, 1965)

2001: A Space Odyssey (Cinerama, 1968)

Blue Velvet (Panavision, 1968)

■ ■ ■ SELECT BIBLIOGRAPHY

BALIO, TINO, ed. *Hollywood in the Age of Television.* Boston: Unwin Hyman, 1990.

BELTON, JOHN. *Widescreen Cinema.* Cambridge: Harvard University Press, 1992.

BERNSTEIN, MATTHEW, ed. *The Velvet Light Trap: American Widescreen,* No. 21 (Summer 1985).

CARR, ROBERT E., and R. M. HAYES. *Wide Screen Movies: A History and Filmography of Wide Gauge Filmmaking.* Jefferson, NC: McFarland, 1988.

HAYWARD, PHILIP, and TANIA WOLLEN. *Picture Visions: New Technologies of the Screen.* London: BFI, 1993.

HILMES, MICHELE. *Hollywood and Broadcasting: A History of Economic and Structural Interaction from Radio to Cable.* Champaign: University of Illinois Press, 1990.

WASKO, JANET. *Hollywood in the Information Age.* Austin: University of Texas Press, 1994.

CHAPTER **14**

The 1960s: The Counterculture Strikes Back

YOUTH AND CHALLENGE

During the 1960s, war was waged on several fronts. From 1964, when North Vietnamese torpedo boats reportedly attacked American destroyers in the Gulf of Tonkin, to 1975, when the United States evacuated its military forces from Saigon, the United States, together with its South Vietnamese allies, fought the Vietcong and the North Vietnamese in Southeast Asia. On the home front, one generation of Americans battled another. Youth (generally considered to be those under 30) found itself in an ideological battle with age. They differed over not only the war but also a host of other issues such as sexual mores, race relations, lifestyle, and just plain style. They belonged to two different cultures. The older members (the "establishment") and the youth movement liked different kinds of music, dressed differently, and wore their hair at different lengths. Indeed, hair became a symbol of the 1960s counterculture and served as a point of departure for one of the decade's most popular stage musicals, *Hair*, the tribal rock opera that ran on Broadway from 1968 to 1972. Hair became a running gag in the Beatles' first film, *A Hard Day's Night* (1964). And it was hair that triggered the redneck violence against the hippie heroes in *Easy Rider* (1969).

The younger, postwar generation, known as "baby boomers," had been raised according to the new permissiveness advocated by Dr. Benjamin Spock, whose *Baby and Child Care* had originally been published in 1946. Indeed, Spock himself subsequently took responsibility for his "children" and became a spokesperson for the antiwar movement in the 1960s. According to Vice President Spiro Agnew, the "problem children" of the 1960s were the fault of Dr. Spock, whose book, according to Agnew, "threw discipline out the window." The products of this revolution in childrearing grew up to challenge the repressive codes established by their more conservative elders, who had been brought up in the hard times of the Great Depression. The children of parents who fought the good and just war against Hitler and fascism in the 1940s questioned the American ideology that had involved the nation on what was apparently the wrong side of a seemingly unjust war in Southeast Asia. And they looked with suspicion on the appeals to patriotism that were used to defend that war.

THE KENNEDY ERA

"The New Frontier"

The 1960s began not with violent confrontation but with the orderly transfer of power from one generation to another. In 1961, 43-year-old John F. Kennedy, a liberal Democrat from Massachusetts, was sworn in as president of the United States, replacing 70-year-old Republican Dwight David Eisenhower. As the youngest president in American history, Kennedy brought the energy and intensity of youth to his program for a New Frontier in American political life. In his inaugural address, Kennedy noted that "the torch has been passed to a new generation of Americans" and called for a new activism, appealing to Americans to "ask not what your country can do for you" but "what you can do for your country."

With Kennedy, a new emphasis on sophistication, style, and wit entered national politics. Jack and his wife Jackie became the ideal couple, and Kennedy's admirers likened his administration to King Arthur's mythical court of Camelot, casting him as both Arthur and Lancelot and Jackie as Queen Guenevere. The White House became their castle, and Washington was transformed into a utopian kingdom full of dreams about the creation of an ideal once-and-future world. Just prior to Kennedy's inauguration, in December 1960, Alan J. Lerner and Frederick Loewe's musical, *Camelot,* had opened on Broadway. And Kennedy's New Frontier naturally evoked Camelot, a world governed by acts of chivalry, trust, passionate idealism, and romance.

With Kennedy, the style of government changed. Kennedy invited noted artists such as cellist Pablo Casals to play in the East Room of the White House. New England poet Robert Frost, who was asked to read one of his poems at the inauguration, became Kennedy's poet laureate. The president's interest in literature ranged from Frost and Shakespeare to Ian Fleming. Fleming's slickly written spy novels about the exploits of Secret Agent 007, James Bond, doubled in popularity after JFK's fascination with them became public knowledge. At the same time, Kennedy cultivated the image of a movie star, bringing glamour to the White House. The president socialized with members of the movie colony—with his "Rat Pack" buddies, including brother-in-law Peter Lawford, Frank Sinatra, Dean Martin, and Sammy Davis, and with Marilyn Monroe.

However, the novelty of the Kennedy style did not necessarily make him the spokesperson for 1960s youth, who questioned the substance of his political program. With the notable exception of his creation of the Peace Corps, Kennedy's foreign policy won him few supporters in the new left student movement. His attempted invasion of Fidel Castro's Cuba, in April 1961, at the Bay of Pigs resulted in severe criticism of his tactics by student activists and others. His handling of the Cuban missile crisis in October 1962 escalated cold war tensions and the danger of nuclear war, infuriating anti-nuclear protestors at home. Under Kennedy's leadership, the presence of American military advisors in Vietnam dramatically increased, expanding an involvement of Americans in Southeast Asia that would ultimately result in the Vietnam War.

The Civil Rights Movement

Kennedy's domestic policy, which focused attention on civil rights, was readily embraced by liberal high school and college students across the nation. The civil rights movement became the cornerstone of 1960s activism, setting an agenda and establishing a strategy of nonviolent intervention that would inform subsequent student protests against the Vietnam War and other political and social problems. But the civil rights movement was well under way even before Kennedy took office. In 1960, four black students staged a peaceful sit-in at an all-white lunch counter at Woolworth's in Greensboro, North Carolina. By the end of the year, these nonviolent protests had successfully integrated lunch counters in over 126 southern cities. In 1962, James Meredith became the first black student to attend the University of Mississippi, though he needed the assistance of federal marshals to attend classes. In support of demands for civil rights set by black organizations such as SNCC (Student Nonviolent Coordinating Committee) and CORE (Congress of Racial Equality), black and white students marched on Washington in 1962 and 1963. They registered black voters in the South during the summers of 1963 and 1964; the latter became known as "Freedom Summer." In 1964, three civil rights workers named Michael Schwerner, Andrew Goodman, and James Cheney were murdered in Mississippi—a crime that became the subject of investigation in Alan Parker's *Mississippi Burning* (1988).

After a summer of civil rights work in the South, in 1964 Mario Savio returned to Berkeley, where he set up a table to recruit additional volunteers. When university officials banned him from organizing on campus and outlawed all other political activity as well, Savio and others protested, launching the Berkeley Free Speech movement. When eight student leaders were summarily suspended by the university administration, students using sit-in tactics developed by the civil rights movement in the South passively protested the university's violation of their freedom of speech. Over the course of the strike, 814 Free Speech Movement supporters were jailed before Berkeley faculty finally voted to permit political activity on campus.

Civil rights marches by Martin Luther King and others led to the passage of the Civil Rights Act of 1964, the Voting Rights Act of 1965, and the Civil Rights Act of 1968, which prohibited discrimination on the basis of color, race, religion, or national origin in public places, at the polls, and in housing. Nonviolence, however, soon gave way to violence. Kennedy was assassinated in November 1963. Blacks rioted in Harlem in the summer of 1964. Malcolm X was killed in February 1965. Blacks rioted in Watts in August 1965, and in Newark and Detroit in 1967. In 1966, Huey P. Newton and Bobby Seale founded the Black Panthers, a black militant organization that advocated violence as a means to secure black liberation and favored separatist objectives instead of integration. Martin Luther King was gunned down in April 1968, and Robert Kennedy was slain in June 1968.

Against the War

In the mid-1960s, as students shifted attention from purely domestic to foreign issues, they adopted the techniques of symbolic protest that had proven effective in the civil rights movement. In 1965, they organized a March on Washington to End the War in Vietnam, which drew national attention to the antiwar movement. By 1968, the escalation of the Vietnam War, the complicity of Columbia and various other universities with war research, and continuing racial injustice at home prompted students at Columbia University to escalate the sit-in into the strike. Students occupied administration buildings and other university property in an attempt to focus attention on the war and racism. When the administration had the students forcibly and violently removed by police, a strike ensued in which students protested the administration's action by shutting down the university. A number of other university campuses followed suit in 1968 and 1969, and in May of 1970, after President Nixon announced a further escalation of the war—an incursion of U.S. forces into Cambodia—there was a nationwide strike on over 200 college campuses. At Kent State University, Ohio National Guardsmen fired into a crowd of student protestors, killing four of them and wounding nine others. Meanwhile, during the summer of 1968, antiwar protestors at the Democratic National Convention in Chicago were savagely beaten by police while network news cameras looked on. Live broadcast of the spectacle in the streets shocked home viewers, who were outraged at

Campus unrest and the student strike at Columbia University served as the basis for *The Strawberry Statement* (1970), which portrays police response to the student occupation of university buildings.

Courtesy of M-G-M

the excessive violence employed by the Chicago police in arresting the demonstrators. These events subsequently served as the background for Haskell Wexler's *Medium Cool* (1969), which followed the movements of a fictional television news cameramen who was caught up in the police riots.

Liberation: The Women's Movement

Conflict resulting from generational and racial differences provided a broad background against which traditional relationships between the sexes underwent a reevaluation. In 1963 Betty Friedan published *The Feminine Mystique*, in which she examined the ways women had been disempowered and repressed. Women in the new left soon found that the student movement was as sexist and patriarchal (that is, male-dominated) as the larger society and began to set up their own activist organizations, such as the National Organization of Women (NOW), which was formed in 1966 with Friedan as its president.

For feminists, the traditional oppression of women was seen as rooted in the institution of marriage, which confined them to the home, and in the dominance of certain cultural assumptions about women, which excluded middle-class women from the workplace and restricted working-class women to a narrow range of permissible jobs. Certain sectors of this institutional oppression relaxed somewhat in the 1960s. The availability of the first reliable oral contraceptive for women (introduced with the marketing of Enovid in 1960) gave women more control over their bodies than they had ever known before, enabling them to choose whether or not to have children and when to have them. Political activism during the 1960s resulted in the overthrow of antiabortion laws in a number of states, with New York at the forefront in 1969.

At the same time, more and more women enrolled in and graduated from college; their numbers increased by 47 percent in the 1950s and 168 percent in the 1960s. As college graduates, women entered the workforce qualified for white-collar jobs traditionally held by men. Working women had been a factor in the American economy throughout the twentieth century, but middle-class women had never entered the workforce in great numbers prior to the 1960s. The women's movement served as an advocate for equality in the workplace, demanding equal pay for equal work, and campaigned to make women economically self-sufficient.

Yet women's liberation entailed new forms of subjugation. Radical feminists complained that the sexual revolution proved more of a benefit for men, who had a field day, than it did for women, who became victims of sexual exploitation. The Pill may have liberated women, but it also changed the attitudes of men toward women, who were now expected to be more accessible than they had been in the past. In other words, it became harder for a woman to say no to a man. Nor was the trade-in of unpaid domestic drudgery as a homemaker for a 40-hour workweek necessarily liberating, especially when men began to expect women to be breadwinners and lovers as well as homemakers.

The 1960s saw some success for the civil rights movement, which put an end to (overt) segregation in schools, public places, and housing, and for the antiwar movement, which helped to force American troops out of Vietnam. The limited success of the women's movement, however, was undercut by women's larger disempowerment within patriarchy. The women's movement's chief political victory proved to be the legalization of abortion, which came in the 1973 U.S. Supreme Court's *Roe v. Wade* decision. Its chief political failure was its inability to secure the passage of the Equal Rights Amendment, which would have guaranteed women the same rights enjoyed by men under the Constitution and the Bill of Rights.

PROJECTIONS: WOMEN ON SCREEN

As far as the films of the 1960s were concerned, the women's movement became the sexual revolution; that is, its political agenda was translated into a series of superficial changes in sexual mores. Women were depicted as sexually liberated or aggressive. But Hollywood's women were modeled less after the revolutionary women who fought for equal rights in NOW (National Organization of Women) than after the centerfolds found in the misogynistic pages of *Playboy. Lolita* (1962) and *Cleopatra* and *Irma la Douce* (both 1963) celebrate the sexual power of the new woman, as does *Barbarella* (1968), the futuristic film in

The backlash against 1960s feminism: Sexual politics were translated onto the screen in terms of sexual display: for example, Jane Fonda as the title character in *Barbarella* (1968).

Rutgers Cinema Studies

which Jane Fonda revolutionizes life in the 41st century by making love "the old-fashioned way." James Bond films introduced a host of sexually available women, including Pussy Galore (Honor Blackman) in *Goldfinger* (1964). The sexual revolution culminated (for men, at least) in the wife-swapping craze celebrated in *Bob & Carol & Ted & Alice* (1969).

Hollywood's response to the women's movement involved more backlash than backing. Parts for women reverted to stereotype: actresses played either madonnas or whores. The only working women were motherly governesses or prostitutes. Julie Andrews enjoyed a spectacular career as the former, playing nannies in both *Mary Poppins* (1964) and *The Sound of Music* (1965). Jane Fonda excelled as the latter, playing an unfaithful wife in *The Chase* (1966) and prostitutes in *Walk on the Wild Side* (1962) and *Klute* (1971). As one of the few white-collar women workers, Doris Day successfully straddled the fence in *Lover Come Back* (1961), in which she played an account executive for an advertising firm. But she also paid the price, winning the screen persona of a sexual tease (that is, a madonna-whore). An exception that proved the rule was Sandy Dennis in *Up the Down Staircase* (1967), playing an inner-city school teacher, Sylvia Barrett. Engaged in one of the few professions traditionally open to respectable women, her dedicated English instructor combined the nineteenth-century idealism of the nanny-to-the-aristocrats with the twentieth-century, down-to-earth realism necessary for survival in the New York public school system.

It was not until the late 1970s and early 1980s that white- and blue-collar working women made it back to the screen. Films such as *Network* (1976), in which Faye Dunaway played a ruthless television executive; *The China Syndrome* (1979), in which Jane Fonda played a television reporter; and *Norma Rae* (1979), in which Sally Field was a textile worker, reflected the real-life achievements of professional working women. They led the way for the new image of the independent woman that dominated the 1980s in films starring actresses such as Sigourney Weaver, Meryl Streep, Glenn Close, Kathleen Turner, Whoopi Goldberg, Debra Winger, Cher, Sissy Spacek, Diane Keaton, Bette Midler, Shelly Long, and Melanie Griffith.

YOUTH FILMS: ACTIVISM AS LIFESTYLE

Women's liberation was not the only movement to fare poorly in its representation on the movie screen. With one or two exceptions—that is, in certain noncommercial works produced by the alternative media—the student movement tended to find itself reduced to confused college kids whose ideas were half-baked and who were drawn to political activism and protests in search of sex and cheap thrills. Documentary and student filmmakers brought some seriousness to the underlying issues, covering peace marches, protests, and student strikes, while radical filmmaking groups such as New York Newsreel and San Francisco Newsreel attempted to represent the perspectives of minority groups and student radicals in films such as *Black Panther* (1968) and *Columbia Revolt* (1968). *Medium Cool* (1969), which was made independently but distributed by Paramount, straddled the fence between documentary honesty and Hollywood glitz, combining the raw fervor of the new left with the stylish trappings of old-fashioned narrative cinema. It deals with the adventures of a television news cameraman whose encounters with black militants, affair with a woman whose husband was killed in Vietnam, and experiences during the police riots at the 1968 Democratic Convention radicalize him.

At the very end of the decade, the student protest movement gave rise to a number of fairly conventional Hollywood features designed to exploit the new youth market. In 1970, after the astounding commercial success of youth-cult movies such as *The Graduate* (1967), which looks at postgraduation career angst, and *Easy Rider* (1969), which glamorizes counterculture lifestyles, the major studios released a series of films concerned with student protest, including *Zabriskie Point, Getting Straight,* and *The Strawberry Statement,* as well as *The Magic Garden of Stanley Sweetheart, The Revolutionary,* and *R. P. M.* (all 1970). *Pursuit of Happiness* (1971) rounded out this unusual, short-lived subgenre dealing with the equally short-lived student movement. In *The Strawberry Statement,* which was

Would-be student radicals in jail: Mark Frechette (left) embodies the hipness of alienated youth in *Zabriskie Point* (1970).

based on the Columbia protests, a student becomes involved in campus demonstrations because he is interested in a girl who belongs to the movement. The hero in *Getting Straight,* a former civil rights worker and Vietnam veteran, returns to school, discovers that demonstrations are sexy, and becomes a committed radical only when victimized by the bureaucracy of the academic establishment and unprovoked police brutality.

Though somewhat more interesting, Michelangelo Antonioni's *Zabriskie Point* similarly obscured the underlying political issues that prompted student unrest. The film reduced student radicalism into an extremely generalized and universal male anxiety, suggesting that the age-old identity crisis is what was at the bottom of student unrest in 1960s America. Its hero, an innocent suspect in a cop killing, sets off on a cross-country flight in a stolen airplane from the West Coast. Easily distracted from his goal by a girl driving on the highway below, he lands and joins her on her trip to Zabriskie Point in Death Valley. At the end of this absurdist reworking of Alfred Hitchcock's *North by Northwest* (1959), he returns to California to surrender to the police but is killed before he can give himself up. The circular story pattern demonstrates the futility of student activism, and its politically incorrect conclusion suggests that the pleasures of mental revolt can be more satisfying than material action in the real world. The film ends with the girl's fantasmatic, imaginary destruction of the symbols of American materialism: as she looks at the house of her bourgeois boss, it explodes, and close-up slow-motion shots of commercial products fill the screen.

In other words, the heroine's psychic act of rebellion proves to be as powerful as—even more powerful than—the hero's physical acts of rebellion.

Finally, *Pursuit of Happiness* documents the identity crisis of a former student activist who campaigned for Gene McCarthy in 1968 and was arrested at the police riots in Chicago that summer, but who gradually became more and more alienated from the movement, his girlfriend, and his family, and from the identity each of them tries to impose upon him. Again, politics are papered over and the film becomes a depoliticized, more individualized saga about the hero's flight from society and search for a personal utopia. The hero gives up on his efforts to change the world and flees it instead, after declaring, "There's a nervous breakdown going on out there and I don't want to be part of it!"

"SOLVING" THE RACE PROBLEM

Neither the women's movement nor the student movement found adequate representation in mainstream American cinema. The controversial political issues they both raised were transformed into the melodramatic stuff of conventional film narratives. Equal rights for women became sexual liberation, and war resistance became existential adolescent angst. Race relations tended to be dealt with a bit more directly, but even well-meaning liberal films such as Stanley Kramer's Academy Award–winning *The Defiant Ones* (1958) "solved" racial problems without uncovering their root causes in the fundamental political and economic inequality between blacks and whites. In the Kramer film, two convicts—one a white bigot (Tony Curtis) and the other a bitter black (Sidney Poitier)—flee the police while handcuffed together, learning that the survival of each depends upon the assistance and cooperation of the other.

Hollywood films of the 1960s exposed bigotry and racism but did so without exposing their sources. The major studios ignored the *politics* of racism. Their films contained no sit-ins, no marches on Washington, no campaigns to register black voters, no attempts to integrate schools and colleges, and no exposés of racial discrimination in housing. There was one notable exception in this silence. *A Raisin in the Sun,* an adaptation of Lorraine Hansberry's play distributed by Columbia Pictures in 1961, treated the attempts of a black family to move into a white neighborhood in Chicago. However, a handful of non-Hollywood films, including documentaries (*King: A Filmed Record . . . Montgomery to Memphis,* 1970) and independently made features (*A Man Called Adam,* 1966), attempt to deal with many of these issues. Unfortunately, they never found wide distribution.

Hollywood concerned itself with racism but did so on its own terms. For Hollywood, racism was not an economic or political but rather a human problem. As such, it could be solved through dramatic means. It was isolated, identified, recognized, and rejected; an Aristotelean catharsis then followed, during which a tenuous accord was reestablished between the races, suggesting that all would be well in the future. Mere acknowledgment of the problem meant that the problem was somehow solved. Sidney Poitier emerged as a perfect problem solver. His skin color provoked racism, but his class status solved whatever problems whites had with his blackness. Playing middle- and upper-middle-class professionals such as a journalist (*The Bedford Incident*, 1965), a doctor (*Guess Who's Coming to Dinner*, 1967), an engineer/school teacher (*To Sir, With Love*, 1967), and a homicide detective (*In the Heat of the Night*, 1967), Poitier is equal, if not superior, to any of his white antagonists, who are forced to recognize his abilities and to purge themselves of their own racism.

In other instances, the cure for racism proves to be white paternalism. The liberal lawyer (Gregory Peck) in *To Kill a Mockingbird* (1962) intervenes to save an innocent black man (Brock Peters) from a white lynch mob, as does a young white priest in *The Cardinal* (1963). Toward the end of the decade, blacks and whites were seen onscreen working together against a common enemy, as was the case in *Hurry Sundown* (1967), in which two young southern farmers—one white and one black—join forces to defeat a white bigot who wants their land. And in *Change of Habit* (1969), black and white nuns work together at a free clinic in the slums to help disadvantaged blacks and Hispanics. These latter two films dramatized the cooperation that takes place between blacks and whites working in the civil rights movement but removed this spirit to a different time (*Sundown* is set in the post–World War II South) and place (*Habit* is set in a northern city). In this way, the films were made more marketable to a contemporary southern (white) audience not quite ready for films dealing with events from the recent past or with ongoing civil rights issues.

ON THE OFFENSIVE: MONEY, FILMS, AND CHANGING MORALITY

Controversy and Conservatism

The political conservatism of Hollywood in the 1960s was, in large part, driven by economics. The industry was still making films for a general audience, in spite of a growing awareness that the traditional moviegoing audiences of the past had begun to disappear in the 1950s, replaced by a younger, better-educated, and more diverse audience. The economics of the general audience explained Hollywood's reluctance to tackle subject matter that was politically controversial. It might have offended some sector of the viewing public—such as the South. The big money-making films of the 1960s reflected this conservative taste. They included war films, such as *The Guns of Navarone* (1961) and *The Longest Day* (1962); widescreen historical spectacles, such as *El Cid* (1961), *How the West Was Won* (1962), *Lawrence of Arabia* (1962), and *Cleopatra* (1963); Disney family films, such as *One Hundred and One Dalmations* (1961), *The Absent-Minded Professor* (1961), *The Sword in the Stone* (1963), and *Mary Poppins* (1964); and musicals, such as *West Side Story* (1961), *The Music Man* (1962), *My Fair Lady* (1964), and *The Sound of Music* (1965).

In the previous decade, the restriction on controversial social subjects such as sex and drugs had been relaxed. But the films that spearheaded this challenge to the Production Code—*The Moon Is Blue* (1953), *The Man with the Golden Arm* (1955), and *Baby Doll* (1956)—did not rank among the top 10 box-office attractions of their respective years. Sex continued to sell in the 1960s with the release of films such as *Lolita* (1962), *Cleopatra* and *Irma La Douce* (1963), and James Bond films, especially *Goldfinger* (1964), *Thunderball* (1965), and *You Only Live Twice* (1967). But other forms of social controversy, such as violence, drug use, and the open rebellion of contemporary youth against the conformity of the older generation, remained relegated to the marginal status of cheaply made exploitation films. As such, they rarely appeared on the big screens of major theaters and, thus, rarely made enormous sums of money. But all of this began to change in the late 1960s, when a viable market opened up for exploitation films—that is, for films containing sex, violence, drugs, and willfully disobedient youth (of the sort found in low-budget teen pics of the 1950s and 1960s made for drive-ins by Roger Corman and American International Pictures). The change was gradual.

A New Vocabulary

In 1966, Warner Bros. tested the waters, as it were, with its film adaptation of noted playwright Edward Albee's prestigious play *Who's Afraid of Virginia Woolf?* Directed by Broadway director Mike Nichols, it features language that violated even the tolerant Production Code of the mid-1950s. Its stars, Richard Burton and Elizabeth Taylor, traded expletives that had never been heard on the screens of first-run theaters before. There are eleven "goddamns," five "sons of bitches," and seven "bastards" as well as "screw you," "hump the hostess," and "up yours." Rated R (restricted to those over the age of 18), the film grossed over $14.5 million and was nominated for 13 Academy Awards, winning 5. But Albee was hardly exploitation material.*

The next year, Avco/Embassy earned more than $44 million with another Mike Nichols picture, *The Graduate* (1967). Though its hero, played by Dustin Hoffman, engages in an adulterous relationship with the sex-starved wife of his father's business partner, the film violates few taboos. Yet, it foregrounds the situation of disaffected youth in ways that appealed to the under-30 market. None of the adults in the film understand Hoffman's alienation; all of them—including his parents and the infamous Mrs. Robinson (Anne Bancroft) who seduces him—try to manipulate him or shape his future. But he simply refuses and, finally, rebels against them.

---

*All box office revenues cited in the book refer to earnings made in the film's initial theatrical run; revenues for rereleases include rental income for all releases up to 2003 unless stated otherwise.

Live Fast, Die Young: *Bonnie and Clyde*

That same year, Warner Bros. released *Bonnie and Clyde,* an outlaw-couple film that earned almost $30 million. Combining large doses of sex (or, more accurately, sexual frustration) and violence, the film appealed to an emerging audience that was both young and antiestablishment. Posters and other publicity material for the film proclaimed that its central characters were "young," "in love," and "kill[ed] people." Depression-era folk heroes cast in the mold of figures from populist mythology such as Robin Hood and Jesse James, Bonnie and Clyde robbed the banks that foreclosed on rural farmers. At the same time, in living out their lives moment by moment, they looked back to the more recent, existentialist, antiheroes of the films of the French New Wave, such as the Jean-Paul Belmondo character in Jean-Luc Godard's *Breathless* (1959), who was also an outlaw on the run.

Bonnie and Clyde's cross-country spree captured the spirit and energy of the youth movement and epitomized the revolt against institutional authority that found support among young moviegoers of the mid-1960s. The stars of the film, Warren Beatty and Faye Dunaway, even made the cover of *Time* magazine. The characters they played were immediately appropriated as cult figures by the new generation of college-age audiences, who were fascinated by their style—by the way they dressed, by the way they talked, by the way they defied custom and convention, and by the way they died. Young men and women began wearing fashions from the 1930s, and the "Bonnie Parker look," which consisted of a V-neck sweater, miniskirt, shoulder-length hair, and beret, became the rage in women's fashion magazines.

And audiences were profoundly moved by the romantic way in which Bonnie and Clyde died. Caught in a police ambush in a hail of bullets, they first look at one another and then rush for one final embrace. Filmed in slow motion, they jerk spasmodically as the bullets tear into them. It is as if they are in the throes of some great passion or of some ultimate sexual experience. Overnight, they became the counterculture's Romeo and Juliet—star-crossed lovers who lived fast, died young, and left good-looking (but bullet-ridden) corpses.

The increasing violence of mainstream Hollywood films such as *Bonnie and Clyde* (1967) tested the limits of what had traditionally been permissible on the American screen. The *New York Times* critic, Bosley Crowther, condemned the film's violence and apparent glorification of criminals—two aspects of the film that clearly violated the old Production Code. But the cultural context in which the film had been made differed dramatically from that in which the original Production Code was written (ca. 1930). John F. Kennedy was shot in 1963, and his spasms as the bullets entered his body had been recorded on film and seen by millions of Americans who also saw Jack Ruby shoot Lee Harvey Oswald in front of television cameras. By the mid-1960s, the Vietnam War had begun to escalate, along with its nightly coverage on the network news. Finally, in the spring of 1968, a few months after the film's release, Martin Luther King and Robert F. Kennedy were assassinated; RFK's shooting was also captured, in part, by television cameras and replayed for shocked audiences.

Courtesy of Warner Bros.

The outlaw couple in *Bonnie and Clyde* (1967): Bonnie (Faye Dunaway) and Clyde (Warren Beatty) are young, in love, and they kill people.

Sex, Violence, and Ratings

The sexual explicitness of both foreign and domestic films, such as *La Dolce Vita* (Italy, 1960), *Two Women* (Italy, 1961), *Kiss Me, Stupid* (1964), and *Who's Afraid of Virginia Woolf?* (1966), increased, responding, in part, to changes in the popular perception of acceptable sexual behavior. However, what was acceptable in one culture or community was not necessarily acceptable in another. In April 1968, the Supreme Court delivered two decisions that proved crucial to ongoing debates over the definition of obscenity, permitting local communities to establish their own censorship guidelines. These changes immediately prompted the MPPA (the Motion Picture Producers Association) to transform its timeworn Production Code review process (which was preliminary to the granting or withholding of its seal of approval) into a ratings system.

By clearly distinguishing films from one another in terms of the potentially objectionable nature of their content, the film industry hoped to head off any attempts on the part of local governments to establish their own forms of censorship. At the same time, the new ratings system provided categories for films that would never have received seals of approval in the past. By acknowledging the existence of such films, the MPPA officially admitted them into the marketplace, paving the way for more American films dealing with mature subject matter.

Under the ratings system, which took effect on November 1, 1968, a "G" means that a film is suitable for general audiences; all ages are admitted to theaters showing such a film. An "M" (which was subsequently changed to "PG") designates the film as suitable for mature audiences; that is, for adults and, subject to the guidance of their parents or to "parental guidance" (PG), for children. An "R" means that a film is restricted to adults; children under age 16 (an age that was later changed to 17) are admitted only if accompanied by an adult. In the case of an "X" rating, no one under 16 (later 17) is admitted. The PG rating was subsequently modified, broken down into PG and PG-13, after the release of *Indiana Jones and the Temple of Doom* (1984), which contained graphic violence that was subsequently deemed unsuitable for children under age 13.

In 1969, sex and violence hit unprecedented heights on the screen. *Sexual Freedom in Denmark,* a foreign import, became the first pornographic film to play in a commercial theater in New York; previously, porno films had been shown only in theaters reserved exclusively for hard-core films. Another import, *I Am Curious (Yellow),* pulled in $6.5 million in rentals that year at the box office, becoming the first porno film to rank among the top 12 grossing attractions of the year. Hollywood also tested the waters. *Midnight Cowboy,* a prestige production directed by John Schlesinger and released by United Artists, contained an explicit sex act, which automatically earned it an X, making it one of the first big-budget Hollywood films to receive that rating. In spite of the X, which not only limited admission to it but also restricted advertising for it (many papers, including the *New York Times,* refused to accept advertising for X-rated films), *Midnight Cowboy* earned over $20 million and won Academy Awards for Best Picture, Best Director, and Best Screenplay. That same year saw the release of Sam Peckinpah's apocalyptic Western, *The Wild Bunch,* which was rated R because of the violence of its opening and closing gun battles and bloodbaths. Here, as in *Bonnie and Clyde,* slow motion aestheticized the violence, making it both more graphic and more balletic.

The Great Teen Pic: *Easy Rider*

Drugs, sex, and violence provided much of the spectacle that turned actor-director Dennis Hopper's low-budget ($555,000) R-rated motorcycle picture, *Easy Rider* (1969), into a big hit that grossed over $60 million worldwide. Although distributed by Columbia, the film is essentially an exploitation teen-pic, modeled on AIP (American International Pictures) biker movies such as *The Wild Angels* (1966). Yet, at the same time, the film's intentions went beyond those of the conventional B picture. It looks like an underground film, employing stylistic practices found in the nonnarrative, experimental cinema of Stan Brakhage, Bruce Baillie, and Kenneth Anger. Hopper used flash frames and cuts that flash forward from one sequence to the next; shots filmed with a handheld camera; squeezed, anamorphic images; and a hallucinatory, psychedelic dream sequence. Advertisements for the film, which described its theme, give some sense of its artistic ambitions: "A man went looking for America and

Courtesy of Columbia

Dennis Hopper (left), Peter Fonda, and Jack Nicholson go looking for America in *Easy Rider* (1969).

couldn't find it anywhere." The film's soundtrack, punctuated with music from Steppenwolf, The Byrds, The Band, The Jimi Hendrix Experience, and other major rock bands, guaranteed its credentials as a counterculture teen pic and established a model for the use of rock-and-roll songs as nondiegetic underscoring in films as diverse as *Zabriskie Point* (1970) and *Mean Streets* (1973).

This rambling motorcycle film serves as a picaresque portrait of 1960s America, ranging from utopian hippie communes to bigoted small-town communities in the South. The film's young heroes become countercultural knights in search of a contemporary Holy Grail, journeying from drug deals in the modern wasteland of Los Angeles to a spaced-out Mardi Gras in the old-world city of New Orleans, where, under the influence of LSD, the film's heroes wander through a graveyard. The characters' idealistic search for the American dream proves to be a failure—or, as Wyatt (Peter Fonda) confesses to Billy (Dennis Hopper) near the end of their trip, "We blew it." They search, but they find nothing.

TRANSFORMATION:
THE COUNTERCULTURE GOES MAINSTREAM

The financial success of *Easy Rider* established the existence of a specialized youth market. By the mid-1960s, the traditional movie audience had changed from a middle-aged, high-school-educated, middle- to lower-class viewing group to a younger, college-educated, more affluent, middle-class audience. By the mid-1970s, 76 percent of all moviegoers were under the age of 30; the majority of these—64 percent—came from affluent families and had gone to college. *Bonnie and Clyde* and *The Graduate* had suggested that a younger audience with a taste for more adult themes could dramatically increase the box-office revenues for a major studio production. But *Easy Rider* proved that even a cheaply made, exploitation film that was pitched solely to the college-age crowd could make a great deal of money.

Easy Rider revolutionized the industry, demonstrating that spectacular returns could be realized on a rather modest investment if the film appealed to this new audience. *Easy Rider* led to a series of youth-cult films, including a number of films from those who had been involved in its production. Producer Bert Schneider parlayed the success of *Easy Rider* into a production company (BBS Productions) a distribution deal with Columbia, and a string of films, including *Five Easy Pieces* (1970); *The Last Picture Show* (1971); *A Safe Place* (1971); *Drive, He Said* (1971); *The King of Marvin Gardens* (1972); and finally, the antiwar Academy Award–winning documentary about Vietnam, *Hearts and Minds* (1974).

Director Dennis Hopper was given a blank check to make his next film, *The Last Movie* (1971), a self-reflexive, antiestablishment Western about the exploitation of third-world cultures that was filmed and set in a remote Indian village in Peru. Jack Nicholson, who played a cameo role in *Easy Rider* that brought him instant stardom, was cast as a hippie in *On a Clear Day You Can See Forever* (1970) and played a series of offbeat types in *Five Easy Pieces; Carnal Knowledge* (1971); *A Safe Place; Drive, He Said;* and *The King of Marvin Gardens* before landing his starring, Academy Award–winning role as the nonconformist mental patient, Randel P. McMurphy, in the film adaptation of the ultimate 1960s anti-authoritarian novel, Ken Kesey's *One Flew Over the Cuckoo's Nest* (1975).

In the case of Hopper, Nicholson, and Schneider, the counterculture moved into the mainstream of Hollywood production, though only Nicholson remained there for any length of time. A handful of directors, such as Michelangelo Antonioni (*Blow-Up,* 1966; *Zabriskie Point,* 1970) and Arthur Penn (*Bonnie and Clyde,* 1967; *Alice's Restaurant,* 1969; *Little Big Man,* 1970), gave dramatic form to the lifestyles and beliefs of the dissident generation that fought war abroad and racism at home, but the majority of films that tried to deal with the 1960s youth culture, the civil rights movement, the student protest movement, or the women's movement depoliticized their agendas or disguised them in such a way that they no longer possessed any confrontational power.

As the films became more and more expensive and less and less exploitational, they lost their dissident status as attacks on the mainstream from the fringe and became mainstream themselves. Even *Easy Rider* soft-pedaled the politics of the antiestablishment left and focused on the style rather than the content of the revolt of youth in the 1960s. Westerns such as *Little Big Man, Soldier Blue* (1970), and *Ulzana's Raid* (1972) implicitly criticized American involvement in Vietnam by suggesting that the genocidal warfare by whites against Native Americans in the old West was comparable to that of whites against Asians in

Southeast Asia. But their antiwar stance remained hidden beneath the surface of seemingly conventional genre pictures. In other words, in spite of the production of films specifically targeted for younger audiences, it was through the disguised medium of genre pictures that the counterculture got its message into the mainstream of Hollywood production.

BLAXPLOITATION AND BEYOND

An Emerging Black Audience

One or two of the most radical films of this era came disguised as genre vehicles. In fact, it was again in the area of exploitation films that the counterculture found the least compromised and most powerful presentations of its political concerns. The most compelling instance of this was found in the short-lived cycle of black action pictures made between 1970 and 1973, which were referred to as blaxploitation films by contemporary trade magazines such as *Variety* and also by critics. The phenomenal success of three Sidney Poitier films made in 1967—*In the Heat of the Night; To Sir, With Love;* and *Guess Who's Coming to Dinner*—indicated to Hollywood that black was not only beautiful but box office as well. Polls indicated that one-quarter of all regular moviegoers in the late 1960s and early 1970s were black. This statistic was reinforced by the box-office figures for Poitier's films, but it was confirmed by the amazing success of a number of routine, cheaply made genre pictures starring relatively unknown black actors—pictures that made money in the wake of Poitier's success.

Between 1970 and 1972, over 50 feature films were made specifically for a black audience. In 1970, United Artists began to cultivate this emerging black audience with its release of Ossie Davis's adaptation of a Chester Himes detective novel, *Cotton Comes to Harlem*—starring Godfrey Cambridge, Raymond St. Jacques, and Calvin Lockhart—which earned a hefty $15.4 million, largely in urban markets where there were large numbers of black viewers. In 1971, Melvin Van Peebles' independently made, outlaw-on-the-run, X-rated picture *Sweet Sweetback's Baadasssss Song*, which cost only $500,000 to make, earned over $10 million. Also in 1971, *Shaft*, a private-eye picture directed by the son of still photographer Gordon Parks and released by M-G-M, grossed over $7 million.

Poitier's big-budget A pictures were targeted at a general audience comprised of both blacks and whites who shared the more or less middle-class values embodied in Poitier's screen persona. This was the same audience that came to see Diana Ross play Billie Holiday in Paramount's lavish production of *Lady Sings the Blues* (1972) and to see Cicely Tyson as a southern sharecropper in *Sounder* (1972). Both *Lady* and *Sounder* were directed by whites and earned over $9 million each in rentals. The boom in big-budget black films went bust in 1978 with the disappointing returns from the filmed adaptation of the Broadway Musical, *The Wiz*, starring Diana Ross, Michael Jackson, Nipsey Russell, and others. The film, which cost Universal more than $24 million to produce, returned only $13.6 million in domestic rentals, emerging as one of the biggest flops of the late 1970s.

Blaxploitation films, on the other hand, were inexpensively made exploitation films pitched primarily to middle- and lower-class urban blacks. White audiences raised on a steady diet of the sex and violence found in gangster films such as *Bonnie and Clyde* (1967), war films such as *The Dirty Dozen* (1967), and Westerns such as *The Wild Bunch* (1969) were drawn in considerable numbers to black crime pictures, which featured similarly strong doses of sex, violence, and gritty realism. Though blaxploitation films were often merely the reworking and recasting of traditionally white stories, plot situations, and character types for black audiences with black actors, many of them nonetheless addressed the concerns of the black community in ways that were unprecedented on the American screen.

A Revolutionary Film: *Sweet Sweetback's Baadasssss Song*

Sweet Sweetback (1971)—which was produced, written, edited, scored, and directed by its star, Melvin Van Peebles—emerged as one of the most revolutionary films of this era. The film's hero evolves from a cynical, self-absorbed, morally corrupt superstud into an angry black militant. Sweetback becomes a political outlaw when he intervenes on behalf of a black radical who is being beaten by the police. He fights back and seriously wounds two cops by hitting them on the head with his handcuffs. The radicalized figure of Sweetback emerges as a cult hero for the black power movement. Black Panther chief, Huey Newton, proclaimed the film "the first truly revolutionary Black film made."

Like the hero of Godard's *Breathless*, Sweetback is an outlaw on the run. But his rebelliousness is more political than existential—he resists white authority on behalf of the larger, oppressed black community whom he realizes he now represents. Presenting Sweetback's flight from the law in the form of a contemporary runaway slave narrative, Van Peebles devotes considerable footage to scenes of his hero running across various landscapes, and signals Sweetback's escape to freedom with shots of the dead police bloodhounds he killed. By the end of the film, Sweetback has crossed the border into Mexico, where (the film suggests) he will recover from his wounds and continue his struggle against the white establishment. The film ends with a title that promises things to come: "A BAADASSSSS NIGGER IS COMING BACK TO COLLECT SOME DUES."

Radical hostility underscores many blaxploitation films in which whites tend to be cast as bigots and villains. Even in Poitier's first film as a director, *Buck and the Preacher* (1972), black homesteaders are tracked down and ruthlessly slaughtered by white bounty hunters. Their sole allies prove to be another oppressed group, Indians, who ride to their rescue at the last minute, playing the part usually performed by the U.S. Cavalry, who rescue settlers from attacking Indians in countless white Westerns. White police officers, like Mattelli (Anthony Quinn) in *Across 110th Street* (1972) and McKinney in *Black Caesar* (1973),

Courtesy of Cinemation

Pursued by the Los Angeles police, Sweetback (Melvin Van Peebles) becomes a black folk hero in *Sweet Sweetback's Baadasssss Song* (1971).

tend to be corrupt and brutally racist cops who take bribes from black gangsters and who abuse their authority as police officers to beat up defenseless blacks.

Outlaws or Role Models?

Black Caesar, directed by the white Larry Cohen, serves as an allegory for racial conflict. Its hero, Tommy Gibbs (Fred Williamson), rises from shoeshine boy to small-time hood to hitman for the Mafia. His rise to power is symbolized by his overthrow of the white lawyer for whom his mother worked as a maid. Gibbs takes the lawyer's place, buying him out of his apartment and even buying the clothes off his back; then he "frees" his own mother from servitude. Gibbs's quest for power leads him to take on the Mafia itself. He and his henchmen wipe out the Mafia family for whom he works and take their place.

Near the end of the film, in a showdown with McKinney, the white cop picks up a handy shoeshine box—the film's first symbol of black oppression by whites—and begins to beat Gibbs with it. Though the hero ultimately defeats the representatives of white power and racism—the Mafia and McKinney—he nonetheless falls from power himself in traditional gangster fashion. Abandoned by friends and family and wounded in a series of gun battles with the Mafia who have wiped out his gang, Gibbs (suddenly vulnerable for the first time in his life) is knifed to death in the rubble of a slum tenement by a gang of black teenagers.

Critics in the black community, including representatives from the NAACP, complained that the heroes of blaxploitation films did not represent the black community in a positive manner. These heroes tended to be violent criminals (*Black Ceasar*), superstuds and pimps (*Sweet Sweetback*), or drug dealers (*Superfly*, 1972). The title characters in *Shaft* (1971) and *Cleopatra Jones* (1973) proved to be more traditional heroes, working as a private detective and a government agent, respectively. In fact, Cleopatra Jones provided an image of black womanhood that was considerably more liberated than that found in other blaxploitation films. And the black policeman in *Across 110th Street*, Pope (Yaphet Kotto), is steadfastly incorruptible. But the criminality of most black heroes made them unacceptable to middle-class black audiences.

However, blaxploitation heroes epitomized the outlaw status that the more aggressive and revolutionary members of the black power movement enjoyed in the eyes of both the black and white middle class. In other words, it was perversely appropriate for the black counterculture to find itself identifying with, and identified as, outlaws. Thus, while the white counterculture identified with Bonnie and Clyde or with the drug-dealing antiheroes of *Easy Rider*, black (and white) revolutionaries made folk heroes out of black outlaws who overthrow white authority. Though the majority of Hollywood productions garbled the message of the counterculture, it found a voice—albeit marginal—in a handful of exploitation films that permitted it to strike back against the more conservative mainstream.

SPLIT SCREEN: THE TWO 1960s

In *Field of Dreams* (1989), the heroine (Amy Madigan) lashes out during a PTA meeting at a conservative neighbor who wants to ban the books of a (fictional) radical black writer, Terence Mann (James Earl Jones), who was an inspiration to the youth movement in the 1960s. She accuses the would-be book burner of never having experienced the 60s, insisting that, instead, she had had two 50s and then had gone right on to the 70s. The 1960s has come to mean the civil rights, student protest, antiwar, and women's liberation movements. It has also become the stuff of nostalgia for television sitcoms such as *The Wonder Years*, which presented the 1960s as an age of innocence and idealism.

But the 1960s cannot be so easily labeled. For moviegoers, there were at least two 1960s. There was a 1960s for the conservative, middle-aged, middle-class mainstream who went to big-budget historical spectacles, lavish musicals, Doris Day and Rock Hudson sex comedies, Disney family pictures, and cartoon-like, gadget-filled James Bond spy thrillers. This 1960s was essentially the second of the two 1950s referred to by Amy Madigan in *Field of Dreams*. But there was also a different 1960s for a younger, more liberal, middle- and lower-class audience—the audience that was moved by the books of writers like the fictional Terence Mann. These viewers were gradually drawn away from their parents' movies to film such as *The Graduate, Bonnie and Clyde,* and *Easy Rider* that attempted to address an under-30 age group. For them, the 1960s began sometime after JFK's assassination—after the nostalgic days of Buddy Holly and before the fanatic hysteria that greeted the arrival of the Beatles in the United States. In other words, the 1960s began, for them, when the happy days depicted in George Lucas's *American Graffiti* (1973) came to a close—at the end of the summer of 1962. For this generation of moviegoers, the 1960s stretched beyond the end of the decade into the early 1970s and lasted until the end of the Vietnam War. But their movies did not catch up with them until the late 1960s. Even when they did, few films—with the possible exception of the animated Beatles' film *Yellow Submarine* (1968)—conveyed the spaced-out, utopian pacifism of the hippies or flower children who followed Timothy Leary's advice, took LSD, and "tuned in, turned on, and dropped out." Nor did many major Hollywood productions capture the anger or intensity of the new left, the antiwar movement, or black militants.

By the mid-1970s, the cynicism of Dr. Spock's baby boomers had won the day. A number of their parents' movies—all of them musicals—began to flop one after the other at the box office, beginning with *Dr. Dolittle* (1967), which cost $20 million and earned $6 million; then *Star!* (1968), which cost $15 million and earned $4 million; *Hello, Dolly* (1969), which cost $24 million and earned $15 million; and *Darling Lili* (1970), which cost $22 million and earned only $3 million. Meanwhile, films for the college-age crowd became more and more popular, with *The Graduate* (1967), *Bonnie and Clyde* (1967), *2001: A Space Odyssey* (1968), and *Easy Rider* (1969) returning huge profits to their producers. Bitter social satires and genre send-ups—such as Robert Altman's *M*A*S*H* (1970) and *McCabe and Mrs. Miller* (1971); Mike Nichols' adaptation of Joseph Heller's comic novel about military bureaucracy, *Catch-22* (1970); Arthur Penn's anti-Western, *Little Big Man* (1970); and Stanley Kubrick's adaptation of Anthony Burgess's study of amorality, violence, and repression, *A Clockwork Orange* (1971)—found a ready audience among disenchanted, increasingly skeptical youth who had been raised on the black humor of nightclub comedian Lenny Bruce, cartoonist Jules Feiffer, and novelists Terry Southern, Joseph Heller, John Barth, and Kurt Vonnegut, Jr.

REJUVENATION

Hollywood filmmaking slowly adjusted to its new audience in the 1960s, but, for many, the system moved too slowly. The majority of those who produced, wrote, and directed motion pictures in the 1960s were themselves products of much earlier eras. As Richard Corliss noted, "For most of the Sixties, movies were a business for middle-aged (or old) men: from 1957 to 1966, the Best Film Oscar went to movies directed by men whose average age was 52." Within 10 years, that statistic had changed, and the average age of Oscar-winning (still male) directors had fallen to 38. During the early 1970s, a new generation of filmmakers appeared—filmmakers who had gone to school in the 1960s and who therefore belonged to that generation of filmgoers: Francis Ford Coppola (UCLA, 1958–1968); George Lucas (USC, ca. 1967); Brian De Palma (Columbia, 1962; Sarah Lawrence, 1964); Stephen Spielberg (California State, ca. 1968); and Martin Scorsese (NYU, 1964, 1966).

Although products of the 1960s, these filmmakers came from varied backgrounds and represented a broad political spectrum. De Palma had roots in the 1960s counterculture that cropped up in both *Greetings* (1968), which deals with the draft and the antiwar movement, and its sequel, *Hi, Mom!* (1970), which contains a powerful sequence dealing with race relations. Coppola, on the other hand, eludes easy categorization. His script for *Patton* (1970) combined idolatry for the World War II military hero with a sympathetic critique of the general's authoritarian behavior. Coppola described the Mafia in *The Godfather* (1972) as "a metaphor for America" and suggested that his film was an exposé of the greed and violence that underlie the capitalist system. But, in exposing the criminal underworld's corruption and abuse of power, Coppola also celebrated the family values, loyalty, and sense of justice that lay at the heart of the charisma that made the Corleones attractive to audiences.

Although Hollywood's filmmakers had become younger, the audiences for Hollywood films had grown even younger still. By the mid-1970s, almost half of the moviegoing public was between the ages of 12 and 20. In other words, the college-age spectators of the 1960s had given way to a high school-age audience in the 1970s. By the end of the 1970s, the five top-grossing films of all time—*Star Wars, Jaws, The Godfather, Grease,* and *Close Encounters of the Third Kind*—had all been directed by men under the age of 35. But the combination of young directors and even younger audiences had resulted in a cinema that was stylistically youthful and inventive but politically conservative. Exploitation-type genre films continued to dominate the marketplace, but in the 1970s they cost much more to make, and much more was at risk if they failed. As a result, their potential for subversive statements had been severely restricted. If, in the late 1960s and early 1970s, the counterculture had struck back, then by the mid-1970s it found itself seriously compromised by changes in the marketplace which heralded yet another turn in the revolutionary progress of the cinema.

■ ■ ■ ■ SELECT FILMOGRAPHY

Lolita (1962)	*Bonnie and Clyde* (1967)
Cleopatra (1963)	*The Graduate* (1967)
Irma la Douce (1963)	*Up the Down Staircase* (1967)
Goldfinger (1964)	*Bob & Carol & Ted & Alice* (1969)
Who's Afraid of Virginia Woolf?	*Midnight Cowboy* (1969)
(1966)	*Easy Rider* (1969)

Medium Cool (1969)
Getting Straight (1970)
The Strawberry Statement (1970)
Zabriskie Point (1970)
Klute (1971)

Sweet Sweetback's Baadasssss Song (1971)
Black Caesar (1973)
One Flew Over the Cuckoo's Nest (1975)

■■■ SELECT BIBLIOGRAPHY

ANON. "The Violent Years," in Ann Lloyd, ed., *70 Years at the Movies: From Silent Films to Today's Screen Hits.* New York: Crescent, 1988.

BOGLE, DONALD. *Toms, Coons, Mulattoes, Mammies, and Bucks: An Interpretive History of Blacks in American Films* (new exp. ed.). New York: Continuum, 1989.

CAGIN, SETH, and PHILIP DRAY. *Hollywood Films of the Seventies: Sex, Drugs, Violence, Rock 'n Roll and Politics.* New York: Harper & Row, 1984.

CORLISS, RICHARD. "We Lost It at the Movies: The Generation That Grew Up on *The Graduate* Took Over Hollywood—and Went into Plastics," *Film Comment* 16, no. 1 (January–February, 1980): 34–38.

CRIPPS, THOMAS. *Black Film as Genre.* Bloomington: Indiana University Press, 1978.

GITLIN, TODD. *The Sixties: Years of Hope, Days of Rage.* New York: Bantam, 1987.

GUERRERO, ED. *Framing Blackness: The African American Image in Film.* Philadelphia: Temple University Press, 1993.

HASKELL, MOLLY. *From Reverence to Rape: The Treatment of Women in the Movies.* New York: Holt, 1973.

HILLIER, BEVIS. *The Style of the Century: 1900–1980.* New York: Dutton, 1983.

JAMES, DAVID. *Allegories of Cinema: American Film in the Sixties.* Princeton: Princeton University Press, 1989.

MONACO, PAUL. *The Sixties: 1960–1969.* New York: Charles Scribner's Sons, 2000.

MORDDEN, ETHAN. *Medium Cool: The Movies of the 1960s.* New York: Knopf, 1990.

CHAPTER **15**

The Film School Generation

THE NEW WAVE

During the late 1940s and early 1950s, Henri Langlois screened old movies seven times a day in his small, 50-seat theater at the Cinémathèque Française in Paris. He ran every kind of film from every country in the world that produced motion pictures. Here a new generation of moviegoers saw the silent films of D. W. Griffith, Carl Dreyer, Sergei Eisenstein, F. W. Murnau, Eric von Stroheim, Maurice Stiller, and others for the first time since their initial releases in the 1910s and 1920s. It was here that audiences discovered the American sound films of Howard Hawks, John Ford, Alfred Hitchcock, and Orson Welles. It was here that they also obtained a sense of their own cinematic heritage by watching the work of Louis Lumière, George Méliès, Louis Feuillade, Jean Renoir, and others.

The Cinémathèque became the meeting place for a handful of film fanatics who came to see everything that Langlois showed. Five young men in particular attended regularly, eventually met one another there, and became the center of an emerging film culture. They watched films; talked and argued about them; wrote passionately about them in a new film journal, *Cahiers du cinéma* (Cinema Notebooks); and brought their knowledge of the cinema to films they themselves made. Their names were François Truffaut, Jean-Luc Godard, Eric Rohmer, Jacques Rivette, and Claude Chabrol. They became central figures in what critics referred to as the New Wave, the explosion of films made by young, first-time French directors that took place at the end of the decade.

The New Wave began in 1958, when Chabrol directed his first feature, *Le Beau Serge*. Then, in 1959, Truffaut's *The Four Hundred Blows* and Godard's *Breathless* not only won international acclaim but also earned huge profits at the box office. Their financial success opened the doors for others and, over the next two years, 67 journalists, academics, writers, and students directed their first films in France. New Wave directors did not apprentice for years in the film industry before getting their first films to direct, but many of them had *studied* films for years. They had learned about the cinema in film clubs, at the Cinémathèque, and in movie houses in Paris. Many of the films they made reflected this alternative form of apprenticeship.

A film such as *Breathless* was hardly academic, but it was informed by an understanding of film history rarely seen on motion picture screens prior to the advent of the New Wave. It was dedicated to Monogram, an American studio that produced B films in the 1930s and 1940s. It contains a tribute to Humphrey Bogart, at whose photograph the hero stares intently, as if looking at himself in a mirror. In the movie, a poster for Bogart's last film, *The Harder They Fall* (1956), is prominently displayed outside a neighborhood theater (as well as a poster for a more recent film, starring Jack Palance and directed by Robert Aldrich). The narrative resembles that of an American crime film, and the film's characters—an existential hero on the run (Jean-Paul Belmondo) hopelessly in love with a femme fatale (Jean Seberg)—belong to the world of American film noir. And the hero's death alludes to the final sequences in old Cagney and Bogart pictures directed by Raoul Walsh (*The Roaring Twenties*, 1939; *High Sierra*, 1941). Although the film is also full of allusions to more traditional art forms and artists such as Dylan Thomas, William Faulkner, Rainer Maria Rilke, W. A. Mozart, Paul Klee, Pierre Auguste Renoir, and Pablo Picasso, it steadfastly refuses to distinguish between high and low forms. As far as Godard was concerned, Bogart stands on equal footing with Mozart.

THE AUTEUR THEORY: DIRECTORS AS STARS

Cahiers du cinéma and Andrew Sarris

Godard and other French critics who worked for *Cahiers du cinéma* rewrote the traditional film canon, which had consisted largely of classic, European art films. They included in it commercial American films made by directors (such as Howard Hawks, Alfred Hitchcock, Vincente Minnelli, and Samuel Fuller) who were then generally considered to be mere Hollywood hacks. An American critic, Andrew Sarris, adopted the tactics of the *Cahiers* group, bringing their writings, opinions, and polemics to the United States in the form of what he termed "the auteur theory." Sarris's book on American directors, *The American Cinema* (1968), argued that directors were the principal authors of motion pictures, and set forth a new canon of great filmmakers. More important, the book forced a wholesale reevaluation of American cinema by critics, scholars, students, and film buffs. A cagey journalist, Sarris inspired controversy (and thus secured attention for his project) by ranking directors; for instance, he noted which belonged to the "Pantheon," "Far Side of Paradise," "Expressive Esoterica," "Less Than Meets the Eye," "Strained Seriousness," and other categories. But Sarris's chief contribution, as an educator, was to provide a map of the existing terrain for others to follow, add to, correct, and challenge. (A tribute of sorts to Sarris can be found in *Galaxy Quest,* 1999, in which the screenwriter David Howard, a former student at Columbia—where Sarris teaches—named the film's intergalactic villain "Sarris.")

Sarris forced Americans to take their own cinema seriously—and he had the critical clout, prestige, and intellectual appeal of the New Wave (and its *auteur* theory) behind him. Though not everyone agreed with Sarris's taste, many were so persuaded by the New Wave's enthusiasm for American cinema that further research into current and past Hollywood products was considered necessary. If Truffaut idolized Hitchcock, then Hitchcock must be an artist of considerable talents. American intellectuals rushed to Truffaut's self-effacing, book-length interview with Hitchcock (1968) to find out what all the stir was about.

Retrospective: America Discovers Its Cinematic Past

While Sarris was rediscovering new film *auteurs* in his weekly newspaper column (which began in 1960), American museums and revival theaters began to conduct extensive retrospectives of major directors' work. In New York City, Peter Bogdanovich, influenced by Sarris's criticism, mounted extensive retrospectives of the works of Welles, Hawks, and Hitchcock during the early 1960s at the Museum of Modern Art. Around the same time, Daniel Talbot (along with Bogdanovich, Sarris, and second-string *New York Times* film critic Eugene Archer) programmed a series of film retrospectives at the New Yorker Theater on New York's Upper West Side. Like the *Cahiers* group, Sarris, Bogdanovich, and Archer wrote extensively about the cinema and argued on behalf of neglected American *auteurs*. Like the critics-turned-directors of the New Wave, Bogdanovich became a director himself. After a brief apprenticeship with Roger Corman, he made *Targets* (1968), a movie about a serial killer who murders his family and then terrorizes the patrons of a drive-in theater that is showing a Boris Karloff horror picture. Karloff's presence in the film inspired Bogdanovich to introduce a cinematic quote—a clip of Karloff from an early Hawks film, *The Criminal*

Courtesy of Columbia

Peter Bogdanovich evoked the world of John Ford in *The Last Picture Show* (1971), casting a familiar Fordian actor, Ben Johnson, as Sam the Lion, who represents the spirit of the past.

Code (1931), which the actor is watching on television. Bogdanovich's psychopathic killer serves as the focus for a number of allusions to Hitchcock's films, such as *Psycho* (1960) and *Strangers on a Train* (1951). After *Targets*, Bogdanovich made a documentary for the American Film Institute about John Ford, *Directed by John Ford* (1971). Tributes to Hawks and Ford filled Bogdanovich's next feature film, an adaptation of a Larry McMurtry novel, *The Last Picture Show* (1971); the film after that, a screwball comedy starring Barbra Streisand and Ryan O'Neal called *What's Up, Doc?* (1972), was a loose remake of Hawks's *Bringing Up Baby* (1938).

The Critic as Filmmaker

Bogdanovich proved to be something of an exception—American film critics did not follow their French counterparts to take up positions behind the camera. Two *Esquire* (nonfilm) critics, Robert Benton and David Newman, collaborated on the screenplay of *Bonnie and Clyde*, which they tried to get first Truffaut and then Godard to direct before turning to Arthur Penn. Benton subsequently became a director (*Kramer vs. Kramer*, 1979; *Nobody's Fool*, 1994), but, though movie wise, he never indulged in the sort of cinematic allusionism found in Bogdanovich's early work. After retiring from the *New York Times,* critic Bosley Crowther became an executive at Columbia Pictures. In 1979, *New Yorker* critic Pauline Kael enjoyed a brief stint in Hollywood as a production executive, courtesy of producer-actor Warren Beatty, but her time there did not result in projects that were ever filmed.

The only American *film* critics to make it in Hollywood as creative talents came from much earlier eras and served as unselfconscious screenwriters for Old Wave directors. Frank Woods left the *New York Dramatic Mirror* to write for Griffith (*The Birth of a Nation*, 1915); *New York Times* reviewer Frank Nugent wrote Westerns for John Ford in the late 1940s, as well as *The Quiet Man* (1952); and the film critic for *Time* and *Nation,* James Agee, scripted John Huston's Bogart-and-Hepburn adventure picture, *The African Queen* (1951) and later Charles Laughton's Gothic chase film, *The Night of the Hunter* (1955).

Training Ground: The Rise of Film Schools

Film critics tended to have little status in the eyes of the American film industry, which found them more annoying than enlightening. Indeed, Nugent was reportedly hired by 20th Century-Fox in order to prevent him from writing negative reviews of that studio's pictures. But Hollywood looked more favorably on film students who studied at major film schools and who desperately wanted to enter the industry. They were uncritical of the industry, eager to succeed in it, and appreciative of its history. They could also be paid (at first) considerably less than older, more experienced directors. At the same time, with the collapse of the studio system, film schools functioned to provide a pool of semiskilled talent on which the industry could draw whenever there was a need for new blood. And during the 1960s, an unprecedented number of would-be *auteurs* enrolled in film schools to study the craft and (they hoped) follow in the footsteps of their favorite *auteurs*, whether those were Hitchcock, Hawks, Ford, Welles, or other neglected giants of commercial cinema.

Film gradually became a feature of a contemporary liberal arts education, and more and more talented young filmmakers took up the study of film and television on both the undergraduate and graduate level. In 1967, 200 American colleges and universities offered roughly 1500 courses in film and television. Eleven years later, over 1,000 schools listed 10,000 such courses. Graduate programs at the University of California at Los Angeles, the University of Southern California, and New York University produced a new generation of filmmakers including Francis Ford Coppola (UCLA), George Lucas (USC), and Martin Scorsese (NYU), while the American Film Institute's Center for Advanced Film Studies trained Paul Schrader, David Lynch, and others.

At the same time, the rise of film study in the university produced a new generation of film-smart moviegoers who had taken one or more film courses in college or even in high school. This new young audience sought films that addressed their interest. Like Coppola, Lucas, and Scorsese, they had grown up on the movies, watching them on television, in campus film societies, or in film courses. They not only appreciated the work of the film school generation (because it grew out of the same cultural experiences as theirs), but also understood many of the allusions to earlier films and filmmakers that peppered the movies directed by the members of the American New Wave.

THE COLOR OF MONEY: YOUNG DIRECTORS AND THE BOX OFFICE

Youth Films and Economics

However, it was not entirely the growth in cinematic literacy that opened Hollywood's doors in the late 1960s and early 1970s to a new crop of filmmakers. It was economics that enabled young directors to get their start. During the period from 1969 to 1972, the seven major studios had record losses totaling over $500 million. Experienced directors had bombed with big-budget flops such as *Star!* (Robert Wise, 1968) and *Darling Lili* (Blake Edwards, 1970). At the same time, the phenomenal success of the low-budget, youth-cult film *Easy Rider* (1969), directed by 33-year-old Dennis Hopper, demonstrated to studio executives that experience was not always as profitable as youthful energy. Meanwhile, a number of youth-oriented films (most made by older directors) such as *Butch Cassidy and the Sundance Kid* (1969), *Woodstock* (1970), *Love Story* (1970), and *Summer of '42* (1971) enjoyed outstanding financial success. And Hopper was not the only young filmmaker involved in the making of a hit. Francis Ford Coppola won an Academy Award for his screenplay for *Patton* (1970), one of the top-grossing films of the year. At the same time, Bogdanovich's *The Last Picture Show* and *What's Up, Doc?* were both among the top 10 box-office hits of 1971 and 1972. More important, many of the films produced by this younger crop of filmmakers fared extremely well at the box office. USC once boasted that "as of December 1983, 41 of the 42 all-time highest grossing films have USC alumni affiliated with them."

Spielberg was not from USC; he went to California State College at Long Beach (In 2002 he returned to complete his undergraduate degree). Even so, Spielberg's films, including some produced by Lucas, topped *Variety*'s 2003 all-time box office charts. After a recent rerelease, *E.T.: The Extra-Terrestrial* (1982) earned a total of $434.9 million, *Jurassic Park* (1993) $357 million, *Jaws* (1975) $260 million, *Raiders of the Lost Ark* (1981) $282 million, *The Lost World: Jurassic Park* (1997) $229 million, and *Saving Private Ryan* (1998) $216 million. Lucas's *Star Wars* films once dominated the top-10 all-time film rental champs list; today, after a successful rerelease, the original *Star Wars* (1977) stands at number 2, with $460.9 million, and *Star Wars Episode I: The Phantom Menace* (1999) ranks number 4, with $431 million in box-office receipts. *Star Wars II: The Attack of the Clones* (2002), *Return of the Jedi* (1983), and *The Empire Strikes Back* (1980) remain near the top of the list, pulling in $310.6, $309, and $290 million respectively. James Cameron, who never attended film school, directed the all-time box office champ, *Titanic* (1999), which earned $600.7 million in rentals.

Back in the early 1970s, industry analysts compared the box-office statistics of the 1969–1972 period with their own research data, which told them that the age of the average moviegoer had gotten younger. By 1970–1971, over 43 percent of all viewers were between the ages of 12 and 20. (By the end of the 1970s, this

The most likely to succeed of the film school generation: (*a*) Francis Ford Coppola, (*b*) Martin Scorsese, (*c*) George Lucas, and (*d*) Steven Spielberg.

figure had climbed to roughly 50 percent, where it stood in 2003.) An additional 30 percent of the total audience were between the ages of 21 and 29, making almost 75 percent of the film audience under age 30. Given the age of the audience, the success of youth films, and the promising track record of young filmmakers such as Hopper, Bogdanovich, and Coppola, the studios turned to the source of much of this new talent in search of the next generation of filmmakers.

The Roger Corman School

Hopper, Bogdanovich, and Coppola had all received practical experience in filmmaking by working for the master of the exploitation film, Roger Corman, who produced and directed cheaply made horror films, Westerns, and motor-cycle and gangster pictures for American International Pictures.

Hopper had starred in a number of Corman teen pics, as had his costars in *Easy Rider,* Peter Fonda and Jack Nicholson. Corman not only gave Bogdano-vich a start but also made it possible for a film school type such as Coppola to make his first feature-length film, *Dementia 13* (1963); for Martin Scorsese to direct his second, *Boxcar Bertha* (1972); and for John Milius to direct his first film, *Dillinger* (1973). AIP even gave Woody Allen his start, bankrolling his *What's Up, Tiger Lily?* (1966). A few years later, Corman helped Jonathan Demme and Jonathan Kaplan make their first films. Demme's background in exploitation resurfaced in his picaresque sexual odyssey, *Something Wild* (1986), with Jeff Daniels and Melanie Griffith, and in his horror mystery, *The Silence of the Lambs* (1991), with Jodie Foster and Anthony Hopkins. Kaplan also fared quite well in the exploitation mode with his gang-rape exposé, *The Accused* (1988), starring Jodie Foster, and with his stalker film, *Unlawful Entry* (1992), starring Kurt Rus-sell and Ray Liotta.

In looking to Corman protégés, the major studios tacitly acknowledged a significant shift in the nature of the traditional Hollywood film. During the 1970s, the industry, led by the film school generation, would turn more and more frequently to the kinds of pictures made by Corman—genre pictures. It would draw on the subject matter that had previously been the sole province of the exploitation market—gangster films, teen hot-rod flicks, science-fiction adventures, monster pictures, and horror films.

Exploitation on a Grand Scale

However, in undertaking these low-budget subjects, Hollywood gave them a big-budget treatment. Thus, Corman's *Bloody Mama* (1970), which explores the gangster family of bloody Ma Barker and her equally bloodthirsty boys, gave way to Coppola's more operatic and more lavish family melodrama, *The God-father* (1972). George Lucas's *American Graffiti* (1973) was a souped-up hybrid of an Annette Funicello–Frankie Avalon *Beach Party* movie (1963) and films such as *Hot Rod Girl* (1956), that documented the 1950s teen world of drag-strip racing and juke joints. Lucas's *Star Wars* (1977) and Steven Spielberg's *Close Encounters of the Third Kind* (1977) looked back to Flash Gordon serials and science-fiction films of the 1950s. Spielberg's *Jaws* (1975) drew on familiar monster pictures such as *The Creature From the Black Lagoon* (1954), *Attack of the Crab Monsters* (1957), and *Frogs* (1972). Brian De Palma's *Carrie* (1976), an adaptation of a Stephen King novel about a young girl with telekinetic powers, had roots not only in De Palma's own AIP shocker *Sisters* (1973), but also in earlier teen monster films, such as *I Was a Teenage Frankenstein* (1957) and *I Was a Teenage Werewolf* (1957).

Many of the big hits of the 1970s were low-budget genre pictures in disguise. Some of the biggest, such as William Friedkin's lavishly produced gross-out horror picture, *The Exorcist* (1973), which earned $89 million on its initial release and a total of $232.6 million after its rerelease in 2001, even dropped the disguise. The industry marketed these films according to methods that had proven effective in the exploitation field. Hollywood abandoned its traditional release pattern whereby a film would first open in one or two theaters in the nation's largest cities; then, several weeks later, as word-of-mouth reports from spectators on the quality of the film spread, it would be placed by the distributor in additional theaters in other cities and in the suburbs, with the number of theaters in which to play it calculated in accordance with audience response.

Starting with *Jaws*, the major studios adopted the distribution patterns developed in the exploitation market. That film was released nationwide in approximately 464 theaters at the same time. In addition to saturating the market with prints of the film, Universal (its distributor) saturated the television and radio airwaves with national and local advertising for *Jaws* as well. They soon discovered that, in a wide-release situation, when advertising (and advertising expenditures) were doubled, the returns at the box office increased by at least three or four times. Thereafter, big-budget exploitation films opened in from 800 to 1,000 theaters simultaneously and advertising budgets increased dramatically, averaging about 50 percent of the film's negative cost (that is, what it cost to make the film). The marketing strategy associated with *Jaws* remains the dominant model for current distribution practice—at least for potential blockbusters. Thus, the first two *Harry Potter* films (2001, 2002) opened on more than 3,600 screens, as did *Spider-Man* (2002). *Terminator 3: The Rise of the Machines* (2003), *Scorpion King* (2002) and *Monsters Inc.* (2001) played on more than 3,400 screens.

REFERENCES, MEANING, AND POSTMODERNISM

The Art of Allusion

Though exploitation films provided models for the new Hollywood, young filmmakers were equally drawn to the classics—the European art cinema, *Citizen Kane* (1941), popular American genres, film noir, and an emerging canon of filmmakers and films. Like Godard in *Breathless*, they refused to distinguish between high and low art, borrowing from both with equal abandon. Thus, *American Graffiti* looks back to AIP teen pics, but it also borrows crucial elements, including its basic plot, from Federico Fellini's *I Vitelloni* (1953). Fellini's semiautobiographical film tells the story of the mundane activities of adolescents living boring lives in a provincial Italian village and concludes with the hero's departure for a challenging future in the big city. At the end of *Graffiti*, its central character, Curt (Richard Dreyfuss), similarly escapes the deadening routine of small-town life in California and heads east to go to college. *Raiders of the Lost Ark* (1981) brought Saturday afternoon serials back to life, but it also invoked *Citizen Kane*, suggesting in its last shot that the lost ark is as ultimately unattainable as was Rosebud.

Hitchcock, Hawks, and Ford inspired filmmakers, who patterned their own films after the films of these American masters. *Rear Window* (Hitchcock, 1954), for example, served as the source of Michelangelo Antonioni's *Blow-Up* (1966); Hitchcock's story of voyeurism in Greenwich Village and Antonioni's investigation of perception and photographic truth in London informed Coppola's study of surveillance in San Francisco, *The Conversation* (1974); and all three provided the background for De Palma's thriller about an accidental eavesdropper in *Blow Out* (1981). *The Searchers* (Ford, 1956), *Vertigo* (Hitchcock, 1958), *Rio Bravo* (Hawks, 1959), *Psycho* (Hitchcock, 1960), and *The Birds* (Hitchcock, 1963) served as central texts to which student filmmakers repeatedly alluded, quoted from, or copied. John Carpenter's *Assault on Precinct 13* (1976), which depicts a desolate Los Angeles police station besieged by scores of terrorists, reworked the plots of both *Rio Bravo*, in which John Wayne defends his jail against a gang of gunslingers, and *The Birds*, in which birds attack a California community and trap the film's central characters in their house.

For his part, Woody Allen acknowledged the influence of Ingmar Bergman (*Interiors*, 1978), Federico Fellini (*Stardust Memories*, 1980), Humphrey Bogart and *Casablanca* (*Play It Again, Sam*, 1972), the phenomenon of moviegoing (*The Purple Rose of Cairo*, 1985) and the Hollywood musical (*Everyone Says I Love You*, 1996). Even producers became idols of younger directors. Spielberg, for example, fancied himself as the new Disney. *E.T.* (1982) is filled with repeated allusions to Disney's *Mary Poppins*; *Close Encounters* looks back to the "Night on Bald Mountain" sequence from *Fantasia* (1940) and concludes with Jiminy Cricket's rendition of "When You Wish upon a Star" from *Pinocchio* (1940). *The Color Purple* (1987) borrows from the visual landscape and overall look of Disney's Uncle Remus narrative, *The Song of the South* (1946). *Hook* (1991) lays bare Spielberg's own Peter Pan complex and solidifies his identity as the child of Disney.

De Palma and Hitchcock

In *Sisters* (1973), Brian De Palma borrowed extensively from *Rear Window* and *Psycho*. Like the James Stewart character in the former film, De Palma's heroine sees a murder committed by her neighbor across the courtyard and spends the rest of the film trying to prove it. The killer turns out to be a Norman Bates–type psychopath who murders men to whom she is attracted. De Palma's *Obsession* (1976), based on a script by Paul Schrader, combined *Vertigo* with *The Searchers*. Its hero (Cliff Robertson) watches helplessly as his wife and daughter are first kidnapped, then (apparently) killed in an explosion. Like the Stewart character

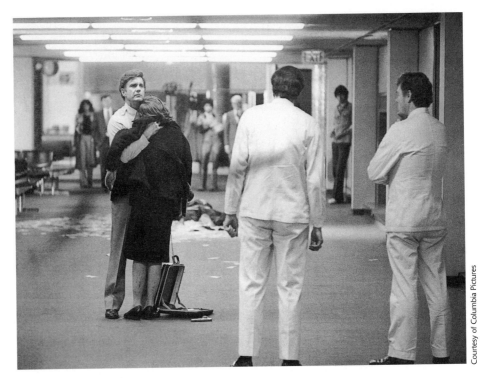

Courtesy of Columbia Pictures

At the end of *Obsession,* this remake of *Vertigo* turns into a remake of *The Searchers*: Michael Courtland (Cliff Robertson) is reunited with his lost daughter (Genevieve Bujold) at the airport.

in *Vertigo* after Madeleine's (Kim Novak's) supposed death, Robertson is traumatized by what he sees, and his recovery consists of remaking a woman who resembles his wife into the image of his wife. Like his counterpart in *Vertigo,* he remains unaware that this woman is actually his daughter ("Madeleine," in the Hitchcock film).

The Searchers comes to the rescue of this semi-incestuous melodrama in the form of a final scene in which the hero, like the John Wayne character in the famous Ford Western, recognizes the woman as his long-lost daughter and lifts her into his arms. De Palma's obsession with Hitchcock, to whose films the younger director repeatedly alluded, extended to imitations of specific shots—such as the 360-degree, circular tracking shot from *Vertigo* that crops up in *Obsession* and *Carrie* (both 1976) and even in *The Untouchables* (1987). For De Palma, the borrowing of this shot enabled him to adopt the stylistic mask of another, behind which he could hide. In effect, De Palma does not speak directly to his audiences but instead communicates *through* Hitchcock. Of all the movie brats (that is, the generation of filmmakers who grew up watching old movies on television, in repertory houses, or in film school), De Palma proves to be the most postmodern, though they are all—in varying degrees—products of the postmodern era.

"The Failure of the New"

As the work of Fredric Jameson suggests, American cinema of the 1970s was a postmodern phenomenon that reflected the sense of alienation and fragmentation brought about by late capitalism. For Jameson, contemporary consumer society possesses a culture that is postmodern. By that he means that postmodernism not only comes after modernism but arises in reaction to it. Modernist art works, such as those by James Joyce, T. S. Eliot, and Igor Stravinsky, responded to the advent of the machine age and mass society, which threatened the uniqueness of the individual with the anonymity of mass production and mass consumption by asserting the integrity and creativity of the artist. Revolting against tradition, modernist artists sought to say something new and different, to be original in a world dominated by mechanical reproduction(s). Postmodernism represents a reaction to the canonization of modernist aesthetics. It refuses to make the traditional distinctions drawn by modernists and premodernists between high culture and popular culture. In the Metropolitan Museum of Art sequence in *Dressed to Kill* (1980), for example, De Palma, as J. Hoberman pointed out, alluded to high art in the form of German Symbolist painter Max Klinger's "Glove" series and popular art through a reference to Hitchcock's *Vertigo* (1958). De Palma's heroine (Angie Dickinson) is framed looking at an Alex Katz portrait of a woman in yellow in a composition that duplicates that of Hitchcock's Madeleine looking at a portrait of Carlotta. At the end of the sequence, De Palma duplicated Plate 2 from Klinger's "Glove" series, as the hand of an unseen man picks up a glove dropped by Dickinson.

In terms of stylistic practices, postmodern artists rely on *pastiche*, a form of imitation of the unique style or content of earlier works that lacks any trace of the satire or parody that characterizes traditional forms of imitation. Pastiche is an entirely *neutral* practice: it conveys no perceptible attitude towards the original. De Palma's Hitchcockian stylistics, such as his 360-degree tracking shots, are a form of pastiche. They are expressionless imitations of shots that were highly charged with romantic feeling in Hitchcock.

Postmodern works also acknowledge the primary obstacle confronting contemporary artists—the inability to say anything that has not already been said. If traditional filmmakers such as D. W. Griffith, Alfred Hitchcock, or Orson Welles invented ways of expressing ideas through the medium of the cinema, postmodern directors such as Brian De Palma could only draw on a pre-existent dictionary of shots, character types, situations, themes, and meanings to express themselves. The authentic expression of ideas in the past has thus given way to quotation and allusion to that authentic expression.

Schizophrenia and Incoherence

Jameson relates this inability to be original, which he refers to as "the failure of the new," to another feature of postmodernism—nostalgia for the past. Nostalgia films such as *American Graffiti* (1973) return spectators from the incoherence of the present to the coherence of the past. In this idyllic past, the self was

Spencer Museum of Art, University of Kansas, Museum purchase:
Latha Churchill Walkes Memorial Art Fund

In the Metropolitan Museum of Art sequence of *Dressed to Kill,* DePalma alludes to Max Klinger's "Glove" series (right) with a shot of an unidentified hand picking up the heroine's glove in the foreground as she gets into a cab in the background (below).

Courtesy Cinema 77 Films/Filmways Pictures

whole, not fragmented as it is today, and unified with, not alienated from, a larger community. Postmodern works reflect the schizophrenic breakdown of the normal experience of the world as a continuous, coherent, and meaningful phenomenon. As Jameson says, these works consist of a series of "isolated, disconnected, discontinuous material signifiers which fail to link up into a coherent sequence." Postmodern artists thus convey the incoherence that informs the social and cultural reality of contemporary experience.

Certain aspects of Terrence Malick's *Badlands* (1973), an outlaw-couple film based on the real-life 1950s killing spree of Charles Starkweather and his girl-friend, Carol Ann Fugate, capture this sense of incoherence. The voiceover narration by the film's heroine (Sissy Spacek) fails to cohere or make sense of the events seen onscreen. And Malick's distanced, observational, nonjudgmental perspective (which includes extended descriptive passages featuring inanimate objects, plants, and animals) refuses to submit itself to the traditional logic of discrete causes that produce specific effects. More obviously, the temporal and narrative discontinuity of films such as *Taxi Driver* (1976), *Looking for Mr. Good-bar* (1977), and *Cruising* (1980) prompt Robin Wood to label them "incoherent texts." Unlike classical cinema, which gives a definite order to experience, these works capture the chaotic spirit of their times. As works that did not know what they wanted to say, they simply reflected the cultural conditions that produced them.

A Postmodern Case Study: *Taxi Driver*

A certain level of incoherence, for example, lies at the heart of *Taxi Driver*, embodied in its central character, Travis Bickle (Robert De Niro). Much as Travis's own goals and desires remain unclear and confused, so does the audience's understanding of and attitude toward the character. What does Travis want? The untouchable blonde "angel," Betsy (Cybill Shepherd), whom he irrationally takes to a porno movie on their first big date? The child prostitute, Iris (Jody Foster), whom he attempts to reform? If he hates the filth of the city and speaks of washing the scum off the streets, why is the target of his assassination attempt the populist politician who has promised to clean up the city? Why does Travis suddenly switch his intended target, killing Iris's pimp instead of the politician?

The incoherence of the character carries over to the audience. Spectators remain uncertain as to whether Travis's "rescue" of Iris at the end of the film, which is accomplished by his brutal murder of her pimp and two of his associates, is to be understood as heroic, as the verbal accounts of it in the press suggest, or disturbingly psychopathic, as Scorsese's filming of the sequence implies. Travis emerges as the enigmatic product of the various incoherences in the world around him. The film captures the plight of the alienated individual in contemporary consumer society. Surrounded by the conflicting messages of politicians, pimps, and the media, engulfed by filth, crime, and corruption, he attempts to play the part of the old-fashioned Western hero whose decisive actions would set things right. But traditional heroism is no longer possible in his world; he can only play the part of a somewhat dubious antihero who lashes out at the most obvious and immediate target he can find.

Films such as *Taxi Driver* expose the contradictions that informed 1970s America, describing the conditions that produced phenomena such as Vietnam (Travis is a Vietnam veteran) and Watergate (the film's politician would say or do anything to get elected), but refusing to understand or make sense of those

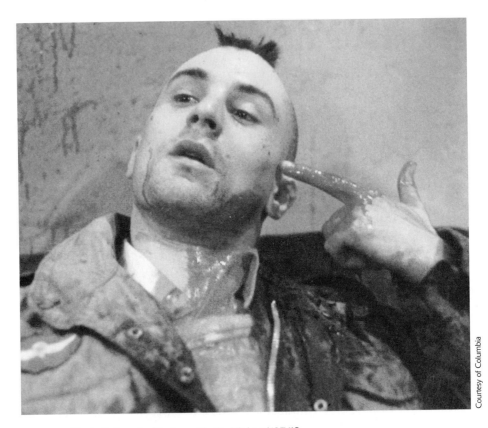

Courtesy of Columbia

What does Travis (Robert De Niro) want in *Taxi Driver* (1976)?

conditions. The film struck a nerve in middle America. One of its repeat view-ers was John Hinckley, the ultimate incoherent spectator, who fell in love with Jodie Foster and shot the politician, President Ronald Reagan, rather than the pimp, in an attempt to rewrite the film and give it a better (that is, more coher-ent) ending. Or perhaps, like Travis, all he wanted to do was get the attention of a girl (Jodie Foster for Hinckley; Betsy for Travis).

REASSURANCE: COMFORT, COMICS, AND NOSTALGIA

A Return to Innocence

Not all 1970s film-school generation films exposed incoherence. A number of them responded differently. As Wood argues, they "papered over the cracks" instead. If Scorsese enjoyed a modest success at the box office describing the alienation and blankness of American identity in the post-Vietnam, post-Watergate, postindustrial, postmodern era of the mid-1970s, then others reaped hitherto unimaginable rewards by returning to a less-troubled, pre-Vietnam, pre-Watergate world when America was still living in relative sociopolitical innocence. *Taxi Driver* earned a paltry $12.6 million; but *American Graffiti*, set in 1962—before the assassination of the Kennedys and King, before the national agony of Vietnam, and before the political cynicism of Watergate—grossed $55.6 million.

   Raiders of the Lost Ark ($282 million) returned us to the innocent action serials of the 1930s and 1940s and restored moral clarity to the screen; we forgot the confusing morality of Vietnam and went back to the clear-cut villainy of Nazis. *Close Encounters* ($128 million) encouraged us to regress to the status of children—to play with our food, indulge our whims and obsessions, and engage in a childlike state of wonder. Indeed, the most characteristic image in a Spielberg film turned out to be that of the rapt face of a child looking up in awe (at a UFO, an extra-terrestrial, or some other marvel)—a look duplicating that of the audience, spellbound in darkness, as it looked up at the screen on which a spectacle of special effects was displayed. *Star Wars* ($460.9 million) was set in a universe "far, far" away and "long, long" ago and, like *Raiders,* evoked the

Photofest

Spielberg's sense of wonder dominates *Close Encounters of the Third Kind* (1977): Melinda Dillon and Carey Guffey stare at offscreen alien activities.

bygone pleasures of children's Saturday matinees at the movies. It also restored the clear-cut distinctions between heroes and villains that had become obscured in post–World War II American cinema. The storm troopers of the (evil) Empire are dressed in Nazi-style uniforms, while Han Solo (Harrison Ford) wears the vest, holster, and boots of a cowboy hero.

Opposing Visions

Scorsese is one of the few directors to foreground the predicament of the modern individual cut adrift from traditional forms of identity construction and confirmation through reaffirming institutions such as the family and the community. Instead, his films explore the disintegration and fragmentation of any sense of a coherent self. The extreme close-up of an Alka Seltzer tablet dissolving in a glass of water in *Taxi Driver* is emblematic of the status of identity in his work as a whole. His characters, who mirror the doubts and confusions of their time, have no unified sense of who they are. Travis and prizefighter Jake La Motta (*Raging Bull*, 1980) are problematically split or divided characters, who, quite symbolically, talk to themselves in mirrors. In *Goodfellas* (1990), Henry Hill, who wants to be a somebody rather than a nobody, models his identity on that of the colorful gangsters who lived and worked in his neighborhood when he was a kid. But this identity proves to be more fantasy than fact, and it slowly disintegrates over the course of the film until Henry returns to the status of a nobody, living anonymously in the witness protection program in the suburbs.

The Dalai Lama in *Kundun* (1997) is alienated and exiled, presented as a figure unable to fulfill his preordained role in life. Like Travis Bickle in *Taxi Driver*, Frank Pierce, the hero of *Bringing Out the Dead* (1999), a paramedic assigned to ambulance duty, wanders the streets of New York City in search of spiritual salvation. And *Gangs of New York* (2002), which celebrates the birth of American identity in Civil War–era New York City, traces that identity to its contradictory origins in the struggle between different generations of immigrants, one largely Protestant and the other mostly Catholic.

Unlike Scorsese, Lucas and Spielberg give us psychologically noncomplex, comic-book characters. They all know who they are. At the same time, they emerge as decisive individuals such as the Richard Dreyfuss characters in *Graffiti, Jaws,* and *Close Encounters,* who are obsessed by blondes in white T-birds, sharks, and UFOs, respectively. Luke Skywalker (Mark Hamill) may not know that Darth Vader is his father or that Princess Leia (Carrie Fisher) is his sister, but he doesn't agonize over who he is, either. He knows, after all, that he is destined to become a Jedi knight and help destroy the Empire. And even if some of Lucas's or Spielberg's characters initially appear indecisive (like the Dreyfuss characters in *Graffiti* and *Close Encounters*), by the end of the films they have definitely discovered who they are and what they want. They not only have it all, but, unlike Henry Hill, they keep it all.

In other words, in the mid- to late 1970s and in the 1980s, the films that proved to be most successful financially were those that reassured rather than disturbed the public. Vietnam, Watergate, and the sociopolitical agenda of 1970s activist America disappeared beneath the surface of the more positive images of an idealized past—of the 1930s, 1940s, or 1950s.

Back in Time

The 1980s saw a nostalgia craze for the 1950s in the form of revivals of 1950s music, fashion, and lifestyles. Teenagers even rediscovered certain 1960s groups such as the Beatles, though the songs that proved most popular tended to be pre–*Sergeant Pepper* (1967). *Grease,* a teen musical set in the 1950s, emerged as the big movie hit of 1978, grossing over $96 million ($188 million after its rerelease in 1998). A few years later, Michael J. Fox, as Marty McFly, took us *Back to the Future* (1985) in one of the first of a series of time-travel films that exploited the nostalgia craze. In this first of what would prove to be (so far) three *Back to the Future* films, the hero returns to the innocence of Eisenhower America in the 1950s.

Taking note of the success of this film, which originally earned $105 million ($208 million through 2003), Coppola sent Kathleen Turner back to the 1950s to relive her life as a teenager, rethink her subsequent life, and reemerge with renewed hope for the future, in *Peggy Sue Got Married* (1986). In both films, the 1950s becomes the site of utopian communities, of baby-boomer Shangri-Las dominated by wholesome values associated with family and community that had somehow disappeared in succeeding decades. Frank Capra's *Lost Horizon* (1937) had sought a populist paradise amid the turmoil of the Depression and prewar years that would provide a retreat for Americans during the chaotic period in which American national identity shifted from an agrarian to a corporate base. Nostalgia films of the late 1970s and 1980s performed a similar function, providing a return to a bygone era that had become identified in contemporary culture with more innocent, happier days.

This was accomplished, in part, by invoking the popular culture of that earlier era, especially its music and its films. Films such as *Peggy Sue, Stand by Me* (1986), *La Bamba* (1987), *Hairspray* (1988), *Sea of Love* (1989), *Great Balls of Fire!* (1989), and *Pretty Woman* (1990) borrowed their titles (and title songs) from 1950s and 1960s rock-and-roll songs, though not all of them are set in the 1950s. Starting with *American Graffiti* (1973) and continuing through *The Big Chill* (1983); *Baby, It's You* (1983); *The Flamingo Kid* (1984); *Dirty Dancing* (1987); *Mermaids* (1990); and *Goodfellas* (1990), more and more films immersed audiences in 1950s and early-1960s music. Fifties' style rock-and-roll songs on the sound track began to function more like a traditional song and dance sequence in a Hollywood musical, serving as an escape from the mundane realities of the present into a more ideal realm associated with the past. Thus, Matthew Broderick's rendition of "Twist and Shout" serves as a utopian centerpiece in *Ferris Bueller's Day Off* (1986), bringing together a community of like-minded rockers who parade together with the hero. And the use of the Righteous Brothers' 1965 version of "Unchained Melody" as the lovers' song in *Ghost* (1990) links their relationship with romantic excesses that more properly belong to their (and post-Watergate America's) youthful past.

Returning to the past: Matthew Broderick sings "Twist and Shout" as the title character in *Ferris Bueller's Day Off* (1986).

Contradictory Impulses

Ironically, the motion pictures to which nostalgia films refer are often less than utopian in their representation of their own times; more often than not, they reflect the contradictory forces that produced them. *Who Framed Roger Rabbit?* (1988) and *L.A. Confidential* (1997) employ the stylistic characteristics of film noir (and of *Chinatown,* 1974) to identify the films' temporal setting as that of the 1940s and 1950s, respectively. Noir lighting also proves appropriate to the murder mystery storyline featuring the investigations of private eye Eddie Valiant (Bob Hoskins) and of police officers Bud White (Russell Crowe) and Ed Exley (Guy Pearce). But the elements of film noir used here no longer convey the profound existential anxiety and social alienation experienced by the individual in postwar America. They function merely as an allusion to these earlier periods rather than as a reflection or expression of them. By the same token, nostalgia films that invoke the 1950s (*Pleasantville,* 1998) ignore the social turmoil that creeps into that era's sex comedies (see Chapter 8), Westerns (see Chapter 10), melodramas, and other genre pictures. Instead, they tend to cast those periods as more or less idyllic. They become projections of contemporary nostalgia for the 1950s rather than reflections of the actual 1950s.

In another version of the time-travel motif, the future comes back in time to fix the present, which poses a threat to future civilizations. In this scenario, the 1980s are rewritten according to the needs of a larger, utopian project. But what informs both kinds of film is a form of wish fulfillment that denies the present and rewrites the past. The first two *Terminator* films (1984, 1991) attempt to provide an escape from the future consequences of past actions by sending agents of the future back into the past to change history. In *Star Trek IV: The Voyage Home* (1986), Captain Kirk (William Shatner) and his crew go back in time to 1980s San Francisco to retrieve a species of whale that has become extinct in the future and that promises to save the Earth from destruction by potential alien invaders. Finally, in *Bill & Ted's Excellent Adventure* (1989), rock-and-rollers from the future dispatch an agent (George Carlin) back to 1980s San Dimas, California, to prevent Bill and Ted (the Wyld Stallyns) from flunking their high school history examination. Their would-be failure threatens to change the course of future civilization, which is rooted in the vision brought about by Bill and Ted's music. Their time travel through past history in a telephone booth enables them to bring back Socrates, Genghis Khan, Napoleon, Joan of Arc, Beethoven, Abraham Lincoln, Billy the Kid, and Sigmund Freud as show-and-tell to their final examination, thus guaranteeing not only that they will pass the course but also that inhabitants of the future will "be excellent" to one another. In *Austin Powers: The Spy Who Shagged Me* (1999), Powers (Mike Myers) travels back in time to the 1960s to fight his nemesis, Dr. Evil (also Myers).

THE BRAT PACK

One film of the 1980s that looks back to the 1950s and 1960s introduced a new generation of actors—"the brat pack"—semitough teens who band together (at least onscreen) in packs and who would prove to upstage and outgross at the box office the earlier generation of directors known as "the movie brats." The film was *The Outsiders* (1983). It was based on an S. E. Hinton novel and directed by an original movie brat, Francis Ford Coppola. It starred Emilio (*Repo Man*, 1984; *Stakeout*, 1987) Estevez, Rob (*St. Elmo's Fire*, 1985; *Austin Powers: The Spy Who Shagged Me*, 1999) Lowe, C. Thomas (*Soul Man*, 1986) Howell, Matt (*The Flamingo Kid*, 1984; *There's Something about Mary*, 1998) Dillon, Ralph (*The Karate Kid*, 1984) Macchio, Patrick (*Dirty Dancing*, 1987; *Ghost*, 1990; *Point Break*, 1991) Swayze, and Tom (*Top Gun*, 1986; *Rain Man*, 1988; *Eyes Wide Shut*, 1999) Cruise. Actually, the brat-pack phenomenon began several years earlier with the release of two films about troubled teens—Jonathan Kaplan's *Over the Edge* (1979), starring Matt Dillon and Vincent Spano; and Tim Hunter's *Tex* (1982) with Dillon, Estevez, and Meg Tilly, which is also based on an S. E. Hinton novel.

The brat pack expanded its circle of members in films such as the sequel to *The Outsiders*—*Rumble Fish* (1983), another Hinton/Coppola effort, starring Dillon, Mickey Rourke, Vincent Spano, Nicholas Cage, and Christopher Penn. It grew further with *Sixteen Candles* (1984), starring Molly Ringwald; and *The Breakfast Club* (1985), with Ringwald, Estevez, Judd Nelson, and Ally Sheedy. By

The brat pack: *The Outsiders* (1983) grouped together (from left to right) future teen stars Emilio Estevez, Rob Lowe, C. Thomas Howell, Matt Dillon, Ralph Macchio, Patrick Swayze, and Tom Cruise.

Courtesy of Zoetrope

the late 1980s, members of the brat pack, who had initially represented the rise of a new movement in the group performance—that is, ensemble, nonstar acting—had themselves become individual stars performing in vehicles designed especially for them.

THE REAGAN YEARS

"This Time Do We Get to Win?"

If the low-budget exploitation films of the late 1960s and early 1970s captured the chaotic temper of the times, then the big-budget exploitation films of the 1980s reflected the new conservatism of Reaganite America. A handful of films and filmmakers resisted this reactionary tide, but, with the exception of Oliver Stone's war film *Platoon* (1986), which earned $137.9 million and wound up in the top-150 all-time box-office champs, they failed to match the success of the more conservative, mainstream films at the box office. For every *Platoon*, there were a couple of *Rambos* and three or four *Rockys*. As for Stone, he was the exception that proved the rule. He took film courses taught by Scorsese at NYU. He not only refused to paper over the cracks introduced into the American psyche during the 1960s and early 1970s, but he also spent the 1980s with his head firmly planted in the 1960s. A Vietnam veteran, he made not only *Platoon* but also *Born on the Fourth of July* (1989) and *Heaven & Earth* (1993). In the 1990s, he continued to look back to the dark side of the 1960s—to Jim Morrison's rise, decline, and death in *The Doors* (1991) and Kennedy's assassination in *JFK* (1991).

Rambo: First Blood Part II (1985) epitomized the new conservatism, which was based, in part, on the desire to rewrite the recent past and put a positive face on our nation's more negative experiences. Sent on a mission to rescue American prisoners of war held captive in Southeast Asia, Sylvester Stallone's John Rambo, referring to the original Vietnam conflict, asks his superior, "This time do we get to win?" The plot of the film is a symbolic reworking of the American right wing's perception of the war—Rambo's mission is undermined by political bureaucrats, military brass, and the CIA, who don't want him to win. If America lost the Vietnam war back in 1975 on both the military and political fronts, Rambo won it for us in the mid-1980s, single-handedly killing hundreds of the enemy and rescuing a chopperful of American MIAs. President Ronald Reagan led the cheering section for the film. After Lebanese terrorists released 39 American hostages, Reagan declared, "I saw *Rambo* last night. I know what to do the next time this happens."

A similar sort of heroic defiance lies at the heart of the *Rocky* series (1976, 1979, 1982, 1985, 1990), though in these films it is not so much history that is being reversed as the fortunes of the underdog. Through hard work, exhaustive physical training, and a tenacious determination to win, Rocky Balboa's lower-class, down-and-out prizefighter battles against all odds to win fight after fight and to prove, contrary to whatever Scorsese might have suggested in *Raging Bull*, that the American dream still works. Unfortunately, as Robin Wood has suggested, this dream is bound up with certain reactionary values, including racism and sexism. White racists cheered as Rocky, the Italian Stallion, went the distance with the champion Apollo Creed (Carl Weathers) in the first film; and although Rocky and Apollo become friends in subsequent films in the series, Apollo plays the acknowledged inferior sidekick to Rocky's obviously superior ethnic hero. If boxing history sees Rocky's prototype, Rocky Marciano, eclipsed by black heavyweights such as Floyd Patterson, Sonny Liston, Joe Frazier, and Muhammed Ali (on whom the character of Apollo was based), the movies reverse that chronology, making Rocky the great white hope of the 1980s.

Physical Culture: Biology as Destiny

Muscle men Stallone and Arnold Schwarzenegger emerged as the ultimate figures of male adolescent fantasy in the 1980s. These He-Men of the Universe provided a form of bodily spectacle and visual pleasure that answered the growing obsession with technology and special effects that dominated the science-fiction film. Rambo returns us to basics; he dresses like a Native American and his chief weapon is an enormous knife. With these simple tools, he takes on the superior technology of the enemy. Rocky merely uses his fists. Schwarzenegger's initial success as *Conan the Barbarian* (1982) and *Conan the Destroyer* (1984) depends, in part, on his swordplay. And as the Terminator, Schwarzenegger comes into the world unarmed and naked, although he is a high-tech cyborg. Special effects enhance the *Terminator* films, but it should not go unnoticed that when Arnold finally gets to play the good guy in *Terminator 2* (1991), his Terminator is technologically inferior to (and thus more human than) his liquid metal antagonist. Rooted in the most rudimentary form of the celebration of the individual—the fetishization of the (male) body—the new conservatism of the 1980s elevated biology to the status of destiny. Both success and survival depended more on physical might than political, social, or economic right. The rugged individualist ruled.

ANOTHER GENERATION

The 1980s witnessed the advent of a new generation of filmmakers. Lucas, Spielberg, De Palma, and Scorsese continued to make films inspired, directly or indirectly, by Hollywood in its heyday. Coppola also continued to work, although his films proved less successful. But they had been joined by a new wave of directors, screenwriters, and actors who were the products of a different cultural experience. A number of the hot new directors, including Martin (*Beverly Hills Cop*, 1984) Brest, John (*Die Hard*, 1988) McTiernan, Spike (*Do the Right Thing*, 1989) Lee, Joel (*Miller's Crossing*, 1990) Coen, Susan (*Desperately Seeking Susan*, 1985) Seidelman, Alex (*Repo Man*, 1984) Cox, Penelope (*Wayne's World*, 1992) Spheeris, and John (*Boyz N the Hood*, 1991) Singleton, went to film school. But they did not grow up, as the earlier generation of movie brats had, on the films of the 1950s, nor did their films contain extensive allusions to earlier American cinema. Indeed, they didn't have the same sort of unlimited access to old Hollywood movies enjoyed by these earlier directors. In the 1970s, commercial television had more or less abandoned old films in favor of made-for-TV movies. When this new crop of directors did pay homage to the past, they tended to cite the seminal works of their own youth, such as television sitcoms, rather than films like *The Searchers*, which their predecessors had seen a generation earlier in movie theaters. At the same time, the new generation of audiences grew up on sitcoms and made-for-TV movies rather than on the classic films of the 1950s. Their expectations of what the cinema could be tended to be radically different from those of their parents.

Laverne and Shirley, a spin-off of *Happy Days* (which was itself a TV adaptation of Lucas's *American Graffiti*), became the source for a series of gags in films such as Spheeris's *Wayne's World*, while one of the sitcom's stars, Penny Marshall, brought her TV experience to bear on her direction of successful screen comedies such as *Big* (1988), *A League of Their Own* (1992) and *Renaissance Man*

(1994), and melodramas such as *Awakenings* (1990) and *Riding in Cars with Boys* (2001). Other young directors, such as Tim (*Batman,* 1989) Burton, Ivan (*Ghostbusters,* 1984) Reitman, James (*The Terminator*) Cameron, and Chris (*Home Alone,* 1990) Columbus, not only lacked formal training in film school but also betrayed few, if any, classical influences on their work. By the mid-1980s, the fascination with the cinema of studio-era 1930s to 1950s Hollywood that had inspired the French New Wave and the original film school generation had dissipated. Film schools no longer produced would-be Hitchcocks, Hawkses, and Fords. They found that their students wanted to be Lucases, Spielbergs, Coppolas, and Scorseses. Hitchcock, Hawks, and Ford had all died in the 1970s, becoming history in the most negative sense of the term. Young filmmakers found they had little patience for the films of D. W. Griffith, F. W. Murnau, Ernst Lubitsch, Frank Capra, Ford, Hawks, or even Hitchcock, who belonged to earlier eras when films were silent, black-and-white, or both.

At the same time, the demands of the marketplace became more and more constrictive. Negative costs escalated and exhibition and distribution strategies became more and more geared toward the new techniques of exploitation marketing. Though everyone wanted to make a new *Citizen Kane,* they also wanted it to gross $100 million or more, wanted to make a bundle on T-shirts and tie-ins, and hoped to be immortalized by having their film transformed into a ride at Disneyland, Disney World, or Universal Studio Tours. Contemporary Hollywood stopped looking to the past and began to look to its future—to cable television sales, video sales and rentals, network broadcasts, and syndication. In other words, filmmakers who had been raised on television began to look *through* television for their audiences. Since the great majority of the viewers of their films would see them in one form or another on the tube, more and more films began to define themselves in relation to the contemporary world of television rather than to the suddenly old-fashioned world of film. By the 1980s, the continuity of the Hollywood tradition had begun to fall apart. Each new film existed in an aesthetic vacuum, though it continued to compete with the box-office statistics of its predecessors. Audiences who expected little were enthralled by the little they got. And they had even less with which to compare. If you have never seen *Intolerance, Sunrise, Citizen Kane, The Searchers,* or *Vertigo,* you can't expect more than *Cocktail* or *Tequila Sunrise* (both 1988).

CREDITS: THE FILM SCHOOL GENERATION AND THEIR FILMS

American Film Institute Center (AFI) for Advanced Film Studies served as a training ground for young filmmakers such as these:

Martin Brest (*Beverly Hills Cop, Midnight Run, Meet Joe Black*)
Caleb Deschanel (*The Black Stallion, The Right Stiff, The Natural*)

Amy Heckerling (*Fast Times at Ridgemont High, Look Who's Talking, Clueless*)
Tim Hunter (*Tex, River's Edge*)
Jeremy Paul Kagan (*The Chosen, The Adventures of Natty Gann*)
David Lynch (*Eraserhead, The Elephant Man, Blue Velvet, Mulholland Dr.*)
Terrence Malick (*Badlands, Days of Heaven, The Thin Red Line*)
John McTiernan (*Die Hard, The Hunt for Red October, The Thomas Crown Affair*)
Tom Rickman (*Coal Miner's Daughter*)
Matthew Robbins (*The Sugarland Express, Batteries Not Included*)
Paul Schrader (*Taxi Driver, Hardcore, Mishima, Light Sleeper, Affliction*)
Ed Zwick (*Glory, Courage Under Fire, The Siege*)

New York University (NYU) has produced others, such as the following:

Joel Coen (*Blood Simple, Barton Fink, Fargo, O Brother, Where Art Thou?*)
Jonathan Kaplan (*White Line Fever, The Accused, Unlawful Entry*)
Spike Lee (*Do the Right Thing, Jungle Fever, Malcolm X, Get on the Bus, Bamboozled*)
Martin Scorsese (*Taxi Driver, Raging Bull, Goodfellas, Gangs of New York*)
Susan Seidelman (*Desperately Seeking Susan, Making Mr. Right*)

The University of California at Los Angeles (UCLA) educated the following filmmakers:

Carroll Ballard (*The Black Stallion*)
Paul Bartel (*Eating Raoul, Scenes From the Class Struggle in Beverly Hills*)
Charles Burnett (*Killer of Sheep, To Sleep With Anger, The Glass Shield*)
Francis Ford Coppola (*The Godfather, The Conversation, Apocalypse Now, Bram Stoker's Dracula*)
Alex Cox (*Sid and Nancy, Repo Man*)
Colin Higgins (*The Best Little Whorehouse in Texas, Foul Play, 9 to 5*)
Gloria Katz (*American Graffiti*)
Paul Schrader (see AFI)
Penelope Spheeris (*The Decline of Western Civilization II, Wayne's World, Senseless*)

Alumni of the University of Southern California (USC) include these filmmakers:

Hal Barwood (*Sugarland Express*)
Ben Burtt (*Star Wars*)
John Carpenter (*Halloween, Escape From New York, They Live, Vampires*)
Walter Hill (*48 Hours, The Warriors, Wild Bill, Last Man Standing*)
Willard Huyck (*American Graffiti, Howard the Duck*)
Irwin Kershner (*The Eyes of Laura Mars, The Empire Strikes Back*)
Randal Kleiser (*Grease; The Blue Lagoon; Honey, I Blew Up the Kids*)
Gary Kurtz (*Star Wars, The Empire Strikes Back*)
Michael Lehmann (*Heathers, Hudson Hawk*)
George Lucas (*American Graffiti, Star Wars*)

Paul Mazursky (*Bob & Carol & Ted & Alice, Down and Out in Beverly Hills*)
John Milius (*Conan the Barbarian, The Wind and the Lion*)
Walter Murch (*The Conversation, Apocalypse Now, Return to Oz*)
Kevin Reynolds (*Robin Hood: Prince of Thieves*)
John Singleton (*Boyz N the Hood, Poetic Justice, Rosewood*)
Robert Zemeckis (*Romancing the Stone, Back to the Future, Who Framed Roger Rabbit?, Forrest Gump, Contact, What Lies Beneath, Cast Away*)

■ ■ ■ SELECT FILMOGRAPHY

The Last Picture Show (1971)	*Star Wars* (1977)
The Godfather (1972)	*Grease* (1978)
American Graffiti (1973)	*Apocalypse Now* (1979)
The Conversation (1974)	*The Empire Strikes Back* (1980)
Jaws (1975)	*Dressed to Kill* (1980)
Assault on Precinct 13 (1976)	*Raiders of the Lost Ark* (1981)
Carrie (1976)	*Rambo: First Blood Part II* (1985)
Taxi Driver (1976)	*Platoon* (1986)
Close Encounters of the Third Kind (1977)	

■ ■ ■ SELECT BIBLIOGRAPHY

BYRON, STUART. "Industry," *Film Comment* **16,** no. 1 (January–February 1980): 38–39.

CAGIN, SETH, and PHILIP DRAY. *Hollywood Films of the Seventies: Sex, Drugs, Violence, Rock 'n Roll and Politics.* New York: Harper & Row, 1984.

CARROLL, NOEL. "The Future of Allusion: Hollywood in the Seventies (and Beyond)," *October* **20** (Spring 1982): 51–81.

COOK, DAVID A. *Lost Illusions: American Cinema in the Shadow of Watergate and Vietnam, 1970–1979.* New York: Charles Scribner's Sons, 2000.

CORLISS, RICHARD. "The Seventies: The New Conservatism," *Film Comment* **16,** no. 1 (January–February 1980): 34–38.

HOBERMAN, J. "De Palma: Dazzling," *Village Voice* July 23–29, 1980): 42.

JACOBS, DIANE. *Hollywood Renaissance.* Cranbury, NJ: Barnes, 1977.

JAMESON, FREDRIC. "Postmodernism and Consumer Society," in Hal Foster, ed., *The Anti-Aesthetic.* Seattle: Bay Press, 1983.

MONACO, JAMES. *American Film Now.* New York: Oxford University Press, 1979.

PYE, MICHAEL, and LYNDA MYLES. *The Movie Brats: How the Film Generation Took Over Hollywood.* New York: Holt, 1979.

ROGIN, MICHAEL. *Ronald Reagan: The Movie.* Berkeley: University of California Press, 1987.

VON GUNDEN, KENNETH. *Postmodern Auteurs: Coppola, Lucas, De Palma, Spielberg and Scorsese.* Jefferson, NC: McFarland, 1991.

WOOD, ROBIN. *Hollywood from Vietnam to Reagan.* New York: Columbia University Press, 1986, rev. 2003.

CHAPTER **16**

Into the Twenty-First Century

CONTRADICTIONS:
FROM THE GIPPER TO *BLUE VELVET*

To some extent, the American cinema of the 1980s and early 1990s can be viewed in terms of the social, political, and cultural landscape of the Reagan–Bush and Bush–Quayle political administrations. "Reaganite" entertainment, as the films of this period have been dubbed, is, in part, a cinema of reassurance, optimism, and nostalgia—qualities embodied in the political persona of Ronald Reagan.

As Robin Wood has argued, national traumas of the 1970s, in particular the Vietnam War and Watergate, served to undermine public confidence in the nation's leaders. Reagan attempted to restore this lost confidence. He did this, in part, by encouraging Americans to forget Watergate and to view Vietnam less as a national defeat than as a failure in American resolve to win, caused, in part, by a loss of faith in traditional American values. Reagan represented a restoration of those values. As a public figure, he evoked an earlier, more innocent era of American social, political, and cultural identity with which he was himself, as a former movie star, identified. As "acting" president, Reagan created for himself a political persona that was built on his earlier screen persona and on the more immediate demands of rekindling popular trust in national leadership.

His screen persona was that of the optimist; the upwardly mobile, self-made man; the war hero; the rugged yet God-fearing individualist; the Western hero who dies saving the life of his best friend; and (offscreen) the dedicated anti-Communist. As a politician, Reagan even began to play the patriarch who, like Notre Dame football coach Knute Rockne (whom Pat O'Brien played opposite Reagan's George Gipp in *Knute Rockne, All American,* 1940), could charismatically rejuvenate the spirits of all Americans by imploring them (as Reagan repeatedly did in political speeches) "to win one for the Gipper." This persona is itself a product of the pre-Vietnam, pre-Watergate 1940s and 1950s when it was constructed. Reagan, as president, automatically evoked this earlier period for most Americans who grew up with him as a Hollywood movie star. To many, Reagan symbolized the 1950s—at least, the idyllic, small-town, 1950s Eisenhower America as it existed in the popular imagination. Thus, when Marty McFly (Michael J. Fox) time-travels back to 1955 in *Back to the Future* (1985), a Ronald Reagan Western, *Cattle Queen of Montana* (1954), is playing at the small downtown movie theater.

Reaganite cinema exploited many of the values and qualities that Reagan himself espoused, as well as the conservative concerns of an emerging new right—the young upwardly progressive professionals—the yuppies of the "me" generation. Indeed, one of the goals of Michael J. Fox (who starred as the young Republican Alex Keaton on a television sitcom, *Family Ties*) in the 1950s segment of *Back to the Future* is typical of the concerns associated with the me generation: he serves as a matchmaker between his future mom and dad and thus ensures his own birth.

Yet, the films of the 1980s and early 1990s cannot be identified entirely in terms of the policies of one or two particular political regimes. They also embraced major liberal countercurrents that undermined the conservative thrust associated with Reagan's agenda for handling foreign policy and domestic affairs. In fact, the Reaganite cinema that dominated the early 1980s seemed to spawn an oppositional cinema that set forth a dramatically different image of America in the late 1980s. During the middle of the decade, around the time of public disclosures concerning the Iran-Contra guns-for-hostages affair (1986), more and more films were being made in Hollywood that were increasingly skeptical of this Reaganite vision of America. They included films highly critical of life in 1980s, small-town America. Thus, David Lynch's *Blue Velvet* (1986) and his short-lived television series *Twin Peaks* (1989–1991) depicted a world of brutality, vice, and corruption that lay beneath the surface of everyday life in an apparently innocent and deceptively ordinary small town in middle America. The world that his characters inhabited was inane and absurd. Tim Hunter's *River's Edge* (1986), a chillingly distanced portrait of teenagers growing up in the

Reaganite cinema: Adapting himself to the 1950s, Marty McFly (Michael J. Fox) does his Chuck Berry imitation at a 1955 high school dance in *Back to the Future* (1985).

deadening atmosphere of contemporary American suburbs, looked at the boredom, the banality, and the selfish insensitivity that characterized the lives of a flaked-out, younger generation of lower-middle-class Americans who are not so much heroic rebels without a cause as dysfunctional misfits without feelings.

REAGANITE CINEMA: "MORNING IN AMERICA"

Regeneration

During his presidential campaigns, Ronald Reagan attacked the pessimism of his Democratic opponents; once elected, Reagan pronounced that the long night of Democratic misrule was over and that it was "morning in America."

This 1984 Republican campaign theme attempted to renew national identity and unity and tell Americans that they were about to witness a new beginning, an economic and spiritual rebirth. Reagan promised to bring America back to life, much as he himself had bounced back after John Hinckley's unsuccessful attempt to assassinate him in 1981. Reagan's own recovery served as a symbolic enactment of things to come; his presidency would make the light in the nation's heart go back on, much as it does near the end of *E.T.: The Extra-Terrestrial* (1982), when the sympathetic alien miraculously recovers from apparent death.

The notions of rejuvenation and starting over informed countless films of this period. In *Cocoon* (1985), three senior citizens in their seventies (that is, about Reagan's age) accidentally discover a fountain of youth in a Florida swimming pool where aliens have stored mysterious cocoons. The film, however, ultimately criticizes their desire for an unnatural, physical youth. The secret of rejuvenation, it insists, lies not in any fountain of youth but in spiritual renewal. In 1986, wealthy businessman Rodney Dangerfield goes *Back to School* where he enjoys a second childhood while attempting to provide a role model for his wayward son.

The rejuvenation theme even finds its way into a cold war science-fiction saga dealing with the threat of a nuclear holocaust. In *Star Trek II: The Wrath of Khan* (1982), "we" (i.e., the United States), including Admiral Kirk (William Shatner) and the crew of the starship Enterprise, battle "them" (i.e., the USSR), led by the vengeful Khan (Ricardo Montalban) who relies on Soviet-like mind-control techniques for possession of a missile-shaped device developed by the Genesis Project. If used properly (i.e., by us) and exploded on a dead planet, the Genesis Effect could transform the planet into a Garden of Eden; if the device falls into the wrong hands (i.e., the Russians) and is set off on an inhabited planet, it would do the same thing but would destroy all existing life in the process. Although Captain Spock (Leonard Nimoy) sacrifices his own life to save those of his comrades, the film concludes with a Reaganite happy ending—with the successful creation of a new world out of a barren, lifeless planet.

Nostalgia: Coming of Age in the Past

More often than not, new beginnings in Reaganite cinema involved a nostalgic return to the past. The magic of the movies enabled audiences to go back in time in an attempt to recover the small-town, affluent American paradise of the Eisenhower era, before poverty, crime, homelessness, and the demise of both the family and the community began to erode the American dream. Indeed, much of Reagan's domestic economic policy looked back to an even earlier era—to that of the Calvin Coolidge administration in the 1920s, when "the business of America was business." At any rate, a number of films, in particular the highly successful *Back to the Future* series (1985, 1989, 1990) and *Peggy Sue Got Married* (1986), feature characters who return to the golden age of the 1950s (and to other time periods) and come back to the present full of the promise and spirit of this idyllic past, reenergized and ready to confront the future.

A time warp of sorts also lies at the heart of *Field of Dreams* (1989). In this film, the hero, Ray Kinsella (Kevin Costner), responds to a mysterious, unseen voice that tells him "if you build it, they will come" and constructs a baseball field in the middle of a cornfield in 1980s Iowa. His apparently irrational behavior blindly reaffirms the essential innocence of America and Americans—in large part through his celebration of the country's national pastime, baseball. But in *Field of Dreams,* the central character doesn't go back in time. Instead, he builds the field and the past comes to him. Famous (dead) ballplayers from different decades in the past, including Shoeless Joe Jackson (Ray Liotta), gather to play baseball on his field in the present. Yet, the effect of this particular variation on the time-travel motif remains the same—contact with the past renews the spirits of those in the present.

The pre-Vietnam era serves as the time frame for a number of more realistic 1980s films, ranging from *Diner* (1982) and *The Right Stuff* (1983) to *Stand By Me* (1986). Although the 1950s of *Diner* and *Stand By Me* is experienced primarily from below—that is, from the perspective of lower- and lower-middle-class teenagers, these films nonetheless present a nostalgic and somewhat romanticized vision of coming of age in Eisenhower America before the traumatic events of the 1960s and 1970s. Both films depict an intense male camaraderie in a disparate group of (white) boys from somewhat different ethnic and social backgrounds and thus reaffirm the mythic notion of an American melting pot.

Paradise Lost/Paradise Regained

The theme of innocence regained takes a variety of forms. One involves a rejection of life in the big city for that in the suburbs, in rural America, or in the untouched world of nature. During the Reagan-Bush period, the shift in population that had begun in the post–World War II years finally resulted in the creation of a new national demographic profile. For the first time in our history, more Americans lived in the suburbs than in either the city or the country. Shopping malls replaced cities as centers of American culture. From one perspective, the suburbanization of America marked a return to small-town values. City slickers, like those in the 1991 film of the same name, find a renewed sense of community and a new, more positive sense of themselves as a result of their encounter with a more primitive, more innocent, rustic America.

Reworking a basic situation presented in the television series *Northern Exposure, Doc Hollywood* (1991) exploits the urban anxieties of an ambitious young doctor who is accidentally trapped in an out-of-the-way rural town. The doctor, played by Michael J. Fox, desperately seeks to escape this impossibly provincial place in order to take up a lucrative practice as a plastic surgeon in Los Angeles. The film climaxes with his ultimate discovery that he belongs in this backwoods Garden of Eden. *Return of the Jedi* (1983) concludes with the victory of the rebels over the forces of the Empire on the forest moon of Endor, where the furry Ewoks live in a utopian world of nature. The *Crocodile Dundee* films (1986, 1988, 2001) present the legendary hunter/adventurer (played by

Back to nature: Allie Fox (Harrison Ford), his wife (Helen Mirren), and his children (River Phoenix, Hilary Gordon, and Rebecca Gordon) abandon civilization for a remote island in the Caribbean in *The Mosquito Coast* (1986).

Paul Hogan) whose values have been shaped by his contact with nature and who serves, along with the globe-trotting archeologist Indiana Jones (Harrison Ford), as a paradigm for the new, masculine hero of the 1980s.

The back-to-nature drive reached its climax in a series of more or less liberal films that reject the values of urban and suburban America. *Witness* (1985) and *The Mosquito Coast* (1986), for example, imagine a more innocent world—Amish Pennsylvania and the jungles of a Caribbean island—in which the hero (Harrison Ford in both films) recovers a simplicity and naivete that are absent in contemporary urban America. Indeed, *Mosquito Coast* emerges as an implicit indictment of the antienvironmental policies of the Reagan and Bush administration. For Ford, this return-to-innocence scenario culminates in an urban drama, *Regarding Henry* (1991), in which he plays an aggressive, cutthroat, yuppie lawyer whose near-death experience forces him to restart his life from scratch and reject his earlier behavior. In a similar vein, in *Medicine Man* (1992), Sean Connery lives in the slowly disappearing rain forests of South America, where he discovers (and loses) a cure for cancer while he also instructs research scientist Lorraine Bracco in the ways of nature, which ultimately prove more attractive than those of civilization.

The most obvious attempts by filmmakers to return to a world of nature that was responsible for bringing characters back to life or for introducing vitality into their otherwise humdrum lives can be found in films such as *Out of Africa* (1985), Danish author Karen Blixen's semiautobiographical account of her life in Kenya from 1914 to 1931; *Crocodile Dundee* (1986), which juxtaposes the relative innocence of the Australian outback to the manifest decadence of New York City; *Gorillas in the Mist* (1988), which looks at anthropologist Diane Fossey's efforts to study and protect African gorillas; and *Dances With Wolves* (1990), in which Kevin Costner's Lt. John Dunbar rejects his own supposedly more advanced culture for that of the Sioux Indians.

At the opposite end of the nature/culture spectrum, the less edifying world of the shopping mall provides a background for the narratives of a number of teen dramas, including *Fast Times at Ridgemont High* (1982), *Bill & Ted's Excellent Adventure* (1989), *Scenes from a Mall* (1991), and *Clueless* (1995). Though the mall can be fun, as Genghis Khan, Joan of Arc, and Beethoven discover in *Bill & Ted*, it is nonetheless a space of ultimate conformity where everyone's leisure-time activity is the same—shopping. Malls represented the rampant consumerism that drove the 1980s economy and provided a semiautonomous setting in which the individuality of those who frequented them gave way to a dehumanizing anonymity. The love-hate relationship that mall shoppers routinely have with malls finds unique expression in these films, which both exploit and expose the shallowness of mall culture.

Striking Back

Strands of Reaganite conservatism can be found in the no-nonsense action films starring super-heroes Sylvester Stallone (in the *Rocky* and *Rambo* films) and Arnold Schwarzenegger (in the *Conan* and *Terminator* films). This ideology even cropped up in the rugged individualism of less muscular types such as Paul Hogan in the *Crocodile Dundee* films (1986, 1988, 2001) and Bruce Willis in the *Die Hard* films (1988, 1990, 1995).

Even would-be antiestablishment action movies of the 1980s, such as Eddie Murphy's *Beverly Hills Cop* films (1984, 1987, 1994) and Mel Gibson's and Danny Glover's string of *Lethal Weapon* films (1987, 1989, 1992, 1998), came down firmly on the side of mainstream values. They promoted law and order, interracial harmony, police camaraderie, and a celebration of the family. At the same time, they realized widely held, popular desires to strike back at what the Reagan administration identified as the chief threats to the security and well-being of 1980s America—terrorism and drug-trafficking.

Of course, Murphy's comic irony and street-smart wit is worlds apart from the single-minded tenacity and straightforwardness of a Schwarzenegger or Stallone. But the fact is that the character of Axel Foley in *Beverly Hills Cop* was originally written as a part for Stallone. Though rewritten for Murphy, the role retains traces of a moral righteousness, a bitter desire for vengeance, and a brutal violence more closely associated with a Rocky or a Rambo than with a Billy Ray Valentine from *Trading Places*.

CASTLES IN THE AIR: REIMAGINING TRADITIONAL INSTITUTIONS

Having It Both Ways

In the Vietnam and Watergate era, the movies dramatized the essential hostility that lay beneath the relationship between individuals and the system. This earlier cinema celebrated outlaws and nonconformists, as seen in *Bonnie and Clyde* (1967), *Easy Rider* (1969), *The Wild Bunch* (1969), *Butch Cassidy and the Sundance Kid* (1969), and *One Flew Over the Cuckoo's Nest* (1975). By exposing the decadence and corruption of lifestyles in the 1980s, motion pictures reaffirmed traditional populist values and proclaimed their own independent status as critics of the system. The female characters in *9 to 5* (1980), for example, encounter a corrupt system in the workplace, which they then make better by change from within.

In Reaganite entertainment, the system works. *Wall Street* (1987) lets us indulge our own desires for success while condemning those of ruthless junk bond speculators such as Michael Douglas's Ivan Boesky-like inside trader, Gordon Gekko. Thus, audiences can identify with Gekko's ambitious young informant, Bud Fox (Charlie Sheen), who uses insider information to rise to the upper strata of the Wall Street elite. But, unlike Gekko, Fox has second thoughts about the morality of his actions; he renounces his ways and uses his skill as a trader to help the government get the goods on his former boss. *Wall Street* demonstrates American business at its worst and at its best, but its chief message is that the business community remains principled; it can, it will, and it does clean up its own act.

In a similar way, *Broadcast News* (1987) lets us criticize the news media, in the person of the handsome but empty-headed news anchorman, Tom Grunick (William Hurt). At the same time, we are also encouraged to appreciate those in television journalism who are either first-rate reporters, like Albert Brooks' Aaron Altman, or hotshot producers, like Holly Hunter's Jane Craig, who also criticize the network's preference for style over substance in its quest for ever-greater ratings. Because it presents the news media as its own worst critic, the film restores our faith in the essential honesty of the institutions of television news as a whole. It's okay because it acknowledges its faults.

Trading Places (1983) seems to criticize the inhumanity of the Duke brothers, played by Ralph Bellamy and Don Ameche, who are Philadelphia stock futures manipulators; but the film refuses to indict the economic system that produces characters like the Dukes. The Dukes emerge as eccentric aberrations of an industry that proves to be perfectly capable of regulating itself. Thus, the film depicts as villains the Dukes, who treat both Eddie Murphy's Billy Ray Valentine and Dan Ackroyd's Louis Winthorp III quite callously. Yet, it does not condemn capitalism. Indeed, it endorses the aggressive, market-manipulating strategies of Valentine and Winthorp, who use the system to destroy the Duke brothers and, more important, to enrich themselves. It's okay for some people—

for the good guys, in particular—to make a lot of money. Capitalism is not inherently evil; in fact, it even has a sense of humor. What's more, the system can be conned by the have-nots of this world, such as a formerly homeless and impoverished black street beggar (Murphy) and a destitute blue-blood turned street person (Ackroyd). In other words, the system works; it rewards those with initiative and industry and punishes those who abuse their power and position for purely personal reasons.

Although Reaganomics did not always provide a stimulus for small business, it did promote individual enterprise. Entrepreneurial experimentation provides the background to *Risky Business* (1983), a teen comedy in which Joel Goodsen (Tom Cruise) targets admission to an Ivy League college as his goal in order to pursue a career in business. While his parents are out of town, Joel enters the world of business on the ground floor with a local corner on the world's oldest profession—prostitution. His success wins him the admiration of a college recruiter who secures his admission to Princeton. The lesson: greed and ingenuity pay, provided they are attractively packaged in the form of Tom Cruise. (In Marshall Brickman's original script, Joel doesn't get into college at the end. This downbeat conclusion was filmed and tested on preview audiences who clearly preferred a happy ending, which was then tacked onto the film.)

Being All That You Can Be

The image of another institution—the military, which had been tarnished as a result of Vietnam—underwent both revision and glamorization in the 1980s. Films about Vietnam, such as Oliver Stone's *Platoon* (1986) and *Born on the Fourth of July* (1989) and Brian De Palma's *Casualties of War* (1989), continued to portray the insanity of the American military establishment, but non-Vietnam service films presented a different face. The military was humanized somewhat when it became the site for comedy in *Private Benjamin* (1980) and *Stripes* (1981). In the former film, Jewish princess Goldie Hawn joins the "new" Army, which includes more women. And in the latter film, Bill Murray and Harold Ramis turn the Army into a fraternal organization of *Animal House* types who spearhead an unauthorized invasion of Czechoslovakia.

Hotshot pilots became something of a movie staple in the 1980s. When watching *An Officer and a Gentleman* (1982), audiences rooted for Zack Mayo (Richard Gere) in his attempt to get through the Naval Aviation Officer's Candidate School and for Debra Winger's local factory girl, whose pride prevents her from trapping an officer (Zack) into marriage and thus from realizing her ambition to better her lot. For the first time in decades, life in the Navy began to look attractive. *The Right Stuff* (1983) documented the early days of the space program when military and civilian pilots trained to become astronauts. Though the film looked somewhat satirically at the politics and public relations that inspired the Mercury flights and debunked the mystique of NASA's first astronauts, it also celebrated the more traditional heroism of the legendary test pilot, Chuck Yeager (Sam Shepard), who definitely had "the right stuff."

Recruitment posters: In *Top Gun* (1986), Maverick (Tom Cruise) has it all, finding adventure and romance (with Kelly McGillis) as a hotshot pilot in the Navy's fighter weapons school.

Courtesy of Paramount

Top Gun (1986), which was filmed with the full cooperation of the Navy, emerged as the cinematic equivalent of a Navy recruitment poster. Directed by Tony Scott, a veteran in the field of television commercials, the film starred Tom Cruise as Maverick, a trainee in the Navy's elite fighter weapons school. The drama hinges on Maverick's competition with his archrival, Ice (Val Kilmer), for the coveted status of "top gun" in the squadron, and on his affair with an astrophysics instructor (Kelly McGillis). Transformed by the film into the military's equivalent of a rock star, Maverick shoots down a couple of Russian MiGs and also wins the heart of McGillis. After the film's release, the Air Force instructed its ad agency to produce commercials with the *Top Gun* look.

The restoration of public confidence in the military, which began onscreen in revisionist celebrations of the military such as *An Officer and a Gentleman* and *Top Gun*, culminated offscreen in the 1983 invasion of Grenada, which was celebrated in Clint Eastwood's *Heartbreak Ridge* (1986); the invasion of Panama in 1989; and the 1990–1991 Persian Gulf war with Iraq. American intervention in third-world countries was perhaps best represented in the cycle of *Indiana Jones* films, which looked back to the neocolonialist spirit of turn-of-the-century Europe and the United States (a spirit remarkably captured in Spielberg's television spin-off series, *The Young Indiana Jones Chronicles*). As Peter Biskind points out, the *Indiana Jones* films celebrate "the figure of the dashing colonialist adventurer who plunders and pillages antiquities from Third World countries for First World collectors." Indy raids the jungles of South America, the mountainous wastes of Tibet, and the deserts of Egypt in search of the Ark of the Covenant in *Raiders of the Lost Ark* (1981). He visits the Far East (somewhere beyond the Himalayas), where he matches wits with Asian thugs in *Indiana Jones and the Temple of Doom* (1984). And in *Indiana Jones and the Last Crusade* (1989), he quests after the Holy Grail in the Holy Lands of the Middle East.

Oedipus with a Happy Ending: The Return of the Father

The hidden agenda behind the Indiana Jones films, as well as that behind the *Star Wars* films; the numerous nostalgic returns to the pre-Vietnam past, from *Back to the Future* (1985) to *Dirty Dancing* (1987); the eager demonstrations that the system works, in films such as *Trading Places* and *Broadcast News*; and the recruiters' visions of the military that can be found in *An Officer and a Gentleman* and *Top Gun*, became clearer as the decade moved to a close and as Lucas's and Spielberg's trilogies moved toward their resolutions. As Robin Wood notes, the dominant tendency of Reaganite cinema is "the restoration of patriarchal authority."

Films of the late 1960s and 1970s, ranging from *Bonnie and Clyde* (1967) and *Easy Rider* (1969) to *The Graduate* (1967) and *One Flew Over the Cuckoo's Nest* (1975), dramatized the generation gap and celebrated the defiance of authority. Nonconformist youth in *Alice's Restaurant* (1969), *Getting Straight* (1970), *Zabriskie Point* (1970), and *Hair* (1979) struggle against the system. Children in *The Graduate*, *A Clockwork Orange* (1971), *Badlands* (1973), *The Exorcist* (1973), and *Carrie* (1976) rebel against their parents (or against parental figures). But in the 1980s, the younger generation sought to repair the relationship between themselves and their parents that had been ruptured in the films of the previous decade.

Most significantly, one of the chief leaders of the (1970s) rebellion against the symbolic father (the repressive Empire) in *Star Wars* (1977), Luke Skywalker (Mark Hamill), makes his peace with his father in the 1980s. In *The Empire Strikes Back* (1980), Luke discovers that his archenemy, Darth Vader, is really his father; and in *Return of the Jedi* (1983), as Vader dies, father and son are reconciled. Thus, as the series comes to an end, Luke redeems his father, winning him back to the good side of the Force. For Spielberg, the evolution was significant. *Close Encounters of the Third Kind* (1977) looked at the inadequacy of the family, which both little children and parents (Richard Dreyfuss's Roy Neary) abandon in quest of the utopian world of the aliens. *E.T.: The Extra-Terrestrial* (1982), which is situated in a broken home, is all about the quest for the absent father, whose place is filled, in part, by the alien, E.T. In *Indiana Jones and the Last Crusade* (1989), Indy's long-standing hostility toward his father, with whom he has not spoken in over 20 years, is put aside as the two join forces to achieve a common goal. Or, rather, they agree to give up that goal—the Holy Grail—in order to save one another.

(a)
(b)

Fathers and sons: (*a*) Indiana Jones (Harrison Ford, right) and his father (Sean Connery) embark on a joint quest for the Holy Grail in *Indiana Jones and the Last Crusade* (1989); (*b*) Ray Kinsella (Kevin Costner, right) is reconciled with his dead father (Dwier Brown) on the *Field of Dreams* (1989).

The ritualistic nature of the restoration of the father found its most magical expression in *Field of Dreams* (1989), in which the oedipal conflict of the 1960s and 1970s was quite literally resolved in the 1980s. Ray Kinsella (Kevin Costner), a former student activist who left home after ridiculing his father's passion for baseball, hears voices and, as a result, compulsively builds a baseball diamond in the middle of an Iowa cornfield. Soon, his dead father's favorite baseball players from the past—such as Shoeless Joe Jackson (Ray Liotta)—show up and begin to play ball on the field. Meanwhile, Ray hunts down his own alternate father figure, black activist-writer Terence Mann (James Earl Jones), and brings him back to Iowa, where black and white, radical and conservative, and father and son resolve their differences by playing baseball together. (Of course, none of the legendary ballplayers who play on the field of dreams are black, a fact that undermines Mann's stirring speech at the end about baseball and the American dream). In the final scene of the film, Ray plays a game of catch with his father, who has come back as a young catcher in his 20s. In this way, the film symbolically effects a reconciliation between the older and younger generations that Vietnam and other social, political, and cultural issues had previously cast into opposite camps.

As Wood and Britton note, a surprising number of films from this period had as their central project the reaffirmation of the father. In several films, including *Kramer vs. Kramer* (1979), *Ordinary People* (1980), *3 Men and a Baby* (1987), and *Boyz N the Hood* (1991), this restoration of the father takes place at the expense of the mother, who either abandons or otherwise gives up her children and leaves them to the father or to other males. Father figures, including trainers such as Burgess Meredith's Mickey in the *Rocky* films, Yoda and Obi-Wan Kenobi in the *Star Wars* films, and Pat Morita's Mr. Miyagi in *The Karate Kid* films (1984, 1986, 1989); or mentors such as Christopher Lloyd's Dr. Emmett

Brown in the *Back to the Future* films or Jones's Terence Mann in *Field of Dreams*, serve as crucial agents for change, providing the necessary stimulus for heroes to realize their goals and desires.

Films of the 1980s regularly dealt with the melodramatics of family relations, with the (attempted) reconstitution of the nuclear family. *Terms of Endearment* (1983) explored the love-hate relationship between a domineering mother (Shirley MacLaine) and her independent-minded daughter (Debra Winger), who rediscover their affection for one another as they both grow older. In a reworking of *Terms of Endearment, Nothing in Common* (1986) explored a similar relationship between a father (Jackie Gleason) and his somewhat distant son (Tom Hanks), who have even less in common than MacLaine and Winger. In 1988, the reunification of separated brothers serves as the basis for the melodramatic comedy of *Rain Man* and for the more improbable comedy of *Twins,* in which Arnold Schwarzenegger and Danny DeVito play twins separated at birth. The family melodrama also provided a vehicle for the representation of more unconventional female characters. In *A League of Their Own* (1992), which dealt with the creation of the short-lived All-American Girls Professional Baseball League, highly competitive sisters played by Geena Davis and Lori Petty battle with one another for recognition as athletes. They eventually go their separate ways, but the film climaxes with their emotional reconciliation years later.

Parents and Babies: A Wide Spectrum

The obsession of recent cinema with questions of family comes as no surprise. During the late 1970s and 1980s, the baby boomers began to have babies themselves. Parenting, whether conventional (i.e., by married, heterosexual couples) or unconventional (i.e., by single parents, unmarried couples, homosexual couples), became one of *the* dominant experiences of the post-Vietnam, post-Watergate era of national recuperation. The cycle began with *Kramer v. Kramer* (1979), in which Dustin Hoffman, abandoned by his wife, learns how to become a father to his six-year-old son. This semimelodramatic scenario was comically reworked more than a decade later—in *Hero* (1992), which also featured Hoffman's attempts to be a good father to his estranged son. In between these two works lay an astounding spectrum of parenting situations. *Baby Boom* (1987) dealt with a workaholic management consultant, J. C. Wiatt (Diane Keaton), who inherits a 12-month-old baby from her cousin who dies in a traffic accident. Like Hoffman in *Kramer,* her attempts to be a good mother come at the cost of her career at a high-powered public relations firm but inadvertently lead her into another career, making and bottling baby food.

The basic formula of *Kramer vs. Kramer,* exploring the redemptive nature of parenting for self-absorbed men who care only for their careers, cropped up in a series of highly successful 1990s films. *Mrs. Doubtfire* (1993), a cross between *Tootsie* (1982) and *Mr. Mom* (1983), combines cross-dressing and role reversal as Robin Williams disguises himself as a female nanny in order to continue seeing and caring for his estranged kids. In *Liar, Liar* (1997), a reworking of the plot premise of a 1941 Bob Hope comedy (*Nothing but the Truth*), duplicitous lawyer Fletcher Reede (Jim Carrey) is punished for continually breaking promises to his son. The boy makes a wish on his birthday that his father should be forced to tell the truth for 24 hours. When the wish is miraculously granted, the truth plays havoc with Carrey's courtroom techniques but leads to an ultimate reconciliation with his son. In *Jerry Maguire* (1996), sports agent Tom Cruise experiences a moral crisis of sorts and attempts to restore integrity to his profession, but it takes his relationship with a little boy named Ray, the son of his accountant (Renee Zellweger), to transform him into the loyal and loving man he says he wants to be.

One of the subplots of Lawrence Kasdan's nostalgic requiem for the 1960s, *The Big Chill* (1983), involves a thirtysomething, unmarried corporate lawyer, Meg (Mary Kay Place), who is racing against her own biological clock and who wants to have a baby—fathered, if possible, by one of her former college friends. In *3 Men and a Baby* (1987), a six-month-old baby girl is left on the doorstep of three bachelors, played by Tom Selleck, Steve Guttenberg, and Ted Danson. This national obsession with getting kids found its wackiest expression in Joel and Ethan Coen's parody of the parental urge, *Raising Arizona* (1987). In this tongue-in-cheek comedy, a small-time crook (Nicholas Cage) and his parole officer/wife (Holly Hunter) are unable to have children, so they kidnap a baby from a couple who just had quintuplets.

Parenting: Peter (Tom Selleck, left) and Michael (Steve Guttenberg) fill in as fathers in *3 Men and a Baby* (1987).

A string of films about parenting were released in 1988, including *She's Having a Baby* and *The Good Mother*. After the notoriety of the Baby M case, Jonathan Kaplan gave us *Immediate Family* (1989), a film about a childless couple in Seattle who contract with a pregnant teenager to adopt her baby. Amy Heckerling's *Look Who's Talking* (1989) and *Look Who's Talking Too* (1990) detailed the adventures in parenting of an unwed mother (Kirstie Alley) and the New York cabby (John Travolta) who drives her to the hospital and sticks around to help her out with raising her son (whose voice is provided by Bruce Willis).

Former child star, now director, Ron Howard explored somewhat more conventional family structures in *Parenthood* (1989), which stars Steve Martin as a comically conscientious family man who tries to become the father he never had. His costar, Rick Moranis, follows in Martin's footsteps, playing a comic inventor who accidentally changes the size of his family in a pair of extremely successful family comedies, *Honey, I Shrunk/Blew Up the Kids* (1989, 1992). At the same time, the *Home Alone* films (1990, 1992, 1997), which play on parental nightmares involving lost children and look at the remarkable survival skills of contemporary kids, have proved to be phenomenal hits among preteen, teen, and post–teen viewers at the box office.

COUNTERCURRENTS

Martin Scorsese: Against the Grain

The Reagan-Bush years did feature a number of filmmakers and films that undermined the feel-good, happy-ending cinema of America in the 1980s. As noted in the previous chapter, Martin Scorsese's films lacked the optimism, reassurance, and box-office grosses of the era's blockbusters and continued to go against the dominant grain. *Raging Bull* (1980) deconstructs the cult of male machismo that Stallone had fostered through his highly successful celebrations of the Rocky character's come-from-behind victories against superior opponents. Robert De Niro's Jake La Motta emerges as a brutally violent, physically abusive, self-destructive antihero whose success in the ring is ironically framed by his subsequent attempts to exploit that image in his act as a nightclub entertainer.

The King of Comedy (1983) inverts the return-of-the-father scenario that runs through so many films of the Reagan-Bush era by focusing on an oedipal conflict that remains unresolved. As would-be TV comic Rupert Pupkin, Robert De Niro both loves and hates a father figure, the comic late-night television host Jerry Langford, who is played by real-life substitute host for the Johnny Carson show, Jerry Lewis. Rupert overthrows the father, kidnapping Jerry and taking his place on TV, but his victory is brief, for he is eventually caught and sent to jail. Though he has achieved fame of sorts, Rupert is reduced at the end of the film to the status of a freak whose celebrity derives primarily from his notoriety in the media rather than from his talents as a stand-up comic.

EMS driver Frank Pierce (Nicholas Cage, left) tends to a near-dead patient named Noel (Marc Anthony) on the streets of New York in *Bringing Out the Dead.*

Rutgers Cinema Studies

Scorsese looks at the dark side of the American dream in *After Hours* (1985), *The Color of Money* (1986), *Goodfellas* (1990), and *Casino* (1995). He explores and calls into question the process of mythmaking in *The Last Temptation of Christ* (1988), in which Christ, doubting that he is *the* Christ, undergoes the same sort of identity crisis experienced by Travis Bickle, Jake La Motta, Henry Hill, and other Scorsese heroes. Even *Cape Fear* (1991), one of Scorsese's most popular films at the box office, portrays a nightmare vision of middle America, in which a yuppie lawyer (Nick Nolte) and his somewhat dysfunctional family are terrorized by a former convict, Max Cady (Robert De Niro), a demonic embodiment of all the violence and sexuality that mainstream Reaganite cinema attempted to hold in check.

The Age of Innocence (1993) and *Kundun* (1997) focus on male characters paralyzed by their failure to realize their goals. In *The Age of Innocence*, a film that trades in the concealment of feelings, Newland Archer (Daniel Day-Lewis) is forced to repress his feelings for the exotic, somewhat scandalous countess Ellen Olenska (Michelle Pfeiffer) and live a less-than-fulfilling life with her cousin May (Winona Ryder). Newland's sterile life with May is condensed, like the famous breakfast table montage in *Citizen Kane*, into a series of circular pans around his study, tracing what he calls the "real events" of his life with her, from her announcing her pregnancy to her death, which all take place within the confines of this little room. *Kundun*, Scorsese's film about the Dalai Lama, is the story of a man, trained from his youth to become a great spiritual leader, who is forced into exile, unable to realize his destiny. *Bringing Out the Dead* (1999), a project that reunites Scorsese with screenwriter Paul Schrader, presents a dark, expressionist, Bressonian tale of two lost souls who find one another on the nightmarish streets of New York. Scarred by their experiences with drugs and death, their mutual alienation from the urban landscape around them makes them a couple and provides the common ground on which they each undergo a religious passion that culminates in their spiritual redemption.

At the same time, Scorsese's earlier films—in particular, *Mean Streets* (1973)—and other offbeat films of the 1970s continued to inspire a number of younger filmmakers whose work combined a similar interest in violent exploitation genres and independently made art cinema. For example, Ethan and Joel Coen's *Blood Simple* (1984), like *Mean Streets,* looked back, but in a decidedly more self-conscious way, to the themes and visual style of film noir, while ironically transposing Scorsese's vision of violent urban relationships to the unlikely, wide-open spaces of Texas. It also captured the visual look and eccentric narrative perspective of Terrence Malick's philosophically meditative *Badlands* (1973). *Miller's Crossing* (1990), released the same year as *Goodfellas,* also explored the inner workings of the mob, but the story was again transposed from an urban setting to a Midwestern no-man's-land that resembled the Personville of Dashiell Hammett's proto-noir, hardboiled novel *Red Harvest.* And, unlike the Scorsese film (or Coppola's *Godfather* films), it gave the gangster genre an existential twist. For the Coens, traditional genres and audience expectations about genre serve as the background against which they can perform their surfacy, postmodernist reworkings of conventions.

As Jim Hoberman and Emanuel Levy suggest, Scorsese's work has spawned a younger generation of hard-boiled filmmaking, as can be seen in the work of New York–based filmmakers such as Abel Ferrara and Nick Gomez, and in that of West Coast directors such as Quentin Tarantino and Paul Thomas Anderson. Ferrara has made a series of disturbed and disturbing urban crime dramas, including the ultraviolent *King of New York* (1990), the sordid *Bad Lieutenant* (1992), and the Leonesque Mafia melodrama *The Funeral* (1996). Gomez's *Laws of Gravity* (1992), made for only $38,000, documents the bleak world of two small-time Brooklyn hoodlums, second cousins to Scorsese's Charlie and Johnny Boy in *Mean Streets. New Jersey Drive* (1995), a story about black teenagers in Newark who steal cars for pointless joyriding, combines Scorsese's sensitivity for life on the streets with Spike Lee's interest in rite-of-passage *bildungsroman.*

Tarantino imitates Scorsese's mean streets machismo and his ear for lower-class vernacular in *Reservoir Dogs* (1992), which stars Scorsese icon Harvey Keitel, and *Pulp Fiction* (1994). But Tarantino's influences include Kubrick, whose 1956 heist film *The Killing* (along with Hong Kong classic, *City on Fire,* 1987) provided the plot premise of *Reservoir Dogs,* and Malick, whose film *Badlands* inspired Tarantino's scripts for *True Romance* (Scott, 1993) and *Natural Born Killers* (Stone, 1994). Tarantino also draws on foreign sources, ranging from Jean-Pierre Melville and Jean-Luc Godard, to Japanese animé and Hong Kong martial arts films (*Kill Bill,* 2003).

Levy describes Anderson's *Boogie Nights* (1997), a study of the porn industry in disco-era Los Angeles, as a reworking of Scorsese's *GoodFellas* (1990) in which a good-looking nobody (Mark Wahlberg) becomes a porn star named

Dirk Diggler, briefly enjoys life at the top, becomes addicted to drugs, and then loses it all, returning to anonymity as a street hustler. Anderson's *Magnolia* (2000) retains a Scorsesean interest in masculinity in crisis, but its emphasis on exposing male bravado (in the form of Tom Cruise's inspirational lecturer) as a cover for deeper anxieties and insecurities takes the film in a direction that Scorsese would never go. Its focus on childhood emotional traumas and midlife moral dilemmas foregrounds male pain and suffering in a series of big scenes that substitute cathartic, emotional testimony for Scorsese's noncathartic acts of physical violence. Scorsese's *Gangs of New York* (2002) indulges in a similar narrative of oedipal conflict between Amsterdam Vallon (Leonardo DiCaprio) and Bill the Butcher (Daniel Day-Lewis), the man who killed his father, but the emotional aspects of the confrontation are repressed and the characters emerge as stoic representatives of opposing historical forces that interact in order that a unified national identity can be forged.

The Gay New Wave

Minorities have consistently been represented either marginally or not at all in Hollywood films. During the 1980s, however, a handful of minority filmmakers began making films that enjoyed both critical acclaim and (limited) success at the box office. There has always been a gay underground, but during the postwar era, it became increasingly prominent, especially in the "beat" movement and, in particular, in the poetry of Allen Ginsberg. By the 1980s, it had finally broken into the mainstream. Elements of underground movies of the 1960s by gay filmmakers such as Jack Smith, Andy Warhol, and George Kuchar cropped up in what Hoberman refers to as the queer cinema of Gus Van Sant's *Drugstore Cowboy* (1989) and *My Own Private Idaho* (1991), Todd Haynes's *Poison* (1991), Tom Kalin's *Swoon* (1992), and Gregg Araki's *The Living End* (1992). The notion of queer cinema refers to a deliberately oppositional stance that certain gay filmmakers take toward conventional Hollywood cinema. In *Idaho,* which is a male hustler's version of Shakespeare's *Henry VI, Part I,* Van Sant combines fantasy sequences, à la Smith's *Flaming Creatures,* with the road exploits of his two *Easy Rider*–like heroes. In the 1990s, though he continued to focus on outsiders, Van Sant turned from queer cinema to more mainstream subjects, directing films such as *Even Cowgirls Get the Blues* (1984), *To Die For* (1995), his quasi-independent box-office hit *Good Will Hunting* (1997), a shot-for-shot remake of *Psycho* (1998), and *Finding Forrester* (2000).

Poison interweaves three unrelated stories—or, as Haynes puts it, "three tales of [homoerotic] transgression and punishment." One tale takes the shape of a documentary interview with a woman who tells how her seven-year-old son murdered his father and then magically flew off out a second-story bathroom window. Another, cast in the form of a science-fiction thriller, follows a scientist who experiments on himself and then turns into a leprous serial killer. The third, set in a prison, involves a sadomasochistic relationship between two male prisoners.

Dr. Graves (Larry Maxwell) distills the sex drive, a formula which will later accidentally transform him into the Leper Sex Killer, as a female admirer, Dr. Olson (Susan Norman), looks on, in *Poison* (1991).

Safe (1995) tells the story of a housewife (Julianne Moore) who suffers from environmental illness (i.e., allergies to the chemicals in the atmosphere) and goes to a secluded New Age retreat where others like her live. The staff guru at this "Wellness Center" provides therapy in the form of a 12-step program designed to reconcile patients with their diseases and to restore their positive self-images, a form of treatment that, according to Haynes, became the last resort for men with AIDS in the late 1980s and early 1990s, making the film a veiled allegory about the social isolation created by that disease. In *Far From Heaven* (2002), Haynes reworks Douglas Sirk's *All That Heaven Allows* (1955), refiguring the earlier film's focus on class into a tale of gender and race in which the husband of the white heroine (Julianne Moore again) leaves her for another man and she turns to the black gardener for a sympathetic ear, prompting a miniscandal in her social circle (and the gardener's).

Set in the 1920s, *Swoon* redramatizes the real-life Richard Leob and Nathan Leopold affair, detailing how the homosexual couple kidnapped and murdered a young boy and exploring the general public's homophobic reaction to their crime over the course of their subsequent trial and execution. In *The Living End* (1992) and *The Doom Generation* (1995), gay filmmaker Gregg Araki reworks classic outlaw-couple films, such as *They Live by Night* (1949) and *Bonnie and Clyde* (1967), to deal with the self-destructive, nihilist urges of a new generation

A SERIOUSLY SEXY COMEDY

SHE'S GOTTA HAVE IT

Driven by desire: Spike Lee's *She's Gotta have It* (1986).

Courtesy of Island Pictures

of social outcasts. In *The Living End,* his two central characters (both HIV positive) go on a crime spree because they've got nothing to lose. In *Doom Generation,* two guys and a girl cut a violent path through a landscape of 7-Elevens and QuickieMarts while engaging in a sexual round-robin that blurs the boundaries erected by traditional notions of sexual orientation.

Spike Lee: Into the Mainstream

Somewhat less marginalized in terms of their status in the film industry than these homosexual filmmakers, a number of black directors moved from the fringes of independent filmmaking to the mainstream of commercial cinema during the 1980s and 1990s. NYU graduate Spike Lee won critical success with his first feature, *She's Gotta Have It* (1986) and soon found financial support for his projects from major studios such as Universal, which distributed *Do the Right Thing* (1989), *Jungle Fever* (1991), *Crooklyn* (1994), and *Clockers* (1995), and Warner Bros., which handled *Malcolm X* (1992). Lee can be credited with preparing the stage for the rise of a new generation of black filmmakers in the 1980s and 1990s, including John Singleton (*Boyz N the Hood,* 1991; *Poetic Justice,* 1993; *Higher Learning,* 1995; *Rosewood,* 1997; *Shaft,* 2000), Mario Van Peebles (*New Jack City,* 1991; *Posse,* 1993; *Panther,* 1995), and Lee's own cameraman, Ernest Dickerson (*Juice,* 1992).

She's Gotta Have It opens with a quote from Zora Neale Hurston's *Their Eyes Were Watching God*, and the film takes up issues related to female subjectivity raised in Hurston's novel. Lee's central character, Nola Darling (Tracy Camilla Johns), like Hurston's, struggles to define herself rather than be defined by the three men with whom she is involved (simultaneously in Lee rather than successively as in Hurston). Lee's film calls attention to the double standard that permits males to have relationships with multiple women but designates women who do the same as "freaks." Black feminists view Lee's Nola less as an independent woman than as a negative stereotype, a sexual siren recalling images of black female promiscuity found in Hollywood (i.e., white-made) films, such as *Carmen Jones* (1954), in which Dorothy Dandridge played an updated version of the heroine of Bizet's opera. Nola undoubtedly traces her ancestry back to the various Lolas and Lulus of European cinema (the Lulu of Wedekind/Pabst's *Pandora's Box*, 1928; the title character of Max Ophuls's *Lola Montes*, 1955, and of Jacque Demy's 1961 and R. W. Fassbinder's 1982 *Lolas*; and of Nabokov's and Kubrick's *Lolita*, 1962), but her role is more that of victim than of victimizer.

Nola's status as a symbol reflects Lee's approach to narrative as a site for the allegorical restaging of contemporary racial politics. In *Do the Right Thing* (1989), each character stands in for a larger social and/or racial type in the Bedford-Stuyvesant community, from the outsiders (Italian-American pizza parlor owners, white cops, Korean store owners) to the insiders (the black residents of this single block in Brooklyn). The Mayor (Ossie Davis) and Mother Sister (Ruby Dee) represent different aspects of the failed older generation of blacks that sought accommodationist policies; the three Corner Men complain about the problems facing their community but take no action; Buggin' Out (Giancarlo Esposito) symbolizes a more radical, confrontational attitude, insisting that Sal include "brothers" among the photos on the pizza parlor's all-Italian Wall of Fame. Mookie (Lee) functions as a bridge between his white employers and the community, but he finally rebels against this heavily compromised position as mediator to join Buggin' Out in the symbolic destruction of a white-owned business in a black neighborhood. As the pizza parlor burns to the ground, another local type, the retarded character named Smiley, pins a photo of Martin Luther King and Malcolm X standing together onto Sal's wall; his act of defiance is accompanied by the lyrics of Public Enemy's "Fight the Power."

Lee's subsequent work continued to explore the semiotics of racial politics. *Malcolm X* (1992) begins on the symbolic register with images of a burning American flag and a black man—Rodney King—being beaten by Los Angeles police officers, as well as excerpts from Malcolm's speeches denouncing white colonialism, imperialism, and racism. For Lee, Malcolm's story becomes the story of the postwar development of black consciousness in the African American community and the actualization of that consciousness in the civil rights and Black Power movements. The film ends with a scene in which Nelson Mandela stands in front of a classroom of black children chanting, "I am Malcolm."

Malcolm the man may have died in the Audubon Ballroom in Harlem in 1965, but Malcolm the symbol lives on in the figures of Mandela and the children.

Get on the Bus (1996) is about the Louis Farrakhan–sponsored Million Man March on Washington, an event symbolized through the interactions of 20 black men on a cross-country bus trip from Los Angeles to Washington, D.C. *Bamboozled* (2002) emerges as perhaps the loudest statement on Lee's part about the power of images as signs. The film explores the way in which the media construct images of blackness for mass consumption, creating a modern-day minstrel show with a pair of black performers—Mantan and Sleep 'n' Eat—in blackface. The film suggests that many contemporary forms of black culture, such as gangsta-rap music videos, are the modern equivalents of nineteenth-century minstrel shows.

Like Spike Lee, NYU film student Susan Seidelman successfully combined the techniques of independent and commercial cinema in her second feature, *Desperately Seeking Susan* (1985; her first film, *Smithereens*, 1982, remained largely an underground classic). Seidelman provided a portrait of suburban society and its stifling effects upon a middle-class New Jersey housewife, Roberta (Rosanna Arquette). Intrigued by a personal advertisement "desperately seeking Susan," Roberta is drawn to New York's lower East Side, where she develops a case of amnesia and lives the more liberated and adventurous life of Susan (Madonna). Though her memory is ultimately restored, by the end of the film she realizes that she can now never return to her former existence as a yuppie housewife. Seidelman subsequently scored another hit with a quasi-feminist satire about male androids, *Making Mr. Right* (1987).

Jim Jarmusch and Julie Dash: On the Fringe

Not all independent filmmakers of the 1980s moved into the mainstream. Another NYU graduate, Jim Jarmusch—who directed *Stranger Than Paradise* (1984), *Down By Law* (1986), *Mystery Train* (1989), *Night on Earth* (1991), *Dead Man* (1995), and *Ghost Dog* (2000)—continues to work on the fringes of the film industry. Though his films rely on story and character, his narrative exposition remains minimal. Things happen to one set of characters, then they or similar things happen again to a different set of characters. Thus, in *Down By Law*, a New Orleans pimp, Jack (John Lurie), is set up by his enemies and sent to jail; then a local drunk, Zack (Tom Waits), is framed for a murder and winds up in the same cell as Jack. They escape, along with another cell mate, only to find themselves hiding out in a room that looks exactly like their former prison cell.

Often, as in *Stranger Than Paradise, Down By Law, Mystery Train,* and *Dead Man*, a foreigner observes what takes place, providing a somewhat estranged perspective on the proceedings and exposing the essential blankness and vacuity of the Americans. Roberto (Roberto Benigni), an Italian who speaks only broken English, plays this role in *Law*. This alien perspective resembles that of the director himself, who looks on bemusedly at the absurdity of the narrative conventions that govern most Hollywood films. Thus, Roberto comments, after

Courtesy of Kino International

Julie Dash, director of *Daughters of the Dust* (1991).

they make good their miraculous jailbreak, that it was "just like they do in American movies." The Native American Nobody (Gary Farmer) serves a similar function in *Dead Man*, exposing the decadence of white culture and constantly referring to white men as "stupid."

Daughters of the Dust (1991), one of the more successful independent films of the early 1990s, provided new models for independent filmmaking. It gave a voice to a group that had traditionally been either unrepresented or misrepresented in mainstream cinema—black women. But it also made money, earning more than $1.6 million and remaining on *Variety*'s list of top-grossing films for over 30 weeks. As Jacqueline Bobo points out, Julie Dash's film was promoted by a dedicated group of two black women and one black man, who publicized it by direct mailings to black churches and social organizations, black radio and television stations, and black newspapers. In other words, the film did not just find its audience—an audience was found for it.

Set at the turn of the century, *Daughters of the Dust* looks at an African American family living on an island off the coast of the southern United States, on the eve of the family's departure for the North. The narrative examines the unique world of the Gullah, the people who inhabit the island, and lovingly observes their customs, many of which will be left behind when the family leaves the island. Like the photographer in the film, *Daughters of the Dust* (which takes the shape of a family album) functions as a means of recording a cultural memory, reconstructing it out of a world that has long since disappeared and transmitting it to a new generation of viewers.

A handful of other female African American filmmakers have followed in Dash's footsteps, including Leslie Harris (*Just Another Girl from the IRT*, 1993), Darnell Martin (*I Like It Like That*, 1994), Kasi Lemmons (*Eve's Bayou*, 1997; *The Caveman's Valentine*, 2001), Maya Angelou (*Down in the Delta*, 1998), and Gina Prince-Bythewood (*Love & Basketball*, 2000).

INTO THE 21ST CENTURY

Since 1992, mainstream Hollywood cinema has continued to adjust itself in response to a variety of factors. Foremost among these is the shift in cultural concerns and practices brought about by the personal computer, the Internet, and the new infotainment marketplace. Hollywood has had to compete for customers with new leisure-time activities that appeal to its traditional target audience of 12- to 24-year-olds. In part, this competition is made easy by the new corporate structure in the film industry that combines music and book publishing and cable, satellite, and Internet subscription services with entertainment software, including films, music, and video games.

Hollywood in the Information Age: Game Logic

Competition with new digital media in the form of video games, music CDs, and the Internet has resulted in certain changes in the nature of Hollywood narratives. The distinction between films and video games has become more and more obscure. Initially, blockbuster films generated an "after market" (an ancillary market for the subsequent exploitation of consumer products generated by the film itself) that included video games based on characters and situations in the original film. In the late 1980s and early 1990s, some of the most popular video games were based on films such as *RoboCop*, *Terminator 2*, *Star Wars*, *Jurassic Park*, *Beauty and the Beast*, and *Aladdin*. With the *Lara Croft* films (2001, 2003), a video game became the source for a series of motion pictures. At the same time, the way in which Hollywood blockbusters structure narrative action increasingly resembles that of video games. *XXX* (2002), for example, begins with a series of "tests," consisting of narratively unrelated, *Mission: Impossible*–type actions, that the player/hero Xander (Vin Diesel) must pass before he can get to do "the really good stuff." Though repeatedly instructed that his part in the game is over, Xander insists on continuing to play until he wins. The *Mission: Impossible* films (1996, 2000), as suggested above, provide a paradigm for game narratives.

Computers and Boolean Logic

The digital age supposedly produces new thought patterns, encouraging us to interrogate the world of information with a Boolean logic. It's a logic that is abstract, symbolic, and systematic—and detached from any direct experience of the world. The logic of Boolean search terms transforms traditional thought habits. Texts become data identified in terms of keywords. Movement from keyword to keyword channels thought, facilitating a high-speed movement through a sea of information that does not lend itself to meditation or to traditional forms of browsing.

This form of thought has seeped into what one could call cinematic, hypertextual narratives. Narratives are constructed around a series of scenes that, like Web pages, provide a variety of options; the narrative moves, at digital speed, from one set of options to another, from one screen to another. As Joseph Natoli suggests, it's a narrative movement that is digital rather than analog. Earlier, book-reading generations consume narratives analogically, making connections between "word and world." The new computer generation consumes narratives digitally, moving from screen to screen without making linear or temporal connections between or among them. Natoli argues that digital movement does not demand that spectators connect the previous shot or scene to the next, constructing story out of raw audiovisual data; it does not rely on memory. Virtually anything can happen, as it does in *The Matrix* (1999), which is Natoli's example of cybernarration. The film's hero, Neo (Keanu Reeves), can "reprogram himself to do anything." He can even reprogram the film's one hard-and-fast rule—that if you die in the Matrix, you die "for real." Neo dies in the Matrix but, like Christ, is resurrected to fulfill his destiny as "the One." *The Bourne Identity* (2002) is another good example. A plot-heavy spy film, *The Bourne Identity* features an amnesiac hero (Matt Damon)—cut adrift from any past or future—and a series of action sequences whose relationship to one another seems purely reflexive, rather than logically motivated.

In this context, *Memento* (2000) can be seen as a commentary on this new narrative logic. The film's hero (Guy Pearce) suffers from short-term memory loss; his mental state provides the perfect example of this sort of Boolean consciousness in which the hero moves back and forth from one page or screen to another in his quest for vengeance. But the film as a whole resists this logic, demanding a completely different sort of mental activity from its audiences, who must have extraordinary powers of memory and superior abilities at story-construction to make sense of the narrative. With every step backward, the film moves relentlessly forward.

Independent Cinema

Hollywood has also struggled to meet challenges from the rise of so-called independent film, associated with the advent of the Sundance Film Festival in 1985 and offshoots of Sundance such as Slamdance, which was launched in 1995 by filmmakers who had not made the cut to get into Sundance. Robert Redford created Sundance as a forum for the support of independent cinema. The exact definition of the term "independent" is a matter of some dispute, because virtually all films are constricted by economic, social, and political forces in the motion picture marketplace. But, in general, the term is used to

Leonard (Guy Pearce) attempts to compensate for chronic short-term memory loss by documenting his activities with Polaroid photographs in *Memento*.

Rutgers Cinema Studies

refer to those films made outside the traditional Hollywood studio system (i.e., independently financed) and thus, presumably, made free of any outside controls. The term "independent" is often associated with a film's budget relative to that of a studio-made film (e.g., Kevin Smith's *Clerks*, 1994, was reportedly made for $27,575 at a time when the average negative cost for a Hollywood feature was approximately $30 million). Or the term is associated with a film's dramatic content (e.g., John Sayles's *Brother from Another Planet*, 1984, and *Lianna*, 1983, deal with marginalized peoples, such as African Americans and lesbians).

In 1987, Tim Hunter's *River's Edge* premiered at Sundance and went on to receive wide critical acclaim as a postmodern masterpiece about disaffected youth in small-town America. In 1989, Steven Soderbergh's *sex, lies, and videotape* created a sensation at Sundance, where it premiered alongside *True Love* and *Heathers*. The film was picked up for distribution by Miramax and went on to earn $24.7 million at the box office, an unprecedented sum, until that time, for an independent film. A string of similar successes from Sundance followed. Reginald Hudlin's *House Party* (1990) secured distribution through New Line and earned $26.4 million. Charles Burnett's *To Sleep With Anger* (1990), Dash's *Daughters of the Dust* (1990), Haynes's *Poison* (1991), Jennie Livingston's documentary *Paris is Burning* (1991), Quentin Tarantino's *Reservoir Dogs* (1992), Araki's *The Living End* (1992), Alison Anders's *Gas Food Lodging* (1992), Victor Nunez's *Ruby in Paradise* (1993), Robert Rodriguez's *El Mariachi* (1993), Harris's *Just Another Girl on the IRT* (1993), Steve James's documentary *Hoop Dreams* (1994), David O. Russell's *Spanking the Monkey* (1994), Smith's *Clerks* (1994),

Ann (Andie MacDowell) turns the video camera on Graham (James Spader, off-screen) in *sex, lies and videotape.*

Rutgers Cinema Studies

Edward Burn's *The Brothers McMullan* (1995), Terry Zwigoff's documentary *Crumb* (1995), Mary Harron's *I Shot Andy Warhol* (1996), Todd Solondz's *Welcome to the Dollhouse* (1996), Neil LaBute's *In the Company of Men* (1997), Chris Ehre's *Smoke Signals* (1998), Jenniphyr Goodman's *The Tao of Steve* (2000), Ken Lonergan's *You Can Count on Me* (2000), Karyn Kusama's *Girlfight* (2000), Todd Field's *In the Bedroom* (2001), and Shari Springer Berman/Robert Pulcini's *American Splendor* (2002)—all of these films premiered at Sundance.

By the mid-1990s, independent cinema had become hot, providing some of the most innovative and exciting motion picture entertainment available with films such as *The Joy Luck Club* (1993), *The Crow* (1994), *Dead Man Walking* (1995), *Leaving Las Vegas* (1995), and *Selena* (1997). But it was Tarantino's *Pulp Fiction* (1994)—which was the first independent (or "Indie") to earn over $100 million ($108 million) and which also received seven Academy Award nominations (winning only in the Best Original Screenplay category)—that truly transformed the independent cinema marketplace into a high-stakes commercial arena.

With *sex, lies, and videotape* (1989), Hollywood had begun to take notice of indie cinema, sending acquisitions executives to all the major indie festivals to buy distribution rights to whatever seemed the least bit commercial. While Hollywood looked longingly at independent cinema, much of independent cinema returned that look, becoming more and more like classical Hollywood cinema. Indies began to cast major Hollywood stars such as John Travolta, Julia Roberts, Bruce Willis, George Clooney, Dustin Hoffman, and Robert De Niro in major (and minor) roles. Indie scripts came to resemble those of their

Hollywood cousins more closely. Independent filmmakers have turned away from the edgy, experimental, often minimal narratives of independent pioneers such as John Cassavetes (*Shadows*, 1959; *Faces*, 1968) and toward classical Hollywood fare, making action films such as *El Mariachi* (1992), which Robert Rodriguez filmed for only $7,000. Rodriguez's low-budget effort was just dying to be remade properly, so a few years later, for $3 million and with two big stars (Antonio Banderas, Salma Hayek), Rodriguez turned *El Mariachi* into *Desperado* (1995). In 2003, Rodriguez drew on the same El Mariachi character and the same stars (Banderas, Hayek) for a $30 million sequel to *Desperado* called *Once Upon a Time in Mexico*.

Independent filmmakers have long worked on the fringes of another successful Hollywood genre—the horror film. George Romero's *Night of the Living Dead* (1968, and also its sequels) returned from the grave in Kathryn Bigelow's *Near Dark* (1987), then in *From Dusk till Dawn* (1996, Rodriguez again) and in the astoundingly successful *The Blair Witch Project* (1999), which cost $35,000 to make and $15 million to market and earned $140.5 million in rentals as of 2003.

By the early-1990s, Miramax—one of the major distributors of independent films—had become a subsidiary of Disney, and New Line/Fine Line and Castle Rock, two other major players in the indie market, had been acquired by Ted Turner's TBS, which was subsequently absorbed by the giant Time Warner conglomerate.

In the wake of *Pulp Fiction,* more independent films began to receive nominations for and even win year-end awards. *Leaving Las Vegas* (1995) won the New York and Los Angeles Film Critics Awards for 1995, and star Nicholas Cage won the Academy Award for Best Actor. 1996 was heralded as "the year of the independents," with Anthony Minghella's *The English Patient, Fargo* by the Coen Brothers, *Shine, Secrets and Lies, Breaking the Waves,* and *Sling Blade* winning top awards at a variety of ceremonies. Miramax, in particular, became notorious for its aggressive and expensive Oscar campaigns that resulted in securing Best Picture nominations for one or more of its releases for 11 consecutive years.

When Miramax produced *Good Will Hunting* in 1997 with a budget of $10 million, it became clear that the distinctions between independent cinema and Hollywood cinema had begun to blur. The film starred Robin Williams, Matt Damon, and Ben Affleck and went on to earn over $138 million in rentals. In the late 1990s, both Miramax and New Line began to include big-budget blockbusters in their production lineups. In addition to its long-standing run of *Nightmare on Elm Street* films, New Line distributed the highly profitable *Austin Powers* films and acquired the *Lord of the Rings* franchise, which generated $314 million and $340 million in revenues for the first two films in the trilogy. Miramax's biggest box-office hit to-date has been *Chicago* (2002), winner of the Academy Award for Best Picture (and five other Academy Awards) in 2003, which brought in $171 million in revenues. New Line and Miramax are in big business today: each of *The Lord of the Rings* films cost over $93 million to make (not to mention what it cost to market them); *Chicago* was relatively cheap to produce, with a negative cost of $45 million.

If independent films such as *Pulp Fiction* or *Good Will Hunting* cost $10 million to make, can they still be considered independent? Clearly, as the costs of making and marketing films increase, their relative independence becomes more difficult to maintain. Independent producer James Schamus has noted that "today the economics required to make oneself heard even as an 'independent' are essentially studio economics." Independent cinema in the twenty-first century is no longer what it was in the twentieth.

Fantasy Films

Over the years, Hollywood has consolidated its strengths, becoming the premiere producer of children's animation, fantasy films, and big-budget, effects-laden action films. In fact, the term "fantasy" encompasses all of these genres, including in its domain animated children's films such as *Finding Nemo* (2003), *The Lion King* (1994), *Shrek* (2001), and *Monsters, Inc.* (2001); fairy tales such as the *Lord of the Rings* films (2001–2003) and the *Harry Potter* films (2001, 2002); action-adventure films such as *Spider-Man* (2002), *The Matrix* films (1999–2003), and the *Indiana Jones* films (1981, 1984, 1989); horror films such as the *Jurassic Park* films (1993, 1997, 2001) and *The Mummy* films (1999, 2001); and science-fiction films such as the *Star Wars* series (1977–2002) and the *Terminator* films (1984, 1991, 2003). Fantasy films that take us to worlds unlike our own where marvelous, supernatural, or uncanny events occur dominate the list of all time box-office champs (the top 30 all-time moneymakers might reasonably be called fantasy films—certainly *Titanic,* 1997, and *Forrest Gump,* 1994 qualify; even *Home Alone,* 1990, contains elements of fantasy.)

In these fantasies, the entire world can be understood as a fantastic construction, as in the *Star Wars* or *Lord of the Rings* films. A world of fantasy can exist within our everyday world of mundane reality—all one need do is go there or find a portal into it, as in the *Jurassic Park* films, the *Harry Potter* films, or *Being John Malkovich* (1999). A world of fantasy often exists "underground," hidden beneath the surface of everyday reality where only special individuals can see it, as in the *Men in Black* films (1997, 2002), the *Matrix* series, and *The Sixth Sense* (1999). Fantastic beings live alongside normal people in the *X-Men* (2000, 2003) and *Ghostbusters* films (1984, 1989).

In fantasy films, characters can do uncanny things. Though dead, Sam (Patrick Swayze) communicates with Molly (Demi Moore) through a spirit-world medium (Whoopi Goldberg) in *Ghost* (1990). John Coffey (Michael Clarke Duncan) has psychic powers and can feel others' pain in *The Green Mile* (1999). Ad executive Nick Marshall (Mel Gibson) has the temporary ability to hear women's thoughts in *What Women Want* (2000). Bruce (Jim Carrey) briefly enjoys godlike powers in *Bruce Almighty* (2003).

Fantasy and make-believe have always been features of Hollywood cinema, as can be seen in films such as *The Wizard of Oz* (1939), in which a young girl from black-and-white Kansas finds herself in the fairy-tale, Technicolor land of Oz. But in previous eras, fantasy was never the predominant genre, as it has become today. Fantasy films of old Hollywood tended to motivate fantasy

Rutgers Cinema Studies

Special effects enable Spielberg to combine live action footage with computer generated dinosaurs to produce fantasy: Tim (Joseph Mazzello, left) and Lex (Ariana Richards, right) help Dr. Alan Grant (Sam Neill) feed a friendly Brachiosaurus in *Jurassic Park.*

realistically (Oz was Dorothy's dream; the pooka in *Harvey,* 1950, was a figment of Elwood P. Dowd's vivid imagination) or to use the fantastic as a premise or background against which a relatively realistic narrative unfolded. Angels (*It's a Wonderful Life,* 1946; *The Bishop's Wife,* 1947), ghosts (*A Guy Named Joe,* 1944), and make-believe figures such as Santa Claus (*Miracle on 34th Street,* 1947) functioned as spiritual presences who oversaw and sometimes guided the activities of realistic characters with normal human powers engaged in realistic narrative action. It was always a matter of the real characters' working things out for themselves. At the same time, classic fantasy films tended to acknowledge fantasy as such, clearly distinguishing it as that which is unreal in an otherwise real world.

Contemporary film fantasies, which became increasingly popular in the wake of the first *Star Wars* (1977), have routinely refused to make such distinctions, blurring the lines between what is real and what is not. The dinosaurs of *Jurassic Park* are real, as are the fantastic creatures (from the Wookiees and Ewoks to the Mon Calimaris) that inhabit the world of *Star Wars.* Supernatural beings, ranging from comic book characters such as Spider-Man, the X-Men, and Batman to the psychic seers in *The Sixth Sense* (1999) and *The Green Mile,* regularly intervene to advance narrative action or to solve problems. In *The Sixth Sense,* Cole (Haley Joel Osment) sees dead people who want him to do things for them. He does.

To some extent, contemporary Hollywood fantasy is a commodified, North American version of the Latin American and South American "magic realism" exemplified in the novels of Gabriel Garcia Marquez (*One Hundred Years of Solitude*) and others. A product of contemporary advertising and media manipulation, Hollywood fantasy understands that the truth is the product of just how convincingly things are presented, and Hollywood has mastered the creation of a homogeneous verisimilitude out of the heterogeneous material of the real and the fantastic.

The Digitization of the Cinema

The digitization of the dream factory brought Hollywood into the age of information, but the information that it traded in was largely make-believe. Make-believe had always been a Hollywood specialty, but in earlier generations, Hollywood had always had to overcome the ontological nature of the photographic image (i.e., the fact that images automatically corresponded, point-by-point, to the thing they were images of), a process that inevitably left signs of strain on the final product. Now it was being done completely and effortlessly in films such as *Titanic* (1997).

Lev Manovich suggests another way of understanding fantasy in the new, digitized Hollywood. He argues that, in the digital age, Hollywood cinema has become a subset of animation, driven by computer-generated imagery (CGI); digital painting, image processing and compositing; and 2-D and 3-D computer animation. "Live action footage is now only raw material to be manipulated by hand—animated, combined with 3-D computer-generated scenes, and painted over."

The digitization of the cinema began in the 1980s in the realm of special effects. By the early 1990s, digital sound (Dolby Digital, DTS/Digital Theater Systems, SDDS) was widely innovated, providing spectators with six-channel stereo sound in most theaters. During the same period, nonlinear digital editing began to supplant linear video-editing systems for postproduction in Hollywood. By the end of the 1990s, filmmakers such as George Lucas had begun using digital cameras for original photography and, with the release of *Star Wars Episode I: The Phantom Menace* in 1999, Lucas spearheaded the advent of digital projection in motion picture theaters. *Star Wars Episode II: The Attack of the Clones* (2002) was filmed entirely with digital technology.

Digitization and Fantasy

The digitization of cinema technology has undoubtedly played a crucial role in the contemporary predominance of fantasy films; it permits filmmakers to manipulate the image from within to make it do whatever they want it to do. The final product enjoys a fantasy quotient previously unattainable. In fact, digital live-action fantasy approaches that of children's animation in its affective power. Like watching a live magician performing, digital fantasy compels our total belief in what we are seeing, even though we know it is faked. The animated or fantasy image has an effect that differs from other cinematic affects—the image is more totally constructed, unreal, and artificial, yet it is simultaneously more real and credible. It bears away our belief. In short, digital fantasy is as dreamlike and compelling as animated films are for children. We become an audience of children in the presence of contemporary film fantasy.

Seeing through Fantasy

The meaning of this turn toward fantasy in the cinema is best revealed in a handful of fantasy films that attempt to explore the factors that led to its production. Two films written by Charlie Kaufman and directed by Spike Jonze, *Being John Malkovich* (1999) and *Adaptation* (2002), expose fantasy as an avenue of escape for troubled characters unable to realize their goals on their own. In *Malkovich,* each of the three main characters uses Malkovich and his celebrity to satisfy their otherwise frustrated desires (for an artistic career, for sexual fulfillment, and for economic gain). In *Adaptation,* the hero, Charlie (Nicholas Cage), struggles to adapt Susan Orlean's book about orchids into a film script without compromising his artistic principles or the integrity of her original work. Charlie insists that in his adaptation he doesn't want to make it a "Hollywood thing" with sex, drugs, guns, or car chases or with "characters learning profound life lessons, or growing, or coming to like each other, or overcoming obstacles to succeed in the end. The book isn't like that and life isn't like that. It just isn't." But the film, which stages the adaptation process through a visualization of Charlie's evolving ideas about how to adapt the book, ultimately has Charlie betray his principles. His adaptation turns Orlean's book about flowers into a formulaic Hollywood film about sex and drugs, complete with guns and a car chase at the end. Fantasy emerges as the result of Charlie's own inadequacies—his insecurity as a writer, his sexual anxieties as an unattractive male, and his self-loathing. In writing himself into his script, Charlie makes the script all about himself and ultimately about his own failings, from his inability to represent what life is really like to his betrayal of his principles as an artist. Fantasy becomes a cover for (male) inadequacy.

David Fincher's *Fight Club* (1999) suggests that fantasy is the necessary product of individual and collective alienation in corporate capitalism. Only through fantasy can we endure the dehumanizing anonymity of consumer culture in modern mass society. The film's hero, Jack (Ed Norton), a recall coordinator for a major automobile manufacturer, suffers from insomnia. Instead of prescribing medication, his physician sends him to group therapy sessions for testicular cancer survivors. Embracing one such victim, Bob, and weeping with him enables Jack to get a good night's sleep. But, when he meets Tyler Durden (Brad Pitt), Jack rejects his earlier identification with feminized males and discovers a more masculine remedy for the mysterious malaise that ails him—fist-fighting. Together, Jack and Tyler form an underground organization of similarly disaffected men, calling their secret society "Fight Club." Shortly after

In *Fight Club,* Tyler Durden (Brad Pitt, right) prepares to administer a chemical burn to Jack (Ed Norton) to take him one step closer to hitting bottom and achieving total freedom.

meeting Tyler, Jack's apartment, which he had meticulously decorated himself with furnishings from a mail-order Ikea catalogue, mysteriously blows up and he finds himself, now homeless, thrust into Tyler's world.

The narrative situation has fairly obvious symbolic significance. Corporate, consumer culture has resulted in the emasculation of modern man, a threat earlier identified and addressed by Theodore Roosevelt, who espoused the "strenuous life." Jack initially identifies with men who have lost their testicles. At the same time, Jack's identity, like that of many in mass culture, has been carefully constructed through his consumption—Tyler contemptuously refers to him as "Ikea boy." Fight Club enables men like Jack to recover their essential masculinity through the pain and suffering of physical combat. It becomes the foundation for a much larger struggle against corporate capitalism that Tyler dubs "Operation Mayhem." Operation Mayhem is designed to destroy the symbols of corporate capitalists—a series of skyscrapers housing the headquarters of various banks and credit card companies.

Prefiguring September 11, 2001

Made in 1999, *Fight Club* is narrated by Jack and takes the form of a flashback that begins at what Jack refers to as "ground zero" (a window overlooking the targeted buildings) and ends with the explosions that result in those buildings collapsing to the ground. The fantasy imagined here ominously foretells the events of 9/11. Jim Hoberman begins his post-9/11 discussion of Hollywood disaster films of the 1990s with a quote from Theodor Adorno: "He who imagines disasters in some way desires them." If the cultural imaginary in turn-of-the-millennium America was focused on apocalyptic events such as alien invasions, unprecedented maritime disasters, meteors crashing into Earth and other instances of national trauma (celebrated in films such as *Independence Day*, 1996; *Titanic*, 1997; *Armageddon*, 1998; *Deep Impact*, 1998; and *Pearl Harbor*, 2001), Hoberman gives this cultural imaginary a new twist, translating "fear of" into "desire for." In doing so, he understands fantasy in Freudian terms as a form of wish fulfillment in which the individual's unconscious desires are acted out. The imagination of disaster in movies and other cultural forms becomes a means of managing those desires. If Hollywood cinema has, over the years, become extremely adept at staging our unconscious desires, the events of 9/11 have forced us to confront them in ways we never quite imagined.

Hollywood's Response to 9/11

Hollywood's initial response, as Hoberman points out, was that of guilt for ever having produced apocalyptic images, followed by attempts at repression. Unreleased films containing images of the World Trade Center were airbrushed (or even reshot, as was the case with *Spider-Man*, 2002, and *Men in Black 2*, 2002) to eliminate crucial scenes containing the Twin Towers. Warner Bros. delayed the release of *Collateral Damage* (2002), a film in which terrorists blow up a Los Angeles skyscraper. M-G-M cancelled plans for a film called *Nose Bleed* in which Jackie Chan was to play a window washer who discovers a terrorist plot to blow up the World Trade Center. Publicity materials for *Spider-Man* were redesigned; the original trailer (which was already in release) contained a scene in which Spidey caught a pair of bank robbers by stringing his web between the Twin Towers; its original poster featured the towers reflected in Spider-Man's eyes. Posters for the prison drama *The Last Castle* (2001) were recalled; they featured the image of an upside-down American flag, the universal sign of distress; the image was deemed inappropriate in the wake of the recent terrorist attack.

For the most part, Hollywood has avoided direct references to 9/11. Director Sam Raimi did insert what he called "a tribute to New York City" in *Spider-Man*. When the Green Goblin (Willem Dafoe) endangers a cable car full of children near the Queensboro Bridge, local citizens throw rocks at him and one New Yorker defiantly shouts: "You mess with one of us, you mess with all of us!"

Though Laura Hillenbrand had been working on the story of Seabiscuit since the late 1990s, the popular reception of this epic of national recovery suggests that it spoke powerfully to post-9/11 movie audiences (spectators in the theater where I saw the film cheered loudly during each of the horse races). Set in the Great Depression of the 1930s, *Seabiscuit* (2002) focuses on three central characters, all of whom seem to be the victims of personal trauma. Seabiscuit's owner, Charles Howard (Jeff Bridges) lost his only child in an automobile accident; the jockey Red Pollard (Toby Maguire) was separated from his family and sent to live with strangers; trainer Tom Smith (Chris Cooper) suffers from an unidentified melancholy that has turned him into a vagrant. The narrative gradually brings all three characters together and documents their return to spiritual and emotional health through their collaborative efforts to make Seabiscuit a winner. As if these backstories were not enough, both Pollard and Seabiscuit are sidelined with leg injuries—physical traumas from which they recover to win the big race. In the feel-good language of Hollywood, America is resilient and can recover from any traumatic experience.

New York's Response to September 11, 2001

Two New York filmmakers, Martin Scorsese and Spike Lee, did directly address the World Trade Center disaster. Released in December 2002, *Gangs of New York* is an epic film about the birth of a national identity out of the bloody conflicts between separate generations of immigrants in New York City. The film concludes with Amsterdam's voiceover declaration that "our great city" was "born out of blood and tribulation." Time-lapse shots of the city, viewed from a graveyard in Brooklyn where Vallon's father and Bill the Butcher are buried, depict the city's growth from the 1860s to the present, ending with the addition of the World Trade Center to the city's skyline. Scorsese resurrects the Trade Center, suggesting that New York will continue to struggle to survive in spite of recent events.

Lee's *25th Hour* (2002), released one day before the Scorsese film, is also a saga of survival—a theme announced in the opening sequence when the hero Monty (Ed Norton) rescues a dog left for dead on the Queensboro Bridge and nurses the animal back to life. The opening credits of the film display shots of post-9/11 lower Manhattan with the twin columns of light that functioned as a memorial for a few months after the disaster. At one point in the film, Monty visits the apartment of his stockbroker friend Frank, which overlooks the former site of the World Trade Center at ground zero. As crews clear debris at the site below, Monty and his friends discuss his future. This is Monty's last night of freedom before reporting to authorities the next day to begin serving a seven-year prison sentence for drug dealing. The film contains a fantasy sequence in which Monty, having decided to run away, finds a new life under a new name somewhere in the anonymity of the Midwest. Monty decides, however, to face up to his responsibilities and to serve his sentence (rather than never to be able to return to New York City). In other words, Lee's film is about New Yorkers' refusal to abandon New York City and their determination to do whatever it takes to start over and to rebuild their city and their lives.

Lee's *25th Hour* rejects escapist fantasy. But Hollywood needs fantasy if it is to survive. As American cinema moves into the twenty-first century, it continues to chart a complex course, addressing the concerns of an increasingly

Photofest

In *The 25th Hour,* Frank (Barry Pepper, left) and Jacob (Phillip Seymour Hoffman) talk about the prospects of their mutual friend, Monty, in a scene overlooking ground zero at the World Trade Center.

diverse mass audience. The body of American cinema includes both progressive and conservative works—films that disturb, films that entertain, and films that do a little of both. What's important is that we must be able to see which films are doing what and to understand why they are doing what they do.

This book attempts to provide strategies for identifying, describing, and analyzing how American cinema and individual films work to negotiate our relationship to the new, constantly-changing world around us. The movies have survived for more than 100 years, in part, because they have satisfied the demands of an ever-changing mass audience. That audience's initial need for its own form of mass-produced entertainment brought the movies into being, and its continued need for amusement governs the transformations in the movies and in the moviegoing experiences that are described in this book.

■ ■ ■ SELECT FILMOGRAPHY

Kramer vs. Kramer (1979)
The Empire Strikes Back (1980)
Ordinary People (1980)
Raging Bull (1980)
Raiders of the Lost Ark (1981)
E.T.: The Extra-Terrestrial (1982)
An Officer and a Gentleman (1982)
Star Trek II: The Wrath of Khan
   (1982)
The Big Chill (1983)
The King of Comedy (1983)
Return of the Jedi (1983)
Trading Places (1983)
Beverly Hills Cop (1984)
Blood Simple (1984)
Back to the Future (1985)
Desperately Seeking Susan (1985)
Blue Velvet (1986)
Down By Law (1986)
Peggy Sue Got Married (1986)
River's Edge (1986)
She's Gotta Have It (1986)
Top Gun (1986)
Baby Boom (1987)
Broadcast News (1987)
Raising Arizona (1987)
3 Men and a Baby (1987)
Wall Street (1987)
Rain Man (1988)
Twins (1988)
Bill & Ted's Excellent Adventure
   (1989)
Do the Right Thing (1989)
Field of Dreams (1989)
Parenthood (1989)
sex, lies, and videotape (1989)
Daughters of the Dust (1991)
Poison (1991)
Laws of Gravity (1992)
Medicine Man (1992)
Reservoir Dogs (1992)

Malcolm X (1992)
The Living End (1992)
Bad Lieutenant (1992)
El Mariachi (1992)
The Age of Innocence (1993)
Pulp Fiction (1994)
Clerks (1994)
New Jersey Drive (1995)
The Doom Generation (1995)
Clueless (1995)
Safe (1995)
Dead Man (1995)
Get on the Bus (1996)
Jerry Maguire (1996)
The Funeral (1996)
Liar, Liar (1997)
Eve's Bayou (1997)
Good Will Hunting (1997)
Boogie Nights (1997)
Titanic (1997)
Smoke Signals (1998)
Down in the Delta (1998)
Fight Club (1999)
The Matrix (1999)
Being John Malkovich (1999)
The Green Mile (1999)
Bringing Out the Dead (1999)
The Sixth Sense (1999)
Star Wars Episode I: The Phantom
   Menace (1999)
Magnolia (2000)
Memento (2000)
Bamboozled (2000)
Far From Heaven (2002)
XXX (2002)
The Bourne Identity (2002)
Spider-Man (2002)
Adaptation (2002)
25th Hour (2002)
Gangs of New York (2002)
Seabiscuit (2003)

■ ■ ■ **SELECT BIBLIOGRAPHY**

BISKIND, PETER. "Blockbuster: The Last Crusade," in Mark Crispin Miller, ed., *Seeing Through Movies*. New York: Pantheon, 1990.

BOBO, JACQUELINE. *Credible Witness: Black Woman, Film Theory, Spectatorship*. New York: Columbia University Press, 1994.

BRITTON, ANDREW. "Blissing Out: The Politics of Reaganite Entertainment," *Movie* 31/32 (1984): 1–42.

BRODIE, DOUGLAS. *The Films of the Eighties*. New York: Citadel Press, 1990.

COMBS, JAMES E. *American Political Movies: An Annotated Filmography of Feature Films*. New York: Garland, 1990.

DAVIES, PHILIP JOHN, and PAUL WELLS, eds. *American Film and Politics from Reagan to Bush, Jr.* Manchester, UK: Manchester University Press, 2002.

GOMERY, DOUGLAS. *Shared Pleasures: A History of Movie Presentation in the United States*. University of Wisconsin Press, 1992.

HEIM, MICHAEL, "Logic and Intuition," in *The Metaphysics of Virtual Reality*. New York: Oxford University Press, 1993.

HOBERMAN, JIM. "Back on the Wild Side," *Premiere* (August 1992): 44–46.

____. *The Magic Hours: Film at Fin de Siecle*. Philadelphia: Temple University Press, 2003.

____. "Out and Inner Mongolia," *Premiere* (October 1992): 50–52.

O'BRIEN, TOM. *The Screening of America: Movies and Values from Rocky to Rain Man*. New York: Continuum, 1990.

LEVY, EMANUEL. *Cinema of Outsiders: The Rise of American Independent Film*. New York: New York University Press, 1999.

LEWIS, JON, ed. *The End of Cinema as We Know It: American Film in the Nineties*. New York: New York University Press, 2001.

MANOVICH, LEV. *The Language of New Media*. Cambridge: MIT Press, 2001.

MASSOOD, PAULA J. *Black City Cinema: African American Urban Experiences in Film*. Philadelphia: Temple University Press, 2003.

MURCH, WALTER. *In the Blink of an Eye: A Perspective on Film Editing*. Los Angeles: Silman-James Press, 1995.

NATOLI, JOSEPH. *Memory's Orbit: Film and Culture, 1999–2000*. Albany: State University of New York Press, 2003.

OHANIAN, THOMAS A., and MICHAEL E. PHILLIPS. *Digital Filmmaking: The Changing Art and Craft of Making Motion Pictures*. Boston: Focal Press, 1996.

PRINCE, STEPHEN. *A New Pot of Gold: Hollywood Under the Electronic Rainbow, 1980–1989*. New York: Charles Scribner's Sons, 2000.

_____. *Visions of Empire: Political Imagery in Contemporary American Film.* New York: Praeger, 1992.

ROGIN, MICHAEL PAUL. *Ronald Reagan, the Movie, and Other Episodes in Political Demonology.* Berkeley: University of California Press, 1987.

ROSENBAUM, JONATHAN. *Movie Wars: How Hollywood and the Media Limit What Movies We Can See.* Chicago: A Cappella Books, 2000.

RYAN, MICHAEL, and DOUGLAS KELLNER. *Camera Politica: The Politics and Ideology of Contemporary Hollywood Film.* Bloomington: Indiana University Press, 1988.

WOOD, ROBIN. "80s Hollywood: Dominant Tendencies," *CineAction* 1 (Spring 1985): 1–10.

_____. *Hollywood from Vietnam to Reagan.* New York: Columbia University Press, 1986.

GLOSSARY of Technical and Other Terms

Academy ratio The shape of the image projected on a screen or, more accurately, the aspect ratio or ratio of the width to height of the projected image as it was standardized (at 1.37:1) by the Academy of Motion Picture Arts and Sciences circa 1930. See also *aspect ratio.*

after-markets A term used to describe ancillary markets for merchandise related to the original motion picture, including video sales and rentals, DVDs, cable and pay-per-view distribution, sound track albums, video games, books, amusement park rides, toys, T-shirts, and other products.

anamorphic lens A special lens used for filming and projecting widescreen images. The anamorphic lens in a camera records a wide, panoramic field of view onto standard 35mm film by compressing the image in the horizontal plane. In the theater, an anamorphic projection lens unsqueezes this compressed image, spreading it across a theater screen to produce an image with an aspect ratio of 2.35:1. See also *CinemaScope* and *Panavison.*

art direction The designing and building of the studio sets and the selection of nonstudio locations on which a film will be shot. Also called "set design."

aspect ratio The ratio of width to height of the projected image. Before 1930, the standard aspect ratio of silent films was 1.33:1; that is, the width of the projected image was 1.33 times that of its height, resulting in a somewhat rectangular image. The 1930 Academy

ratio, which remained a standard until 1953, was, at 1.37:1, more or less identical to the silent film aspect ratio. Starting with Cinerama in 1952, which featured a 2.77:1 aspect ratio, American films were filmed and/or projected in a variety of extremely rectangular widescreen formats, ranging from 1.66:1 (Vista-Vision) to 2.35:1 (CinemaScope) and 2.77:1. The current American widescreen standards are 1.85:1, 2.21.1 (70mm), and 2.40:1 (anamorphic Panavision). See also *Academy ratio.*

B films Quickly made motion pictures, usually produced to fill the second half of a double bill that also features an A film. B films generally have a budget (and a running time) that is significantly less than that of A films.

backlight Light used to illuminate the space between characters and their backgrounds to separate the characters from their backgrounds. See also *three-point lighting.*

biopic A biographical film based on the life of a famous historical figure. This genre is generally associated with studios such as 20th Century-Fox (*Young Mr. Lincoln*, 1939) and Warner Bros. (*The Life of Emile Zola*, 1937) during the 1930s and 1940s, though other studios also made biopics and the genre survives today (*Malcolm X*, Warner Bros., 1992).

blaxploitation films A term coined by *Variety* to describe a series of Hollywood genre films made in the early 1970s, featuring black performers, that were produced for a black audience.

blind bidding   A distribution system in which exhibitors are forced to contract for the rental of films prior to seeing them.

block booking   A distribution system in which exhibitors are forced to contract for the rental of groups of (two or more) films to secure the permission to exhibit any one film distributed by a particular studio.

cable television   A system for the transmission of television signals that uses cable wires or fiber optics instead of radio waves broadcast through the air.

camera angle   The angle at or from which the camera looks at the action. In a low-angle shot, the camera looks up from below at the action. In a high-angle shot, the camera looks down from above at the action. In an eye-level shot, the camera looks at the action head-on, from a position that is chest or head high.

camera distance   The relative distance of the camera from the action being filmed (e.g., extreme close-up, close-up, medium shot, long shot, and so on). The scale on which the distance is measured is generally that of the human body. (The content of the shots need not be restricted to human or even animate forms. Each film will establish its own scale of distances, depending, in part, on the subject matter of the film.) Thus, an extreme close-up presents only a portion of the face. A close-up frames the entire head, hand, foot, or other object. Medium close-ups give a chest-up view of individuals, as seen in most sequences in which two characters converse with one another, while medium shots tend to show the body from the waist up. Shots of characters that frame them from the knees up are referred to as medium long shots, while long shots range from full-figure images of characters to inclusion of some of the surrounding space immediately above and below them. In extreme long shots, the human body is overwhelmed by the setting within which it is placed, as in Westerns in which distant figures are seen as specks in a larger landscape.

camera movement   The physical movement of the camera, either through its rotation on an axis (that is, a pan or tilt shot) or through its movement on a track, a dolly, a crane, or other movable camera support. See also *crane shot, dolly shot, pan, tilt,* and *tracking shot.*

CinemaScope   A widescreen process, developed in 1953 by 20th Century-Fox, that relies on an anamorphic camera lens to squeeze a panoramic view onto standard 35mm film and an anamorphic projection lens to display the original view on a theater screen, producing an image with an aspect ratio of 2.35:1. The system was initially accompanied by four-track, magnetic stereo sound. See also *aspect ratio.*

Cinerama   A widescreen process, independently developed and introduced in 1952, that employed three interlocked cameras to record a panoramic view on three separate strips of 35mm motion picture film. In the theater, three interlocked projectors projected the three film strips side by side on a deeply curved screen. This projection produced an aspect ratio of 2.77:1. A separate strip of film carried the stereo magnetic sound, which consisted of six tracks that supplied sound to five speakers behind the screen and additional surround speakers, and a seventh track that was used to control the other six. See also *aspect ratio.*

classical Hollywood cinema   A mode of production associated with American cinema that involves certain narrative and stylistic practices. Narratives are structured around characters who have specific, clearly defined goals and deal with their triumph over various obstacles that stand in the way of the attainment of those goals. These narratives are presented in a manner that is both as efficient and as (stylistically) invisible as possible.

close-up   An image in which the size of the object shown is relatively large. See also *camera distance.*

continuity editing   A system of editing that attempts to create the illusion of temporal and spatial coherence, unity, and/or continuity. It relies on the *180-degree rule,* the *shot/reverse shot,* and various matches.

costume design The style or design of the clothing worn by the actors and actresses who appear in a film.

crane shot A moving shot in which the camera, mounted on a crane, rises or descends as it views the action.

crosscutting A form of editing that involves cutting back and forth between two or more separate scenes. See also *parallel editing.*

cut A simple break in the film where two shots are joined together. In *Rear Window* (1954), there is a cut from James Stewart looking to a shot of what he sees (Miss Torso).

deep focus A style of filming that relies on a wide-angle lens, coated lenses (lenses that have been treated with a special substance that enables them to transmit more light), fast film (i.e., film that is more sensitive to light and thus requires less exposure time than slow film), and powerful illumination to produce an image that possesses extreme depth of field (i.e., in which the extreme foreground and extreme background appear in sharp focus). See also *depth of field.*

depth of field The range in front of an individual lens within which objects will appear in sharp focus. Depending on the focal length of the lens used, the range of sharp focus will be shallow, moderate, or deep.

diegetic/nondiegetic *Diegetic* refers to the space or world of the story. Anything that belongs to this space (that could possibly be seen or heard by the characters in the story) is considered diegetic; that which does not belong to this space (e.g., a film's credits) is considered *nondiegetic.*

diegetic sound Sound that comes from the world depicted in the film, including dialogue, sound effects, and music (from radios, orchestras, or other onscreen sources). This sound is produced within the space of the film and can be (or could be) heard by any characters who inhabit that space. *Diegetic sound* is distinguished from *nondiegetic sound.*

dissolve A fluid form of shot transition that involves fading out on one shot while simultaneously fading in on another; for a brief moment, at the midpoint of the dissolve, both images are visible on the screen at the same time.

dolly shot A shot in which the camera, mounted on a mobile platform or camera support with wheels, moves in any of a variety of different directions parallel to the floor.

DVD The initials stand for either digital video disc or digital versatile disc. The size of a CD (compact disc), the DVD can store over two hours of high-quality digital video and up to eight tracks of CD-quality digital audio.

editing A process that involves the selection of images (in the form of unedited takes or shots) and sounds for subsequent inclusion in the film and the assemblage of this material to produce a finished film. Though some editing occurs during *production,* the bulk of a film's editing takes place during the *postproduction* stage. Editing also refers to the sequence of shots in the finished film.

establishing shot A shot that functions to present the spatial parameters within which the subsequent action of a scene takes place or otherwise introduce a scene.

eye-level shot See *camera angle.*

eye-line matching This feature of continuity editing involves two shots in which a character in the first shot looks offscreen at another character or object. The next shot then shows what that character is looking at from a position that reflects, in its angle, the character's position and the direction in which he or she has looked, but remains more or less objective (as opposed to subjective) in nature. *Point-of-view editing* is a form of *eye-line matching* in which the second shot shows what is being looked at from the character's exact position.

fade The gradual darkening of the image until it becomes black (the fade-out) or the gradual brightening of a darkened image until it becomes visible (the fade-in).

fill light   A light used to fill in shadows cast by the key lights. See also *three-point lighting*.

film noir   Literally meaning "black film," film noir refers to a style or mode of filmmaking, which flourished between 1941 and 1958, that presents narratives involving crime or criminal actions in a manner that disturbs, disorients, or otherwise induces anxiety in the viewer.

flashback   A shot or sequence that shows events that take place at an earlier moment than the present time in the film.

focal length   The distance from the center of a lens to the plane of the film. The focal lengths of lenses vary from relatively short lengths in *wide-angle lenses* to relatively long lengths in *telephoto lenses*.

Genre   A category of filmmaking that is recognized as a type possessing familiar narrative and stylistic conventions. Standard genres are the melodrama, Western, war film, musical, and comedy.

graphic match   A technique used in continuity editing in which the major features of the composition in one shot are duplicated or matched in the next shot, providing a graphic continuity that serves to bridge the edit.

high-angle shot   See *camera angle*.

high-key lighting   A style of lighting found in comedies, musicals, and other upbeat films, in which the fill light eliminates dark shadows cast by the key light, producing an image that is brightly and evenly lit. See also *three-point lighting*.

Independent cinema   A term used to describe films made outside the traditional studio system or made by independent producers (e.g., David O. Selznick, Samuel Goldwyn, Walter Wanger) within it. Contemporary independent cinema is generally independently financed; that is, films are made without funding from (and prior to having a contract with) a major distributor.

iris-in/iris-out   A major transition in the silent cinema in which an adjustable aperture on the camera would gradually open, in an iris-in, to reveal more and more image within an expanding, geometrically shaped frame, or would gradually close down, in an iris-out, to narrow the field of view, which is surrounded by more and more blackness.

key light   The chief or brightest source of light in a scene. See also *three-point lighting*.

letterboxing   A video format that enables widescreen films to be seen on television in (more or less) their original *aspect ratio*. It involves a reduction in the height of the image so that the full width of the image can be seen on the somewhat narrow television screen. If a film has been letterboxed, black (or blue) masking appears above and below the original widescreen image.

lighting   The illumination of the set or filming location by means of natural or artificial lights. See also *three-point lighting*.

long take   A shot that continues for a relatively long period of time (e.g., 20 or more seconds).

low-angle shot   See *camera angle*.

low-key lighting   A style of lighting, found in film noir, suspense, or horror films, in which there is little fill light, resulting in a dark or shadow-filled image. See also *three-point lighting*.

match on action   A technique of continuity editing that uses the carryover of physical movement from one shot to the next to conceal cuts. Thus, as a character begins to sit down in medium long shot, an editor will often cut in to a closer shot as the action continues.

medium shot   An image in which the size of the object or scene shown lies somewhere in between that of a close-up or medium close-up and a medium long shot or long shot; in terms of the human body, a shot that frames characters roughly from the knees up. See *camera distance*.

mise-en-scène   A French term that literally means "putting on the stage." Mise-en-scène encompasses a variety of theatrical categories related to the staging of action for the camera.

These range from purely theatrical areas of expression (such as set design, costume design, the blocking of actors, performance, and lighting) to purely filmic techniques (such as camera movement, camera angle, camera distance, and composition). Strictly speaking, mise-en-scène includes the relation of everything within the shot to everything else within the shot—of actors to the décor; of décor and actors to the lighting; of actors, décor, and lighting to the camera position; and so forth.

mode of production The particular system in which films are made. These systems range from home movies, in which amateur equipment is used by individuals to record everyday events for family viewing, to Hollywood productions, in which state-of-the-art equipment and experienced professionals (screenwriters, directors, actors, and other craftspersons) are used to produce commercial products for a mass audience.

montage The French word for "editing"; a style of editing associated with Soviet films of the late 1920s.

montage sequence A sequence in a film that relies on editing to condense or expand action, space, or time. In a travel montage, for example, a lengthy journey of a character might be condensed to a handful of shots of various places which that character has visited that are connected by a series of dissolves. This kind of montage can be seen in *Mr. Smith Goes to Washington* (1939), when Jefferson Smith (James Stewart) takes a sight-seeing bus around Washington, D.C., and shots of various buildings and monuments are edited together to reflect his tour of the nation's capital. On the other hand, the shower sequence in Alfred Hitchcock's *Psycho* (1960) is also a montage sequence. It breaks the action down into over 75 separate shots, relying on montage to expand (and thus magnify the horror of) the brutal murder of the film's heroine.

movie palace An enormous motion picture theater with lavish, often exotic, décor. Located in a large urban area, a movie palace typically had enough seats for several thousand spectators at once. The New York Roxy, for example, had 6,200 seats. The first movie palaces were built in the decade from 1910 to 1920.

multiplex A cluster of several theaters under a single roof, economically operated by the same size staff required to run a single theater. Typically, three or four small theaters, each seating about 200 spectators, will be grouped around a single large theater, seating 500–800, to form a movie arcade.

nickelodeon A small storefront motion picture theater, approximately 25 feet wide and 75–100 feet long, seating about 200 spectators. Introduced in about 1905, nickelodeons were so named because they charged customers a nickel (or a dime) for a full program of motion picture entertainment.

nondiegetic sound Sound (generally music) that does not originate in the world depicted onscreen but comes from the space occupied by a nondramatized narrator. The music provided by the film's composer that underscores dramatic action (and that is not heard by the characters in the film) is nondiegetic. Voiceover narration provided by someone who is not a character in a film, such as the voice-of-God narration found in newsreels and certain documentaries, is nondiegetic.

normal lens A camera lens that possesses an angle of view somewhat similar to that of the human eye, which thus provides a view of the action that seems less exaggerated or distorted than that provided by a *wide-angle* or *telephoto lens*. The range for normal lenses is roughly 40mm–50mm.

180-degree rule A convention observed in filmmaking that ensures continuity in screen position and screen direction from one shot to the next. In cutting from shot to shot, the camera remains on one side of an imaginary line (the 180-degree line) that runs through the main actors or action. If the camera were to cross this line during a conversation sequence, for example, the screen position of players in the first shot would be reversed in the second.

pan   A camera movement in which the camera rotates horizontally on its axis, presenting a panoramic view of the scene by rotating from right to left (or from left to right) a certain number of degrees to reveal what lies before the camera on either side.

Panavision   An anamorphic, widescreen process similar to *CinemaScope*. Panavision replaced CinemaScope as an industry standard for anamorphic filmmaking during the early 1960s.

Panning and scanning   A process employed in the adaptation of widescreen motion pictures for broadcast on television. In the transfer from original motion picture to television master, a special telecine device crops the film to make it fit on the television screen, introducing edits and pans from one part of the original image to another.

parallel editing   A style of editing that involves cutting back and forth between two or more scenes in which the action is taking place simultaneously or in which one action is compared or contrasted with another. See also *crosscutting*.

Pay-per-view   A *cable television* distribution system that enables cable companies to charge home viewers a fee for watching an individual film rather than a subscription fee for a particular premium cable channel such as HBO or Showtime.

persona   The "mask" or projected personality of an actor or star.

point-of-view editing   A form of eye-line matching that involves a series of three separate shots—a shot of a character looking offscreen, a point-of-view shot of what the character sees, and a reaction shot of the character as he or she reacts to the thing that has been seen.

point-of-view shot   A shot that is clearly marked as subjective in nature and that duplicates the optical perspective of a specific character in the film.

populism   A dominant myth that celebrates a certain kind of American identity based on preindustrial, agrarian ideals, such as that of Jefferson's yeoman farmer, the small businessperson, the opponent of big government, the anti-intellectual, and the good neighbor.

postproduction   The phase of motion picture production during which footage filmed during production is edited and assembled, special effects are created, music is composed and recorded, and the sound track is mixed.

preproduction   The phase of motion picture production during which a screenplay is written, parts are cast, a crew is assembled, and sets and costumes are designed and constructed.

production   The phase of motion picture production during which actual filming takes place.

Production Code   Rules and regulations, established (and subsequently revised) at various periods during the history of the studio system, that indicated particular subjects, ranging from nudity, white slavery, drug addiction, and other criminal acts to miscegenation, that were not permitted to be represented on the screen.

ratings   A system of film classification that rates films on the basis of the amount of sex, violence, or objectionable language contained in them. The Motion Picture Association of America has six ratings: G (suitable for a general audience), PG-13 (parental guidance recommended for children under the age of 13), PG (parental guidance suggested), R (restricted to persons over 17 unless accompanied by an adult), NC-17 (no child under 17 permitted), and X (prohibited to persons under 17). The difference between NC-17 and X is that the former rating is used for serious films with mature themes, such as *Henry and June* (1990), and the latter is now used solely for pornographic films.

roadshowing A specialized distribution system, modeled on the legitimate theater, in which a film is shown at first-run theaters and tickets are sold, in advance, on a reserved-seat basis.

runs, zones, and clearances A pattern of exhibition in which certain theaters secure the rights to exhibit films before other theaters are permitted to show them. *Runs* are broken down into first run, second run, and subsequent runs. New films are initially licensed only to first-run theaters, which are thus protected from competition with second- and sub-run theaters. Only one theater in a certain *zone* or geographical area will be permitted to exhibit the film in any particular run. And between each run, a certain period of time or *clearance* will be established to enable the various runs to maximize profits.

scene The film's smallest dramatic unit; it consists of one or more shots presenting an action that is spatially and temporally continuous.

'Scope A shortening of the term "CinemaScope." It has become a generic term for any film made in an anamorphic process. See also *Cinemascope*.

segmentation The breaking down of a film into its basic parts for purposes of analysis of the relationship of one part or segment to another.

set design See *art direction*.

shot An unbroken strip of film made by an uninterrupted running of the camera and edited at the beginning and end in preparation for its inclusion in a film. See also *take*.

shot/reverse shot A multishot system (involving at least two shots), frequently used in filming conversations and other kinds of sequences, that observes the 180-degree rule. The shots alternate back and forth between an angled shot from one end of the 180-degree line and another from the other end. The second shot views the action from the same angle as the first, though that angle is now reversed, that is, the shot is taken from the opposite direction. In other words, the shot/reverse shot pattern involves an initial shot, from one angle favoring one character, followed by another shot, from another angle favoring the other character. The relative screen positions of both characters will be maintained from shot to shot and the camera will remain on the same side of the 180-degree line that runs through the center of the action.

sound mixing The combination, during the phase of postproduction, of three different categories of film sound—dialogue, sound effects, and music.

stereo magnetic sound A sound system that relies on magnetic recording and playback in the theater, using magnetically striped projection prints to produce stereo sound coming from three or more speakers in the theater.

take An unbroken strip of yet unedited film made by an uninterrupted running of the camera; to be distinguished from a *long take*.

telephoto lens A camera lens that has a long focal length and takes in a relatively narrow angle of view in comparison to a *normal lens*. Any lens that is longer (e.g., 75mm, 100mm) than the standard 40–50mm normal lens is a telephoto lens.

3-D A system of motion picture production and exhibition, (re-)introduced in the 1950s, that involved the creation of an illusion of depth/emergence, which was based on the principles of binocular vision.

three-point lighting The standard lighting set-up employed in Hollywood. The three points to which the term refers are the dominant sources of illumination—the key light (or chief directional light source), the fill light (or weaker light source that fills in the shadows cast by the key light), and the backlight, the minor light that illuminates the space between the back of the set and the characters in order to separate or distinguish the characters from the background.

tilt A form of panning in which a stationary camera tilts upward or downward on its axis.

tracking shot A shot in which the camera, mounted on any one of a variety of mobile camera supports (e.g., cranes, dollies, Steadicams, or tracks), moves bodily through space in any of a variety of directions parallel to the floor. In some situations, the camera is placed on tracks laid on the floor or built into the ceiling.

VCR Abbreviation for "video cassette recorder."

vertical integration A system of motion picture production, distribution, and exhibition in which these three sectors are controlled by a single economic entity, such as a studio, that both makes and distributes a product exhibited in its own theaters. This particular structure was outlawed by the courts in 1948.

VHS Abbreviation for "video home system," a special system of *VCRs* and tapes that rely on a half-inch videotape format.

VistaVision A widescreen process developed by Paramount in 1954. It relies on a special 35mm camera that exposes two frames of film horizontally (rather than one frame exposed vertically as in standard cameras) to record a panoramic view. It produced an extremely sharp image that was projected in an aspect ratio of 1.66:1.

voice-over narration Speech that accompanies a previously filmed sequence but does not come from the sequence itself. The voice may be that of a character in the film who is describing onscreen events that are seen in a flashback or it may be that of an omniscient, unseen, offscreen commentator whose voice accompanies onscreen images, as in newsreels and certain forms of documentaries.

wide-angle lens A camera lens that possesses a short focal length and takes in a fairly wide angle of view, relative to that captured by a *normal lens*. A 25mm lens (or any lens shorter than the 40–50mm normal lens) is a typical wide-angle lens.

widescreen Any film production or projection format that uses an *aspect ratio* greater than the *Academy ratio*, that is, an aspect ratio of 1.66:1 or more.

wipe A form of shot transition in which the second shot appears to wipe the first shot off the screen.

zoom A special lens possessing a variety of different focal lengths that range from wide-angle to telephoto. Manipulation of the lens produces the impression of movement toward or away from objects by shifting from wide-angle to telephoto focal lengths or vice versa. These shifts simply enlarge or decrease the apparent size of the image but involve no actual movement of the camera.

INDEX

Note: Pages in *italics* indicate pictures or photographs.